Foucault's Technologies

Another Way of Cutting Reality

Kaspar Villadsen

Great Clarendon Street, Oxford, OX2 6DP,
United Kingdom

Oxford University Press is a department of the University of Oxford.
It furthers the University's objective of excellence in research, scholarship,
and education by publishing worldwide. Oxford is a registered trade mark of
Oxford University Press in the UK and in certain other countries

© Kaspar Villadsen 2024

The moral rights of the author have been asserted

All rights reserved. No part of this publication may be reproduced, stored in
a retrieval system, or transmitted, in any form or by any means, without the
prior permission in writing of Oxford University Press, or as expressly permitted
by law, by licence or under terms agreed with the appropriate reprographics
rights organization. Enquiries concerning reproduction outside the scope of the
above should be sent to the Rights Department, Oxford University Press, at the
address above

You must not circulate this work in any other form
and you must impose this same condition on any acquirer

Published in the United States of America by Oxford University Press
198 Madison Avenue, New York, NY 10016, United States of America

British Library Cataloguing in Publication Data

Data available

Library of Congress Control Number: 2024937680

ISBN 9780198819400

DOI: 10.1093/oso/9780198819400.001.0001

Printed and bound in the UK by
Clays Ltd, Elcograf S.p.A.

Links to third party websites are provided by Oxford in good faith and
for information only. Oxford disclaims any responsibility for the materials
contained in any third party website referenced in this work.

Acknowledgements

I could not have written this book without the invaluable help of the colleagues and friends who gave me their input over the course of this five-year writing odyssey. To all of them I express my heartfelt thanks for the time and efforts they took to comment on drafts of the manuscript. Neither could this book have come to fruition without the institutional support I have received, including two essential scholarships that enabled me to make extended research visits to the USA. The first, a collective research grant organized by Trygve Wyller at Oslo University, allowed me to spend twelve months at the Department of Philosophy, University of California, Berkeley. I sincerely thank Trygve for heading the Nordhost project behind this stay, and I deeply appreciate the stimulating collaboration and friendship that he has afforded me. At UC Berkeley, I was hosted by Hans Sluga, who, in addition to his great hospitality, generously offered me his views on my book project, including his important suggestion that I discuss Jacques Ellul's critique of modern technology.

My friend and long-standing collaborator, Thomas Dumm, also kindly invited me to visit Amherst College as a Lowenstein guest professor. I enjoyed eight months of excellent research and teaching conditions at the Department of Political Science as well as many inspiring talks with Thomas. This second scholarship also enabled me to hire two research assistants from among my brilliant students at the college, John Kim and Ryan Yu, whose immense help with my book project I am incredibly grateful for. Not only did they judiciously edit my writing, but also frequently engaged in profound conversations concerning my arguments, the chapter structure, and my choice of wording. I continued to benefit from their support and thought-provoking conversations long after returning to Denmark.

I also wish to acknowledge the enormous, unfailing help my old friend and collaborator, Mads Peter Karlsen, offered me during the book's long gestation. Karlsen read and carefully commented on several chapters, suggesting crucial references, especially on Althusser and Nietzsche. The same is true of Johannes Lundberg, who first served as a research group assistant in my department and later became a PhD student under my co-supervision. Lundberg helped organize the large bibliography and he gave detailed, impactful comments on three of the chapters, bringing several important references

vi   Acknowledgements

to my attention. Providing me with his views on my writing, Jeremy Tauzer, whom I worked with at UC Berkeley, came up with many suggestions that greatly improved the manuscript. Another more recent collaborator, Johan Gøtzsche-Astrup, also generously commented on several chapters and the introduction in detail, greatly improving the overall manuscript.

The book also owes much to the tireless support of my research group colleagues at the Department of Business Humanities and Law, Copenhagen Business School. Several members kindly acted as designated commentators on my draft chapters at research seminars. Sverre Raffnsøe offered highly productive comments on Chapter 2, especially regarding the Heidegger–Foucault encounter; Cathrine Bjørnholt Michaelsen gave her astute input on Chapter 5, especially on methodological issues; Marius Gudmand-Høyer provided numerous insightful suggestions on Chapter 1 and the Introduction, insisting that I present my argument on Foucault's technological thinking more boldly; and Morten Sørensen Thaning made many fruitful observations on Chapter 4, especially regarding Foucault's work on ancient self-formation. My former master's thesis student, Peter Græsbøll Holm, was both an enthusiastic supporter and keen interlocutor during the last phases of the project, offering carefully considered comments on large portions of my writing. My sincerest thanks to each of them for their generosity, knowledge, and tireless support, which I hope one day to have the chance to return! As much as I have strived to implement all of their careful suggestions, the usual disclaimer applies.

I also extend my thanks to Adam Swallow, editor at Oxford University Press, and Phoebe Aldridge, project editor at Oxford University Press, for their wonderful help and exceptional support in processing a manuscript long overdue. Although encouraging my original book proposal, the anonymous delegates for Oxford University Press insisted that I include a discussion of Heidegger—an insistence I have come to highly appreciate.

Finally, my wife, Adriana, and my two daughters, Lucia and Emilia, have undoubtedly carried the greatest burden during this extensive book project. For their patience, love, and understanding, I am always deeply thankful.

Parts of Chapter 4 draw on my 2023 article: 'Goodbye Foucault's "Missing Human Agent"? Self-formation, capability and the dispositifs'. *European Journal of Social Theory* 26 (1): pp. 67–89. Portions of Chapter 3 present an argument which runs parallel to my article: 'Foucault's "The Subject and Power"—Four Decades Later'. *Foucault Studies* (36, August 2024). Finally, sections of Chapter 2 appear in my article 'Heidegger and Foucault on Modern Technology'. *Journal of Political Power* 17 (2).

Contents

List of Abbreviations		viii
	Introduction	1
One.	Foucault's Concept of Technology	29
Two.	The 'Eye' of Technology	87
Three.	The Production of 'Normal' Citizens	151
Four.	Techniques of Self-Formation	208
Five.	Critique and Questions of Method	267
Six.	Three Studies	304
Bibliography		325
Index		338

List of Abbreviations

The following abbreviations are used in the text to designate the works by Foucault, Heidegger, Nietzsche, and Althusser that are most frequently cited or referred to.

Michel Foucault

AB: Foucault, M. 2004. *Abnormal: Lectures at the College of France 1974–1975*. Basingstoke: Palgrave Macmillan.

AK: Foucault, M. 1971. *The Archaeology of Knowledge*. New York: Pantheon Books.

BP: Foucault, M. 2008. *The Birth of Biopolitics: Lectures at the Collège de France, 1978–1979*. New York: Palgrave Macmillan.

CF: Foucault, M. 1980. 'The Confession of the Flesh'. In *Power/Knowledge: Selected Interviews and Other Writings 1972–1977*, edited by Colin Gordon, pp. 194–240. New York: Pantheon Books.

CT: Foucault, M. 2011. *The Courage of Truth: The Government of Self and Others II: Lectures at the Collège de France 1983–1984*. New York: Palgrave Macmillan.

DP: Foucault, M. 1977. *Discipline and Punish: The Birth of the Prison*. New York: Vintage Books.

GE: Foucault, M. 1998. 'On the Genealogy of Ethics'. In *Ethics, Subjectivity and Truth: Essential Works of Foucault 1954–1984, Volume 1*, by Michel Foucault, pp. 253–280. London: Penguin.

GL: Foucault, M. 2012. *On the Government of the Living: Lectures at the Collège de France, 1979–1980*. New York: Palgrave Macmillan.

GSO: Foucault, M. 2010. *The Government of Self and Others: Lectures at the Collège de France*. New York: Palgrave Macmillan.

HES: Foucault, M. 2005. *The Hermeneutics of the Subject: Lectures at the Collège De France 1981–1982*. New York: Picador.

HS1: Foucault, M. 1979. *The History of Sexuality, Volume 1: An Introduction*. London: Penguin Books.

HS2: Foucault, M. 1984. *The History of Sexuality, Volume 2: The Use of Pleasure*. London: Penguin Books.

HS3: Foucault, M. 1985. *The History of Sexuality, Volume 3: The Care of the Self*. London: Penguin Books.

PP: Foucault, M. 2006. *Psychiatric Power: Lectures at the Collège de France, 1973–1974*. London: Palgrave Macmillan.

PS: Foucault, M. 2015. *The Punitive Society: Lectures at the Collège de France 1972–1973*. Houndmills: Palgrave.

PTI: Foucault, M. 2019. *Penal Theories and Institutions: Lectures at the Collège de France, 1971–1972*. New York: Palgrave.

SMD: Foucault, M. 2003. *Society Must Be Defended: Lectures at the Collège de France 1975–1976*. New York: Picador.

SP: Foucault, M. 1982. 'The Subject and Power'. *Critical Inquiry 8* (4): pp. 777–795.

STP: Foucault, M. 2007. *Security, Territory, Population: Lectures at the Collège de France, 1977–1978*. New York: Palgrave Macmillan.

TJ: Foucault, M. 2000. 'Truth and Juridical Forms'. In *Power: Essential Works of Foucault, 1954–1984, Volume 3*, by Michel Foucault, pp. 1–90. New York: New Press.

WK: Foucault, M. 2013. *Lectures on the Will to Know: Lectures at the College de France 1970–1971 and Oedipal Knowledge*. London: Palgrave Macmillan.

Friedrich Nietzsche

GM: Nietzsche, F. 1994. *On the Genealogy of Morality*. New York: Cambridge University Press.

GS: Nietzsche, F. 1974. *The Gay Science*. New York: Random House.

TSZ: Nietzsche, F. 1999. *Thus Spoke Zarathustra*. Mineola, NY: Dover Publications.

WP: Nietzsche, F. 1968. *The Will to Power*. New York: Random House.

Louis Althusser

FM: Althusser, L. 1969. *For Marx*. Harmondsworth: Penguin Books.

ISA: Althusser, L. 1971. 'Ideology and Ideological State Apparatuses (Notes towards an Investigation)'. In *Louis Althusser: Lenin and Philosophy and Other Essays*, pp. 127–189. New York: Monthly Review Press.

x List of Abbreviations

Martin Heidegger

B&T: Heidegger, M. 2010. *Being and Time*. Albany: State University of New York Press.

DT: Heidegger, M. 1966. *Discourse on Thinking: A Translation of Gelassenheit*. New York: Harper & Row.

LH: Heidegger, M. 2000. 'Letter on Humanism'. *Global Religious Vision 1* (1): pp. 83–109.

NV2: Heidegger, M. 1984. *Nietzsche Volume 2: The Eternal Recurrence of the Same*. San Francisco, CA: Harper & Row.

NV3: Heidegger, M. 1991. *Nietzsche Volume 3: The Will to Power as Knowledge and as Metaphysics*. San Francisco, CA: Harper & Row.

NV4: Heidegger, M. 1982. *Nietzsche Volume 4: Nihilism*. San Francisco, CA: Harper & Row.

QT: Heidegger, M. 1977. 'The Question Concerning Technology'. In *The Question Concerning Technology and Other Essays*, by Martin Heidegger, pp. 3–36. New York: Garland Publishing.

T: Heidegger, M. 1977. 'The Turning'. In *The Question Concerning Technology and Other Essays*, by Martin Heidegger, pp. 36–53. New York: Garland Publishing.

WN: Heidegger, M. 1977. 'The Word of Nietzsche: "God is Dead"'. In *The Question Concerning Technology and Other Essays*, by Martin Heidegger, pp. 53–115. New York: Garland Publishing.

WP: Heidegger, M. 1977. 'The Age of the World Picture'. In *The Question Concerning Technology and Other Essays*, by Martin Heidegger, pp. 115–136. New York: Garland Publishing.

Introduction

Michel Foucault is rarely viewed as a philosopher of technology, yet academics and students routinely refer to his terms 'technologies of power', 'governmental technologies', and 'technologies of the self'. This book is a response to the contradiction between the paucity of research into Foucault's thinking on technology and the richness of technological vocabulary and metaphors in own his writings as well as in the commentary literature. Foucault's use of terms such as technologies, mechanisms, diagrams, grids, machinery, production, and manufacture conveys that his objects of inquiry—sexuality, illness, crime, the economy, language—have been fabricated throughout the course of history. In an extra twist, however, Foucault did more than simply *borrow* a technological vocabulary to describe how important cultural phenomena are constructed. Surprisingly, he often spoke of a variety of things as though they themselves *were* technologies, including practices (e.g. the confession), institutions (e.g. the asylum), architecture (e.g. the panopticon), concepts (e.g. civil society), the soul (a technique of power over the body), and even philosophy itself (a reflexive technology of the self). In an oft-cited interview, Foucault went so far as to describe his own studies as a 'fabrication' (COF: 212). So, did Foucault occasionally couch his writing in technological vocabulary as a means of engaging in various critical pursuits, for example, to display power's productivity, or did he fundamentally think technologically? This book contends that the latter is true.

If this claim is correct, then technological elements serve neither as *objects* of Foucault's analysis nor solely as convenient *metaphors* for making arguments, but are rather *integral* to his thinking and writing. As the title, *Foucault's Technologies*, indicates, this book explores not Foucault *and* modern technology, such as technical devices or systems like television or industrial machinery, but rather his particular approach to the theme of technology, specifically the analytical concepts he developed for thinking technologically. Indeed, he recovered several distinct technologies, including discipline, security, and pastoral power, all of which have become signposts of his historical works and underlie some of his huge influence across the social and human sciences. With technology so forceful an element of Foucault's enduring

Foucault's Technologies. Kaspar Villadsen, Oxford University Press. © Kaspar Villadsen (2024).
DOI: 10.1093/oso/9780198819400.003.0001

2 Foucault's Technologies

appeal, I seek in the book to unpack the origins of his technological thought, lay out the advantages he achieved by thinking technologically, and consider the potential of pursuing this approach in future studies.

Foucault offers a unique concept for thinking technologically: the *dispositif*, which interlinks his three central themes of knowledge, power, and subjectivity. As Paul Rabinow and Nikolas Rose (2003: xv) put it, Foucault's *dispositif* can 'cut reality in a different way', a notion that inspired my subtitle. Conventional social theory relies on categories like institutions, classes, and ideologies, but Foucault's *dispositif* brings new relations to light, slicing not only through class and institutional divisions but also between the basic oppositions of the discursive, the social, and the material.

Foucault's thinking breaks sharply with the customary understanding of technology as a set of instruments or systems that repeatedly generates specific results. Foucault also abandons the omnipresent cause/effect model, which posits technology as the reliable cause of a distinct effect. Rather than treat technology as a cause, or 'false origin' prompting actions, Foucault insists, as Nietzsche did, that effects be the point of departure. Analytically, one cannot isolate the *dispositif* from its effects as a kind of unmovable mover, partly because it transforms through its own effects. As I argue later, Foucault's *dispositif* is more 'insubstantial' than allowed by our common-sense view of technology as artefacts. For instance, insofar as the *dispositif* induces a particular effect in social relations, say, a doctor's proclivity to normalize bodies, the effect is less a matter of what the *dispositif is* than what it *does*. In brief, in claiming that Foucault 'thinks technologically', I mean that 1) he uses technological terms to *conduct analysis*, 2) he sometimes describes things *as if they were* technologies, and 3) he often understands practices of discourse, social struggle, and subjectivation *as dispositioned* by technology or *dispositifs*. Through these moves, Foucault offers a highly original take on how particular phenomena emerging in early modernity became central to our contemporary world view and self-perception.

Foucault never arrived at an ultimate analytical approach, instead ever modifying, transforming, or replacing his analytical concepts—a practice that makes reconstructing his technological concepts quite challenging. I begin this rather ambitious undertaking by reconstructing Foucault's concept of technology, to this end examining the related notions of techniques, diagrams, and, especially, the *dispositif*, and thereby building an analytical toolbox for use in one's own studies. As such, the book will systematically reconstruct many of Foucault's key terms and well-known ideas as components of his technological thought. To enhance the understanding of Foucault's technological thought, I then consider how his work speaks to

Introduction **3**

key precursory and contemporary thinkers. Finally, I illustrate how Foucault himself deployed his analytical tools to study the historical emergence, development, and transformation of technology. Considering some of today's contexts, I also show how Foucault's framework is effective for the study of such recent issues as welfare recipients' inner motivation, how to manage risky migrants, and the war against Covid-19.

Technology in Foucault's words

To explore how thinking technologically helped Foucault carve out his distinct analytical approach, let us begin with his own words. People tend not to speak of technology as 'producing' sexuality, the body, or civil society, but Foucault did precisely that when, for example, he famously wrote in *Discipline and Punish* that the soul is the 'correlative of a certain technology of power over the body'. This soul 'is not a substance', Foucault declared, as it is the 'reality-reference' on which objects of analysis like psyche or subjectivity have been carved out: 'on it have been built scientific techniques and discourses, and the moral claims of humanism' (DP: 29–30). Here, Foucault was pointing out the historical correspondence between 'man's' emergence as a positive object of knowledge and the expansion of disciplinary techniques. This correspondence is produced and solidified by the disciplinary *dispositif*, which relies on and, simultaneously, propels the knowledge of psychology and psychiatry. For Foucault, disciplinary techniques and the psy-disciplines thus 'fabricate' the soul. His comments to this effect reached a critical tenor when he discussed the 'anthropological figures', such as *homo criminalis*, invented by the psy-disciplines to categorize and normalize law-breakers. However, by insisting that the soul is not a substance but rather technologically fabricated by discipline, Foucault escaped having to critique discipline from a humanist perspective and its 'moral claims' and assumptions about an estranged inner essence needing liberation from the grip of disciplinarity. At a later point he went on to say that 'it is not that the beautiful totality of the individual is amputated, repressed, altered by our social order, it is rather that the individual is carefully fabricated in it, according to a whole technique of forces and bodies' (DP: 217). In brief, by thinking technologically about 'the soul', Foucault escapes humanism and its 'moral claims' for an inner essence.

In another influential statement from *The History of Sexuality, Volume One*, Foucault rejected 'the repressive hypothesis' that sex in the modern West has been essentially repressed, basing this rejection on a technological approach

4   Foucault's Technologies

to sexuality aligned with his famous dictum that power is productive, not repressive. Foucault actually disputed the idea that a prohibitive Victorian morality had inhibited sex, arguing that the politics of sex actually mobilized 'an entire technical machinery' from which arose 'the production of sexuality rather than the repression of sex' (HS1: 114). He declared that knowledge about sex and techniques of control, in fact, have expanded in tandem ever since the late sixteenth century. Accordingly, 'the techniques of power exercised over sex have not obeyed a principle of rigorous selection, but rather one of dissemination and implantation of polymorphous sexualities' (HS1: 12). Replacing the idea that sex expresses inherent, yet largely inhibited natural drives, Foucault concluded that sex is 'a complex idea that was formed inside the [*dispositif*] of sexuality' (HS1: 52). Chapter 6 explores how Foucault came to see sexuality as produced by the *dispositif* of sexuality, a move by which he replaced presumed universals like 'sexuality' and 'desire' with a technological analysis centred on the productivity of discursive practices and political interventions. In this analysis, Foucault showed how the gradual interlinking of techniques, practices, institutions, and concepts came to underpin our modern notion of sexuality—and perversions.

Throughout his work on crime and sexuality, Foucault generally insisted that power is exercised far less by law than by techniques, an insistence that required a technological rather than judicial grid of analysis. In 1976, he said, 'I will try, where sexuality is concerned, not to envisage power from a juridical point of view, but from a technological one' (2007a: 158). Foucault was speaking of an entire political technology of life, noting that modern instruments of power over life break with the model of sovereignty. If the juridical discourse adequately represented a power centred on the right to decide life and death, Foucault declared, 'it is utterly incongruous with the new methods of power whose operation is not ensured by right but by technique ... We have been engaged for centuries in a type of society in which the juridical is increasingly incapable of coding power' (HS1: 89). He added that from the eighteenth century onwards modern society has 'created so many technologies of power that are foreign to the concept of law' (HS1: 109). Similarly, in a 1977 interview, Foucault (1980e: 184) said that 'the study of the penal system convinced me that the question of power needed to be formulated not so much in terms of justice as in those of technology, of tactics and strategy'. These quotes show that Foucault's discovery of 'productive power' pertained to not only sexuality and crime but also the exercise of power as such in modern, European societies. Significantly, discussions of Foucault and technology often overlook that Foucault's repeated use of technological terms in the 1970s occurred not simply because he stylistically preferred them but because they expressed

Introduction 5

his diagnosis that techniques as a mode of governing modern societies have gained ground at the expense of law.

Foucault also emphasized that every technique has its own history, beginning with its invention, moving through its gradual modification, and on to its repurposing to new ends. He also shed light on how techniques often intersect into larger clusters, or *dispositifs*, where they acquire new functions, are modified and perhaps entirely redirected. Foucault advanced this important point in relation to 'the technology of security' (STP), a mode of governing highly pertinent today. According to Foucault, although security has gained predominance over law and discipline as a response to market fluctuations, epidemics, crime, and other problems, legal and disciplinary techniques can still be reactivated in security strategies. In fact, such techniques are often redeployed even if crime prevention becomes an economic calculation of the risks/rewards involved in specific punishments or other means of deterrence. As such, Foucault argued, a security technology 'consists to a great extent in the reactivation and transformation of the juridico-legal techniques and the disciplinary techniques' (STP: 9). His general analytical point (Chapters 1 and 5) is that techniques are not discrete and stable entities for the reasons that they transform over time, are taken up in conflicting strategies and are given new justifications. From Foucault's works, I will thus reconstruct a distinction between relatively isolated, modifiable *techniques* versus *technologies* that link up techniques within a broader strategy.

Another example of Foucault's unexpected technologies comes from his discussion of liberal governance as a technology that 'produces freedom' (STP, BP). This notion accords with the general principles of liberalism advanced in early eighteenth-century political economy, which insisted that limiting political government was necessary to respect individuals' inviolable freedom and the natural self-regulation of society. In the liberal tradition, freedom can only be exercised under certain conditions, and liberalism therefore aims to organize 'the conditions in which one can be free'. Foucault, in analysing this tradition, presented freedom as something produced, thereby circumventing a universal notion of freedom as a substance one can gain or lose: '[W]e should not think of freedom as a universal which is gradually realized over time ... The formula of liberalism is not 'be free'. Liberalism formulates simply the following: I am going to produce what you need to be free. I am going to see to it that you are free to be free' (BP: 63). Paradoxically, of course, because organizing the conditions for freedom carries the risks of undermining the very freedom they seek to foster, there is a 'problematic relationship between the production of freedom and that which in the production of freedom risks limiting and destroying it' (BP: 63–64). Foucault called this regulation of freedom a technology: 'It is not an ideology; it is not exactly, fundamentally, or primarily an ideology. First of all and above all it is a technology of power' (STP: 49). Invoking the term technology, Foucault avoided engaging in an ideology critique, which, crudely put, claims that liberal notions of freedom and natural order are ideological obfuscations that blind people to their unfreedom. In his study of liberal thought, technology manifests as a 'politico-epistemological technology' in that it conditions how the object of government can be known and how it must be regulated to achieve a particular modality of freedom.

Foucault, digital society, and surveillance capitalism

What does Foucault's framework for thinking technologically offer in today's world, where digital technology increasingly mediates the government of both self and others? Chapter 3 asks how we have come to conduct ourselves according to the tenets of today's advanced capitalist economy. What techniques have produced the 'normalized citizens' now living their lives in the confines of wage labour, mass consumption, and, more recently, digital self-exposure and the commodification of their personal data. In this connection, I introduce Foucault's 'matrix' of totalizing and individualizing power (SP), suggesting that interventions such as personal health records, credit score ratings, and consumer risk profiles intermesh totalizing power with individualizing power. In other words, individuals become objectified as data points in health statistics, consumer credit markets, and loan default registries even as they are obliged to recognize themselves as the unique 'person' produced by such statistics. Foucault's own analysis focused on state institutions such as psychiatry, medicine, and the penal system. Today, however, more and more private corporations use, or trade in, techniques of individualizing power: criminal records, health risk profiles, background consumer reports, and credit scores. Amid the rise of big data, algorithmic decision-making and predictive profiling, Foucault's analytical matrix remains analytically helpful, albeit in need of some adaption.

The traces of ourselves we leave scattered around the web are pure gold to today's data miners, and the bottomless wealth of data accumulated has transformed the private sector, public health, and higher education. Every time we shop, travel, post a selfie, stream a movie, or simply scroll, we generate data that can predict our future behaviour. Shoshanna Zuboff (2019) has described a new economic order, 'surveillance capitalism', where human experiences are claimed as free raw material to be exploited for behavioural predictions. 'Although some of these data are applied to product or service improvement', Zuboff (2019: 8) writes, 'the rest are declared as a proprietary *behavioral surplus*, fed into advanced manufacturing processes known as "machine intelligence", and fabricated into *prediction products* that anticipate what you will do now, soon, and later'. In this new capitalist order, people have willingly exchanged their privacy for access to 'free' services and customer benefits, but machine-learning has led to an unchecked acceleration of predictive profiling that reaches far beyond the boundaries of our consent.

On the other hand, we often allow large corporations and social media platforms to collect our data, and Bernard Harcourt (2015a) has argued that the internet giants capitalize on our boundless desires for digital exposure. For Harcourt, our desire to access everything all the time has driven the unprecedented levels of digitalized surveillance, but so has our insatiable desire for attention and publicity through self-exposure. Indeed, 'our increasingly confessional digital presence: our selfies, our "quantified" data, our reality videos' have boosted commercial and governmental actors' capacity to monitor and seduce us (Harcourt, 2015a: 129). So, our own craving for virtual experiences has largely propelled us towards this 'expository society' in which 'the digital age has effectively inserted the surveillance capability into our everyday pleasures' (Harcourt, 2015a: 24), and the constitution of subjectivity is becoming ever more closely tied to our 'internet alter egos' on social media and mediated through constant smartphone communication routines.

The intricate relationship between our subjectivity and digital technology is also central to Colin Koopman's (2019) genealogy of 'the informational person', which traces the emergence of mass-scale population records such as birth certificates and social security numbers, as well as the rise of 'racialized data'. Drawing on Foucault, Koopman rejects the idea that 'datafication' estranges us from our human essence: 'When we feel alienated by data, then, it is not because we are cut off from our essence, but rather because we have become estranged from other, prior, technologies of the self' (Koopman, 2019: 8). According to Koopman, the opposition between an individual and data about that individual cannot be sustained: 'My argument is that our data are not mere *externalia* attached to us from which we might detach our truer selves as we please, but are rather constitutive parts of who we can be. Who we are is therefore deeply interactive with data' (Koopman, 2019: 8). Put differently, our intricate relationship with our (largely digitalized) data

8 Foucault's Technologies

has become a condition for subjectivity, not something from which we can ultimately hope to escape.

Under surveillance capitalism, the individual is simultaneously a data point inputted to algorithmic processes that predict the behaviour of a statistical 'figure' and a 'unique person' encouraged to expose their true self. In his influential essay 'The Subject and Power' (SP), Foucault suggested that modern state power has developed around two poles: a 'totalizing' one based on population statistics and jurisprudence and an 'individualizing' one centred on the guidance of each person's conscience. These poles can be viewed as heuristic devices that neither are mutually exclusive nor preclude instances where specific techniques integrate the two. Where once individualizing techniques tied a subject to a predetermined identity, say, someone with a criminal proclivity or economic responsibility, now individualization increasingly relies on patterns recognized in their digital behaviour. These 'totalizing' data are analysed to generate predictive profiles representing the average behaviour in a user segment but no individual in particular. Such profiles offer us a virtual identity, continually affirmed or refined according to our digital practices, at a new nexus of totalizing and individualizing power. John Cheney-Lippold (2011) has termed this virtual identity-making associated with social media behaviour a 'new algorithmic identity'. Companies engage in this identity production by using statistical models to predictively profile an individual on characteristics such as gender, age, religion, and race. Such data analyses are also used to measure and forecast companies' sales performance, customer satisfaction, and productivity. Companies also base decisions on data analyses that indicate managers' and employees' impact on business goals—a data-based management practice befittingly referred to as 'people analytics'.

For decades now, scholars and students have looked to Foucault for help studying these sweeping technological developments. One stream of research has focused on 'social' or 'governmental technologies'. Some of the topics examined are the constitutive role of insurance technology in the welfare state (Ewald, 1991), the importance of accounting as a governmental technology (Hopwood and Miller, 1994), the management of pregnancy through clinical risk techniques (Weir, 1996), the use of 'empowerment' as a technology to turn the poor into responsible citizens (Cruikshank, 1999), the proliferation of dialogue technology in 'non-authoritarian' management (Karlsen and Villadsen, 2008), the use of biotechnology to assess 'risky' people's genes, race, and gender (O'Malley, 2010), standards and standardization as tools for governing conduct (Higgins and Larner, 2010), the social struggle around defining sustainability standards (Silva-Castañeda and Trussart,

2016), how service standardization is negotiated among health workers (Villadsen, 2021a), and how pension fund decisions are 'securitized' through risk/reward calculations (Himick, 2023).

Although Foucault never experienced the rise of digital society, surveillance capitalism, or the revolutionary presence of the internet, big data, and algorithms, his work still provides a toolbox apt for analysing these developments. A second stream of Foucault-inspired studies has examined digital technology in its many, diverse manifestations. Scholars in this stream have used his concepts to study the creation of an algorithmic identity from monitored internet behaviour (Cheney-Lippold, 2011), the exposure of people to data-mining through their digital self-exposure (Harcourt, 2015a), the historical emergence of the 'informational person' as a carrier of profitable data (Koopman, 2019), how diverse human experiences serve as input to surveillance capitalism (Zuboff, 2019), the depoliticizing effects of algorithmic decision-making (Weiskopf, 2020), the archaeological affinities between the Christian pastorate and algorithmic authority (Cooper, 2020), the governmental use of mobile surveillance during Covid-19 (Bigo et al., 2021), and ESG (Environmental, Social and Governance) derivatives as a tool for financially engineering the climate (Morgan, 2023).

Although these studies offer rich insights, the specific concepts of technology applied can be somewhat unclear. At times, technology refers to specific technical devices, such as a clinical risk technique, but technology can also represent a set of technical devices *as well as* the body of technical knowledge involved in deploying these devices. For example, insurance technology encompasses both actuarial science and the correlated techniques for risk mitigation. The latter rendering of technology, as I argue in this book, comes closest to Foucault's own use of the term. In Chapter 1, I focus on the role of concepts in Foucault's work, explicating how Foucault often actively shaped concepts in the service of opening up empirical fields. He often provided descriptions that confronted other histories, theories, and concepts using his own concepts as tactical interventions into already conceptualized domains. At a more granular level, Chapter 1 traces how Foucault gradually shifted from using the rather unspecified term 'technology' to the more analytically refined *dispositif* in his writings and lectures of the 1970s.

Does 'technology' lack analytic precision?

What exactly did Foucault mean by 'technology' and 'techniques' as well as his most elaborated term, the *dispositif*? About the *dispositif*, Nick Hardy

10 Foucault's Technologies

(2015: 191) notes that 'while a small number of analyses have moved understanding forward, it remains stubbornly opaque'. In fact, Foucault never presented the *dispositif* as systematically as assumed in the commentary literature, and in writing this book I hope to help bring more clarity to this term.

The lack of a single, firm definition as well as precise criteria for identifying technology in Foucauldian terms has frustrated both conventional historians and sympathetic commentators of Foucault. Paul Rabinow (2003: 41) observes, 'Foucault never provided the sort of criteria that would satisfy a positivist social scientist or empiricist historian, or even that would enable others to judge unambiguously whether Foucault's [*dispositifs*] were discoveries or inventions. Clearly they were both' (note that I have replaced 'apparatus' with *dispositif* for consistency). I discuss this ambiguity in Foucault's approach at length in Chapters 1 and 5, making the key point that, although the *dispositif* results from an act of construction, Foucault firmly based it on an extensive examination of the historical archive. Rabinow also notes that Foucault helpfully introduced the *dispositif* to get beyond his earlier, exclusive focus on discourse, but 'the analytic unpacking of the object remains minimal. The elements composing or taken up in a network apparently could be anything' (Rabinow, 2003: 51). To reach greater precision, Rabinow emphasizes that a *dispositif* can become transferable when its techniques prove useful for tackling problems other than those for which they were initially invented. The *dispositif* transforms into a technology:

> That initial response to a pressing situation can gradually be turned into a general technology of power applicable to other situations. The apparatus is a kind of formation. What may have begun, for example, as a pressing problem of urban policing may turn into a set of diverse techniques applicable to other populations, at other times and in other places: the apparatus can be turned into a technology. (Rabinow, 2003: 54)

I suggest, however, that the notion of *dispositif* is preferable to Rabinow's 'technology', which Foucault often used with little qualification in the early 1970s (see Chapter 1). In my view, the term 'technology' signals too much material solidity, permanence, and repetitive efficacy, whereas the *dispositif* carries permanent modifiability as well as a production of unexpected, sometimes self-undermining, effects.

Mitchell Dean (1996) similarly points to weaknesses in the Foucauldian concept of technology, finding a 'multiplying tendency' in the use of the concept both in Foucault himself and in governmentality studies. This scholarship, Dean argues, has multiplied technology's domains of reference, which have come to span from 'a political technology of the body, through technology of power and technology of government, to—as a subset of the latter—intellectual technologies and calculative technologies' (Dean, 1996: 53). Dean also posits that the concept of technology 'suffers from a certain indeterminacy', and that it is 'worthwhile to match its rhetorical effects with greater analytic precision' (Dean, 1996: 54). Although precision is of course a longstanding scientific virtue, I contend that Foucault's technological concepts have a versatile, open-ended character that have advantages for undertaking philosophically informed studies of our relationship with technology (Andreasen, 2016). The critique of 'conceptual imprecisions' risks overlooking these advantages, as it fails to fully explore the philosophical and analytical motivations guiding Foucault's technological thought.

Admittedly, Foucault's own usage of technology and *dispositif* is often modest and seemingly underdeveloped, at least at first glance. The few analytical premises he has offered can make the *dispositif* seem an imprecise and therefore slippery notion. Importantly, however, Foucault intended to keep his analytical concepts free of preconceived content and thereby enable them to take shape in specific historical contexts. In the following chapters, I show that the *dispositif* neither possesses any inherent content or meaning, nor carries any thinly veiled ideology. Some readers may also be frustrated to discover that the *dispositif* is not a conventional theoretical concept or model whose adequacy can be tested on different empirical materials: it is a concept that only emerges through patiently pursuing extensive descriptions of a historical process. This is why Foucault largely refrained from offering general definitions and, when asked to do so, chose instead to describe the singular, accidental emergence of *dispositifs* like discipline, sexuality, and security.

Foucault's technological thought echoes the French and European tradition of conceptualizing technology as both a body of knowledge and a set of techniques, but the emphasis on strategy and power distinguishes Foucault's thinking. For example, in an oft-quoted interview, Foucault considered whether architecture is a scientific discipline. Remarking that the opposition between exact and inexact science was uninteresting, he firmly inserted the history of architecture in the 'general history of technê' (Foucault, 2000a: 364), his aim being to keep the term *technê* separate from the more narrowly defined 'technology':

The disadvantage of this word technê, I realize, is its relation to the word 'technology', which has a very specific meaning. A very narrow meaning is given to

12 Foucault's Technologies

> 'technology': one thinks of hard technology, the technology of wood, of fire, of electricity. Whereas government is also a function of technology: the government of individuals, the government of souls, the government of the self by the self, the government of families, the government of children, and so on. (Foucault, 2000a: 364)

In this statement, Foucault avoided the widespread understanding of technology narrowly defined as instruments for manipulating natural resources and materials. Noting that architecture is not simply a technical knowledge, Foucault broadened the meaning of technology to include the intersection of power and knowledge in practices of government.

Notoriously elastic, the term technology has changed meaning over time and between North America and Continental Europe. Eric Schatzberg (2006) notes that, although distinct terms in Continental linguistic practices, 'technique' and 'technology' are generally translated into English as simply 'technology', thereby blurring important distinctions. In the Continental tradition, Schatzberg (2006: 488) explains, 'technique refers to the methods and procedures of material culture, especially in engineering and industry, while technology is concerned with the study of these activities, their principles'. Back in the nineteenth century, the English, French, and German renditions of technology all connoted the science of the practical arts. In the early twentieth century, American social scientists merged elements of the German notion of *Technik* with the English term technology, 'shifting the latter from its original definition as the science or study of the useful arts to a new one that embraced the industrial arts as a whole, including the material means of production' (Schatzberg, 2006: 487). By 1930, 'technology' had transformed from the science of the arts into 'applied science', concludes Schatzberg, a development resulting in 'an awkward combination of Technik and applied science' (Schatzberg, 2006: 511)—a hybrid notion of technology linked firmly to the idea of progress.

The influential French critic of modern technology Jacques Ellul (1912–1994) argued that a sharp distinction needed to be drawn between *technique* and *technologie*. In his seminal book, *The Technological Society*, first published in 1954 and released in English in 1964, Ellul (1980: 32) declared, 'It is a grave error, often made by French intellectuals imitating Anglo-American usage, to speak of technology when they really mean technique.' The two terms differ, Ellul insisted, in that 'technique' refers to a general discourse on varying technologies and therefore diverges from the science of industry and production. Ellul retained this sense of technique as a general concept, reasoning that 'individual technologies must not be

Introduction **13**

isolated and analysed apart from an understanding of the wider technical phenomenon'. In this way, his work performs a 'philosophical reflection' centred on 'the concept itself' (Ellul, 1980: 31–32). Ellul's thinking broadly resonates with that of Foucault. For one, both saw technology as inseparable from subjectivity and social institutions, as evident in Ellul's (1980: 33) focus on 'the reality constituted by technology's relationship to man or society'. Both also viewed technology as inseparable from its economic, political, and intellectual contexts. Finally, Ellul conceived of technique as 'a system in which the technologies correlate to one another' (Ellul, 1980: 31) to form a quasi-autonomous, interconnected whole—a formulation whose relational character resembles Foucault's *dispositif.*

Nevertheless, Ellul's philosophical reflection on technology as a ubiquitous and all-inclusive system separates his ideas from Foucault's genealogies of the emergence and evolving interplay of *dispositifs*. Ellul wrote about his intellectual procedure:

> The countless studies on alienation, the impact of television, work organization, the effects of mass media on voting, urbanization, etc. can be useful afterwards. They can then help us understand certain aspects of the technological system. But we cannot take off from them to work out the concept of technology. We have to begin on the highest level of abstraction and then proceed to the reality constituted by technology's relationship to man or society. (Ellul, 1980: 33)

Ellul's appeal to work at the 'highest level of abstraction' contradicts Foucault's strategy of tracing 'scattered origins', that is, tracing how practices and techniques first emerge in response to specific, local problems and, then, gradually begin to connect, converge, and operate in conjunction. In another departure, Ellul somewhat idiosyncratically saw technique as an exclusive, dominant 'mode of involvement' that answers all questions from a perspective of maximum efficiency: 'the technological mediation, which imposes itself and becomes total' (Ellul, 1980: 35). Ellul's dystopian critique of 'technique' as a tyrannical imposition on humanity is a far cry from Foucault's more tempered question regarding 'what price we pay' for specific technological arrangements (see Chapter 4).

Despite these differences, the two philosophers' views of technology converge in their mutual scepticism of 'technology' in its contemporary meaning, which is strictly tied to technical devices and machines to the exclusion of the more diffuse economic and political relations that condition the advent of specific techniques in the first place. Indeed, Foucault declared that the history of specific techniques contrasts 'another history', namely his genealogical

14 Foucault's Technologies

approach, which is 'the much more general, but of course much more fuzzy history of the correlations and systems of the dominant feature' (STP: 8). Because this 'general' history conditions the emergence of technologies such as discipline or security, a narrow focus on a specific technique (e.g. the stethoscope) or institution (e.g. the hospital) fails to consider the broader social strategies (e.g. public hygiene) that govern people as particular subjects or, in Ellul's terms, the mode of involvement defining 'technology's relationship to man'. However, Foucault abstained from Ellul's all-encompassing view of technology, insisting on the irreducibility of a general strategy (the level of technology) and its concrete elements (techniques). This principle of irreducibility highlights how a strategy can intensify, be tempered, fail, or create unexpected effects. By keeping both the general analysis of technology and the concrete analysis of specific techniques at his disposal, Foucault made an original contribution to the study of technology. This empirical sensitivity and his tempered analytical critique separate Foucault from 'deductive' technology critics like Ellul and Heidegger. Even when culturally diagnosing the general relationship 'between man and technology', Foucault saw the careful work of genealogy as indispensable.

Reconstructing Foucault's technological thought

Towards the end of the 1970s, Foucault elucidated that technology was not a 'thing' but rather a nexus of interlinked elements, including institutional practices, techniques, and forms of knowledge. Together, these elements create a particular disposition in the social body towards, for example, normalization. This is why I disagree with Jim Gerrie, who claims that 'like many people [Foucault] simply may have felt more comfortable confining the term "technology" to artefacts' (Gerrie, 2003: 23). Indeed, when Foucault spoke of 'disciplinary technology' or 'the technology of security', he was *not* referring to distinct artefacts but to the interlinkage of techniques and knowledge and used the *dispositif* to explicate this understanding of technology.

The *dispositif* constitutes *a cluster* of techniques *invested with a strategy*. Such a *dispositif* induces a particular inclination into social practices and knowledge production. Or, put differently, the *dispositif* brings about a formatting of society that conditions the emergence and reconfiguration of techniques, forms of knowledge, and institutions. Below, I briefly reconstruct Foucault's technological approach through a series of steps in which I specify the *dispositif* from various vantage points, with the final step offering potential analytical pathways.

Technologies are creators of visibility

Readers of Foucault will notice how he relied on visual evidence such as plans for partitioning towns, the physical layout of military camps, or architecture designed for surveillance to drive home his persuasive analyses. He presented this visual material, so integral to his writing, as techniques for mastering others and oneself. Thomas Flynn declares that *'The argument is in the architecture'* (italics in original), arguing that Foucault's visual artefacts create lines of sight that are essentially strategic, and therefore, says Flynn (2010: 116), 'the contours inscribe relations of control, not just forms of intelligibility'. Hence, when Foucault used terms like 'disciplinary gaze', 'the normalizing gaze', or 'permanent visibility', he meant not the act of looking as such, but rather how technologies make things visible as well as governable. This theme of technological visibility, as I show in Chapter 2, is where Foucault approximates but ultimately departs from Martin Heidegger.

Foucault's *dispositif* bears some resemblance to Heidegger's notion of modern technology as a *way of disclosing* the world (see Chapter 2). The *dispositif* makes objects visible under the light of a certain normativity, but, unlike Heidegger, Foucault does not see modern technology as a prevailing mode of world-disclosure, which turns everything into a stockpile of meaningless and exploitable resources. Instead, Foucault demonstrates that technology has no fixed functionality or inner essence. Generally, Foucault's *dispositif* enables the production of truth about what an object is (e.g. crime) and a normativity for how to evaluate and govern it (e.g. normalization). Further diverging from Heidegger, Foucault shows that how the *dispositif* shapes our world depends on its specific social and historical contexts, including the social struggles that invest (and reinvest) techniques with specific aims and rationalities. In other words, the *dispositif* establishes the conditions under which to visualize and articulate the world, but eschews reference to the subject's interior consciousness or attunement to the world. Hence, one must reconstruct the *dispositif* in the exterior world, as a social-material arrangement that emerges from tactical responses to urgent problems and colliding interests.

Although accepting the argument that reading Foucault through a Heideggerian lens can greatly clarify Foucault's thinking (Elden, 2001; Dreyfus, 1996), I nevertheless conclude that Foucault's genealogy is ultimately distinct from Heidegger's critical philosophy of technology. Whereas Heidegger established 'the essence of technology' from within a history of metaphysics, Foucault emphasized the 'fluid meaning' of techniques. Schematically, his genealogy substitutes Heidegger's double ontology (being versus beings) with the visibilities that emerge from a Nietzschean field of interacting forces.

In Chapter 2 I discuss the importance of Heidegger's and Foucault's divergent readings of Nietzsche, suggesting that Foucault's technological thinking evolved at the intersection between his attention to visualizing objects associated with Heidegger and a Nietzschean concern with techniques of domination. Analytically, the *dispositif* creates a double intelligibility, one created by material elements (institutions, practices, techniques) when they interlink in a particular set-up and the other created by the *dispositif* as a *conceptual tool* used by the genealogist (see Chapter 5). Alluding to Heidegger, Foucault rejected the view that philosophy is meant to remind us of an essential but forgotten question, preferring instead to trace multiple historical trajectories through which technological objectification has emerged in specific ways inseparable from our sociopolitical reality.

Technologies are linked to subjectivity and social struggle

In contrast to a natural science perspective on the history of technology, which describes how technologies are developed for manipulating the physical world, Foucault describes law, security, and discipline as 'social technologies' (Raffnsøe and Gudmand-Høyer, 2015: 191). I take the word 'social' to mean that the invention of technologies cannot be disentangled from social organization and the constitution of subjectivity. Commentators often emphasize the anonymous character of power in Foucault, expressed as 'intentionality without a subject, a strategy without a strategist' (Dreyfus and Rabinow, 1982: 187), assigning this anonymity to the *dispositif* as well. Following this emphasis, the literature on Foucault and technology thus tends to neglect the question of social struggle and the role social actors play as instigators of *dispositifs*.

This book foregrounds how *dispositifs* emerge out of social struggle in which social actors initiate *tactics* in response to urgent problems. Physiocrats, hygienists, town planners, industrialists, and prison reformers carry out such tactics, which include the invention and deployment of various techniques for controlling and moulding individuals. For instance, eighteenth-century military training, scholastic discipline, and labour regimentation operated through techniques like drills, timetables, and workers' mandatory records. Foucault's work from the 1970s particularly displays the way such tactical responses to urgent problems push the forming of *dispositifs*, but also propel their disintegration. Rabinow makes this point about two texts from that period, but it applies to most of the significant publications from that decade: 'Foucault cast the elements in an apparatus as joined and disjoined by a strategic logic and a tactical economy of domination' (Rabinow, 2003: 52). Hence, power relations are integral to Foucault's genealogies. History does not evolve through meaning and better knowledge but through tactics and social strategies, Foucault asserted, reflecting his use of the civil war model for historical analysis in the mid-1970s. Similarly, he often focused on the tactical appropriation of techniques—that is, how older techniques are readopted and put to work for new ends, describing these shifts in terms with military, tactical connotations, such as 'reactivation' and 'displacement'. Insofar as Foucault replaced meaning with 'civil war' as a model of historical intelligibility, this shift calls for extending the working definition of the *dispositif* to say: a cluster of practices and techniques supporting, and supported by, *types of knowledge*—and propelled by *strategies*.

Technologies evolve in a dynamic interplay

In the 1970s, Foucault's work developed in ways of general analytical value. Particularly, he entered into a repeated dialogue with Althusser's theoretical Marxism as well as developed his somewhat overarching analysis of 'disciplinary society' from 1975 (DP) into a finer-grained analysis examining how several *dispositifs* interplay in 1978. In the first lectures of his 1978 course, *Security, Territory, Population*, Foucault described the tripartite *dispositifs* of law, discipline, and security as sometimes reinforcing and assimilating, other times challenging and infiltrating, one another (STP: 8–12). This complex field contradicts Althusser's model of ideological state apparatuses (Chapter 3). Foucault explored the link between state formation and techniques of subjectivation in dialogue with Marxist thought, while also dislodging himself from Marxist vocabulary. Using this dialogue, I highlight several points at which Foucault and Althusser intersect: the two poles of state power, the divine voice of ideology, and the paradox of freedom in interpellation.

Foucault, however, moved beyond Althusser's dual model of state power (repressive/ideological), offering much more historically sensitive analyses of how social groups seek to influence state legislation and the state's responsibilities as an 'agent of moralization' (Chapter 3). Compared to Althusser, Foucault described social struggle as occurring in far more fluid and mobile relations, but he also transcended Althusser's theoretical model by laying out the dynamic interplay between *dispositifs*. In such processes of interplay, one *dispositif* can infiltrate another and transform it from within (see Chapters 1 and 3). De Certeau describes this infiltration vividly: 'Indeed, this

18   Foucault's Technologies

system of discipline and surveillance, which was formed in the nineteenth century on the basis of pre-existing procedures, is today in the process of being "vampirized" by still other ones which we have to unveil' (de Certeau, 1986: 189). Such tactical displacements, whereby techniques become reappropriated and inserted into new institutions, require a detailed genealogical analysis, and are indiscernible if the analysis is confined to the official texts on penal reform. Hence, a genealogy of the penal system's reorganization must trace the tactical reutilization of techniques for corrective punishment, a tactic that cannot be reduced to the explicit formulations in penal theories. In sum, Foucault's technological thought foregrounds the transversal relations between elements (techniques, concepts, architecture, etc.) over any 'hidden meaning' or underlying structure that only a privileged observer can excavate.

Overall, Foucault's emphasis on the heterogeneity of history draws from a Nietzschean genealogy in which a multiplicity of forces interplay and create new forms, including specific *dispositifs*. It follows that the *dispositif*, neither solid nor unified, exists in continual transformation. It is 'over-determined', producing unintended and sometimes self-undermining effects, just as it transforms by interacting with other *dispositifs*. Chapter 1 reconstructs four different modalities of such interplay: 'appropriation and reutilization of elements', 'internal infiltration', 'competing constructs of the same object', and 'the emergence of new *dispositifs* at the intersection of existing ones'.

Analytical pathways

Foucault never systematically presented the key concepts of his technological thought, a gap this book tries to fill by developing the notions of technology, techniques, and *dispositif* as analytical tools. Unfortunately, Foucault's stark reservations against turning his work into generalizable methods may have justified scholars' neglect when it came to his methodological principles. Colin Koopman argues that this neglect has led to a somewhat careless use of his concepts, since 'the prevailing norm in contemporary uses of Foucault involves the adoption and elaboration of his conceptual material without paying corollary attention to his methodological repertoire' (Koopman, 2015: 573). Specifically, an overall aim of the book is to integrate the study of self-techniques with the analysis of *dispositifs* and thereby bridge Foucault's mid-career analytics of power in the 1970s with his work on ethics in the early 1980s. This integration does not treat the *dispositif* as a unified 'thing' but as an arrangement and social propensity under continual enactment, with individuals being involved in this enactment, giving shape to it, rather than simply being determined or constrained by it.

The capacities by which individuals engage with power/knowledge arrangements are rooted in the *dispositif* itself (e.g. disciplinary training) as well as forged through self-techniques. In Chapter 4, I discuss Foucault's limitations regarding the sociopolitical conditions that shape individuals' capacity to practise reflexive self-techniques. Against the widespread critique of Foucault's 'missing human agent', I argue that his limitations in this regard are not a neglect of humans per se, as his books are full of hygienists, prison reformers, industrialists, truth-tellers, and others that act to solve urgent problems, defend their interests, or transform themselves. Rather, given his stern critique of welfare institutions, Foucault hesitated to explore how power/knowledge structures of medical and educational institutions could constitute the very conditions that enable individuals to resist, manoeuvre, negotiate, or transform the forces subjugating them. Human agency is therefore a matter to be considered in light of the different relations in which subjects can engage with the *dispositifs*. Chapter 4 examines such relations, including counter-conduct, truth-telling, and limit-experiences.

Chapter 6 offers examples of how Foucault's technological approach can be put to work empirically, presenting a retrospective reading of three illustrative studies focused on the general analytical points raised above. The first example is Foucault's own analysis of 'the *dispositif* of sexuality', discussed at the outset of the Introduction. The other two examples, which are studies from my own research, help to explicate Foucault's technological approach through the lines of reasoning I used to make my own analytical and methodological choices. The second example, then, is a 'history of the present', which examines how recent Scandinavian social policies rearticulate key nineteenth-century philanthropic doctrines of 'self-help', 'poverty of the soul', and 'advice is better than handouts'. The study traces how contemporary social policy increasingly foregrounds the client's 'inner self-worth' over social structures, formal rights, and redistributional justice. The third example is a brief genealogy of 'the risky migrant' in Danish policy discourse: a thorny figure straddling the *dispositifs* of law, discipline, and security. Finally, I offer some tentative comments on 'the war' against Covid-19, which entailed border closures, lockdowns of entire countries, unprecedented stimulus packages, and tracking devices by which governments monitored citizens' movements. From the perspective of this book, the pandemic prompted responses from within our existing *dispositifs*, just as it provoked realignments between them. Hence, I speak of a pandemic-driven

20 Foucault's Technologies

recomposition in which the legal *dispositif* expanded, becoming increasingly dominant as it mobilized disciplinary techniques and security predictions.

The literature on Foucault and technology

In the vast corpus of literature on Foucault, only a handful of studies address technology's central role in his writing (de Certeau, 1986; Feenberg, 1999; Rabinow, 2003; Latour, 2005; Dorrestijn, 2012; Andreasen, 2016), with some going so far as to assert that Foucault cannot be understood without recognizing the key role he attributed to technology (Behrent, 2013; Gerrie, 2003; Matthewman, 2014). Although making pertinent observations on Foucault's technological thinking, none of these scholars systematically and analytically reconstructs his technological approach.

Bruno Latour (2005) has repeatedly praised Foucault for standing among the few historians who have studied 'intellectual technologies' (documents, charts, files, maps, and organizational devices) and recognized their agency (Latour, 2005: 76). Latour points out Foucault's careful attention to the minor elements that concretely constitute the means of power, and how this attention effectively counters the overwhelming sociological emphasis on power as some invisible substance to be revealed and denounced. As Latour sees it, however, Foucault's genius was lost in his 'transatlantic destiny':

> No one was more precise in his analytical decomposition of the tiny ingredients from which power is made and no one was more critical of social explanations. And yet, as soon as Foucault was translated, he was immediately turned into the one who had 'revealed' power relations behind every innocuous activity: madness, natural history, sex, administration, etc. (Latour, 2005: 86)

Latour astutely highlights Foucault's effort to desubstantialize the notion of power, noting the acute attention Foucault paid to the unremarkable practices and techniques through which power is exercised. Foucault's emphasis on relationality, that is, how techniques, procedures, and material arrangements become linked up, may put him in the vicinity of actor-network theory (ANT) and the sociologists of associations, but I am not convinced that Foucault aligns so easily with this tradition, especially its principle of generalized symmetry (see Chapter 5). Notably, Foucault's work from the 1970s consistently explored social struggles and the associated asymmetries in which social groups mobilize and readjust techniques that once served other purposes. Whereas Latour wants to enlist Foucault squarely in his fight against social explanations, I opt to spend time establishing how Foucault treated social conflict, with all its discursive and material subtleties, as inseparable from his technological thought.

In 'Micro-Techniques and Panoptic Discourse', Michel de Certeau (1986) discusses the crucial role of techniques in Foucault's texts, focusing on the narrative strategy in *Discipline and Punish*. Although narrowed to surveillance and discipline, de Certeau's discussion provides highly relevant insights into how to approximate Foucault's technological thinking. In de Certeau's reading, Foucault described a twin process whereby the reformist, humanitarian project of the eighteenth century onwards dovetailed with, or was 'colonized by', minor disciplinary techniques that gradually saturated the social body (de Certeau, 1986: 185). As we know, no planners or rulers implemented the disciplinary colonization 'from above', just as Foucault had no overall theory or model to explain the advance of disciplinary techniques. 'Foucault's theory', writes de Certeau, 'does not escape its object, that is, the micro-procedures. It is an effect and a network of these procedures themselves' (de Certeau, 1986: 191). He goes on to say that Foucault's real originality lies in his resolute adoption of disciplinary representations into his own text: 'There is no hierarchical break between the theoretical text and the micro-techniques. Such a continuity constitutes the philosophical novelty of Foucault's work' (de Certeau, 1986: 191). De Certeau's focus on secrecy, however, fits poorly with a central analytical argument of this book.

To describe Foucault's approach, de Certeau uses the terms 'secret and aphasic practices', which I take to mean historically distant and, perhaps, objectionable for present-day readers. By recovering the incipient, half-forgotten techniques of surveillance in schools, barracks, and workshops, Foucault showed us contemporary society's ordering principles 'in a mirror'. 'This strange operation', writes de Certeau, 'consists in transforming secret and aphasic practices into the central axis of a theoretical discourse, and making this nocturnal corpus over into a mirror in which the decisive reason of our contemporary history shines forth' (de Certeau, 1986: 190). Notably, the way I analytically reconstruct the *dispositif* parallels how de Certeau portrays Foucault's strategy of adopting techniques fully into his own discourse, but diverges in the sense that I do not view the procedures and techniques that come to constitute a *dispositif* as 'secret' or 'unspoken'. Conversely, I accept Foucault's insistence that 'everything is said' and 'the rationalities are clearly visible' (see Chapters 3 and 5) when it comes to justifying the deployment of specific techniques in response to urgent problems like workers' unrest or deadly epidemics.

22   Foucault's Technologies

Some commentators emphasize how these techniques shape humans to the extent that they become 'body-machines'. Steven Dorrestijn (2012: 14) terms this merging of the human with the technological 'technical mediation', which happens through the training of technically mediated routines. Dorrestijn draws extensively on *Discipline and Punish*, in which Foucault related how conducting repeated drills for correctly aiming, holding, firing, and reloading rifles merge the soldier and the device into 'a body-weapon, body-tool, body-machine complex' (DP: 153). Dorrestijn underscores how strategies of power interweave humans and technology, specifically through training that naturalizes individuals' relationship with techniques (Dorrestijn, 2012: 10). Foucault provided evidence for this interpretation when writing, for example: 'The human body was entering a machinery of power that explores it, breaks it down and rearranges it' (DP: 138). Clearly, *Discipline and Punish* richly describes practices of training and manipulating individuals through routines, equipment, and spatial arrangements, but Dorrestijn—like many other interpreters of Foucault—highlights the moulding of the human body while relegating the human actors' active technology work to the shadows. In this book, particularly Chapter 4, I seek to recalibrate this imbalance by reinserting individuals' self-constitutive work into the analysis of *dispositifs*.

Some commentators make the stronger claim that one cannot fully understand Foucault without taking the centrality of technology to his work into account. Comparing Foucault's thinking with ANT, Steve Matthewman suggests that Foucault, too, analysed technology in four dimensions: technology 'as objects (in relation to stethoscopes and rifles), activities (such as disciplinary techniques and other exercises of power), knowledge (particularly medical and penological) and modes of organization (hospitals and prisons)' (Matthewman, 2014: 274). This fourfold definition is helpful because it resembles Foucault's own conception of technology as a cluster of techniques and practices linked to modalities of knowledge. Still, as important as noting Foucault's use of these dimensions may be, it still falls short of fully accounting for technology's fundamental role in Foucault's work. Moreover, although true that Foucault's 'major concepts are couched in technological terms' (Matthewman, 2014: 275), the precise implications of this terminology for Foucault's concepts are left unexplored.

In 'Foucault and Technology', Michael Behrent sets out to consider all the instances where Foucault uses 'technique' or 'technology' in his work. In this article, Behrent makes two interesting arguments. First, Foucault moved from having a critical attitude towards modern technology—an attitude characteristic of French intellectual culture in the 1950s and 1960s—to using technological terminology more analytically from the early 1970s onwards. Second, although Foucault analysed technology as a means of social control and regimentation of the body, he refused humanism as a basis for his critical analysis, 'denying himself the most common theoretical basis for this position—a celebration of the human being in its non-technological essence' (Behrent, 2013: 58). From the early 1970s until completing his final works on Greco-Roman antiquity in the 1980s, Foucault conceptualized power in technological terms above all because of his philosophical anti-humanism. 'During his final phase', writes Behrent, 'Foucault continued to use "technology" in its positive or methodological sense because, even in his analysis of the self, he steadfastly refused to return to the categories of philosophical humanism' (Behrent, 2013: 58). Ultimately, Behrent's central claim is that Foucault used a technological idiom to avoid the drawbacks of humanism.

Foucault indeed repeatedly expressed scepticism against humanist thinking, especially the division between truth and power, and against the assertion that any liberating political project must realize 'the truth of our humanity'. He identified these broad humanist doctrines in various traditions, including Christianity, Marxism, existentialism, fascism, National Socialism, and Stalinism (e.g. Foucault, 1988b: 14). Significantly, Behrent notes that Foucault simultaneously critiqued technology as a means of social control and embraced a technological idiom to avoid humanism. I would caution, however, that Behrent probably overstates this point, as Foucault frequently utilized technological terms in ways with little or no relationship to humanism. Take, for example, his analysis of eighteenth-century debates on grain supply or his scrutiny of mass vaccination techniques (Chapters 1 and 6). Nevertheless, I agree with Behrent that Foucault's work from the 1960s to the early 1980s shifted from a largely critical tenor regarding technology to a more tempered analytical language. This is why I attempt to show how Foucault resolved the tension in his technology discourse by developing the notion of the *dispositif*. With this notion, Foucault could introduce an analytical concept immune to assumptions of transcendent truth and inner, human essences, while also steering clear of an underlying moral critique.

Foucault's technologies and intellectual history

This book explores Foucault's exchanges with other important thinkers (mentioned above) in developing his technological thought, thus presenting inquiries that can be termed intellectual history. Importantly, however, these inquiries are secondary to my principal aims of reconstructing the key concepts by which Foucault thought technologically and thereby rendering them both effective and flexible for future studies. As such, the analytical implications and critical potentials of Foucault's concepts supersede questions central to intellectual history, including those regarding 'influence' (direct or indirect), 'Foucault's intention' (explicit or inexplicit), or 'the role of Foucault's intellectual context'. These overriding aims require that I primarily work 'at the surface' of the concepts themselves without seeking to deeply interpret other thinkers' intentions; the symptoms of underlying ideology; or the role of tradition, milieu, or epoch.

On this point, I take inspiration from the issues Foucault took with what he termed the history of ideas and its search for authors' intentions, references to major historical epochs, preference for canonical texts, and use of hermeneutical methods. Importantly, Foucault's scepticism was largely directed at the traditional history of ideas and not recent intellectual history, which has eclipsed that tradition since the 1950s. Although the typical author-centred focus of intellectual history deviates from the approach Foucault takes, he still has certain commonalities with intellectual historians, who have endeavoured to situate concepts in the specific contexts of their emergence, to emphasize the political and social effects of concepts, and generally to bring intellectual history closer to social history.

Foucault recurrently critiqued the traditional history of ideas for its tendency to stray from the statement itself towards another non-discursive level and thus avoid the need to carefully analyse statements as they emerge. Foucault (1998e: 283) said: 'Thus faced with a change, a contradiction or an incoherence, one resorts to an explanation by social conditions, mentality, world view and so on.' Methodologically, Foucault cautioned against approaching historical texts, artefacts, and events as documents with hidden meanings not fully expressed by their creators and requiring the historian to decipher and present them anew. A book on 'Foucault's technological thought' guided by a conventional history of ideas would probably recover Foucault's 'intended meaning' when he used technological terms; trace specific authors' influence on Foucault; and use explanatory categories like 'oeuvre', 'tradition', or 'the spirit of the time'. Foucault would undoubtedly figure as 'author' and, hence, the unifying entity in such a piece of intellectual history.

Behrent's (2013) above-mentioned study lucidly illustrates how a careful (and self-declared) intellectual historian examines Foucault's use of the term technology. Behrent (2013: 56) writes that he will 'identify the relevant instances in which Foucault employs the terms "technique" or "technology" in an effort to reconstruct how he understood them and what philosophical or rhetorical ends he intended them to serve'. Note the explicit aim to reconstruct Foucault's intention in using technological terms. Behrent also invokes the terms 'intellectual context', 'collective common sense', and 'shared intellectual outlook', all references encompassed by the explanatory models of intellectual history. By comparison, Foucault posited that the history of ideas organizes historical events according to certain pre-given categories including tradition, spirit of the time, author, influence, and origin. Behrent makes no claim that contemporary French critics of technology directly influenced Foucault's thinking: 'Rather, what this comparison suggests is that Foucault's view of technology and its function in the modern world belonged, to some degree, to the common sense of French intellectuals of the postwar era' (Behrent, 2013: 65). As such, Behrent's study centres on a key theme in intellectual history concerning the reception of concepts, their dissemination, appropriation, and influence. Finally, Behrent correctly notes that the period from 1971 to 1979 is when Foucault's use of the term 'technology' evolved most profoundly (Behrent, 2013: 57). However, unlike Behrent's essay, in this book Foucault's lectures from that period are particularly important sources, as they contain Foucault's most elaborate comments on the *dispositif*. Behrent's delimitation on this front is hardly in itself objectionable, and his study certainly yields valuable insights, even if his methods conflict with Foucault's critical stance to certain ways of writing history, including author-centred ones. Again, I pursue elements of intellectual history in parts of this book in order to create a richer analytical account of Foucault's technological thought than currently available and to indicate the types of inquiries for which it can be used.

I have also eschewed taking an intellectual biography approach as Stuart Elden has so cogently done with his recent three-volume collection covering Foucault's entire intellectual history. In the volume *The Early Foucault* (2021), Elden traces Foucault's intellectual career from his student days to the publication of *Madness and Civilization*, explaining Foucault's development through the explicit or 'silent' presence of an inspirational figure, a well-known intellectual history device. Elden claims, as he did earlier (Elden, 2001), that Foucault read not only Nietzsche through the lens of Heidegger, but he 'was also reading Kant through Heidegger' (Elden, 2021: 162). Discussing Foucault's introductory essay on Kant's anthropology (Foucault, 2008), Elden further concludes that 'Heidegger is a silent presence in Foucault's examination' (Elden, 2021: 162). Elden shares Hubert Dreyfus's view that Foucault's thinking was deeply inspired by—and reconcilable with—that

26 Foucault's Technologies

of Heidegger. I evaluate this claim in Chapter 2 but bring it up now to point out my intention to avoid any reference to 'silent presences' and instead stick to analysing texts and concepts as actually articulated.

The practice of tracing specific ideas back to influential figures is fundamentally questionable from a Foucauldian perspective. He repeatedly cautioned against taking 'the founding subject', 'the originating subject', or 'the subject of knowledge', as an unproblematic starting point. The history of ideas generally took this starting point, Foucault believed, and hence turned historical analysis into a futile search for origins. Martin Saar (2011: 41–42) notes that, for Foucault, the history of ideas remained 'obsessed with the identity-conferring categories of "work" and "author"'. Analytically, this obsession prevents historians from grasping the interplay of multiple elements in history, due to their fixation on specific works and authors. Although submitting to the biographical necessity of treating Foucault as a unified 'author', Elden counters this false 'unification' by showing the numerous twists and turns Foucault took in his career as he responded to the various experiences and situations that came his way. I aim, however, to move my analysis further from the unifying, explanatory category of the author by foregrounding how Foucault responded to events and intellectual encounters with *conceptual and analytical inventiveness*—the key focus of this book.

As Foucault saw it, the history of ideas pivots on the authority of the author and the book, an authority he objected to on the grounds that the historian can then establish false causes and vague relationships, especially by using the concept of 'influence'. Foucault's critique of 'the author function' broadly parallels Nietzsche's claim that the subject's sovereignty is a fictitious idea that misconstrues the subject as the cause of action when, in fact, actions are part of a multilayered process of dispersed events (Chapter 4). Historians operating from the assumption of the founding human subject risk failing to analyse such events and thus ordering texts and statements with reference to this subject. Foucault saw the notion of historical continuity and the postulate of the founding subject as constitutive of all knowledge as 'twins' in the same thought system. If a historian sets out to analyse dispersed events, Foucault declared, then '[t]he cry goes up that one is murdering history'. What the critics essentially mourn, 'is not the disappearance of history, but the eclipse of that form of history that was secretly, but entirely related to the synthetic activity of the subject' (AK: 14). The postulate of human consciousness as the original source of history resonates in notions like creation, oeuvre, originality, influence, all central to the history of ideas. A key problem with 'founding subjects' is that the historian, confined to searching for such origins, becomes blinded to the processes whereby elements are repeated, reappropriated, and gradually intertwined. Writing the genealogy of technologies, however, Foucault could trace these precise processes marked less by originality and much more by recurrences, transfers, and modifications.

Foucault repeatedly distinguished his approach from the history of ideas throughout his career. In *The Archaeology of Knowledge*, he described his work as 'an enterprise in which the methods, limits, and themes proper to the history of ideas are questioned' (AK: 15), and in his inaugural 1970 lecture, 'The Order of Discourse', he emphasized that 'the exterior conditions' of discourse are at once institutional, political, and technical, as they consist of not only linguistic rules but also the entire institutional and material set-up in which one produces discourse: rules, conventions, procedures, and rituals, as well as technical media like graphs, tables, and geometrical figures. Treating sources as 'documents' whose essential meaning must be uncovered, the conventional history of ideas has often ignored their 'exterior' institutional, political, and technical conditions. In examining Foucault's *dispositif*, I will show how the concept effectively gets around authors and books as the original sources of meaning. As a cluster of interconnected techniques, practices, and modalities of knowledge, the *dispositif* neither expresses nor conceals anything, but rather produces a *propensity* to visualize and render objects governable in a particular way.

Unlike the history of ideas, Foucault's genealogy insists on connecting the textual and the social. Paul Veyne explains how, in Foucault's particular version of nominalism, the object must be seen as inseparably bound to a set of practices and techniques, since 'we cannot separate the thing in itself from the dispositif or "the set-up", in which it is bound up for us' (Veyne, 2010: 11). Although, for example, civil society does not 'exist in-itself', a whole set-up of discursive and social practices have recourse to it and organize themselves by invoking it. The produced object, civil society, is the effect of such intersecting processes, yet also has its own effects. As a result, an analysis of *dispositifs* centres on the power effects that ensue when practices and actions are evaluated according to 'the truth' of, for example, civil society (Chapter 5).

In Foucault's technological thought, objects are never invariable or universal but rather continually constituted within—and between—specific *dispositifs*. Saar explains that while certain aspects of Foucault's thinking and recent intellectual history converge, they also diverge substantially. Although perhaps open to insights from social history, sophisticated intellectual historians remain principally focused on ideas and 'will never travel all the way along the road leading to a history of discourses and practices, where authors and texts are not the primary referent any more' (Saar, 2011: 45). Put differently, the *dispositif* creates realities irreducible to the textual and author-centred explanations of most intellectual history.

Although aligning Foucault and intellectual history is a complicated undertaking, as demonstrated above, I pursue some elements of the latter, taking a cue from Quintin Skinner, who took the study of concepts from the conventional history of ideas and developed it into a 'contextualist approach' to intellectual history. Foucault's genealogy crucially differs from Skinner's emphasis on understanding the author's position in a polemical context, but both thinkers maintain that statements and concepts must be understood as forms of action with concrete effects in a given context. Skinner (2023: 196) declares, 'To grasp the use of a concept involves understanding what it is for, what can appropriately be done with it.' He further argues that what a concept can do remains unknown until its meaning is grasped and the specific context of its use explored: 'We must try to re-enter the different intellectual and political worlds in which each individual text constituted an intervention in an existing debate if there is to be any prospect of understanding them' (Skinner, 2023: 196). This book makes efforts to help the reader understand the contexts in which Foucault made his conceptual inventions for thinking technologically. Still, I have undertaken this task with the primary aim of reconstructing Foucault's analytical concepts—specifically intended for 'users'—rather than of retrospectively recovering the intellectual and political milieus that Foucault addressed.

In this spirit, I have followed a route paved with discussions of how Foucault's work intersects with that of other key thinkers, but have kept my gaze ultimately focused on the analytical implications. So, join me now as I embark on this journey through Foucault's technological thinking, beginning with his mature concept of technology, the *dispositif*. I then proceed to a reconstruction of his technological thought in the lights of Heidegger, Althusser, Nietzsche, and Deleuze. Next, I seek to integrate the *dispositif* and the analysis of self-techniques in a single framework and, finally, consider how contemporary studies can benefit from Foucault's technological approach.

Chapter One
Foucault's Concept of Technology

Concepts are the building blocks of academic research and its public dissemination. Max Weber made a conceptual breakthrough with his study on 'the Protestant Ethic'; Erving Goffman's concept of 'facework' is known almost universally among academics; and Ulrich Beck became famous by coining 'the risk society'. Foucault was great at picking concepts and owes part of his fame to influential concepts like 'discipline', 'biopolitics', 'governmentality', and, increasingly, '*dispositifs*'. In fact, one of the key attractions of Foucault across the humanities and social sciences is that he has offered scholars concepts that help guide research: genealogy, discourse, microphysics of power, subjectivation, and of course technologies of power. The use of concepts makes a difference to the impact of our research in the academic community and beyond.

However, using concepts drawn from Foucault's work is not uncomplicated and involves a set of questions that the reader has probably already faced: are the selected concepts adequate to the study and material in question? Have the concepts been chosen and developed in a manner that is sufficiently sensitive to the empirical material? Or did they predetermine the analysis, hence foreclosing the complexities of the social and historical reality? Could concepts from alternative theoretical traditions be used with greater effect? Such questions concerning concepts are crucial in most disciplines, including philosophy, linguistics, history, sociology, ethnography, and political science, both in the formulation of research questions and the synthesis of findings. What can we then learn from how Foucault himself developed and used concepts? If we want to work in a manner inspired by Foucault, we need to ask how he worked with concepts, and why he worked with concepts in this way. Here, the concept of technology, I suggest, offers a privileged avenue for exploring Foucault's particular approach to concepts as tools of analysis.

Schematically, it is possible to distinguish between three modalities of using concepts in academic work. First, application of concepts on empirical data; second, contestation and reworking of concepts; and third, turning empirical concepts into analytical categories. The first modality is

Foucault's Technologies. Kaspar Villadsen, Oxford University Press. © Kaspar Villadsen (2024).
DOI: 10.1093/oso/9780198819400.003.0002

commonplace and uses a concept as a way to encapsulate and present the overall findings of a research project, thereby advancing its relevance and traction beyond the particular study in question. The concept may serve to guide the choice of data, the focus points of attention, and the final presentation of the entire research project. For instance, a hypothetical research project may set out to study the 'governmentalization' of unemployment services in Sweden. It might conclude that services are being submitted to 'neoliberal rationalities' and that new self-technologies reshape the encounters between clients and professionals. In this case, the project may be assessed both in terms of how well it gives an account of Foucault's original concept and how effectively it is retailored for the relevant setting. In other words, to what extent does the project generate original, unexpected insights that extend the concept beyond its original formulation? Is the concept carefully rearticulated in the context of the specific material, or is it simply injected there without careful contextualization? Surely, writing, as Foucault did, about self-technology in Ancient Greece is one thing, but studying motivational counselling for self-development in present-day Sweden is another. We must adjust for such contextual differences; otherwise, there is a risk of treating the concept as if it existed eternally and fixed, prior to its deployment. We immediately see that the use of concepts, and the way they inform the inquiry and unfold, becomes central to evaluating the quality of the research project. In sum, in this first usage, the concept serves to guide, articulate, and encapsulate empirical findings, while it also provides certain criteria for assessing the adequacy of these findings.

Second, we may aim to critically challenge and reformulate an existing concept. The premise is that concepts do not fall from the sky ready-made. We must hence avoid treating concepts as if they existed in a vacuum, untouched by their deployment—this often involves scientific disagreement and political struggle. In this case, our criterion of success is not whether a concept is 'applied' in an adequate manner, but rather whether the study effectively succeeds in contesting a given concept. Such contestation may take place in several ways: one can present empirical data to contest the validity of a reified, self-evident concept; or analytical work may demonstrate the logical contradictions and limitations of a concept; while recovering historical processes may display the fundamental contingency of a given concept. For instance, demonstrating how the binary of state versus economy rests upon a set of discursive constructs can contest the binary itself; revising the concept of ideology to denote practices rather than ideas directs focus to the techniques and practices that produce 'the free market'; and describing the shifting historical lines of division and intersection between state and economy displays the non-universality of 'the free market'. This research strategy recognizes that there is no innocent concept in and by itself, and hence it explores how concepts underpin particular social relations in terms of inequality, gender, race, class, etc. In brief, this approach centres on the concept itself, seeking to problematize its universality, discuss its applicability, and highlight its effects in terms of power relations.

Third, we may mobilize a concept from our empirical archive and turn it into an analytical category. This means that we actively utilize the concept in our own writing, deploying it to describe new material, perhaps reconstructing the concept altogether. This strategy could be termed conceptual experimentation, which assumes that constructing a concept is inevitably an act of creation and intervention in a particular historical context. Gilles Deleuze defined philosophy as the activity of creating concepts, which he famously advanced together with Felix Guattari (Deleuze and Guattari, 1994). Concepts must lay out the transformative potentials, the possibility of something new, inherent in all systems, which would otherwise be hard to conceive of. The task is not simply to criticize or defend a concept, since, wrote Deleuze (1991: 321), 'a philosophy's power is measured by the concepts it creates, or whose meaning it alters, concepts that impose a new set of divisions on things and actions'. The strategy of marshalling concepts for critical and experimental purposes is evident in much of Foucault's work. He would mobilize a concept that he found in the archive, sometimes dislodging it from its historical embeddedness and putting it to work for new purposes. In an interview late in his life, Foucault described the use of concepts as a life-enhancing intervention:

> Forming concepts is a way of living and not a way of killing life; it is a way to live in a relative mobility and not a way to immobilize life; it is to show, among those billions of living beings that inform their environment and inform themselves on the basis of it, an innovation that can be judged as one likes, tiny or substantial: a very special type of information. (Foucault, 1998d: 475)

The following chapters will in particular consider 'the disciplinary gaze', 'instruments of normalization', 'techniques of the self', and the '*dispositifs*' of law, discipline, and security, which are a subset among Foucault's reservoir of concepts. Often, Foucault's conceptual rearticulations served, at the same time, as a means for describing a historical process, for example the rise of 'modern biopolitics' or 'the governmentalization of the state', and as critical commentaries on his intellectual and social context. As such, genealogies, guided by disembedded concepts, would indirectly shed light on urgent concerns at Foucault's own time. In this strategy, the concept both serves as a category of analysis and as a tool of problematization, which entails transforming the original concept and putting it to work in unexpected ways. The three modalities of concept deployment are not exhaustive but are rather intended to help the reader reflect on and situate his or her use of concepts drawn from Foucault's work.

***

Foucault never wrote a text on his own use of concepts, although *The Archaeology of Knowledge* discusses concept formation as part of his elaboration of discourse analysis. In Foucault's genealogical work from the early 1970s onwards, reflections on his use of concepts in writing genealogy are scant, and research on Foucault's relationship to concepts is similarly sparse. This chapter clarifies Foucault's use of concepts, and especially his conceptual inventions around the theme of technology, which demands some work of reconstruction. First, it explores the issue of how concepts generally function in Foucault's work and then zooms in on how he approached technology. Second, the chapter takes up the task of reconstructing Foucault's notion of technology as a system of techniques and practices, emphasizing that technology is a response to urgent needs and social struggle. This section also considers Foucault's gradual displacement of technology by the concept of *dispositif*. The third section on 'diagram and micro-dispositifs' describes two analytical directions in Foucault's analysis of *dispositifs*. One traces how local tactics and techniques are enrolled in overall strategies, while the other describes how a strategic imperative begins to saturate institutions. Fourth, we explore how, in the late 1970s, Foucault foregrounds interplay, mutual support, and contradictions between multiple *dispositifs*. The fifth section considers some complexities in Foucault's framework, including 'over-determination' and 'strategic elaboration', which bring into view unintended effects that propel the *dispositif* into perpetual transformation.

The analytical clarifications undertaken in this first chapter should help prepare the reader for the following chapters: Chapter 2's discussion of the theme of technology and visibility, Chapter 3's exploration of normalizing techniques, Chapter 4's examination of self-formation, and the discussion of critique and methodological questions in Foucault in Chapter 5, and, finally, Chapter 6's presentation of studies inspired by Foucault's technological approach.

Technology: between analytics and concept

Foucault's use of the term 'technology' fits best into the third modality above—turning empirical concepts into analytical categories—and hence it evades conventional thinking on concepts as representations. He mainly utilized the concept of technology for describing how modern systems of knowledge and practices emerged in historical processes like discipline, sexuality, or biopolitics. However, more elaboration is needed to fully flesh out Foucault's approach to technology, including why he used technology to describe things that could be—and often have been—described otherwise, for example as suppression, class dominance, functionality, or individual ethics. Foucault said, in the lecture 'What is Critique' from 1978, that he used concepts like 'knowledge' or 'power' not to designate entities in reality or something transcendental. Instead, these terms served only the methodological function of opening up the field for description: 'It is not a matter of identifying the general principles of reality through them, but of somehow pinpointing the analytical front' (Foucault, 2007b: 60). This statement is a warning against abstract conceptualization, for example 'state ideology', and an insistence on the need for empirical description, for example of how power and knowledge interrelate in a specific process and a specific domain. For Foucault, concepts like knowledge and power are not universals always-already possessing some content that can be invoked to legitimize or denounce what is under scrutiny. Rather, the task is to describe how power and knowledge are interrelated, and in this sense the concepts serve only as an 'analytical grid'.

> It is also important at every stage in the analysis, to be able to give knowledge and power a precise and determined content: such and such an element of knowledge, such and such a mechanism of power. No one should ever think that there exists one knowledge or one power, or worse, knowledge or power which would operate in and of themselves. Knowledge and power are only an analytical grid. (Foucault, 2007b: 60)

Here, Foucault reworks the concepts of power and knowledge in order to render them as analytical tools, 'the grid of power/knowledge', capable of describing a concrete, historical relation between the two. The question is, however: what status can we assign to Foucault's other 'signature' concepts—archaeology, genealogy, discipline, biopolitics, and governmentality? Considering the vast amount of scholarship that has deployed Foucauldian concepts, surprisingly few contributions have focused explicitly on the role of concepts in Foucault's authorship (exceptions include Deleuze, 1992; Davidson, 2004; Koopman and Matza, 2013). In a rare article, Colin Koopman and Tomas Matza (2013) propose a set of useful distinctions for clarifying Foucault's concepts and their functions. Particularly pertinent is their differentiation between 'analytics', 'concepts', and 'categories'.

First, *analytics*, Koopman and Matza (2013: 821–822) suggest, 'are the broadly methodological constraints that Foucault brought to bear upon his inquiries', namely his methods of archaeology and genealogy. Second, on the specific level of analysis, we find *categories*, which 'function like lenses through which inquiry takes place'. Examples of categories are discourse, power/knowledge, and techniques, which make up analytical grids in Foucault's descriptions of how language, power relations, and institutions have been organized. Third, *concepts* emerge out of the work of inquiry and are hence embedded in the specific contexts that Foucault studied. Examples include discipline, biopolitics, and pastoral power, which all 'specify the formulations through which Foucault made sense of the objects of his inquiry' (Koopman and Matza, 2013: 822). Eschewing speculative and abstract conceptualizations, Foucault often mobilized his empirical material when he wanted to convey a theoretical critique, hence acting as a 'critical empiricist' (Koopman and Matza, 2013: 821). A complication to this set of distinctions is that many of Foucault's concepts appear both as *objects* of analysis and *tools* for inquiry. Hence, Foucault's genealogies put under scrutiny historical concepts (three) derived from the archive, but during the analysis, the concepts can begin to serve as analytical categories (two) in their own right.

The concept of biopolitics, for example, was not coined by Foucault but came to prominence in the early twentieth century in biologically informed reasoning on the nation state, natural selection, and war between groups. Foucault's use of the term is similarly placed at the intersection between human biology and politics, but he first introduced biopolitics in 1974 in a discussion of social medicine, using the term to denote the political regulation of the biological aspects of human beings as members of groups, cities, or nations (Gudmand-Høyer and Lopdrup-Hjorth, 2009: 104). In 1976, Foucault put the concept to use in describing how modern nation states in the nineteenth and twentieth centuries began to wage war against harmful individuals within their own populations. Hence there was a deadly biopolitics of 'internal purification' in Foucault's genealogy of state formation in the register of race-war (SMD). Another variant of the concept of biopolitics emerged in Foucault's descriptions of how medical and 'psy-sciences' work to normalize deviances through less dramatic, daily practices of welfare state institutions (HS1). And finally, in his studies of neoliberalism,

Foucault returns to biopolitics—now with a framework that he views as indispensable for understanding neoliberalism as governmental rationality (BP). In this context, eighteenth-century quasi-biological notions of the market as a 'natural order', with its 'natural' prices, fluctuations, and mechanisms, become central to understanding the premises of twentieth-century biopolitical economic thought (Villadsen and Wahlberg, 2015).

These brief comments are meant to show that, for Foucault, the concept of biopolitics serves different purposes and takes very different shapes depending on the context of his inquiry. This fact has not precluded a tendency in contemporary debates to speak about biopolitics as if the concept were a clearly defined descriptor which is straightforwardly applicable in studies of present-day issues, where the state is involved in regulating individuals' biological lives. This is not to say that Foucault's concepts cannot be fruitfully redeployed in our own research. But insofar as Foucault's concepts are empirically grounded, emerging out of his genealogies, careful work of reconstruction is required if the concept is to serve as an analytical category. Whereas Foucault's analytics, such as genealogy, can be transplanted to new contexts relatively easily, his concepts must be disembedded from their specific historical embeddedness to operate on new material. Hence Koopman and Matza argue:

> While concepts require a high degree of careful disinterring in order to be redeployed, analytics are much more portable in their original form. Foucault's work gains much of its rigor and mobility on the basis of analytics, whereas concepts are what lend his work its vividness and force. (Koopman and Matza, 2013: 825)

One could object that Koopman and Matza's reconstruction creates a systematicity out of Foucault's highly experimental work, positing clear distinctions between his a priori analytics and categories on the one hand, and the concepts resulting from his inquiries on the other. Hence Jeremy Tauzer describes Koopman and Matza's schema as 'highly tamed and academic', insofar as it creates 'a directionality from a stable toolbox to a variable field and a variable collection of results which does not do proper justice to the empirical openness and experimental flexibility of Foucault's approach' (Tauzer, 2023: 2).

Nevertheless, the distinction between concept and analytics is a good starting point for exploring Foucault's technological thinking. This thinking entails, as we will see, a shift by which, in the 1970s, Foucault leaves his relatively loose use of the word technology in preference for the more carefully elaborated concept of the *dispositif*. The notion of *dispositif* can be

36 Foucault's Technologies

situated, I suggest, somewhere 'in between' the empirical concept and the analytical category. In other words, it straddles or interconnects the two, insofar as it requires the scholar to give historical content to the concept. Accordingly, technology does not figure as a universal or unspecific term in Foucault's work, or as 'technology as such', like Heidegger's conception of technology as the prevailing modern world view (discussed in Chapter 2). For Foucault, technology always figures as a technology 'of something', for example 'technology of discipline', 'technology of security', or 'technology of sexuality'.

Foucault's use of the term emphasizes, as we will see, what a technology produces and how it organizes social practices, rather than what it essentially 'is'. The avoidance of using the concept in a universal or general sense is evident in Foucault's repeated insistence on giving historical content to the concept. It is thus possible to rewrite Foucault's (2007b) above-quoted dictum that concepts merely mark up 'the analytical front', to say: 'We should not think that there exists one technology which would operate in and of itself.' This is both because technologies always come in the plural and because they are entangled with their socio-historical context. Therefore, to again paraphrase Foucault, when undertaking a study of technology, we must at every stage in the analysis be able to give the concept a precise and determined content. Indeed, technologies emerge and operate within historical processes. They arise in response to particular problems, they are invested by particular strategies, they produce a particular knowledge, and they interplay with other technologies.

The way that Foucault uses concepts, including the concept of technology, displays his strategy of testing out different frameworks for approaching the historical material. His premise is that concepts are never simply neutral descriptors of reality but are always inserted into already conceptualized domains. Here, they can have transformative effects insofar as they allow us to redescribe, for instance, historical processes, state formation, or the function of power. Foucault's experimentation with concepts could be encapsulated in this simple formula: what would happen if we deploy X conceptual framework to redescribe Y? For example, what would happen if we redescribe the subject not in terms of its essence, but in terms of its fabrication? Or, what would happen if we redescribe sexuality not in terms of its repression but in terms of its production? Pursuing such experiments, Foucault seems to follow the premise that concepts are not eternal or unrevisable, as mentioned above, but come into existence in particular contexts where they serve certain purposes. Such an activist approach to concepts in Foucault is suggested by Arnold Davidson (2004: 181): '[C]oncepts are to be identified by the uses that are made of them, by the connections that govern their employment and that allow them to enter into what Foucault thought of as specific "games of truth".

Often, Foucault pursued an experimental strategy in critical dialogue with dominant intellectual traditions, like Freudian Marxism or Hobbesian social contract theory, and as indirect comments to political and social issues of his time. Foucault's work thus displays a broad resonance with Deleuze and Guattari's proposal that philosophy's essential task is to 'create concepts for problems that necessarily change' (Deleuze and Guattari, 1994: 28). The experimental character of Foucault's inquiries is most evident in his lectures, which also, along with his many interviews, contain Foucault's occasional comments to sociopolitical issues. At times these comments would be explicit, while at other moments Foucault made thinly veiled connections between his lecture themes and what he saw as critical issues of his day, such as the treatment of prisoners in France, the ideology of the French communist party, or the rise of left-wing terrorism in Italy.

At stake in these exchanges was how to reconceptualize a domain, for example psychiatry, punishment, or sexuality, and Foucault sometimes described his work as the recovery of 'subjugated knowledge' (SMD: 8–9). Mobilizing such marginalized knowledge would be an insurrection against institutionalized knowledge that claims the superiority of science. Hence, for Foucault, concepts do not simply work in a representational manner, that is, as descriptors of clearly demarcated entities in reality. Concepts are rather superimposed upon a field that is always-already stabilized by concepts, with which new concepts will intertwine or clash. Accordingly, Foucault's concepts do not just describe struggles but inevitably themselves partake in struggles. This emphasis on the concept's intervention into a field of forces was presaged in Nietzsche's philosophy. Hence Deleuze says in the foreword to his Nietzsche book: 'A Nietzschean "aphorism" is ... a proposition which only makes sense in relation to the state of forces that it expresses, and which changes sense, which must change sense, according to the new forces which it is "capable" (has the power) of attracting' (Deleuze, 2006: xix).

At times, Foucault was drawn towards the view that writing history is never impartial and neutral; instead it takes sides in struggles of the past as well as the present (SMD: 173). Against the premise that phenomena like madness or sexuality posses universal characteristics, Foucault's concepts mark out coordinates around which past struggles have occurred and ongoing contestation evolves. This does not, however, amount to propagating what Foucault called 'an imperative discourse' that orders one to 'strike against this and do so in this way' (as I discuss in Chapter 5). Rather, it is a matter of producing

38 Foucault's Technologies

a 'tactically effective analysis' (STP: 3) which, in a given domain, marks out the field of forces and obstacles for those who wish to engage in struggle.

What did Foucault mean by technology?

On the following pages, I will reconstruct Foucault's thinking on technology based on formulations scattered across his books, lectures, and interviews. Works from the 1970s constitute the peak of Foucault's use of such technological terminology, but prior writings from the 1950s and 1960s as well as subsequent publications from the 1980s contain many technological terms too. Consider the brief survey in Table 1.1 showing the occurrences of key technological terms from selected works, predominantly from the 1970s. I use the French originals published by Gallimard.

The survey shows that all of the six selected works by Foucault contain quite an abundance of technological terms. *Discipline and Punish* and *Security, Territory, Population* display the highest frequencies, which is perhaps unsurprising given the instruments of power, control, and regulation that Foucault treats in these works. The first deals with the plethora of techniques that proliferated in the seventeenth and eighteenth centuries for moulding the body in punishment, military training, factory work, hospitals, and schooling, whereas the latter analyses eighteenth-century innovations for organizing cities in order to control crime levels, infectious diseases, food supply, efficient prices, and more. Hence *Discipline and Punish*, and to some extent also *Psychiatric Power*, focuses on disciplinary techniques aimed at the human body, including the distribution of bodies in space, the control of activity, and the division of time: timetables, work rhythms, drills, physical exercises, examinations, surveillance arrangements, prison calendar, production line stopwatch, savings schemes, and the medical case file.

In *History of Sexuality, Volume 1* and *Security, Territory, Population*, Foucault shifts emphasis from the body to the health of the population. Foucault's targets of analysis in these works include techniques for analysing sexual desire and producing it in discourse, which he often traced back to the examination of conscience, the 'technology of the flesh', in sixteenth-century Christianity. With the modern medicalization of sexuality, the 'technology of the flesh' is refined into a series of diagnostic and corrective techniques, targeting especially sexual anomalies in relation to children's sexuality and women's sexual physiology. Technologies like population statistics, public hygiene, demographics, statistical prediction, vaccination campaigns, and preventive crime measures take centre stage in the *Security, Territory,*

Table 1.1 Technological terms in selected works by Foucault (source: the author)

Term	*Le Pouvoir psychiatrique* (1973–1974)	*Surveiller et punir* (1975)	*Historie de la sexualité, Tome 1* (1976)	*Sécurité, territoire, population* (1977–1978)	*Historie de la sexualité, Tome 4* (1982)	*Historie de la sexualité, Tome 2* (1984)
Mécanisme(s)	54	105	61	127	10	0
Technologie(s)	44	31	32	52	10	2
Technique(s)	81	158	43	128	27	17
Instrument(s)	57	58	16	82	17	5
Dispositíf(s)	107	59	116	72	3	0

40   Foucault's Technologies

Population lectures. The latter are 'vital' technologies of power, insofar as their aim is to maximize life by reducing the risks that epidemics, crime, and economic crisis pose to the population's health and vitality.

Turning to Foucault's last works in the early 1980s, one still finds the use of technological terminology, although it is notably less frequent than in his 1970s works. Our survey here reflects Foucault's self-declared move in the early 1980s from *dispositifs* of subjugation to practices of self-constitution. In an interview from 1982, he says: 'Perhaps I've insisted too much on the technology of domination and power. I am more and more interested in the interaction between oneself and others and in the technologies of individual domination, the history of how an individual acts upon himself in the technology of self' (Foucault, 1988b: 18–19). Accordingly, 'techniques' now figures as the most frequent technical term, whereas *dispositifs* almost completely disappears.

In his 'ethical phase' from the 1980s, Foucault uses his technological approach to describe the transformations of moral experience in human history. In contrast to a history of moral codes, Foucault focuses on techniques by which individuals are led, either by themselves, or under the direction of others, to conduct themselves as ethical subjects. Accordingly, he defines ethics as 'the elaboration of a form of relation to self that enables an individual to fashion himself into a subject of ethical conduct' (HS2: 251). With this focus, Foucault studies the shifting moral attitudes and techniques related to self-conduct over five to six centuries from the Greco-Roman world to the emergence of Christianity. Examining ancient Greco-Roman thought, he centres on three major techniques of the self: dietetics, economics, and erotics. A key goal guiding these self-techniques was to be able to direct and temper one's desire, not in order to submit to a universal moral code, but as part of one's work to achieve self-mastery. Foucault wrote that 'not only did the Greeks not seek to define a code of conducts binding everyone, neither did they seek to organize sexual behavior as a domain governed in all its aspects by one and the same set of principles' (HS2: 251). The techniques of self-mastery that Foucault finds in ancient philosophy also differ, as he sees it, from techniques for guidance of the soul through the revelation of inner truth, emerging in early Christianity (see Chapter 5).

An important analytical point arising from Foucault's 1980s works is that the same practical techniques can be sustained over time, while being invested with new goals and rationalities. Focusing on the theme of obedience, Foucault described how early Christians sustained ancient Greco-Roman techniques of self-conduct, fundamentally transforming them in the process:

> So, from the fourth century, within monastic institutions there is the transfer of a number of fundamental techniques of ancient philosophical life into Christianity. But this transfer of techniques, and in particular of the technique of direction, is brought about, principally around the relationship of obedience, with a veritable inversion of all the effects produced by this technique. In other words, the procedure of direction, the technique of direction, is now inscribed in a general apparatus (dispositif) or, if you like, in a technology of direction that alters and inverts all its effects. (GL: 274–275)

Here, Foucault was comparing how ancient Greeks and Romans defined obedience and deployed its associated techniques to how Christianity rearticulated and modified the same theme. In antiquity, obedience was closely tied to the ideal of self-mastery, which served as the path to a well-lived life. Exemplified by Stoic autonomy, the techniques of 'ancient direction' help the individual attain a self-sufficiency and autonomy in relation to others and in the face of contingent events. Christianity demands the exact opposite: indeed, the Christian principle of obedience through humility, asserted Foucault, 'puts me below everyone and makes me want nothing' (GL: 274). Foucault's analysis of obedience and its Christian transformation parallels other comparisons he made between the ancient practice of self-care through 'the use of pleasures' and the Christian asceticism, which entails self-scrutiny and renouncing desire (GE; HS2).

Most importantly, the long quote above illustrates two general points. First, in rendering self-reflection and self-conduct as a matter of practical techniques, Foucault clearly demonstrated that the problem of subjectivity—of how to become a subject for oneself and for others—is central to his technological thinking. Second, Foucault complicated his own schematic contrast between antique and Christian moral codes by emphasizing that the self-techniques he studied were neither distinct nor neatly partitioned for each epoch (Chapter 5). Generally, techniques are modified and perhaps entirely redirected when enrolled into a new *dispositif*.

Foucault's rather nonchalant use of various and often overlapping technological terms indicates that elaborating a rigorous notion of technology was never the principal concern in any of his texts or lectures. As already mentioned, he generally used the terms in descriptions of specific historical processes, for instance when tracing the emergence of discipline or sexuality. In terms of reconstructing technology as an analytical category, we must be aware that the ways that technology emerges and operates in one historical process might not be transferable to other processes. Foucault favoured shaping a concept in relationship to particular contexts and within specific,

42   Foucault's Technologies

genealogies. Scrutinizing Foucault's scattered uses of the term 'technology' in his books and lectures, we are moreover faced with the problem that his usage displays little effort at conceptual consistency. He very rarely gives precise definitions of the term, and he often shifts between a number of seemingly interchangeable words such as '*mécanisme*', '*appareil*', '*ensemble*', '*système*', and '*dispositif*' without offering any explicit explanation. Despite these limitations, I suggest that a distinct framework for analysing technology in a Foucauldian vein can be elaborated from his authorship.

One reason for this apparent conceptual carelessness is that many of Foucault's most significant uses of the term 'technology' occurred in his lectures, which he never intended for publication. The lectures sometimes display imprecisions, repetitions, and restatements of the same point in slightly different terms. At times, Foucault's oscillations between terms like 'technology', 'system', and 'apparatus' appear to simply bear out his wish to vary his language. Consider, for example, the use of shifting terms in *Psychiatric Power* on discipline as constitutive of the modern individual:

> I think we should equally see the real constitution of the individual on the basis of a certain *technology* of power. Discipline seems to me to be this *technology*, specific to the power that is born and develops from the classical age, and which, on the basis of this game of bodies, isolates and cuts out what I think is a historically new element that we call the individual. (PP: 57, my italics)
>
> Then, at the end of the seventeenth century, and during the eighteenth century, disciplinary *apparatuses* appear and are established which no longer have a religious basis ... You see the appearance of disciplinary *systems*. There is, of course, the army, with quartering to start with, which dates from the second half of the eighteenth century, the struggle against deserters, that is to say, the use of files and all the *techniques* of individual identification. (PP: 70, my italics)

Notable here is that Foucault uses 'technology', 'technology of power', 'system', and 'apparatus' as apparently equivalent terms for discipline ('apparatus' here translates the French '*dispositif*', a translation which we will discuss later). Of course, Foucault might have used the term 'technology' in the first passage quoted above because it connotes the production or crafting of something, namely the individual. However, the notions of 'apparatus' or '*dispositif*' carry a similar meaning, whereas 'system' foregrounds the creation of a coherent structure or order, as in the army's functional divisions and hierarchical ranks. Finally, the term 'techniques' comes in to designate specific devices, like individual case files, that make up the micro elements of the disciplinary technology/*dispositif*/system.

It should be clear that the distinctions suggested here are not explicit in Foucault's lecture hall formulations in 1973, but result from my reconstruction. My conceptual reconstruction will henceforth draw upon Foucault's articulations of technology and *dispositifs* as they evolved during the 1970s. To base conceptual clarification on lecture manuscripts can be challenging due to their typical lack of precision. However, Koopman and Matza (2013: 832) note that while his lectures are 'perhaps not always the most precise guide to the subtle intricacies of Foucault's central concepts, they do nevertheless showcase those intricacies in the context of their analytical refinement'. The lecture series thus allows us to follow Foucault's thought in movement, which is evident in his gradual shift from a rather unspecific use of the term 'technology' to the refinement of 'the *dispositif*'. Towards the end of the 1970s, it becomes clear that technology is not a 'thing' but rather a nexus of elements, as Foucault (CF) explicates his use of the *dispositif*, offering definitions and analytical principles.

As a first approximation, Foucault's concept of technology can be conceived of as *a series* of practices and techniques, *which are invested with a strategy*. For example, the technology of discipline comprises a range of practices and techniques for surveying, comparing, and correcting human bodies. These practices and techniques are all invested with the strategy of 'normalization'—that is, preventing unwanted behaviour and bringing human action to comply with certain norms. The notion of technology as a network guided by a strategy can be further explained by considering the distinction Foucault in some places draws between 'techniques' and 'technologies'. He thus speaks of 'the history of the actual techniques', like the technique of solitary confinement, as opposed to the more general history of technologies, such as the technology of discipline (STP: 8). We will examine this important distinction between the histories of technology versus techniques in more detail in Chapter 2 as part of a comparative discussion of Foucault and Heidegger. Notably, Gavin Kendall and Mike Michael (2001: 3) observe that this distinction is largely overlooked by most Foucauldians, whose usage of the two terms 'technology' and 'technique' 'may sometimes be a little careless'. Kendall and Michael (2001: 6) explain that Foucault uses the French term *technique* to refer to a practical instance, including procedures, tools, forms of analysis and self-reflection, either isolated or linked up with other techniques. *Technologie*, by contrast, designates agglomerations of techniques, which are linked together and cohere with other techniques to form a system governed by an overall strategy.

We note that this definition collapses the division between the social and the technical commonly assumed in the use of the term technology.

44   Foucault's Technologies

This means that we cannot conceive of technical devices or 'hardware' as entities separate from society because, for Foucault, technology does not harbour any inherent, non-social functionality. Moreover, narrowing the meaning of the term technology to 'hard technology', like an electrical transformer, would exclude all those procedures and rationalized practices through which humans seek to produce and modify themselves or others. Foucault recognized that the term technology, like its Greek precursor *technē*, risks denoting only hard technology:

> What interests me more is to focus on what the Greeks called techne, that is to say, a practical rationality governed by a conscious goal ... The disadvantage of this word *techne*, I realize, is its relation to the word 'technology,' which has a very specific meaning. A very narrow meaning is given to technology: one thinks of hard technology, the technology of wood, of fire, of electricity. (Foucault, 2000a: 364)

When analysing technology, as Foucault explains, he wants to emphasize the kind of reasoning which is always invested in techniques. And he wants to give attention to how techniques not only produce something material (wood, fire, electricity) but also produce 'immaterial' things like social relations and self-relations. Although Foucault does not mention the '*dispositif*' in this context, his dissatisfaction with the connotations of technology is likely to have been one of the reasons he eventually preferred the concept of *dispositif*. This term came to define an agglomeration or interconnection of diverse elements, including practices, procedures, techniques, scientific concepts, laws, architecture, and more (CF: 194). Because of its multiple connotations, *dispositif* can be a slippery concept, and it is not easily translatable into English. The *Collins English Dictionary* defines 'dispositive' as 'a thing that disposes, such as a legal document', which partly captures Foucault's usage, but it also notes that the noun is now obsolete. Michael Behrent presents a more extensive definition from the *Historical Dictionary of the French Language*:

> According to the *Dictionnaire historique de la langue française*, dispositif originally designated the final words of a legal ruling, in which a court's decision was announced. The word subsequently entered military language, referring to 'the totality of means arranged [disposés] consistent with a plan.' A usage from 1797, for instance, speaks of a 'dispositif de défense.' Around 1860, the term acquired its most common contemporary sense: the 'way in which the organs of an apparatus are arranged [disposés].' (Behrent, 2013: 87–88)

Similarly, Raffnsøe et al. (2014) explain that in French the term *le dispositif* is a common word, which denotes an arrangement set up for a particular purpose, today often used in relation to information, communication, and media technology. An example is 'un dispositif d'information', which is the monitor at a railway station that displays the departure and arrival times of trains as well as the relevant platform numbers. This device illustrates the basic functions of a *dispositif* insofar as it processes inputs and generates effects according to a specific rationality. Raffnsøe et al. point out that *dispositif* is also used in the military and legal contexts, where it designates the carrying out of a plan or the effectuation of a law. In military terminology, the *dispositif* is distinct from the planning of a strategy, since it 'designates the operation of the plan in time and space, with the means at hand, and with regard to the characteristics of the adversary. In a legal context, a dispositive refers to the closing, effective part of a lawful or administrative text' (Raffnsøe et al., 2014: 9–10). In both cases, the term gives emphasis to the activity of carrying out a strategy or command, while taking diverse contextual factors into account. Raffnsøe et al. examine the etymology of the dispositif from their assertion that the older connotations of the term are important for grasping its significance in Foucault's work:

> Etymologically, in French as well as in English, the notion derives from the Late Latin dispositivus, a substantive form of the adjective under the same name; hence the dispositive refers to a certain 'something' that has certain 'attributes'. Moreover, both the adjective and the substantive are themselves derivatives of the Latin verb dispōnăre (lit. 'to set apart'), which is generally referring to such endeavors as 'to set in order,' 'to arrange,' 'to dispose,' or 'to form.' (Raffnsøe et al., 2014: 9).

Again, we note that the *dispositif* connotes activity rather than substance, especially given that the term originally derives from a substantiation of a verb. In order to retain these connotations Raffnsøe et al. suggest translating the French word with its English equivalent, 'the dispositive', which carries very similar semantics as the French word, even if it is obsolete in contemporary English.

From this brief etymology of *dispositif* we can derive a strategic, military, and legal meaning as well as a technological connotation, all of which Foucault evokes in his usage. The translator of the English version of *Psychiatric Power*, Graham Burchell (PP: xxiii), notes that there is no satisfactory English term that captures Foucault's rendering of the *dispositif* as a 'configuration

46 Foucault's Technologies

of elements' that is at the same time 'strategic and technical'. In this regard, Burchell's argument runs entirely counter to Raffnsøe et al. (2014). In the context of psychiatric power, explains Burchell, the concept carries a dual meaning:

> On the one hand, in relation to 'psychiatric power' the term picks out a sort of strategic game plan for the staging of real 'battles' and 'confrontations' that involve specific 'tactics,' 'manipulations,' 'manoeuvres,' and the overall 'tactical disposition' or 'deployment' of elements … . On the other hand, it also refers to a more or less stable 'system' of 'techniques,' 'mechanisms,' and 'devices'; 'a sort of apparatus or machinery.' (PP: xxiii)

Burchell chooses, like the majority of translators, to translate the *dispositif* as 'apparatus', although he admits that this solution is not optimal, since 'apparatus' also translates *appareil* and therefore risks confusion with Althusser's notion of state apparatuses (PP: xxiii; see also Bussolini, 2010: 106). This is unfortunate, in that Foucault made significant efforts to distance himself from Althusser's notion, as we will see in Chapter 3. I have chosen to keep the French *dispositif* untranslated, since the English word 'dispositive' is obsolete, and none of the English terms used ('device', 'machinery', 'apparatus', 'mechanism', 'deployment') satisfactorily convey Foucault's rendering of the *dispositif*. In particular, the idea that the *dispositif* constitutes an assemblage or agglomeration is lost in these translations. Throughout this chapter, I follow Foucault's own conceptual shift by employing the term *dispositif* in relation to the texts and contexts where he used it.

It is noteworthy that Foucault's own definition transcends the conventional division separating language from practices and materials, since the *dispositif* connects a series of discursive and non-discursive elements. In a 1977 interview, 'Confession of the Flesh', which contains the only elaborate definition of the *dispositif* offered by Foucault and thus has become a mandatory quotation, Foucault said that the term denotes

> a thoroughly heterogeneous ensemble consisting of discourses, institutions, architectural forms, regulatory decisions, laws, administrative measures, scientific statements, philosophical, moral and philanthropic propositions—in short, the said as much as the unsaid. Such are the elements of the [*dispositif*]. The [*dispositif*] itself is the system of relations that can be established between these elements. (CF: 194; 'Apparatus' in the English translation is replaced by *dispositif*, which Foucault originally used in French)

What Foucault seeks to mark out with this definition is an 'ensemble', an intermediary network of connections, which is pervaded by a particular strategy. The network connects up surprisingly diverse elements such as discourses, institutions, architectural forms, regulatory decisions, etc. Again, discipline provides an illustrative case (DP; PS). Using the *dispositif* as 'analytical front', Foucault describes how, in the eighteenth century, discipline began to interlink reformist penal law, new correctional techniques, early psychiatric classifications, and the architectural design of institutions. Analysing how psychiatric institutions became invested with disciplinary technology, Foucault notes how a 'series' is established 'that brings together the subject-function, somatic singularity, perpetual observation, writing, the mechanism of infinitesimal punishment, projection of the psyche' (PP: 55). The focus is not so much on each individual element in the *dispositif*, for example the 'somatic singularity' or 'perpetual observation', since it is the arrangement of the elements that creates effects of power.

We note that Foucault defines the *dispositif* in an unspecific and openended manner: 'a system of relations'. This fact has prompted discussions of what the *dispositif* is, and, given the unspecificity of the term, what is *not* a *dispositif* (Deleuze, 1992; Agamben, 2009; Bussolini, 2010; Pasquinelli, 2015). Paul Rabinow (2003), in his discussion of the above oft-cited definition of the *dispositif*, observes that Foucault's demarcation is principally a negative one. Decisively blending the discursive and non-discursive, '[i]t is a marking of distance from the exclusive emphasis on discourse in the Archaeology' (Rabinow, 2003: 51). On Rabinow's interpretation, Foucault presents the *dispositif* in support of the shift of analytical approach he had pursued in *Discipline and Punish* and in subsequently studying biopolitics.

However, Foucault had already introduced the *dispositif* in 1973, drawing a distinction between a 'representational analysis' that he undertook in *Histoire de la folie à l'âge classique* and the analysis he would pursue in the *Psychiatric Power* lectures. In hindsight, says Foucault, his study of madness had privileged 'the image of madness produced in the seventeenth and eighteenth centuries', while treating this representational level in isolation from strategies of power (PP: 12). Now, Foucault wishes to try out a very different analysis in order to see if it is possible:

> instead of starting from the analysis of this kind of representational core, which inevitably refers to a history of mentalities, of thought, we could start from an apparatus (*dispositif*) of power. That is to say, to what extent can an apparatus of power produce statements, discourses and, consequently, all the forms of representation that may then [...]* derive from it. (PP: 13)

48 Foucault's Technologies

As I will argue throughout this book, Foucault's introduction of the *disposi-tif* as a conceptual tool should be seen from the perspective of Nietzschean genealogy. Rather than the archaeological recovery of 'pure discursive reg-ularities', Foucault now wants to locate genealogically the formation of discursive practices at the points where strategies of power are deployed and intersect. Hence he asks with reference to the *dispositif*: 'How can this deployment of power, these tactics and strategies of power, give rise to asser-tions, negations, experiments, and theories, in short to a game of truth?' (PP: 13). However, Rabinow focuses on Foucault's famous definition of the *dispositif*, which appears in the later interview, 'Confession of the Flesh', from 1977 (CF). And Rabinow is not content with Foucault's lack of spe-cification of the constitutive elements of the *dispositif* or the nature of their interrelationships:

> Although the distancing from his previous work is emphatic, the analytic unpack-ing of the object remains minimal. The elements composing or taken up in a network apparently could be anything. This expansion beyond discourse conse-quently displaces the issue to what kind of relationships such diverse elements maintain one with the other. (Rabinow, 2003: 51)

While the unspecific definition might be frustrating at first, I would suggest that it has certain analytical advantages. Foucault's rendering of the *disposi-tif* would appear to align well with his view of concepts as non-universal, revisable, and historically contingent. In fact, the *dispositif* is defined in such a way—an unspecified 'system of relations' traversed by a strategy—that it requires extensive historical analysis before the concept begins to take shape. The open-ended definition means, first, that the exact nature of the rela-tions between the *dispositif*'s elements cannot be given in advance, and, second, that it is hardly possible to establish a general explanatory model that can be applied to all *dispositifs* to describe their historical developments. This is because *dispositifs* are inseparable from their specific socio-historic conditions. It is these qualities, in my view, that situate Foucault's concept of *dispositif* as straddling 'analytical category' and 'empirical concept'. To repeat the key point: the *dispositif* is always a *dispositif* of the interlink-ing of power/knowledge, just as the precursor concept, technology, always referred to the interlinking of power/knowledge. These are preliminary con-cepts that anticipate the discoveries of genealogical inquiry in order to attain their shape and effect. Hence, for the *dispositif* to emerge from extensive historical material demands the work of detailed genealogical analysis. The open-ended character of the concept becomes an advantage instead of an obstacle; it creates analytical mobility, sensitivity to the historical material, and a preparedness for surprise.

The emergence of technology

It is perhaps no surprise that, in Foucault's work, technology emerges historically, just as it transforms through history. In his genealogical accounts, technologies often arise from a series of local problems, urgencies, and inventions, which means that technologies are of dispersed origins and scattered locations. With reference to Nietzsche, Foucault (1984b) suggests that the genealogical problem is not to find the original source, or *Ursprung*, of historical phenomena, but to trace their emergence, or *Entstehung*. When the genealogist listens to history, she will learn that things do not hide a timeless and essential secret, but only 'the secret that they have no essence or that their essence was fabricated in a piecemeal fashion from alien forms' (Foucault, 1984b: 78). The task of genealogy, therefore, entails showing how technologies have been born from something other than themselves; that is, unravelling how they were assembled from forces and elements dating back in history. These premises reflect Foucault's overall genealogical approach, which dissolves the unity of our identity, displays the non-necessity of events, and splits history into multiple layers and processes. In concrete terms, the genealogical task consists of tracing technologies through the coalescence of the mundane practices and minor techniques that form them. It may involve, for example, describing how techniques for the training of bodies in workshops, schemes for organizing time in reformatories, and the mandatory use of workers' record books gradually began to form a 'nexus' or technology of discipline.

Let us briefly consider Foucault's sketch of the emergence and gradual dispersion of disciplinary technology in *Psychiatric Power* (PP: 62–66). Foucault notes that although disciplinary technologies are especially apparent in the eighteenth century, they actually date all the way back to the Middle Ages. At the time they were marginal and remained so until the eighteenth century, existing principally in religious communities such as convents and monasteries, 'like islands in the general plasma of relations of sovereignty' (PP: 66). Indeed, the sovereign structures of feudal and monarchical sovereignty remained in place as the dominant form of organizing power relations, and disciplinary technology was only tolerated and ancillary to it. Foucault argues that during this time the elaboration or reactivation of disciplinary *techniques* effected a transformation in the church in terms of religious practices, hierarchies, and ideology (PP: 64). For example, disciplinary technology served as a source of innovation by organizing education as an ascetic exercise that interconnects time and progress. This is the idea, says Foucault, 'that one can only learn things by passing through a number of obligatory and necessary stages, that these stages follow each other in time' (PP: 67). The point is that discipline did not constitute an obstacle to social transformation, isolated at the margins of a society governed by sovereignty; instead discipline turned out to be a source of opposition and innovation.

Foucault also mentions the Cistercian reform, a movement in seventeenth-century France led by monks who sought a return to a simpler lifestyle. Paradoxically, while calling for a return to austerity, especially in terms of manual labour in the fields, the Cistercians were major contributors to technological innovation in agriculture and hydraulic engineering. On Foucault's account, the Cistercians demonstrate how their attempts to reconstitute an 'original' disciplinary order drove innovations that diffused across the whole of society. These revived principles and techniques include 'the rule of poverty, the obligation of manual labor and the full use of time, the disappearance of personal possessions and extravagant expenditure, the regulation of eating and clothing, the rule of internal obedience, and the tightening up of the hierarchy' (PP: 64). During the seventeenth and eighteenth centuries there was a 'progressive extension' of these disciplinary elements, 'a sort of general parasitic interference with society', which gave birth to what Foucault 'schematically' calls a disciplinary society (PP: 66). This brief sketch vividly exemplifies the basic genealogical principle, mentioned above: technology emerges historically in a piecemeal fashion from alien forms.

In his genealogies, Foucault marks out a particular propensity or 'strategic imperative' (CF: 195), which gradually emerges in social organization at large. He describes, first, how specific techniques may intensify, interconnect, and proliferate over time until they pass a certain threshold and begin to saturate social space. Hereafter, society is no longer the same, having passed a tipping point just like water that begins to boil (Nealon, 2008: 39). This idea of a threshold, where at a given moment practices are rationalized to such an extent that we may identify the consolidation of a technology, is illustrated, again, by the case of discipline. In *Discipline and Punish*, Foucault meticulously shows how diverse techniques, including stopclocks, modes of classification, architectural designs, and optical schemas, become integrated in diverse institutions: 'Hence also their rooting in the most important, most central and most productive sectors of society. They become attached to some of the great essential functions: factory production, the transmission of knowledge, the diffusion of aptitudes and skills, the war-machine'

(DP: 211). Foucault thus describes the advent of discipline as 'a technical mutation' in power relations, occurring in the nineteenth century (DP: 257). Disciplinary technology crossed a threshold when a series of disciplinary institutions emerged, including clinical medicine, criminal psychiatry, and scientific management (DP: 224). On several occasions, Foucault suggests an analytical strategy that retrospectively explores how local responses to specific concerns gradually became taken up, transformed, and extended by broader strategies for social control. At the local level, tactics are often clearly articulated and hence readily analysable:

> The rationality of power is characterized by tactics that are often quite explicit at the restricted level where they are inscribed (the local cynicism of power), tactics which, becoming connected to one another, attracting and propagating one another, but finding their base of support and their condition elsewhere, end by forming comprehensive [dispositifs]. (HS1: 95)

For Foucault, then, the constellation of a technology does not happen through a spontaneous assembling of isolated elements, but from strategies put to work to tackle pressing problems. It follows that technology does not represent the world in a neutral manner, and it does not simply fulfil a beneficial social function. In the 1977 interview, Foucault said that the *dispositif* is 'a formation which has as its major function at a given historical moment that of responding to an urgent need' (CF: 195). So the technology or *dispositif* responds to 'an urgent need'; but this sounds almost like sociological functionalism, which Foucault stridently opposed as we will see later. 'Urgent needs' can be sudden threats to society as a whole such as the strike of the plague in mid-fourteenth-century Europe or challenges to the early capitalist economy represented by the idle and vagabonds. Urgent needs are sometimes the needs of particular groups, as exemplified by eighteenth-century merchants' need to protect moveable goods against theft or industrialists' need to fix workers to the productive apparatus and tie them to a life of wage-labour.

Foucault recounts forms of worker resistance against wage-labour in the eighteenth and nineteenth centuries: 'There were huge and sometimes collective refusals of Monday work, circuits of nomadism organized according to labor markets, tavern societies, spontaneous forms of organization of the working class' (PS: 191). The analysis of how a range of tactics were applied to suppress such resistance and discipline workers will be discussed in Chapter 4. It suffices to say here that Foucault describes the emergence of a range of punitive and moralizing techniques applied to the labouring

52 Foucault's Technologies

population, which he eventually denotes 'disciplinary technology'. It was, he says, 'necessarily highly complex' and 'multiple in its points of application', since it had to ensure three overall goals: 'protection of the productive apparatus; repression of illegalism; the moral equipping of the proletariat' (PS: 174). While minor tactics are initiated by identifiable actors, these actors tend to retreat into the background as the tactics solidify into strategies that propel *dispositifs*. On Foucault's account, then, the 'urgent needs' to which the *dispositif* responds are the needs of certain groups, although once a *dispositif* is consolidated it is often forgotten who invented its constitutive elements.

In Foucault's account, the innovators of micro-disciplinary techniques—such as merchant guilds, philanthropic associations, and societies for the correction of manners—were not pervaded by a uniform class ideology. Furthermore, the emergence of disciplinary technology cannot be straightforwardly derived from the capitalist system and its 'needs'. Although Foucault asserts that tactics and techniques cannot be deduced from a particular class or capitalist relations of production, such micro-inventions may still become enrolled in more general social strategies. In modern state formation, tactics that are first local, private, amateur, and invented for specific needs can undergo a process of 'statification' whereby they are taken up by state administrations and become professionalized and legally codified. Indeed, techniques of discipline undergo precisely such a piecemeal process of 'stratification', spurred by pressure from privileged groups. But how can we understand the general relationship between tactics and strategies, and how does class come into this relationship? Generally, Foucault begins his analysis at the level of local and piecemeal tactics and ends up with more overall strategies:

> I think we have to analyze the way in which the phenomena, techniques, and procedures of power come into play at the lowest levels; we have to show, obviously, how these procedures are displaced, extended, and modified and, above all, how they are invested or annexed by global phenomena, and how more general powers or economic benefits can slip into the play of these technologies of power. (SMD: 31)

Jacques Bidet gives emphasis to Foucault's attention to social struggle in his work from the 1970s: 'Foucault arranges the battlefield by defining as primary the moment of the particular, construed in terms of "tactic", and as secondary the overall movement, conceived in terms of strategy' (Bidet, 2016: 156). Social groups, which are not restricted to the Marxist binary scheme, play their part in utilizing and reinserting their tactics into strategies. Again, Bidet offers helpful explication:

> The thousand and one tactics that we see at work are not deducible from the strategic imperatives of class: they are utilised by them. But they ultimately converge in grand strategies, which form the context of their reiteration. So we end up with a sort of circular relation between the individual moment and the structural moment. (Bidet, 2016: 156)

The genealogical recovery of the emergence of a *dispositif* must commence at sites where tactics and the elaboration of techniques can be observed. These tactical inventions, says Foucault, 'were invented and organized from the starting points of local conditions and particular needs. They took shape in piecemeal fashion, prior to any class strategy designed to weld them into vast, coherent ensembles' (Foucault, 1980b: 159). Although classes play a role in Foucault's analysis, they do not constitute pre-given, fixed entities from which the analysis begins. Instead of preceding struggle, Foucault emphasizes that classes can arise from the deployment of tactics in struggles, insofar as the experience of struggle may generate collective identities (as we will see in Chapter 3). In passing, one should note that the emphasis on class differs greatly across Foucault's works. The strategies of conflicting groups are pronounced in the 1973 lectures, *The Punitive Society*, whereas strategies become more 'anonymous' in *Discipline and Punish* and in Foucault's late 1970s lectures.

The invention of minor tactics are precursors of larger strategies that, in turn, may become entrenched as technologies or *dispositifs*, as evident in the *dispositif* of discipline. In this perspective, the *dispositif* is created 'from the ground up', which is why what Greg Lambert calls Foucault's 'favourite pair' of concepts for denoting the emergence of *dispositifs* is '*dispersion and generality, rather than totalization and universality*' (Lambert, 2020: 72, italics in original). Analysing discipline, Foucault says that 'it was first to be introduced ... at the local level, in intuitive, empirical, and fragmented forms, and in the restricted framework of institutions such as schools, hospitals, barracks, workshops, and so on' (SMD: 250). Across prisons, armies, schools, hospitals, and factories, a disciplinary *dispositif* was becoming visible. A point of confusion, however, is that Foucault often insists on speaking of *dispositifs* in the plural, as in 'disciplinary *dispositifs*', 'biopolitical *dispositifs*', or '*dispositifs* of security'. One explanation may be that Foucault wanted to signal in this way the generative character of *dispositifs*. As mentioned, the *dispositif* is not an entity but rather a 'formatting' of society that conditions the emergence of manifold new inventions, techniques, and institutions. This interpretation implies that the disciplinary strategy can deploy, or invest itself in, different 'devices', such as the school, the examination, or diagnostic tools for learning disabilities. It further implies that once a strategy has become entrenched, it needs to rely on concrete *dispositifs* for its operation and expansion. Steven Collier (2009: 80) gives this mechanism an instructive formulation when he describes *dispositifs* as 'broad configurational principles' through which new formations of practices and institutions take place. In other words, the strategy that propelled a *dispositif* generates new correlations between practices, institutions, and techniques. It is important to note that these elements were often previously assembled in other *dispositifs*, so the formation of a *dispositif* typically proceeds by reappropriation and reintegration of 'alien forms'.

Diagram and micro-dispositifs

We detect two different 'directions' in Foucault's analysis of the *dispositif* : one of 'generalization' and one of 'micro-dispositifs' (Deleuze, 1997: 184). On the one hand, Foucault's analysis of *dispositifs* describes how a strategic imperative begins to saturate the social body and becomes a ubiquitous propensity across institutions. Under this analytical direction, Foucault describes the generalization of discipline, when it becomes diffused across key institutions like barracks, schools, workplaces, families, and hospitals. On a few occasions, Foucault describes this direction by the term 'diagram'; he said that in our society, which 'may be characterized as disciplinary ... the disciplinary system is the general form in which power is inserted, whether located in a State apparatus or diffused in a general system' (PS: 231). This generalization means that disciplinary observations and solutions become more likely, but it does not mean that the disciplinary imperative becomes omnipotent or deterministic of all social forms.

However, 'the dispositionally prescriptive level is a crucial aspect of social reality', argues Raffnsøe et al. (2016: 292), 'since it has a determining effect on what is taken for granted and considered real'. Foucault at times picked 'signature' models, of which the panopticon is the best known, that lucidly express a distinct strategic imperative, in this case 'panopticism'. He described how this prison-form, that is correctional confinement based on panoptical surveillance, diffused beyond its original setting and became a general strategy for organizing a whole range of institutions. Generalization can take place both over time and across social space. Hence, cellular confinement shifts from a marginal existence under feudalism and monarchical rule to become a significant device when a new disciplinary strategy pushes it across the technological threshold (Deleuze, 1988: 40). The analysis of generalization does not posit a basic antagonism between two classes cleaving society, but it describes how society 'strategizes itself' (Deleuze, 1997: 187). Similarly, the *dispositif* 'strategizes itself' by appropriating and reformatting a number of practices, techniques, and institutions.

On the other hand, Foucault's genealogies recover diverse sites, or 'breeding spots', where tactics and techniques were deployed in response to local problems. This analytical direction at times focused on how these tactics became enrolled in and invested by an overall strategy. At other times, this 'micro-analysis' would describe how, at diverse sites and institutions, the strategic imperative necessarily becomes specified, stratified, or deflected. Foucault spoke of a 'swarming of disciplinary mechanisms' occurring in the eighteenth and nineteenth centuries. Even if there is a growth in disciplinary institutions, he writes, 'their mechanisms have a certain tendency to become "de-institutionalized", to emerge from the closed fortresses in which they once functioned and to circulate in a "free" state; the massive, compact disciplines are broken down into flexible methods of control, which may be transferred and adapted' (DP: 211). In this way, Foucault escaped the idea of a simple dissemination of a given strategy and its techniques by granting irreducibility to the level of what Deleuze (1988: 184) terms 'micro-dispositifs', a 'diffuse and heterogeneous multiplicity'. The nineteenth-century asylums for the mad could be seen as such 'micro-dispositifs' that intensify and distribute but also deflect power. Foucault explored how, in what he called 'the asylum dispositif' (PP), mental patients deflected psychiatric power by producing excessive symptoms of their illnesses, which put in question the authority of the doctors' diagnosis. A specific power game hence played out in nineteenth-century France around the simulation of hysteria 'at the heart of the asylum system' (PP: 137).

We can thus speak of a generalization of the disciplinary strategy, without any ultimate sedimentation of it, since disciplinary *dispositifs* are continually shaped by struggles and accidental events. In analytical terms, a strategy forges connections between diverse elements (e.g. cellular punishment, psychiatric classifications, and penal law) without eradicating their differences. Foucault says: 'The logic of strategy is the logic of connections between the heterogeneous and not the logic of the homogenization of the contradictory'

56 Foucault's Technologies

(BP: 42). In writing genealogy, suggests Deleuze, Foucault oscillated between the two overall analytical directions, 'generalization' and 'micro-analysis':

> This thesis concerning dispositifs of power seemed to me to move in two directions, in no way contradictory, but distinct. In both cases, these dispositifs were irreducible to a State apparatus. But according to one direction, they consisted of a diffuse and heterogeneous multiplicity, 'micro-dispositifs.' According to another direction, they referred to a diagram, a kind of abstract machine immanent to the entire social field (hence panopticism, defined by the general function of seeing without being seen and applicable to any multiplicity). These were, so to speak, the two directions of microanalysis, both equally important, since the second showed that Michel was not satisfied with a 'dissemination.' (Deleuze, 1997: 184)

Hence, on Deleuze's reading, Foucault's approach to the *dispositif* was twofold. On the one hand, he assumed that the strategic imperative, or 'diagram', could saturate the social body, endowing it with a particular propensity, for example for normalization. On the other hand, Foucault maintained that the social body was the site of multiple heterogeneous 'micro-dispositifs', for example monastery, prison, school, and welfare office. Did Foucault not pursue a dual approach, asks Deleuze, by which he managed 'to maintain the rights of a microanalysis (diffusion, heterogeneity, fragmentary character) but at the same time to maintain a kind of principle of unification that is not of the "State", "party", totalization, or representation type?' (Deleuze, 1997: 190). In order to achieve this task Foucault needs to be able to speak both of a diagram, which is the abstraction of a given strategy so that it becomes transferable, and of how the diagram ramifies through and takes various shapes in a multiplicity of instances. We can hence extract two complementary strategies of analysis in Foucault. First, 'generalization' explores how a specific discursive element, e.g. the distinction normal/abnormal, becomes strategically useful and begins to constitute a generalizable schematic. Second, 'micro-analysis' asks how different discursive and technical elements become linked together, e.g. new penal laws, criminal psychiatry, and cellular punishment, forming a *dispositif* that carries a particular strategic propensity.

Deleuze makes much of Foucault's underdeveloped term 'diagram', which merely appears twice in *Discipline and Punish*. In this famous passage, Foucault defines the panopticon as the diagram of disciplinary power:

> [T]he Panopticon must not be understood as a dream building: it is the diagram of a mechanism of power reduced to its ideal form; its functioning, abstracted from any obstacle, resistance or friction, must be represented as a pure architectural

> and optical system: it is in fact a figure of political technology that may and must
> be detached from any specific use. It's polyvalent in its applications. (DP: 205)

There are several significant points in Foucault's definition. First, the panopticon is both a specific technical invention and an idealized model of discipline—i.e. a diagram. As a diagram, the panopticon is highly flexible, since it constitutes a 'polyvalent' formula for organizing spaces and social relations. Foucault had already described how, during the eighteenth and nineteenth centuries, panopticism had infiltrated and become operational in the major institutions of European societies: hospitals, barracks, schools, and armies: 'Whenever one is dealing with a multiplicity of individuals on whom a task or a particular form of behavior must be imposed, the panoptic schema may be used' (DP: 205). Second, the panoptic diagram increases the efficiency of any institution, because it intensifies the internal processes independently of their particular purposes. In each case, 'it arranges things in such a way that the exercise of power is not added on from the outside, like a rigid, heavy constraint, to the functions it invests, but is so subtly present in them as to increase their efficiency' (DP: 206–207). And, third, by introducing the term 'diagram', Foucault explains, in more formal terms, how the generalization of panopticism was possible. He does so by reducing panopticism 'to its ideal form', abstracting it from its materiality, as if it were functioning without all the difficulties, obstacles, and disorder of actual practices and institutions. Foucault explains that the diagram 'can in fact be integrated into any function (education, medical treatment, production, punishment)', where it 'may be precisely adjusted, in the smallest detail, to the processes that are to be supervised' (DP: 206). Having become a pure, unspecific schematic, the panoptic diagram operates as a catalyst in diverse institutions, giving greater intensity to their specialized functions. In brief, the diagram is an abstract logic, which can invest multiple concrete techniques. Analytically, it is important that the panopticon is not simply an expression of modern surveillance. The panopticon can—and must—be analysed both as an invention, which emblematically embodies the disciplinary *dispositif* and as a specific technical instrument in its own right.

For Deleuze, one can identify the abstract logic of a strategy by extracting the strategy from all the contextual tactics and circumstances through which it evolved. Divested of specific content and contextuality, the strategy emerges in its distinct, transferable form. It has become what Deleuze terms a diagram. Because it is an abstract schematic, the diagram can travel from one institution to the next, where it can intermingle with specific functions. Therefore, Foucault writes that the panoptic schema's 'vocation was

58   Foucault's Technologies

to become a generalized function' and an 'easily transferable mechanism' (DP: 207, 209). Hence the panoptic diagram can at one moment serve as a programme for the prison while later it can be integrated into other institutions and practices. Foucault writes about the panoptic diagram that it can be 'precisely adjusted' to the different processes in which it is put to use:

> It can in fact be integrated into any function (education, medical treatment, production, punishment); it can increase the effect of this function, by being linked closely with it; it can constitute a mixed mechanism in which relations of power (and of knowledge) may be precisely adjusted, in the smallest detail, to the processes that are to be supervised. (DP: 206)

In brief, the diagram is sufficiently general or abstract not to have a specific use. For example, the panoptical diagram can reinforce the prison's basic function of ensuring criminals' moral betterment by intensifying anonymous surveillance. Jakub Zedbik explains that, although schools, prisons, and barracks are vastly heterogeneous systems, the same diagram of surveillance—or seeing without being seen—operates in all of them. Zedbik describes the process of abstraction and translation as one of 'contraction':

> How does the diagram travel from one system to another? The minimal elements of surveillance are abstracted from one context—the prison—and shifted to another system—the barracks. This movement, from the concrete case of the prison to the stage at which the forces that constitute the surveillance element of prison are abstracted, is made through contraction or constraint. The superfluous is taken out—walls, bodies, bars—and only the elements of surveillance are left. (Zedbik, 2012: 25)

'Contracting' panoptical surveillance, Deleuze (1988: 34, italics in original) finds that its minimal function is to '*impose a particular conduct on a particular human multiplicity*'. However, I would suggest that *imposing a norm on a human multiplicity* is a better choice for the minimal function of panopticism. When panoptic arrangements make groups of individuals visible, the minimal function is to distinguish between the normal and the abnormal, which can imply, but does not necessitate, imposing on individuals a particular conduct. Such normalizing distinctions are said to emerge out of the very nature of those surveyed, since norms are established by reading off traits inherent to the group under surveillance and classifying them. Foucault says that discipline has the function of being 'anomizing', always 'bringing anomie, the irreducible, to light, and of always being normalizing ... What characterizes disciplinary systems is the never-ending work of the norm in the anomic' (PP: 54). Permanent surveillance makes surfaces visible so that norms can be established in discourse and made sanctionable. Hence, the norm cuts across what can be visualized and what can be enunciated, what can be seen and what can be said.

Deleuze finds in the diagram the 'missing link' that connects the *dispositif*'s discursive and non-discursive components. We recall from Foucault's definition (CF: 194) that the list of elements that make up the *dispositif* was highly diverse, comprising architectural forms, regulatory decisions, scientific statements, and more. Foucault places these elements in two categories, 'the said as much as the unsaid', which Deleuze (1988: 32) describes as 'two forms', namely 'the visible and the articulable'. According to Deleuze, these two forms are distinct and irreducible to each other, since they share 'no common form, no conformity, not even correspondence'. On Deleuze's (1988) account, Foucault's central project was to challenge 'the referential dictum', that is, logical theories of reference which assume that words and objects take up a referential relationship. Foucault carries out his challenge by inquiring into 'the stratum', to use Deleuze's term, which reveals the rules that condition both what is sayable and what is visible. Foucault's inquiry into the referential relationship asks how a correlation can be established between these two distinct regions in the first place, allowing words to be tied to things. Kevin Thompson aptly presents Deleuze's reading of the Foucauldian challenge: 'how can the heterogeneous conditions of language and light be adapted to each other? How can the forms of the sayable, the conditions of spontaneity, be joined with the forms of the visible, the conditions of intuition? (Thompson, 2008: 4–5). The explanation for the integration of the two forms cannot be found in the domain of knowledge. Hence Thompson points out that the third form, which can adapt statements to the visible, is force: 'Force relations thus act as the requisite mediating axis between these disparate forms and thus make possible the joining of words to things, reference itself' (Thompson, 2008: 5).

Deleuze writes:

> When Foucault defines Panopticism, either he specifically sees it as an optical or luminous arrangement that characterizes prison, or he views it abstractly as a machine that not only affects visible matter in general (a workshop, barracks, school or hospital as much as a prison) but also in general passes through every articulable function. (Deleuze, 1988: 34–35)

Deleuze (1988: 33) formulates this question of mediating between forms thus: 'outside forms, is there in general a common immanent cause that exists within the social field?' He suggests that the diagram is such an immanent cause, which creates a kind of correspondence between the visible and the

60 Foucault's Technologies

articulable. He notes that *Discipline and Punish* repeatedly speaks of 'assemblages, adjustments and interpenetration of the two forms' (Deleuze, 1988: 33). The panoptic diagram, declares Deleuze (1988: 34), is 'a machine that not only affects visible matter in general (a workshop, barracks, school or hospital as much as a prison) but also in general passes through every articulable function'. Foucault himself expresses something similar, I think, when he suggests that the history of penal practice (the visible) and the history of the human sciences (the articulable) might run though the same register. The aim is to discover, he writes, 'whether there is not some common matrix or whether they do not both derive from a single process of "epistemological-juridical" formation; in short, make the technology of power the very principle of both the humanization of the penal system and of the knowledge of man' (DP: 23). Deleuze (1988: 34) lucidly portrays the diagram as 'a machine that is almost blind and mute, even though it makes others see and speak'. This means that as an abstract schema, the diagram has no intrinsic meaning or intentionality, but it integrates the visible and the articulable, making more likely certain observations and statements.

On Deleuze's reading, the relationship between 'the two directions' of Foucault's analytics, the abstraction of the diagram and the micro-analysis of institutions, is one of non-identity, since the diagram is operationalized in institutions in heterogeneous ways. Jason Read (2003: 88) describes the relation between the two directions, 'the immanent cause and its specific instances', as one of 'tension'. Comparing Marx's analysis of capitalism with Foucault's study of discipline, Read asserts that the factory is irreducible to the capitalist mode of production, just as the prison is irreducible to disciplinary power. The reason why, in both cases, one phenomenon is not deducible from the other, is that discipline and capitalism alike unfold through dynamic relations that are pervaded by diverse and irreducible logics:

> The immanent social field is constituted by a multiplicity of apparatuses or relations, in the case of capitalism, the mode of production is also constituted by relations of distribution and consumption, which, although constitutive of the social field, have differing and divergent logics from those found in production proper. (Read, 2003: 88–89)

Deleuze refers instead to Nietzsche to explain why the relationship between the diagram and institutions is marked by non-identity. In Deleuze's (1988: 70–71) interpretation, relations also become central, since in Foucault's 'profound Nietzscheanism' forces are exerted upon other forces, and hence power is simply a relation between specific forces. This means that institutions will integrate the diagram according to their specific power relations and the specific knowledge that they produce: '[T]he institution has the capacity to integrate power-relations by constituting various forms of knowledge which actualize, modify and redistribute these relations' (Deleuze, 1988: 77). This assumption of non-identity is analytically valuable for scholars who wish to undertake organizational research inspired by Foucault, since it stresses the potential of studying how techniques are adopted, modified, or resisted in organizations.

Deleuze's premise of non-identity between the diagram and its integration in diverse institutions does not merely imply differentiation or stratification, since 'there is no diagram that does not also include, besides the points which it connects up, certain relatively free or unbound points, points of creativity, change and resistance' (Deleuze, 1988: 44). These 'Nietzschean' premises imply that the diagram passes through all elements of the *dispositif*, which themselves constitute points of intensification, redirection, or resistance. Hence, Nietzsche had Zarathustra inform his reader that in all living things he found the will to power; 'even in the will of the servant I found the will to be master' (TSZ: 77). In his McGill lecture on Nietzsche from 1971, Foucault appears to endorse such a dynamic and immanentist view of power, when he cites Nietzsche from *The Will to Power*: 'The world is essentially different at every point; it weighs on all the points, all the points resist and in every case the results are perfectly non congruent' (WP: 210). Foucault also picks from Nietzsche a formulation which would appear to anticipate Foucault's own assertion that the *dispositif*'s knowledge production intersects with strategies of domination: 'The whole apparatus of knowledge is an apparatus of abstraction and simplification, organized not for knowledge but for mastery over things' (WP: 208). The key implication of this Nietzschean view of power as dynamic and differentiated is that the *dispositif* is never solid and identical to itself, but exists in continual transformation that may open up new potentials—or new 'lines into the future', to use Deleuze's term.

However, notable differences also distinguish Deleuze from Foucault in their rendering of *dispositif* and diagram. Whereas Deleuze assumes that the diagram interconnects the sayable and the seeable, Foucault mainly uses the diagram to highlight the transferable capacity of the *dispositif*. In Foucault's rendering, the diagram exposes the programmatic character of the *dispositif*, which means that the diagram, such as the panopticon, can travel from one context and become useful in diverse other contexts. However, in Foucault's work this travelling typically happens when specific techniques spread from one setting to another (e.g. from monastery to correctional prison), which

62 Foucault's Technologies

means that his analysis resists Deleuze's idea of the diagram as an 'abstract and immanent cause'. Indeed, Raffnsøe et al. emphasize the difficulty in aligning abstract conceptualization with the fragile and contradictory processes in which Foucault's *dispositifs* surface: 'The primary level of dispositional analysis is an ambiguous and fragile social "ordering process" ultimately irreducible to an abstract conceptual articulation, which aims to define general characteristics and clearly demarcate these definitions through binary oppositions' (Raffnsøe et al., 2015: 205).

Deleuze also brings Foucault's concepts into his own philosophy by accentuating the diagram's virtual character over actual institutions and their tangible constraints. Deleuze's 'tonality' of the concept is hence 'antiprogrammatic' (Zdebik, 2012: 111), whereas Foucault insisted on the programmatic nature of the diagram, detailing how asylums, barracks, and prisons were reprogrammed by the imperative of discipline. Deleuze, however, grants ontological priority to the world's immanent creativity, emphasizing the production of difference and resistant subjectivities (Bussolini, 2010: 102). This emphasis reflects Deleuze's general principle of mapping constitutive forces, or constellations of forces, that can be abstracted from institutions and bodies (Deleuze and Guattari, 1994). Deleuze's rendering of the diagram as an 'immanent cause' in the entire social body means that the cause cannot be isolated or identified apart from its effects. Deleuze finds a certain inspiration in Spinoza's dictum that God is a cause entirely immanent in His creation, and here one must recall that God granted man freedom and hence there is no assumption of determinism. The interplay of historical circumstances could have developed in multifarious ways, but after the fact we mistakenly tend to speak of the cause of a specific event.

Foucault saw the diagram as immanent in its effects, and he emphasized it as being historically contingent and singular as opposed to self-grounding, universal, or eternal. Deleuze, similarly, emphasized historical contingency and problematized claims to universality and eternity, but he still asserted the world as constituting ever-present ruptures and possibilities for something new. Deleuze could thus present the diagram as immanent and creative by invoking Foucault's dictum that power runs through multiple points of resistance that generate change and difference. Indeed, Foucault said that 'the swarm of points of resistance traverses social stratifications and individual unities' (HS1: 95–96), affecting disturbances and mutations. Unlike Deleuze, however, Foucault maintains that, at the level of institutions and micro-relations, the diagram tends to extend and reinforce the effects of disciplinary power. He insists that the operationalization of the diagram has concrete consequences in each institution, shaping the relations between the subjects in each setting under the imperative of normalization. Deleuze's interpretation is helpful, however, since it emphasizes that a *dispositif* is not a rigid template that shapes everything according to its own imperative and characteristics. Rather, its diagrammatic character means that the *dispositif* channels, distributes, and reorganizes. The *dispositif* puts the diagram into operation, but its effects might just as much consist of transformations of its network, opening of unforeseen pathways, or even forms of resistance against it.

A plurality of *dispositifs*

In the concluding chapters of *Discipline and Punish*, Foucault pushes his analysis to its loudest register when he speaks of the 'disciplinary society', the 'society of normalization', and the 'carceral continuum'. A few years later, however, he complicated this rather totalizing portrayal of disciplinarity by laying out a framework where multiple *dispositifs* interact in dynamic and complex relations. This framework is particularly salient in the 1978 lecture series, *Security, Territory, Population*, in which Foucault conceives of the social field as pervaded by several *dispositifs* that interact, reinforce, or negate one another. Whereas *Discipline and Punish* and related works had foregrounded the 'internal' workings of the disciplinary *dispositif* (its micro-techniques, its proliferation, and its forms of knowledge), Foucault now turned to the 'external' relations between various *dispositifs* (their mutual support, their opposition, and their exchange of elements). Indeed, recent contributions to Foucault scholarship thus emphasize the complex hetero-geneity of different modalities of power revealed by Foucault in his late 1970s lectures (Collier, 2009; Raffnsøe et al., 2016). There, Foucault presents us with a gamut of distinct *dispositifs*, each imbued with distinct strategic impe-ratives. Collier (2009: 79–80) observes that in the late 1970s Foucault left his analysis of 'disciplinary society' and its diagnostic style marked by syste-maticity, functional coherence, and a totalizing reach. Henceforth Foucault pursued a more subtle approach that allowed descriptions of multiple and heterogeneous configurations of power. In brief, in the analytics that Fou-cault developed in the late 1970s the interrelationship between the *dispositifs* becomes more important than the *dispositif* in itself.

In the first two lectures of the 1978 course, Foucault introduces what he terms three major *dispositifs* of power: 'law', 'discipline', and 'security'

64 Foucault's Technologies

(STP: 4–55). In the published transcript in French, Foucault uses the terms *'mécanisme'*, *'dispositif'*, *'ensemble'*, and *'systéme'* interchangeably. Studying seventeenth- and eighteenth-century texts on city planning in response to crime, diseases, and scarcity of grain, Foucault demonstrates how the three *dispositifs* produce particular problems and solutions unique to their own rules of visualization and enunciation.

The legal *dispositif* is prohibitive and effectuates 'a binary division between the permitted and the prohibited, and a coupling, comprising the code, between a type of prohibited action and a type of punishment' (STP: 5). The essential object of law is a territory and the subjects inhabiting it, and its techniques are codification of acts, prohibitions, and the imposition of sanctions. Foucault often ties the legal *dispositif* to monarchical, sovereign power dominant in Western Europe from the Middle Ages to the sixteenth century. This sovereignty in public law is self-referential since what achieves obedience to the law is the law itself (STP: 99), which means that the law remains insensitive and external to its object: 'A rule is external to that which is governed: it is imposed upon its subjects in relation to an extrinsic standard of authority, morality, virtue, order, duty or obedience.' Disciplinary norms are, by contrast, intrinsic to the object: 'A norm, on the other hand, appears— or claims—to emerge out of the very nature of that which is governed. Its normativity is predicated upon and justified by its normality' (Rose and Valverde, 1998: 544). For Foucault, the law cannot be attributed any universality; instead he describes how the law was gradually infused by, or worked together with, disciplinary and medical norms (HS1: 144). Foucault rarely focuses on law in isolation, but always analysed the legal *dispositif* as related to and continually developed in close relationship with other *dispositifs*.

Within the framework of discipline, 'a series of adjacent, detective, medical, and psychological techniques appear which fall within the domain of surveillance, diagnosis, and the possible transformation of individuals' (STP: 5). The disciplinary *dispositif* is essentially preventive, since 'disciplinary power always tends to intervene beforehand, before the act itself if possible, and by means of an infra-judicial interplay of supervision, rewards, punishments, and pressure' (PP: 51). Foucault often places discipline and law in interrelation, arguing that the normalizing power of the network of disciplinary techniques, the 'micro-law' or 'infra-law', reaches beyond the jurisdiction of the law (DP: 222). As objects of disciplinary normalization, infinitesimal details of individuals' lives can be observed and evaluated in terms of the norm: 'Whereas the juridical system defines juridical subjects according to universal norms, the disciplines characterize, classify, specialize; they distribute along a scale, around a norm' (DP: 223).

By setting up norms that evaluate degrees of normality on a scale, discipline could transgress the juridical binary division between the acceptable and the unacceptable. The disciplinary norm can be brought to bear both on those sanctioned by the legal system (e.g. criminal psychiatry) and law-abiding individuals who can be the targets of normalizing interventions (e.g. schooling, health care, and human resource management). Within the network of the disciplinary *dispositif*, the use of normalizing techniques intersect with psychological and medical knowledge, and this interlinkage continually readjusts norms, hence producing new objects of intervention.

Finally, the security *dispositif* emerged in response to the specific question of 'population' which, in the eighteenth century, began to be viewed as the totality of measurable processes: birth rates, mortality, epidemics, and migration (measured in demographic statistics). The problems of security diverge from both sovereign questions of rule and disciplinary normalization. From the viewpoint of security, the object of government becomes visible not as legal subjects in a territory, but as 'a population with its specific phenomena and processes' (STP: 66). The techniques of security target not the individual to be corrected but the totality of the population, aiming at risk prevention rather than perfection of the body. The object is series of events occurring at the level of society, so they cannot be contained within specific institutions like prisons or hospitals. Foucault analyses attempts to securitize and hence minimize the risk of events that occur at the population level like epidemics, food shortages, and crime.

An essential feature of the population is its intransparency to the sovereign's eye and governmental aspiration, since the processes inherent to the population '[escape] the sovereign's direct action in the form of the law' (STP: 71). Security takes as its premise *the reality* of population constituted by dynamic patterns of production, procreation, migration, and so on. Recognizing that it is impossible to eliminate everything undesired, security takes the more tempered ambition of optimizing and minimizing the risks of the processes inherent in this reality. These processes are essentially conceived of as 'circulations' that can be facilitated or minimized:

> This given will not be reconstructed to arrive at a point of perfection, as in a disciplinary town. It is simply a matter of maximizing the positive elements, for which one provides the best possible circulation, and of minimizing what is risky and inconvenient, like theft and disease, while knowing that they will never be completely suppressed. (STP: 19)

66 Foucault's Technologies

Securitization does not aim for legal prohibition or disciplinary perfection but is concerned with averages, optimal levels, and acceptable intervals. Perhaps a better name than 'security' would be 'prediction' or 'predictive interventions', insofar as security prepares for the future by predicting 'series of probabilities' (STP: 19). Foucault lays out three key characteristics of security: the prediction of probability, the calculation of costs, and the establishment of acceptable levels. Taking the example of crime, Foucault explains:

> First, that security 'inserts the phenomenon in question, namely theft, within a series of probable events'.
> Second, that 'the reactions of power to this phenomenon are inserted in a calculation of cost'.
> Third, that 'instead of a binary division between the permitted and the prohibited, one establishes an average considered as optimal on the one hand, and, on the other, a bandwidth of the acceptable that must not be exceeded'. (STP: 6)

In modern societies, Foucault suggests, security has come to the forefront in comparison to law and discipline. This development does not entail the disappearance of law and discipline, however it means that laws and disciplinary techniques are increasingly deployed for security purposes. As we later discuss in relation to the Covid-19 crisis (Chapter 6), when security is foregrounded as a means of social regulation, the key question in this instance is whether a specific law or disciplinary technique serves to reach acceptable levels of infections given a calculation of the costs and benefits involved in regulating the pandemic.

The strategic imperative of security is thus the effective management of the contingencies of a living population. Anticipating this imperative in his 1976 lectures (SMD), Foucault says that the population constitutes 'serial phenomena', which are 'essentially aleatory events that occur within a population that exists over a period of time' (SMD: 246). Although these events are aleatory, they can be revealed as statistically recurring by 'forecasts, statistical estimates and overall measures' (SMD: 246). To be sure, this securitization of populations or segments by mathematical modelling and forecasting has proliferated since Foucault's lectures. This development inaugurated, in Michael Dillon's (2007: 46) words, 'a government of population (in its very contingency) by the burgeoning new sciences of contingency (statistics and probability) for the contingent (effects-based) promotion of life'. The dissemination of security *dispositifs* submits citizens to an accelerating accumulation of statistical data, compilation of personal information, and the use of predictive analysis and algorithmic profiling on existing data in areas like insurance, consumption, and health care. The primary knowledge form is predictive, which makes calculable unknown futures and uncertain processes, with the aspiration of optimizing such processes. Initiatives for managing populations from traffic management to disaster planning embody this predictive rationality, and recent techniques like remote tracking, real-time screening, and biometrical person registers can be analysed as means of securitization.

Returning to Foucault himself, he says that the essential object of law is a territory and its legal subjects, the object of discipline is the body, and the object of security is the totality of a living population (STP: 11). It is tempting to read this typology as sequential, so that the law belongs to the feudal state, discipline to industrial society, and security to the post-industrial era. However, Foucault cautions that the *dispositifs* do not appear in any sort of sequential order: 'There is not a series of successive elements, the appearance of the new causing the earlier ones to disappear' (STP: 8). Foucault does not seek to outline overarching and irretrievable breaks from one epoch to another, and instead explores the continual interplay between multiple *dispositifs*:

> We should not be looking for some sort of sovereignty from which powers spring, but showing how the various operators of domination support one another, relate to one another, at how they converge and reinforce one another in some cases, and negate or strive to annul one another in other cases. (SMD: 45)

It is well known that during the late 1970s Foucault, in his 'governmentality lectures', strived to challenge the idea of a unified and centralized state (STP, BP). He did so by laying out multiple *dispositifs*, which the state does not pre-exist in any coherent way. The state is rather an 'effect', says Foucault, 'constituted on the basis of a thousand diverse processes' (STP: 239). Analytically, the state cannot serve as the encompassing viewpoint for analysing the procedures, technologies, and tactics of power, because it is itself immanent to these (STP: 119). This view is a far cry from the Marxist idea of a state apparatus that can be seized. As we will see in Chapter 4, Foucault's work on *dispositifs* occurred in an ongoing critical dialogue with Althusser's theory of Ideological State Apparatuses and its 'latent centralization of ideological practices and representations on the basis of a "State Ideology"' (Balibar, 2014: xv). The heterogeneity of *dispositifs* escapes notions of a centralized state agency and a uniform ideology. Instead, the social body appears as fractured

68 Foucault's Technologies

by different imperatives, at times reinforcing and assimilating, at other times contradicting and undermining one another.

Foucault's work from the 1970s contains a number of examples of how several *dispositifs* enter into dynamic interplay, transforming their interrelations as well as their internal composition. I suggest that at least four different modalities of interaction can be reconstructed:

1. Appropriation and reutilization of elements (e.g. cellular confinement, confessional technique).
2. Internal infiltration (e.g. discipline within sovereignty).
3. Competing constructs of the same object (e.g. scarcity of grain).
4. Emergence of new *dispositifs* at the intersection of existing *dispositifs* (e.g. legal psychiatry).

Appropriation and reutilization of elements

In the first modality of interaction, techniques integral to existing *dispositifs* are assembled into another *dispositif*, where they will acquire new functions. Foucault describes this modality well when explaining how the *dispositif* of security gains more pre-eminence, sometimes utilizing techniques derived from the legal and disciplinary *dispositifs*: 'A technology of security, for example, will be set up, taking up again and sometimes even multiplying juridical and disciplinary elements and redeploying them within its specific tactic' (STP: 8–9). This process echoes Nietzsche's principle of 'functional indeterminacy' according to which a practice holds no univocal meaning, but carries diverse interpretations in the course of history (GM: 53–54). In *On the Genealogy of Morality*, Nietzsche argues that techniques of punishment may survive over time, while becoming invested with entirely new meaning and functions. This historical 'fluidity' of meaning entails that the current function assigned to a technique does not explain its origin, the recovery of which requires genealogical inquiry (GM: 52). Genealogical inquiry must also describe how the technique becomes productive in games of power and dominance when it is reappropriated, reinterpreted, and given new functions. Nietzsche thus declares how anything that has come into existence 'is continually interpreted anew, requisitioned anew, transformed and redirected to a new purpose by a power superior to it' (GM: 51). For example, in the movement from sovereignty to discipline, the technique of confinement itself changes as it becomes integrated into a new dominant *dispositif*.

Foucault's Concept of Technology **69**

For the genealogist, the prison is not a substance that receives different properties (Protevi, 2016: 126), since its function is contingent on the system into which it is inserted. Foucault presents an extensive analysis, in *The Punitive Society*, of how older techniques of pastoral power became integrated into the correctional prison system during the late eighteenth century. This process of 'Christianization' of the penal system was surprising, notes Foucault, since the dominant penal theories at the time emphasized very different juridical principles. Penal reformists like Cesare Beccaria (1738–1794) and Jacques Brissot (1754–1793) argued that punishment should essentially protect society, with no vengeance or penance but carefully measured responses to infractions. These penal theories, says Foucault, imply that one only punishes 'inasmuch as society has to defend itself, and ... there cannot be any fundamental relationship between sin and crime, penalty and penance' (PS: 89). Nevertheless, in the eighteenth century the prison became a site of solitary penance which was completely different from the juridical-punitive order envisaged by dominant penal theories. In this process, infractions were reconstructed as originating in moral wrongdoing whose correction required a process of penance supported by moralizing techniques. Foucault says: 'So what we see is a moralization of the penal system, despite the practice and discourse of this system' (PS: 292). This integration of Christian morality into the penal system was part of a general strategy of moralization that the privileged applied to the lower strata of society (discussed in detail in Chapter 3). Here, we focus on the penal system's appropriation of principles and techniques derived from the Christian tradition, which substantially transformed the prison into 'the penitentiary'.

Foucault's genealogy actually presents a slightly more complex storyline, since he distinguishes between the Catholic church and Protestant dissidents when tracing the 'Christianization' of the prison (PS: 86–88). He insists that the penitentiary has no strict descent from the monastic model, even if solitary isolation was key to the monastery. Instead, the penitentiary emerged in its nascent form from Anglo-Saxon Protestant dissenters, among whom the American Quakers were the most innovative in developing correctional confinement. On Foucault's account, it was the Quaker society that established and administered the first prison in Pennsylvania around 1780–1790. This 'prison-form' was guided by the Quakers' conception of power as 'a force of coercion and morality' (PS: 87) and their emphasis on solitary retreat as the technique for soul-searching and subsequent conversion. The retreat to 'the depths of solitude' was essential to provide the conditions for the sinner to encounter God, namely 'the rectitude of a mind undisturbed by the passions and images of the world' (PS: 88). However, the integration of

70 Foucault's Technologies

religious components into the European penal system at the end of the eighteenth century did not entail a simple displacement of the judicial principles of punishment. Rather, the penitentiary induced an internal transformation of the penal system, since 'a new form of juridical-religious connection is established through it' (PS: 92). Foucault notes that the emergence of the penitentiary was 'quite surprising' in its time, 'although for us it has lost that sharpness' (PS: 92). Here, we are reminded of a key genealogical principle: one needs to recover the historical juncture at which the prison was 'assembled' to deprive it of its current self-evidence. Foucault suggests that it is the prison's assimilation of our deep-rooted Christian morality which makes it so difficult to free ourselves from its apparent obviousness and timelessness:

> if [the prison] appears to be so deeply rooted in our culture, this is precisely because it was born weighed down with a Christian morality that gives it a historical depth it does not possess. At the confluence of this Christian morality, with its millenary thickness, and a knowledge, which in reality only arises from the prison but whose function is to justify it, to rationalize it, the prison appears ineradicable, held in a sort of 'obviousness'; in this way it is endlessly revived. (PS: 92)

Of course, the late eighteenth century did not give the correctional prison its essential form that would endure without modification. Foucault does not follow the prison's trajectory past the nineteenth century, but he notes that in that century the Christian technique of retreat was reinforced and recodified by medical and sociological knowledge. Hence the retreat is 'supported and codified by the medical theme of therapeutic isolation and [the] sociological [theme] of a break with the delinquent milieu' (PS: 85). To be sure, the latter notion of removal from a delinquent environment still lives on despite the consistent production of delinquent milieus inside and at the borders of the prison itself.

In brief outline, the above analysis shows that the legal-punitive *dispositif* took up elements derived from pastoral power by integrating Christian moral concepts and techniques of penance. Although Foucault does not use the terminology of *dispositifs* at this juncture, he concludes that the penitentiary brought about three significant reconfigurations of the penal system in a way that is emblematic of how *dispositifs* typically operate in his oeuvre. First, Christian concepts of penance became linked to penal law through the 'grafting of Christian morality on criminal justice' (PS: 82); second, a new form of knowledge became possible, that is, a knowledge of the offender's moral deviances; and third, Christianity invested the penal system with an impetus for scrutiny and guidance of the soul. As a consequence, the legal-punitive *dispositif* was reconfigured and new generative relations were forged. Thus transformed, the *dispositif* creates new visibilities, operates new rules of discourse, and establishes new relations of power between the subjects.

Internal infiltration

The second modality of interaction is when one *dispositif* infiltrates another, investing the latter with its strategic imperative and forms of knowledge in the process. Foucault's analysis in *Discipline and Punish* of how disciplinary techniques and knowledge infiltrated the legal system during the eighteenth and nineteenth centuries is well known. Our example will be discipline's infiltration and overturning of the family's sovereignty found in Foucault's *Psychiatric Power*. There, he analyses how, in the mid-nineteenth century, the family became invested with a psychological and psychiatric discipline that required the parents to scrutinize their child for possible abnormalities. Until this point, Foucault recounts, the family had conformed to the sovereign *dispositif*, which meant that its principal concerns were allegiance and obedience, the hierarchy of births, the order of inheritance, and the significance attached to the family name (PS: 114–115). However, with the generalization of discipline in society, the sovereign family underwent 'a sort of internal disciplinarization', which involved 'a kind of transfer of disciplinary forms and schemas, of those techniques of power given by the disciplines', into the family structure (PP: 115). As a result, a number of disciplinary techniques were transplanted to the family, such as time control, pedagogical supervision, and, most importantly, a disciplinary gaze that distinguishes between the normal and the abnormal child. The family, says Foucault, 'begins to function like a little school: the strange category of student parents appears, home duties begin to appear, the control of school discipline by the family; the family becomes a micro-clinic which controls the normality or abnormality of the body' (PP: 115). Agents with 'psy-expertise' like visiting nurses, child psychologists, and psychiatrists began counselling parents on how to discover abnormal children so that they could be submitted to institutional care and normalization:

> You must find for us the mad, feeble minded, difficult, and perverse, and you must find them yourself, through the exercise of disciplinary kinds of control within family sovereignty. And when, through the operation of this disciplinarized sovereignty, you have found your mad, abnormal, feeble minded, and difficult

members in your home, we, say the disciplines, will put them through the filter of normalizing apparatuses and restore them to you. (PP: 115)

As a result of the disciplinary *dispositif*'s infiltration of family sovereignty, the family assumed the task of deciding between normal and abnormal in order to hand over its abnormal members to the expertise of normalization. On Foucault's account, this process of disciplinary penetration into the family institution led to the latter's internal transformation, and hence 'family sovereignty gradually came to resemble the disciplinary form' (PP: 115). Furthermore, the disciplinary infiltration of the family created new visibilities, such as the child's body, behaviour, character, and especially sexuality. This new 'watchful family eye' (PP: 124) relies upon psychopathological categories, central to which is a growing knowledge of what constitutes normal child development as well as normal parenting. In terms of the aforementioned vocabulary of diagrams, we might say that the disciplinary diagram intensifies, modifies, and overturns the family's supervisory functions. Once integrated into the family, the disciplinary diagram interconnects the visible and the articulable, making possible specific observations and enunciations regarding the child's normality or abnormality. To sum up, in the first modality of interaction, techniques integral to one *dispositif* are assembled into another *dispositif*, whereas in the second, one *dispositif* gradually infiltrates another by investing the latter with its strategic imperative.

Competing constructions of the same object

This modality can occur as part of the process of appropriation, which was described above. However, here I wish to show that the same phenomenon or object may be constructed very differently as a result of *dispositifs*' interplay. An illustrative example of this modality comes from *Security, Territory, Population* (STP: 33–37). Analysing eighteenth-century French debates on how to ensure grain supply, Foucault presents us with distinct and irreconcilable constructions of the same object: scarcity of grain. In eighteenth- and nineteenth-century France, a major concern was preventing the scarcity of grain, since it led to inflated prices and popular revolt in the towns. Foucault sketches up three phases in the regulation of grain scarcity (STP: 35–37), which vividly illustrate the operations of several *dispositifs*.

In the first half of the eighteenth century, grain shortage was targeted by regulations intended to prevent shortages from occurring, including prohibitions on hoarding, price controls, limits on grain exports, and control of

Foucault's Concept of Technology   73

cultivated land. These legal and disciplinary regulations aimed to preclude grain scarcity from happening at all. However, at the end of the eighteenth century, politicians and economic advisors began to argue that the free circulation of grain was a much better mechanism to ensure grain supply. Central to this process were the physiocrats, a group of French economists who came to prominence in the second half of the eighteenth century by advancing early theories of political economy. The physiocratic theories opposed existing traditions, especially mercantilism, which defined wealth based on the nation's balance of trade or the accumulation of gold. Instead, they emphasized that wealth is derived from agricultural labour and land development. The physiocrats intervened in the debate on scarcity, notably in proposals put forward in 1763 by Louis-Paul Abeille which recommended the removal of restrictions by advancing their doctrine of 'freedom of commerce and the circulation of grain' (STP: 33). From the perspective of this new doctrine, security is not about securing a group of individuals against dangers such as famine, but about securing the freedom of distribution. Whereas the legal-disciplinary *dispositif* constructed scarcity as an evil to be eliminated, the emerging security *dispositif* inserted scarcity into a 'reality of fluctuations' that could neither be completely eliminated nor prevented (STP: 37). So, against the idea that scarcity should be eliminated by outlawing it, the physiocrats made the phenomenon of scarcity visible and articulable as an inevitable part of the natural order in its reality.

This natural order is marked by fluctuations (abundance or scarcity and dearness or cheapness) which can be kept within tolerable limits by means of the price mechanism. We here find the idea that the market, if left to function freely and spontaneously, creates a 'natural' price, which secures optimal distribution. This notion of a natural price of the market was central to early political economy, which Foucault studied extensively in *The Birth of Biopolitics*. There, he recovers the advent of the doctrine of non-intervention into the market mechanisms so essential for economic liberalism: 'the market appeared as something that obeyed and had to obey "natural", that is to say, spontaneous mechanisms. Even if it is not possible to grasp these mechanisms in their complexity, their spontaneity is such that attempts to modify them will only impair and distort them' (BP: 31). If allowed to function freely, early political economists argued, the market would generate a price that was not only natural but also 'true', and therefore the market would act as 'a site of veridiction', which told governors whether they governed correctly or not. Foucault explains that 'inasmuch as it enables production, need, supply, demand, value, and price, etcetera, to be linked together through exchange, the market constitutes a site of veridiction' (BP: 32). The introduction of the

74 Foucault's Technologies

price mechanism into politico-economic discourse involved a shift from the 'just price' to the 'true price' of grain as well as other market commodities.

Generally, we can say that each *dispositif* operates what Foucault calls a 'regime of veridiction', that is, a set of procedures that condition how the truth about a given phenomenon can be told. Regimes of veridiction include, for example, political economy, modern psychology, or the confessional, which allow true statements to occur about the market, sexuality, or the soul. Foucault says that 'the problem is to bring to light the conditions that had to be met for it to be possible to hold a discourse on madness—but the same would hold for delinquency and for sex—that can be true or false according to the rules of medicine, say, or of confession, psychology, or psychoanalysis' (BP: 36). Using his technological approach, Foucault can write a history of truth that sidesteps influential approaches to the problem of truth and rationality—a problem, says Foucault, 'which has been constantly taken up in various forms since the beginning of the nineteenth century. From romanticism to the Frankfurt School', including 'the history of truth, the history of error, or the history of ideology' (BP: 35). We will consider his approach more carefully in relation to other intellectual traditions in Chapter 5, but it suffices to say here that rather than ideological obfuscation or progressive rationalization, Foucault views truth as dependent on the regimes of veridiction that arise at particular historical junctures. Instead of asserting the progressive realization of truth, we realize that it is from within our current regimes of veridiction that we can today see past truth claims as erroneous. Foucault explains that 'the regime of veridiction established at a given moment ... is precisely the one on the basis of which you can now recognize, for example, that doctors in the nineteenth century said so many stupid things about sex' (BP: 36). In this case, then, the history of the *dispositif* of sexuality is also the history of the changing regimes of veridiction that condition how the truth about sex can be produced. The analytical point, however, is that, as the object of scarcity moves from the legal-disciplinary *dispositif* to the *dispositif* of security, the truth of scarcity transforms entirely as a result of the *dispositifs'* rules of visualization and enunciation.

Let us briefly return to and conclude on the general point that each *dispositif* operates a 'regime of veridiction', understood as a set of procedures for the production of true knowledge. It is noteworthy that among the set of heterogeneous elements tied together by the *dispositif*, Foucault gives particular attention to formalized knowledge. By formalized knowledge one should understand scientific propositions, legal clauses, or technical procedures, which are all elements of the *dispositif*'s regime of veridiction. Foucault pays special attention to these elements in the reconstruction of *dispositifs*, although never in isolation, since the analysis centres on the evolving processes through which knowledge becomes formalized. As we have repeatedly noticed, these processes are invested by tactics that interlink power and knowledge, hence propelling their continuous co-production.

The emergence of new dispositifs

Finally, new *dispositifs* may be born at the intersection between existing *dispositifs*. This modality of interaction foregrounds how 'urgent needs' at times emerge at the boundaries and from the difficult interchanges between *dispositifs*. One example is legal psychiatry, which was born during the nineteenth century as a response to problems arising at the boundaries between the *dispositifs* of law, discipline, and security (Villadsen, 2021a: 490). Abnormality as an object, Foucault explains (AB: 56–57), is produced through the interplay between legalistic codes regarding offences and medical knowledge of abnormality. Foucault also uses the term 'the human monster', of which the hermaphrodite is emblematic, to denote those rare individuals emerging in the juridico-biological domain: 'However, the monster emerges within this space as both an extreme and an extremely rare phenomenon. The monster is the limit, both the point at which law is overturned and the exception that is found only in extreme cases' (AB: 56). Situated at the limit of what is possible, the figure of the monster contradicts simultaneously the laws of society and the norms of nature, combining the impossible with the forbidden. By being an extreme case, the monster becomes 'the principle of intelligibility' for all the subjects that are circulating 'dangerousness' because of their various abnormalities. 'The monster is the major model of every little deviation', says Foucault (AB: 56). As such, the monster is a solution to a persistent problem of the nineteenth century, 'that of discovering the core of monstrosity hidden behind little abnormalities, deviances, and irregularities' (AB: 56). In brief, psychiatric and biological knowledge resolved an insurmountable obstacle for the legal system by making it possible to speak the truth of a subject—that is, to render it categorically dangerous.

From a bird's eye perspective, then, emerging in the nineteenth century was the dual challenge of identifying 'dangerous individuals' who posed a potential threat to the population, and treating them not merely in accordance with jurisdictional practice but also inserting them into medical knowledge (Foucault, 2000b). From this urgent need, says Foucault (2000b: 194), arose legal psychiatry, 'a knowledge system able to measure the index of danger present in an individual; a knowledge-system that might establish the

76 Foucault's Technologies

protection necessary in the face of such danger'. The rise of legal psychiatry is an illustrative example of how the *dispositif* interlinks power and knowledge, or, specifically in this case, jurisdictional practice with psychiatric diagnosis. Foucault describes how legal psychiatry grew out of a transformation of the legal system, which was first a site of jurisdictional practice but which gradually integrated a new form of veridiction centred on knowing the truth of the criminal. His approach meant studying, says Foucault, 'how this veridictional practice—supported, of course, by criminology, psychology ... —began to install the veridictional question at the very heart of modern penal practice, even to the extent of creating difficulties for its jurisdiction, which was the question of truth addressed to the criminal: Who are you?' (BP: 34–35). Hence the problem of veridiction was crucial in transforming the penal system and giving rise to the development of legal psychiatry as a new power/knowledge constellation, or *dispositif*. Legal psychiatry was also a response to an 'urgent need' on a broader scale, namely from the increasing discordance between the biopolitical imperative of minimizing inherent risks to the population and applying formal jurisprudence.

Foucault gives a broadly similar account of how, in the nineteenth century, the *dispositif* of sexuality achieved its major breakthrough because it interlinked the discipline of the individual body with the quest for securing the vitality of the whole population. In both cases, new power/knowledge configurations arose from the interplay between the strategic imperatives of different *dispositifs*.

'Over-determination' and 'strategic elaboration'

We have so far examined various ways in which *dispositifs* expand or transform as a result of their interplay with other *dispositifs*. However, a *dispositif* is itself unstable, since it is pregnant with contradictions and unintended effects that propel its perpetual transformation through history. This means that a *dispositif* not only transforms because of its interplay, but also creates the conditions of its own transmutation or decay, without ever constituting a closed system. Foucault says that once a *dispositif* has emerged, it develops through a double process of 'functional overdetermination' and 'strategic elaboration':

> On the one hand, there is a process of functional overdetermination, because each effect—positive or negative, intentional or unintentional—enters into resonance or contradiction with the others and therefore calls for a readjustment or a reworking

of the heterogeneous elements that surface at various points. On the other hand, there is a perpetual process of strategic elaboration. (CF: 195)

Let us examine the key terms in this quote in turn: 'overdetermination', 'intentional or unintentional effects', and 'strategic elaboration'. A situation of over-determination occurs when there are multiple causes that could account for, or determine, a particular effect. Analytically, since there are more causes present than necessary to produce the effect, there can be no single or unidirectional causality. It is not clear whether Foucault introduces over-determination with reference to Sigmund Freud or Louis Althusser, both of whom used the term. In *The Interpretation of Dreams*, Freud (2010 [1899]) argued that many events in dreams were usually over-determined, insofar as they derived from multiple factors in the dreamer's life, including 'the residue' from the day's experiences, unconscious wishes, and repressed traumas nested in the layers of the psyche that required repeated interpretations.

There is some resonance between Freud's concept and Foucault's emphasis on multiple interacting causes. Yet Foucault was probably invoking the notion of over-determination as his former teacher, Althusser, had developed it, without committing fully to all its implications. Althusser used over-determination to offer a framework for grasping social transformation that was more complex than the Marxist model of contradiction permitted. In the section entitled 'Contradiction and Over-Determination' in *For Marx*, Althusser (1969a: 101) proposes that society as such should be understood as structured by a complex over-determination of multiple factors. The particular event of revolutions, argues Althusser (1969a: 126), cannot be derived from a simple and purified contradiction, 'the beautiful contradiction between Capital and Labour'. In reality, revolutions are always 'exceptions' to this model which, in Althusser's somewhat simplified rendering, retains Hegel's abstract 'dialectical' schema. Althusser suggested that revolutions, like social formations (e.g. feudalism, capitalism), are conditioned on a series of factors, none of which act as the sole or essential cause of the others. In other words, the class contradiction is 'over-determined' by various processes and events, the interplay of which *may* result in 'a revolutionary situation' or rupture (Althusser, 1969a: 122). Conceiving of social formations as complexly structured, Althusser introduces, as Paul Resch (1989: 524) notes, 'a theatre without an author', effectively eschewing the idea of 'an expressive totality (where all elements express a single immanent principle)'. The key parallel between Althusser and Foucault regarding over-determination is that each social formation/*dispositif* is 'decentred' and hence cannot be derived from a central point or original source.

78 Foucault's Technologies

Over-determination surfaces very rarely in Foucault's work. In *Psychiatric Power* the term appears in a straightforward way to describe 'the tactic' of setting asylum inmates to work in the early nineteenth century. Foucault (PP: 154–156) explains that work became a mandatory practice in the asylum system because it was invested with a range of different motives such as ensuring discipline, creating regularity, and instituting a system of rewards: 'Work is highly over-determined in the asylum system since ... it ensures the necessary order, discipline, regularity, and constant occupation. Thus, very quickly, around the 1830s, work becomes obligatory within asylums' (PP: 154). Foucault emphasizes the fact that asylum work was paid, and thus the inmate could satisfy needs created by the asylum system itself, ameliorating institutionalized deprivations such as insufficient food, and allowing the purchase of extra amenities like tobacco and dessert. However, no single motive could account for the adoption of the technique of 'beneficial occupation in treatment' within the asylum *dispositif.* In his lecture series, *Abnormal,* Foucault uses the term 'double determination' to describe how, in the second half of the nineteenth century, 'perversity' was simultaneously invested by juridical and medical discourse (AB: 32). In this case, an over-determined object is invested with incommensurate forms of knowledge while being inserted into the psychiatric *dispositif.*

Notable among the links between Foucault and Althusser with regard to over-determination is the assumption, first, that a social formation is pervaded by multiple interacting effects and, second, that the elements of a formation do not express any single principle or essence. Althusser sought to expel Hegelian dialectics from historical materialism by theorizing the form of causality operative in complex social formations. Hence it was crucial for Althusser to evacuate what he believed was a reductionist idea of social formations as 'expressions' of an essence. Tim Benton explains this helpfully:

> The Hegelian notion of totality is what Althusser calls 'expressive', in the sense that each specific element or 'moment' of a *seemingly* complex whole is interpreted as 'expressing' in its own particular way some general or essential character of the whole: the appearance of complexity is reduced by the Hegelian philosophical method to an *essential* simplicity. (Benton, 1984: 62, italics in original)

For Althusser, each social transformation is irreducible to the logic of a simple contradiction because multiple irreducible factors interact at a given conjuncture. Several contradictions will coexist, and their interaction with other processes and events may induce transformation. Similarly, for Foucault the strategic imperative does not determine the workings of a *dispositif* 'because each effect ... enters into resonance or contradiction with the others and therefore calls for a readjustment or a reworking of the heterogeneous element' (Foucault, CF: 195). In both cases there is an insistence on the necessity of careful historical analysis. Althusser's materialist premise of the irreducibility of social formations to an inner principle implies, notes Benton, that 'ideological forms, particular forms of the state, and so on ... must be first analysed in their specificity, and only then explained in general terms' (Benton, 1984: 62). This emphasis on beginning the analysis in the specifics and only then conceptualizing them resonates broadly in Foucault's recovery of the gradual assembling of techniques and practices constitutive of a *dispositif*.

Overall, notable parallels can be drawn between Althusser and Foucault around their conceptualization of over-determination and the structuring forces in social formations. At the same time, their works also diverged in significant ways, as we will discuss in Chapter 3. Important dividing lines include Althusser's maintenance of economic relations as determinant 'in the last instance', his psychoanalytic notion of subjects' 'imaginary' relation to their real conditions of existence, and his distinction between ideology and science, all of which Foucault opposed. With respect to the analysis of *dispositifs*, two differences are noteworthy. First, for all its dynamic complexity, Althusser's notion of over-determination was bound to one singular social formation, whereas Foucault analysed multiple *dispositifs* evolving in mutual support, competition, and negation. Second, the Marxist distinction between ideological representation and real antagonism disappears in Foucault's *dispositif*, since, notes Mark Coté (2007: 47), 'the dispositif is not a matter of a contradiction between "imaginary" conditions in relation to "real" conditions of existence. It is only through dispositifs that the "truth" of any real is produced.' For Foucault, 'true objects', as well as distinctions of truth and falsity, are produced by the *dispositif* itself, on its 'surface', without any false naturalization of the dominant ideology which obfuscates the true kernel of class antagonism.

An important implication of Foucault's use of over-determination is that contradictory effects must be expected as part of the *dispositif*'s operation. Because any given *dispositif* is ceaselessly shaped by the tactics, events, and operations of other *dispositifs*, it produces both 'intended and unintended effects' (CF: 195). Along with the transformation ensuing from the interplay between *dispositifs*, it is important to note that each *dispositif* creates its own conditions for transformation. Nick Hardy (2015) argues that much of Foucault's work focuses on responses to aleatory events, which also characterize the *dispositif*'s capacity to ensure social stability. Hardy (2015: 208)

80 Foucault's Technologies

suggests that Foucault used over-determination to denote that *dispositifs* vastly increase the probability of certain outcomes, since they 'produce a field of overdetermination so reducing aleatory possibilities'. A *dispositif* achieves 'aleatory dominance', argues Hardy, 'when the dispositif has proven able to counteract, subsume, or alter unexpected and contradictory events, so maintaining its dominant effects' (Hardy, 2015: 213). While it is correct to emphasize that a *dispositif* makes certain outcomes more likely than others, insofar as it imbues social relations with a specific propensity, Hardy overestimates the *dispositif*'s capacity to dominate the outcome of events.

In fact, rather than pointing to 'aleatory dominance' as the basis of social stability, Foucault uses the concept of over-determination to emphasize the *dispositif*'s unintended, contradictory, and uncontrollable effects. In showing that social struggle is integral to the *dispositif*, Foucault describes how the *dispositif* creates unintended effects that are invested by new actors in their strategies. These tactics may in turn radiate back into the *dispositif*, creating the need for its adjustment or major transformation. The *dispositif*, in other words, produces relations that spur its transmutation, since its expansive operations create resonances which call for readjustments. Again, Foucault shifted focus from subjects and things, and foregrounded instead the relations between these agents and their different forces. This refocusing, argues Alan Schrift, displays Foucault's inspiration from Nietzsche's understanding of power as relations between forces, that is, 'forces of attraction and repulsion, domination and subordination, imposition and reception' (Schrift, 1995: 40). However, whereas Nietzsche often worked with an opposition between two (masters and slaves, Rome and Judaea), Foucault leaves dualisms behind, exploring the relations between sets of three: law, discipline, security; and truth, power, subjectivity.

In the unforeseen effects and resonances we also find the reason why the strategic imperative and its 'actual' implementations are always marked by gaps and discordance. For example, from the imperative of discipline emerged the unintended effect of 'the delinquent milieu' and related subcategories such as juvenile delinquents, requiring specialized correctional expertise, techniques, and institutions. More recently, the growing number of delinquents has been taken up by political-economic strategies around the 'outsourcing' of punishment to expanding profit-generating corporations. The resulting 'prison-industrial complex' comprises a whole set of correctional services, such as skills training, supervised jobseeking, outpatient alcohol treatment, psychological therapy, or parenting classes, that interact in mutually reinforcing ways—we discuss these in more detail in Chapter 3.

Across his works, Foucault mentions multiple unforeseen effects of the spread of the disciplinary *dispositif* (for example, DP: 278–280). These effects include the prison's consistent correctional defects that paradoxically reinforce the disciplinary imperative itself and the production of abnormalities that become useful in new tactics. In both cases, Foucault shows how the unforeseen effects induce into the disciplinary *dispositif* 'a sort of interplay of shifts of position and modifications of function' (CF: 195). Hence the endurance of the correctional prison cannot be explained in terms of its actual results, since the failure of prisons to turn offenders into lawful subjects has not at all eliminated the aspirations for disciplinarity as such. Rather than undermining discipline, the failures provide the disciplinary strategy with new targets against which to pit itself, allowing a reutilization of the unintended consequences. Discipline thus entails a kind of 'stubborn' normativity that persists—or even thrives on—evident failures to reach its own goals. Foucault says: 'the real history of the prison is undoubtedly not governed by the successes and failures of its functionality, but is in fact inserted within strategies and tactics that find support in these very functional defects themselves' (STP: 118). So the prison owes its long lifespan not to successfully correcting offenders but more to the fact that it produced 'defects' useful for social tactics only loosely related to correctional punishment itself.

What useful defects did the prison produce? It is well known that prisons often create a 'delinquent milieu' or 'criminal subculture' which reproduces particular techniques, practices, and subjectivities. Foucault indeed suggests that the prison has produced delinquency with great success, but he also emphasizes that the delinquent was not simply a lawbreaker but produced as an abnormal or pathological individual. Delinquency is, writes Foucault, 'a specific type, a politically or economically less dangerous—and, on occasion, usable—form of illegality' (DP: 277). If the delinquent could potentially be normalized, since he was a 'pathologized subject' rather than inherently evil or a class enemy, he was less dangerous. Furthermore, Foucault notes that from the early nineteenth century onwards there was a reutilization of the delinquent milieu in terms of organized criminal activities like prostitution linked up to the capitalist economy: 'The delinquent milieu came to be reutilized for diverse political and economic ends, such as the extraction of pleasure through the organisation of prostitution. This is what I call the strategic completion [*remplissement*] of the dispositif' (CF: 196). Hence the *dispositif* can expand 'strategically' when its unexpected effects become useful for various political and social strategies. The general analytical point is that the *dispositif* continually transforms as it is affected by its own results, especially those that were unintended.

82 Foucault's Technologies

Notable in this regard are the contradictions that arose in the eighteenth and nineteenth centuries between the formal penal discourse and the social tactics of propertied groups. The latter sought to protect their wealth and production by moralizing workers and seeking to make minor violations, irregularities, and misconduct legally sanctionable. Sometimes, industrialists and tradesmen organized their own practices of surveillance, control, and disciplinary sanctioning, a 'spontaneous superintendence' which, says Foucault, 'seeks to establish continuity between moral control and repression on the one hand, and the penal sanction on the other'. He then continues: 'So what we see is a moralization of the penal system, despite the practice and discourse of this system. All this movement allows penality to spread widely into everyday life' (PS: 107–108). This attack on a range of working-class behaviours detrimental to the capitalist order means, notes Bernard Harcourt (2015b), that moralization is inscribed into the economic process. And soon, writes Harcourt (2015b: 291–292), '[t]his moralization will extend to institutions like the police and other authorities that supervise and target the lower strata of society'. This process demonstrates, first, that the disciplinary *dispositif* extended its points of application through social tactics pursued by privileged groups and, second, that some unexpected techniques emerged from this interconnection of penal law and moral judgements.

Such judicial-moral techniques have proliferated in the twentieth and twenty-first centuries, forming a 'prison-industrial complex' which targets individuals at the borders of the labour market, the psychiatric system, and the prison system. Indeed, long-term unemployed people and ex-offenders often become subjected to mandatory reporting, enforced drug and alcohol treatment, behavioural psychological counselling, curfew restrictions, and compulsory job training (which will be further discussed in Chapter 3). The eighteenth- and nineteenth-century penal reformers would never have envisioned the emergence of major private prison companies, driven by economic profits and linked to other businesses supplying goods and services to government prison agencies. As an unintended effect, then, correctional punishment came to benefit not only the justice system, but also construction companies, job training agencies, surveillance technology vendors, prison food services, and psychiatric facilities.

The general point is that the *dispositif*, understood as a network of practices and techniques, can—and will—generate something that those who set those practices and techniques in motion did not intend. That 'something' can, in turn, be rendered useful for those same innovators or for other agents pursuing other tactics. In this way, the *dispositif* evolves without ever forming a coherent whole, which determines social relations. Foucault repeatedly claims that a *dispositif* also creates the conditions of its own decay or transformation, and produces effects that are invested by new actors or in new modes, and are used in new strategies that will be strong enough in transforming an already stabilized *dispositif* or in creating a new one.

This is where the *dispositif*'s transformability ultimately differs from Althusser's theory of ideology. Whereas Foucault spoke of effects that enter into resonance, creating contradictions and unforeseen outcomes, Althusser conceived of effects as resulting from the stimulus-response of interpellation. We further discuss Althusser's thesis on Ideological State Apparatuses (IDS) in Chapter 3, but, schematically, his notion of interpellation entails that ideology 'calls out' subjects who respond by identifying with ideology and practising its 'commands'. We have seen that Foucault's concept of *dispositif* escapes such linear production of effects, instead emphasizing the multidirectional interplay of effects. Foucault's turn to *dispositifs* in the 1970s can be seen as an attempt to dislodge the analyses of social struggle from the model of stimulus-response (Panagia, 2019: 723), along with associated notions like interiority and alienation that are central to ideology critique. The *dispositif* itself marks out a transversal 'surface' upon which tactics and techniques evolve in interaction. Finally, adopting the concepts of 'over-determination' and 'strategic elaboration', Foucault's genealogy becomes attuned to the possibility of piecemeal social transformations irreducible to the (Marxist) horizon of an overarching revolution.

The above discussions have emphasized the motility of the *dispositif*, insofar as it interacts with its surroundings and continually readjusts its components. These features bring to mind both organic processes and mechanistic functions. Recently, Matteo Pasquinelli (2015) has argued that Foucault's concept of *dispositif* has its principal root in French philosopher of medical epistemology, Georges Canguilhem. Pasquinelli's argument follows two routes: first, Foucault and Canguilhem are linked via 'the norm', which they both saw as a dynamic concept undergoing continuous redefinition in power relations. We have already seen how Foucault examines the norm in his famous analysis of disciplinary normalization (DP). In *Abnormal*, Foucault explicitly invokes Canguilhem's (1991) key work, *The Normal and the Pathological*, explaining how normalization differs from the law, since 'the norm's function is not to exclude and reject. Rather, it is always linked to a positive technique of intervention and transformation, to a sort of normative project' (AB: 50). Second, and more pertinent to the present discussion, Pasquinelli argues that Canguilhem's (2008) essay from 1952, 'Machine and Organism', served as a precursor for Foucault's elaboration of the *dispositif*.

84   Foucault's Technologies

Foucault must have known the essay, writes Pasquinelli, since 'Canguilhem uses the term *dispositif* in a way that is very similar to how Foucault would do so later' (Pasquinelli, 2015: 84, italics in original). This second connection is interesting because it shows how a 'dispositional' notion of power as relational, impersonal, and technological can be found already in Canguilhem.

Canguilhem's key claim in his 1952 essay is that machines function like organisms. Although machines are artificial constructs, Canguilhem (2008: 87, italics in original) argues that '*machines can be considered as organs of the human species.* A tool or a machine is an organ, and organs are tools or machines.' In developing his thesis, Canguilhem specifies that the parts of the machine are transformable, just as their order in 'a system of connections' is modifiable. Furthermore, the outcome or 'movement' produced by the machine is a function of the configuration as a whole:

> A mechanism is a configuration of solids in motion such that the motion does not abolish the configuration. The mechanism is thus an assemblage of deformable parts, with periodic restoration of the relations between them. The assemblage consists in a system of connections with a degree of freedom ... In any machine, movement is thus a function of the assemblage, and mechanism is a function of configuration. (Canguilhem, 2008: 76–77)

The mechanical language employed by Canguilhem invokes the nascent mechanical know-how of the seventeenth century, which paves the way for the technological view of power characteristic of the *dispositif*. More importantly, Canguilhem finds in Descartes a transition from the political command to the machine's execution of mechanical connections: 'According to Descartes, a mechanical device that executes replaces a power that directs and commands' (Canguilhem, 2008: 87). According to Pasquinelli, this is the place where Canguilhem for the first time introduces the notion of the *dispositif*, understood as an impersonal, automated power that substitutes for the personalized power of a ruler: 'What must be emphasized here is that Canguilhem presents the *dispositif* as a form of power but without an explicit and visible command' (Pasquinelli, 2015: 84). A parallel can be drawn here to Foucault's comments in *Security, Territory, Population* on the arrival of a time with the rise of state reason, *raison d'etat*, where history unfolds without a Divine plan or Godly miracles (STP: 257). In Canguilhem's plausible forerunner to Foucault's *dispositif*, we thus find a view of power as impersonal, non-representational, and immanent to a configuration of moveable elements.

Davide Panagia (2019) suggests that Foucault's decision to use the *dispositif* was prompted by his dissatisfaction with Althusser's thesis on ideological dominance as achieved through the linear mechanism of interpellation. Hence Canguilhem's formulation helped Foucault in developing his analytics of power 'on the basis of the motility of things rather than on what will appear as a static and linear reflex function implicit in the model of communication that the apparatus will exploit' (Panagia, 2019: 722). The emphasis on disposition, arrangement, and movement in the *dispositif* serves as Foucault's remedy to Althusser's 'inability to register any form of interactivity other than stimulus/response' (Panagia, 2019: 723). We recall that the *dispositif* is always relational rather than substantial, since it designates 'precisely the nature of the connection that can exist between heterogeneous elements' (CF: 194). Indeed, Raffnsøe et al. insist that the *dispositif* is not a 'thing' but a 'transversal set of connections' between diverse components: 'The dispositive is of a *relational* nature rather than of a substantial kind' (Raffnsøe et al., 2014: 10, italics in original). In brief, aiming to describe a specific transversal 'connectivity' in relations sharply separates Foucault's *dispositifs* from models of communication and stimulus/response.

Of course, there are limits to the compatibility of Canguilhem and Foucault in relation to machines/*dispositifs*, since Foucault's elaborations also take inspiration from very different sources (as we will explore in the following chapters). The *dispositif*'s operations are irreducible to biomechanical metaphors of evolutionary mutation. For example, its continuous interactivity does not pair squarely with a biological model of how an organism seeks to sustain its consistency in the face of environmental influences. Nevertheless, the oblique link to Canguilhem brings us back to key features of Foucault's elaboration of technology as *dispositifs*. We have seen that Foucault's 'technological view of power foregrounds relations of forces over expression of essences, explores the generative power of the diagram without reference to ideological misrepresentation, and maps the exchanges between *dispositifs* without referring to the silent motives of individuals or classes. We also noted that Foucault's approach involves extensive genealogical inquiry into the processes of a *dispositif*'s evolving composition. The key questions are, then: through what configurations of practices, technical inventions, relations of force, and modalities of knowledge did a particular *dispositif* emerge? What strategic imperative is at play, making certain connections in the social body more likely than others? And how will the *dispositif* continually (re)construct its own objects such as 'deviance', 'scarcity', or 'pathological crime'? Although the historical path of the *dispositif* tends towards stabilization, the *dispositif* is always open to contradictions, rupture, and discontinuities as elements are exchanged between *dispositifs* in their interplay.

The analytical emphasis on transformation and dynamic interrelations between different forces ultimately separates Foucault's analyses of *dispositifs* from Martin Heidegger's sweeping philosophical critique of modern technology, which is the subject of Chapter 2.

Chapter Two
The 'Eye' of Technology

How do we make sense of a time in which our life is ceaselessly shaped by technology? Today, modern technology is the cause of many urgent problems, but it is nevertheless presented as their ultimate solution, whether in specific domains, like cybercrime and mechanized warfare, or in threats to the planetary ecosystem, like deforestation and global warming. While we recognize that modern technologies often have deleterious effects in our collective and private lives, we refuse to give up on them, instead investing our hopes in the promise of better and more advanced technology to solve our problems. Consider a few examples: in prenatal diagnostics, there is a growing interest in detecting and correcting for hereditary abnormalities, ensuring genetic optimization and the 'technological reengineering' of the human material. This development raises thorny ethical questions regarding the limits to our manipulation of human genetics, and where to draw the division between acceptable and unacceptable qualities of life. Higher education is increasingly subjected to optimization imperatives that transform education into quantifiable data like graduation ratio and optimization of enrolment time, equating quality with graduates' 'employability'. This tendency has sparked debates on whether the standardization of learning, together with digital teaching technology, eradicates the classical ideal of learning as cultivation of the self, by reducing learning to a set of instrumental labour market skills.

Common to these examples is a tendency towards 'empty optimization', that is, the technological exploitation of all aspects of our genetic and mental capacities with seemingly no purpose other than to maximize efficiency for its own sake. It appears that our belief in absolute control of our time, our natural resources, and our own human race is still alive and well, despite the rising climate movement and debates on the Anthropocene. To be sure, the loss of intrinsic meaning, value-blind instrumentalization, and the objectification of nature and humankind is a long-standing theme in modern philosophy and critical social theory. Martin Heidegger and Michel Foucault are both pivotal in creating pathways to think critically about this theme, both discerning a historical trajectory of technological saturation of modern culture that still

Foucault's Technologies. Kaspar Villadsen, Oxford University Press. © Kaspar Villadsen (2024).
DOI: 10.1093/oso/9780198819400.003.0003

88   Foucault's Technologies

carries us forward. Of key significance in this process is the installation of a particular modern world view, or a 'gaze', that turns everything into objects of quantification, manipulation, and optimization. The essence of technology, Heidegger argued, forces us to perceive nature and ourselves as objects of exploitation, restricting the ways in which they can reveal themselves to us simply as meaningless raw material.

Almost anticipating the advent of the data-intensive age, Heidegger warned that modern technology would create a resource-plundering, self-propelling system that would last into the next centuries, transforming all that exists into quantifiable and interchangeable data. Similarly prophetic, perhaps, one of Heidegger's students, Gunther Anders (1902–1992), claimed that human beings suffer from 'thing-shame', which is the feeling of shame over not being a thing, caused by our sense of inferiority to the machine in terms of its efficiency and accuracy (Anders, 2016). Anders would appear to anticipate recent debates on the predictive capacity of machine-learning as superior to human brains with their alleged flaws, like sluggishness, irrationality, and 'emotional bias'. Ironically, today's high tech corporations promise not only to better predict consumer behaviour but also, by feeding algorithms with an endless supply of data points, to make profiling individualized, less discriminatory, and hence more 'humane'. As a result, the ethico-political subject can now be substituted by 'optimized', data-driven profiling and algorithmic decision-making.

Heidegger and Foucault both evade the view that modern technology is a problem for which we must find concrete solutions, because such solutions tend to replicate modern technology itself. Instead, they sought ways in which we can relate differently to technology as our historical condition.

***

In his seminal essay, 'The Question Concerning Technology' (QT), Heidegger argued that 'modern man' not only applies an objectifying gaze upon nature, but also begins applying that same gaze upon himself, endlessly examining the human material for optimization potential:

> Everywhere everything is ordered to stand by, to be immediately at hand, indeed to stand there just so that it may be on call for a further ordering. Whatever is ordered about in this way has its own standing. We call it the standing-reserve [Bestand] ... Does not man himself belong even more originally than nature within the standing-reserve? The current talk about human resources, about the supply of patients for a clinic, gives evidence of this. (QT: 17–18)

At this important juncture in his essay, Heidegger suggests that modern humans not only objectify nature as resources to be optimized, controlled, and processed as commodities, or 'standing reserve' (Ger. *Bestand*); they also objectify themselves as such a resource. As a result, life has become part of an undifferentiated pool of quantifiable and exploitable raw material. This bleak portrayal of the instrumentalization of human existence has broad similarities with Foucault's portrayal of discipline and biopolitics as a series of interventions and regulatory controls of the human species. According to Foucault, human life was captured in a dual movement beginning in the seventeenth century—one that rendered the human being both as a discrete 'body-machine' and as a unit in a 'population-body' to be optimized (HS1: 139). As we saw in Chapter 1, in the same period disciplinary techniques began to form an unprecedented system of examination and classification of human aptitudes that aimed to extract maximum force and time from the body. In modern societies, observes Foucault, the disciplinary gaze became a ubiquitous institutionalized way of seeing, that ceaselessly scrutinizes individuals' behaviour and predispositions for abnormalities. In *Discipline and Punish*, he writes:

> It is the examination which, by combining hierarchical surveillance and normalizing judgement, assures the great disciplinary functions of distribution and classification, maximum extraction of forces and time, continuous genetic accumulation, optimum combination of aptitudes and, thereby, the fabrication of cellular, organic, genetic and combinatory individuality. (DP: 191)

As these opening quotes indicate, important themes connect Heidegger and Foucault, especially in their diagnosis of technology as a modern proclivity to order and optimize all forces of life. In broad outline, both thinkers identify modernity as the age of expansive objectification of human capacities, conceive of historical systems of thought as the condition of thinking, and share a view of truth not as foundation but as event. Furthermore, they both draw significant intellectual inspiration from Nietzsche in diagnosing modernity as deprived of higher values as well as contesting any doctrine of history's inevitable progress.

Nevertheless, as I will argue throughout this chapter, we must recognize the differences between Heidegger's philosophical critique of technology and Foucault's genealogical approach to technologies. In his diagnosis of modern technology, Heidegger depends on a sweeping history of Western thought, from Greek antiquity to the modern age, which culminates

90 Foucault's Technologies

in modernity's interminable quest to turn everything into measurable and exploitable objects. By comparison, Foucault describes in great empirical detail how this objectifying and optimizing gaze emerged historically and how it became useful in factories, schools, military barracks, hospitals, and more. Compared to Heidegger's grandiose history of Western metaphysics, Foucault offers more detailed accounts of the historical emergence and gradual transformations of the techniques through which human subjects become objectified. Indeed, as I will show, Heidegger's philosophical critique of the restricted vision of 'the modern age' ultimately contrasts with Foucault's genealogies of distinct technological 'gazes'.

I accept the argument that reading Foucault's concepts through a Heideggerian lens can greatly clarify Foucault's overall project (Elden, 2001: 6), especially concerning the genesis of Foucault's thinking on modern technology. Overall, I also believe that a comparative discussion with Heidegger allows us to understand Foucault's approach to technology with more depth than is typically offered in the introductory literature to Foucault and the many empirical applications of his concepts. Nonetheless, it is crucial to pay close attention to the differences between the two thinkers, because these differences bring as much clarity to Foucault's thinking as an integrative reading does. Hence the core of this chapter revolves around the comparative discussion of the relationship between Heidegger's and Foucault's thinking on technology. In particular, it explores the extent to which the two can be connected around the 'gaze' of modern technology, given that they both broadly conceive of technology in terms of its production of certain visibilities.

The chapter falls into five overall sections. First, the section 'Was Foucault simply a Heideggerian?' briefly reviews the contentious and unresolved debate on the intellectual relationship between Heidegger and Foucault. The second section, 'Heidegger's question concerning technology', lays out the key premises in Heidegger's philosophical critique of modern technology. A third section discusses how far the parallels between Heidegger and Foucault can be pushed regarding their 'shared obsession' with visibility. The fourth section, 'Does *Gestell* 'correspond perfectly' to *dispositif*?', examines these two key terms, emphasizing how the *dispositif* gives priority to the analysis of relationality and context, and how this priority distinguishes the concept from *Gestell's* metaphysical underpinnings. Finally, the concluding section, 'Where Heidegger and Foucault come apart', compares the two thinkers and their approaches to modern technology in particular.

Was Foucault simply a Heideggerian?

Foucault (1989a: 471) once declared: 'I'm simply a Nietzschean!' At other moments, however, he would grant a similarly fundamental importance to his inspiration from Heidegger, or he would say that reading Nietzsche and Heidegger together was decisive for his thinking (Foucault, 1989a: 470). From the outset, we should note that Foucault only rarely made explicit references to Heidegger, and he never wrote a text devoted to Heidegger. Nevertheless, late in his life Foucault paid a major unexpected tribute to the German philosopher. In an interview from 1982, Foucault answered a question about the intellectual inspirations for his thinking by saying that Heidegger was an 'overwhelming influence', 'but no one in France has ever perceived it' (Foucault, 1988b: 12). In another interview, on 29 May 1984, a few weeks before he died, Foucault declared:

> Heidegger has always been for me the essential philosopher. I started by reading Hegel, then Marx, and I began to read Heidegger in 1951 or 1952; then in 1952 or 1953, I no longer remember, I read Nietzsche. I still have the notes I took while reading Heidegger—I have tons of them!—and they are far more important than the ones I took on Hegel or Marx. My whole philosophical development was determined by my reading of Heidegger. But I recognize that Nietzsche prevailed over him. (Foucault, 1989b: 250)

The intellectual relationship between Heidegger and Foucault remains unresolved, however, and commentators are strongly divided on the issue. Some scholars argue that great affinities connect the two thinkers, while others assert that they stand worlds apart. In his seminal contributions to this debate, Hubert Dreyfus (1996) makes the case that Heidegger's Being (Ger. *Sein*) is comparable to Foucault's concept of power, since both Being and power structure the way that objects can emerge. Dreyfus follows a convention in the commentary literature of spelling Heidegger's 'Being' with a capital B to distinguish it from 'beings', understood as all existing entities (Ger. *Seiendes*). We will adopt this convention here (which also entails that 'being' is changed to '[Being]' in all quotes). The difference between Foucault and Heidegger, suggests Dreyfus, is that Heidegger's philosophy focuses on how we have come to treat nature as object, whereas 'Foucault transforms Heidegger's focus on things to a focus on selves and how they became subjects' (Dreyfus, 1996: 1–2). Foucault thus explored the ways modern subjects have come to constitute themselves under discursive divisions

92 Foucault's Technologies

like reason/madness, sexuality/perversion, and normality/deviance. Stuart Elden observes that 'very striking affinities can be found' between Heidegger and Foucault, asserting that 'whilst Foucault—unlike many of the others—does not directly speak *of* Heidegger, he often speaks in a thoroughly Heideggerian way' (Elden, 2001: 152). Nevertheless, Elden rightly recognizes that not all of Foucault's work is Heideggerian, and that Foucault was sometimes engaged in an implicit critique of Heidegger. Going further, Samuel Ijsseling argues that Foucault's historical inquiry into the nature of reason can only be understood in its true radicalism from a Heideggerian viewpoint: 'Without the profound understanding of Heidegger's thinking that is always presupposed by Foucault, one risks reading Foucault only as a sociologist, an historian of sciences, or as a variation on authors like Max Weber or Habermas and, thus, not to grasp the radicalism of Foucault's enterprise' (Ijsseling, 1986: 420).

Other prolific commentators on Heidegger and Foucault arrive at almost the opposite conclusion. Gianni Vattimo argues that even if Foucault's thought could be described as 'a summa or synthesis of Nietzsche and Heidegger', it is 'Nietzsche who dominates, with too little space given to Heidegger's ontological aspirations' (Vattimo, 2006: 183). Hans Sluga observes that it is most fruitful to read Foucault in Nietzschean terms, insisting that, although Heidegger and Foucault shared a great inspiration from Nietzsche, 'the Nietzsche whom Foucault discovered from his own reading ... is not at all like Heidegger's Nietzsche' (Sluga, 2005: 222). Sluga suggests that Heidegger's metaphysical interpretation of Nietzsche stands at the farthest possible distance from Foucault's genealogical use of Nietzsche, revealing itself 'as the sharpest alternative' to Heidegger's Nietzsche (Sluga, 2007: 118). Jana Sawicki (1987) sides with Sluga, arguing that Foucault, unlike Heidegger, never engaged himself with metaphysics but pursued a particularistic critique of the present. Hence, Sawicki concludes that Foucault never provided an overall account of the 'essence' of modern technology, since 'he simply identifies particular practices in the present, the assumed value of which he is sceptical, and traces their lines of descent in Nietzschean fashion' (Sawicki, 1987: 168). Timothy Rayner asserts that theoretically, Heidegger and Foucault have almost nothing to say to each other, but adds that theory is not the right way to connect them. Establishing a connection at the level of theory, as Dreyfus does, means 'looking for the wrong sort of relationship' (Rayner, 2001: 151). On Rayner's account, Heidegger and Foucault wrote in a similar *critical spirit* that aimed for a radical reversal in our experience of the technological life form. They shared the wish 'to turn our attention from the inner life that characterises technological enframing towards the conditions which establish this way of being', a move which stands in the service of 'transforming our experience of this mode of existence entirely' (Rayner, 2001: 152). Finally, Gilles Deleuze (1988: 113) recalls Foucault's well-known declaration that 'Heidegger always fascinated him, but that he could understand him only by way of Nietzsche'. It is by reading Nietzsche, argues Deleuze, that Foucault escapes phenomenology's 'pacifying' emphasis on meaning, recovering force as that which constitutes life. Deleuze concludes that Foucault's genealogy 'is a Nietzschean rather than a Heideggerian history, a history devoted to Nietzsche, or to life' (Deleuze, 1988: 129). In light of this scholarly division, we must dig deeper into Heidegger's and Foucault's works on technology to better grasp their fundamental similarities and differences.

To start with, we note that Foucault's work displays little explicit influence from Heidegger, especially in comparison with his repeated references to Kant and Nietzsche. The most direct trace of Heidegger is evident in some of Foucault's early publications, including his introduction to Ludwig Binswanger's *Dream and Existence* (Foucault, 1993) and Foucault's *Mental Illness and Psychology*, both published in 1954 (Foucault, 1976 [1954]). These two texts bear extensive witness of Foucault's engagement with Heidegger's thought, which leads Alan Milchman and Alan Rosenberg to conclude that 'the presence of Heidegger is overwhelming' in Foucault's earliest texts, since at that time he had not yet freed himself from the phenomenological perspective with its constituent subject' (Milchman and Rosenberg, 2003: 4). Other significant traces of Heidegger's influence on Foucault surface in subsequent works from the 1960s, in particular his *Introduction to Kant's Anthropology* (Foucault, 2008 [1964]) and *The Order of Things* (Foucault, 1970 [1966]). At that time, however, Foucault had dislodged himself from phenomenological notions of the subject's existential experiences, such as finitude, and instead historicized such experiences as parts of the modern episteme (Palti, 2021: 24–25).

For now, we leave aside the complex discussion of Foucault's different inspirations from Heidegger throughout his career (see McQuillan, 2016) in order to focus on the theme of modern technology. In carrying out this comparative discussion, we avoid speculative assessments of underlying similarities in Heidegger's and Foucault's work or explanations in terms of hidden meaning or unarticulated intentions. Sluga notes that many of the interpreters who search for strong affinities between Heidegger and Foucault 'have been engaged in the sort of deep hermeneutics of which Foucault himself expressed justified suspicion' (Sluga, 2005: 119). Indeed, Foucault (AK) emphasized that he wished to approach the discourse at the level of what was actually said, and that analysing discourse with reference to specific authors typically involves psychological and biographical factors, whereby 'the theme of an originating subject' is reintroduced (Foucault, 1977b: 137). The following exposition will carry out comparisons based on the works of Heidegger and Foucault, while leaving aside subterranean explanations like psychological motives, hidden meanings, or unconscious drives.

The following discussions will focus on texts by Heidegger that Foucault is most likely to have read in the early 1950s, namely the essays published in 1950 in the collection *Holzwege* (Heidegger, 1950). Sluga suggests that Foucault probably read 'The Age of the World Picture' (WP), 'since it elaborates further on the epochal conception of history and addresses, in particular, the question of the history of modern rationality', along with Heidegger's essay 'The Word of Nietzsche: "God is Dead"' (WN) from the same collection (Sluga, 2005: 222). These selected texts by Heidegger constitute a still largely underexplored source of inspiration for Foucault's thinking on technology and related themes like discipline and objectification. Our analysis of these works by Heidegger will be supported by other significant texts, including 'The Question Concerning Technology' (QT), *Being and Time* (B&T), *Discourse on Thinking* (DT), 'The Turning' (T), and 'Letter on Humanism' (LH), as well as *Nietzsche Volumes 2 and 3* (NV2; NV3). First, as a prelude to the comparative analysis, it is necessary to reach a more detailed understanding of Heidegger's philosophical critique of what he often termed the technological age.

Heidegger's question concerning technology

Modern technology had concerned Heidegger since at least the 1930s, and in his later years it became *the* pre-eminent theme of his work. Heidegger believed that technology was not merely another aspect of our existence; rather, it fundamentally defines our prevailing way of thinking in the modern West. He depicted a world in which both nature and humans are ceaselessly ordered, calculated, and turned into exploitable resources to such an extent that seeing reality in any different way has become almost impossible. In a memorial address from 1955, Heidegger painted a dystopian picture of humanity's technological destiny. In his talk, *Discourse on Thinking*, Heidegger described modern technology as an evolving movement in which man's encroachment on nature ultimately uproots him and he becomes enslaved by that which was to serve him:

> In all areas of his existence, man will be encircled ever more tightly by the forces of technology. These forces, which everywhere and every minute claim, enchain, drag along, press and impose upon man under the form of some technical contrivance or other—these forces, since man has not made them, have moved long since beyond his will and have outgrown his capacity for decision. (DT: 51)

Heidegger's thinking on technology reached a high point in the 1940s and 1950s with his landmark essay 'The Question Concerning Technology', which was based on a lecture he gave in 1949 and published in 1954. The essay was originally called 'Das Gestell', a key term in Heidegger's critique of modern technology. It is often translated as 'enframing', the adequacy of which I discuss below. In 'The Question Concerning Technology', Heidegger gave a diagnosis of his own time as one of unprecedented technological domination, placing modern technology within a larger history of Western thought and posing the question of how we might reach a freer relationship to technology. Heidegger thus wanted to reopen the question of what technology is, a question whose multidimensionality has been increasingly restricted as calculative reasoning became the prevailing mode of discovering the world and fully integral to life in the techno-industrial age.

It is a fundamental premise for Heidegger, since his early works, that human beings distinguish themselves from other animals by our unique capacity to pose the question of how we assign meaning to our world: hence 'the inescapability of the question of the meaning of [Being]' (B&T: 25). Heidegger argued that philosophy should serve as the primary means of such primordial questioning by following 'a problem-awakening model' (Heidegger, 1992: 259), which interrogates the 'conditions of possibility of any world-view as something to be questioned' (Heidegger, 1992: 368). For philosophy to be able to question modern technology as a fundamental world view, however, certain obstacles must be eliminated.

Heidegger thus begins 'The Question Concerning Technology' by rejecting two interrelated ideas of technology: first, that technology is exclusively defined as instruments that serve certain ends and, second, that technology is fully under human control. He terms these ideas 'the instrumental and anthropological definition of technology' (QT: 5). While the instrumental notion of technology is 'correct', it is not 'true', Heidegger argues, since it obscures how we have come to think technologically in the first place. To pursue this question, he distinguishes the narrow sense of 'technology', defined as technical devices and procedures, from 'the essence of technology', defined as a mode of disclosure. 'The essence of technology is by no means anything

96 Foucault's Technologies

technological', asserts Heidegger (QT: 4), which permits him to move from specific technical devices to consider instead the kind of fundamental world view that such devices merely embody and exemplify. In brief, questioning 'the essence' of technology allows us to examine the epochal, ubiquitous character of the kind of world-disclosure that technical devices merely crystallize.

Heidegger's philosophical critique of modern technology advances four main propositions. First, technology is not an instrument; it is a mode of disclosing everything that exists. The name for this mode is *Gestell*. Second, technology charges humanity to take an objectifying attitude not only towards nature but also to itself. Third, subjectivism and modern metaphysics, as diagnosed most aptly by Nietzsche, is the inner logic of modern technology. Finally, we can prepare for a freer relationship to modern technology by taking an attitude to the world defined as *Gellasenheit* ('readiness towards things'). The following sections briefly examine these key propositions.

Technology is 'a mode of disclosure'

Heidegger begins by tracing modern technology back to the ancient Greek word *technē*. The ancients did not define *technē* merely as human production through manipulation and forging of natural materials, but instead as a larger phenomenon of bringing things into an intelligible form. Hence '*technē* is the name not only for the activities and skills of the craftsman, but also for the arts of the mind and the fine arts. *Technē* belongs to bringing-forth, to *poiesis*; it is something poietic' (QT: 13). Recovering this ancient definition, Heidegger argues that technology is not simply a means of production but a way of revealing the world. Even if this revealing of things was believed to happen by means of craftsmanship and knowledge, the material itself was also seen as a 'co-responsible' cause for how the objects came into being. Heidegger now invites us to understand *modern* technology as a mode of revealing as well: 'It is of utmost importance that we think bringing-forth in its full scope and at the same time in the sense in which the Greeks thought it' (QT: 10). What is crucial in *technē*, Heidegger stresses, 'does not lie at all in making and manipulating nor in the using of means, but rather in the aforementioned revealing' (QT: 13). Whereas the ancients believed that there was something intrinsic in natural materials, never fully graspable or available to them, modern technology suppresses the question of the inner qualities of materials that was so significant in the ancient Greek conception.

Schematically, while the ancient craftsman 'cooperated' with natural materials in creating an artefact as envisioned, the modern industrialist 'imposes upon' nature, approaching it as undifferentiated inventory to be stored up, reserved, and exploited for optimal yields. Hence production in the modern age means aggressively ordering nature's resources for human use, deploying processes that do not follow naturally from the material itself, but are forced upon it. Heidegger explains that we have come to think of production in this reductive sense because we identify human intervention as the exclusive grounds for causation, instead of seeing human actions and natural materials as co-responsible for production.

This is where Heidegger revisits Aristotle's theory of causation, or 'the doctrine of the four causes' (QT: 7–9). According to this ancient theory, things owe themselves to four causes, which may all partake in the explanation of the existence of something.

- First, *the material cause* is the matter out of which a thing is produced (for example, the bronze that goes into making a statue).
- Second, *the formal cause* is the account of the form of what is to be produced (bronze is melted in order to acquire the shape of a statue).
- Third, *the efficient cause* is the craft and knowledge required to produce something (the skills of the sculptor and the art of bronze-casting which the sculptor relies on).
- Fourth, *the final cause* is the ultimate end, or *telos*, for which the productive activities are carried out (the goal of creating the bronze statue guides each step of the artistic process as their final cause).

Notably, Aristotle developed this fourfold theory of causation primarily for the study of nature, as is evident, for instance, when he posits an organism's flourishing and survival as a final cause to explain the formation of an animal's organs and its behavioural tendencies (Falcon, 2015). Most importantly, then, the Aristotelian framework de-emphasizes the human subject as the ultimate cause of the production of things.

However, in the age of modern technology, argues Heidegger, we think exclusively in terms of what ancient philosophers called the efficient cause. Whereas in Aristotle's time the theory of causation disclosed things as indebted to all four causes, our contemporary culture has largely blinded us to causes other than effective causality. However, when production is construed solely in terms of effective cause, insists Heidegger, 'we bar to ourselves the way to the primal meaning of that which is later called causality' (QT: 9). He uses the hyphenated words 'bringing-forth' (Ger. *hervorbringen*)

98   Foucault's Technologies

to denote the four elements working together in bringing something into existence. This bringing-forth is a rendering of the Greek word *poiēsis*, which means to bring something 'out of concealment into unconcealment', a mode of production which respects and brings forth the inherent qualities of materials. By contrast, in modern times technology is a *challenging-forth* (Ger. *herausfordern*), a mode of disclosure aimed entirely at calculability, manipulation, and commodification. This forceful disclosure, declares Heidegger, 'puts to nature the unreasonable demand that it supply energy that can be extracted and stored' (QT: 14). Such imposition means that nature is disclosed solely as standing reserve, that is, a stockpile of meaningless resources waiting to be dissected, stored, and redistributed (QT: 17). When nature is understood as such a stockpile, it cannot make any demands on us, since it no longer rests-in-itself or harbours any inherent meaning. Nature appears as resources or commodities, which only serves the purpose of further ordering and maximizing of the *Bestand*, or standing reserve.

Heidegger uses the term *Gestell* to denote this technological mode of disclosure, a key notion of his which will be crucial in our subsequent comparison with Foucault's *dispositif*. Heidegger writes that *Gestell* denotes 'the gathering together of that setting-upon which sets upon man, i.e. challenges him forth, to reveal the real, in the mode of ordering, as standing-reserve' (QT: 20). *Gestell* is often translated as 'enframing', which indicates how the world today appears to us through frameworks of meaning that turn everything into standing reserve. The term is of broad significance for Heidegger, since it describes the defining characteristic of our contemporary world view and the modern age as such. *Gestell*, writes Ian Thomson (2014: 57), 'is Heidegger's famous name for the technological understanding of [Being] that underlies and shapes our contemporary age'. However, *Gestell* does not simply mean that some object or another is 'framed' so that it appears in a particular way; it rather defines the very ordering of all our experiences and relations, or the entire 'set-up', which orders for us the meaning, value, and essence of things that exist. Notably, Heidegger uses the compound term *Ge-stell*, where 'Ge' indicates gathering, or encompassing, while 'stell' means challenging-forth or ordering (as in *stellen* or *bestellen*).

Heidegger's translator, William Lovitt, lists the variety of meanings that the verb *stellen* (to place or set) has: 'It can mean to put in place, to order, to arrange, to furnish or supply, and, in a military context, to challenge or engage' (QT: 15). Lovitt explains that in 'The Question Concerning Technology' 'Heidegger sees the connotations of *herausfordern* (to challenge, to call forth, to demand out hither) as fundamentally determinative of the meaning of *stellen*' (QT: 15). *Gestell* therefore manifests all the modalities in which humans disclose their world as an aggregate of exploitable resources, and on this point *Gestell* runs parallel to Foucault's *dispositif* in its far-encompassing effects and transversal reach. In Heideggerian terms, *Gestell* encompasses all the modes of ordering that order man to disclose his world as standing reserve. *Dictionary of Untranslatables* (Cassin et al., 2014) explains that *Gestell* is very hard to translate, since Heidegger created it from an unusual compound of two words that describe man's thrownness into technological world-disclosure. Davis Pascal defines *Gestell* thus:

> It is used by Heidegger in a broad, unexpected, unusual sense to designate the whole or the collection (which is indicated by the prefix Ge-) of all the modes of setting (Ger. stellen) that causes man's way of wanting to impose modern technology on the whole planet ultimately to enslave him as the servant of what he intended to have at his service. (Pascal in Cassin et al., 2014: 1988)

Susanna Lindberg (2015: 226) rightly objects that the common translations of *Gestell* into English as 'Enframing' or 'Framing' are terms that are 'misleadingly concrete'. Here, we follow scholars like Lindberg by preserving the German term *Gestell* in order to avoid the misleading connotations of 'frame' and 'enframing'.

Clearly, while *Gestell* defines a mode of experiencing the world, it is nothing like a subjective response. Heidegger describes it in terms of a 'sending' or 'destining', which forces humanity onto the path that discloses everything as standing reserve. The *Gestell* has been foisted upon us, insofar as man is thrown into the mode of ordering disclosure, which in Heidegger's words 'challenges' and 'claims' him: 'When man, investigating, observing, ensnares nature as an area of his own conceiving, he has already been claimed by a way of revealing that challenges him to approach nature as an object of research, until even the object disappears into the objectlessness of standing-reserve' (QT: 19). Heidegger then argues that *Gestell* can 'claim' us, giving us the restricted view of technology solely as a tool of human action, because this world view had already rooted itself prior to the advent of the physical sciences that take nature as an object of dissection and manipulation. As Krzysztof Ziarek explains: 'Experience in modernity has been "framed" as technological, it is preset or positioned as various modalities of the Gestell, or enframing' (Ziarek, 1998: 183). Hence calculative science and technical advances are made possible by the essence of technology, and they are not the prior cause of it.

Heidegger posits that *Gestell* underpins both science and technical inventions, thereby rejecting the conventional idea that advances in the technical

100 Foucault's Technologies

sciences conditioned the advent of modern technology. Modern science, as Heidegger sees it, is a calculative thinking that promises effectivity and happiness but keeps us from ever reflecting on the meaning of our own time, 'the atomic age' (DT: 56). This is because science forgets to ask: 'What is the ground that enabled modern technology to discover and set free new energies in nature?' (DT: 50). The examples of modern science that Heidegger gives emphasize its manipulative character, including atomic science, computing, synthetic biology, and the knowledge involved in petroleum chemistry and industrial agriculture. For Heidegger, explains Sawicki (1987: 158), 'technology is "ontologically prior" to science', and, since scientific thinking is pervaded by the *Gestell*, 'scientific theorizing is fundamentally inseparable from practices of ordering and controlling'. As a result, nature can henceforth only appear as mathematically calculable causal relations. Albert Borgmann observes that

> the scientific view, due to its prominence, obscures the moral and poetical force of nature. It follows that technology in its broad epochal sense is the temperament of an era that enables humans to grasp the lawful mathematical structure of nature and that gives that structure a prominent, perhaps an unduly important, place in its culture. (Borgmann, 2005: 427)

As ordering disclosure becomes the sole standard of what counts as real, it conceals other ways of revealing, including the *poiēsis* of ancient technology. Heidegger takes as the fundamental premise that disclosure and concealment are two interrelated dimensions of human intelligibility, since any revealing always carries concealing with it.

This premise brings us to Heidegger's central question of Being, which, as noted earlier, he believed distinguishes human beings' capacity for reflecting upon how we render our lives meaningful in light of our own finitude. Heidegger wished to reintroduce 'the ontological difference', which allows us to speak of Being (that which both elicits and escapes our conceptualization of the world) in its difference from *beings* (i.e. the totality of entities that exist). The ontological difference often appears in Heidegger's early works in order to distinguish *beings* from *Being*. In *Being and Time*, Heidegger thus defines his principal inquiry as 'the being of beings, or the meaning of Being in general' (B&T: 26), an inquiry which extends Husserl's phenomenological dictum that the disclosure of one thing requires the concealment of another. Heidegger posits that our world-disclosure is always tied to a framework, which we cannot interrogate without at the same time presupposing it, since 'this, the self-showing that makes appearing possible, is not appearing itself'

(B&T: 28). That which elicits appearances, Being, is not itself appearing, and Being should thus be understood insubstantially, as an event or process of *coming into being*. Being, explains Michael Zimmerman (2021: 722), does not denote 'the substantial essence of entities as in traditional metaphysics, but rather the event of disclosure itself'. Disclosure is, as Zimmerman (2021: 725) puts it, 'the self-concealing interplay of presencing and absencing'. Heidegger argues, then, that the inquiry into the question of Being must start from the recognition that Being can never be finally conceptualized or mastered, since it is not a thing but a permanent question posed by our essential openness to the world's inexhaustibility.

For the later Heidegger, Being denotes an ontological abundance or excessiveness that escapes full conceptualization, insofar as it 'gives itself and refuses itself simultaneously' (Heidegger, 1998: 255). By speaking of how Being both *appears* and *withdraws*, Heidegger seeks to articulate Being, that which gives the condition of existence to all beings, without reifying this 'giving' as a substance that transcends beings. This premise brings us back to the problem of concealment in disclosure. Our fixation on what appears conceals something, but that 'something' is not a hidden substance but rather Being's withdrawal, or, as Heidegger says, 'concealedness is the very heart of coming into appearance' (T: 36 n2). 'Being as such' names an abundance of meaning that only partly shows itself but can never be exhausted by any metaphysical framework. The reason for this inexhaustibility, suggests Thomson (2018), is that the relation between '[Being] as such' and 'the being of entities' should be understood as one of excess:

> For the later Heidegger, [Being] itself—that is, '[Being] as such' in its difference from the historical succession of metaphysical ways of understanding 'the being of entities'—is what partly lends itself to and yet always also partly exceeds every metaphysical attempt to capture its meaning in a single metaphysical framework. (Thomson, 2018: 180)

Against this backdrop, the question is how we inquire into our world-disclosure, given that what sets the conditions of our disclosure is not readily open to such interrogation.

Gestell blinds us to this essential question, since it conspicuously 'exposes' nature within a one-dimensional scale, depriving it of any inherent meaning or mystery. Thomson thus explains the oblivion of the question of Being under the rule of *Gestell*: 'For, we are in the technological "understanding of the being of entities" whenever we presuppose that to be an entity means to be nothing but an inherently meaningless "resource"'

102 Foucault's Technologies

(Thomson, 2018: 179). Modern technology reveals *and* conceals, like all other metaphysical frameworks with their respective *technē*, but it carries a more fundamental danger, namely, in Heidegger's words: '[T]he challenging [*Gestell*] not only conceals a former way of revealing, or bringing-forth, but it conceals revealing itself and with it' (QT: 27). On account of Heidegger's diagnosis, modern technology is uniquely positioned to conceal 'revealing itself', since it culminates in a kind of ontological one-dimensionality or 'flatness'. Modern technology is, as Heidegger announces, 'the supreme danger', since it can ultimately conceal that it is yet another historical mode of intelligibility that makes entities knowable as entities: 'the destining of revealing is in itself not just any danger, but danger as such. Yet when destining reigns in the mode of [*Gestell*] it is the supreme danger' (QT: 26–27). Heidegger further declares that 'the rule of the [*Gestell*] threatens man with the possibility that it could be denied to him to enter into a more original revealing' (QT: 28). The real danger for Heidegger, then, is that once humanity has been claimed by modern technology, other modes of revealing might fall into eternal oblivion, including the very question of Being itself. When this question is forgotten, Being ceases to be an infinitely intriguing question and is instead understood as if it were a thing or, perhaps better, a totality of discrete and controllable entities.

Heidegger's work on modern technology contains two other important themes—subjectivism and modern metaphysics—which we examine before closing our discussion with Heidegger's ethical response to modern technology in his notion of *Gelassenheit* ('readiness toward things' or 'receptive waiting').

Subjectivism: a prelude to modern metaphysics

We have already noted that modern technology 'charges man' to objectify himself as a mere resource. For Heidegger, the unprecedented objectification of nature propelled by modern technology goes hand in hand with subjectivism—the human subject's elevation of itself as the constitutive centre of all knowledge. In 'The Age of the World Picture', he suggests that modern science places man as the being upon which all that exists is grounded, since 'observation of and teaching about the world change into a doctrine of man, into anthropology' (WP: 133). Here, Heidegger uses the term anthropology to describe a situation where 'man' has placed himself as the ultimate value- and meaning-bestowing source in the universe. 'Anthropology' defines, for Heidegger, 'that philosophical interpretation of man which explains and evaluates whatever is, in its entirety, from the standpoint of man and in relation to man' (WP: 133). Man positions himself in absolute mastery, argues Heidegger, since he 'exalts himself to the posture of lord of the earth' (QT: 27), contending to become 'that particular being who gives the measure and provides the guidelines for everything that is' (WP: 134). Subjectivism thus denotes humanity's self-assertive quest for achieving control over all aspects of our reality on a global scale, and as such it constitutes a key precondition for the ceaseless advance of technological objectification. Thomson (2018: 57) suggests that 'what Heidegger calls "subjectivism" is a conceptual and historical precursor to what he will soon call "enframing" (or Gestell)'. For modern metaphysics, asserts Heidegger with reference to Nietzsche, 'every being is an object for a subject', and yet this 'interpretation of beings in terms of subjectivity is itself metaphysical' (NV3: 216). Subjectivism is thus a constitutive part of Western metaphysical thought, with its central dualism of a self-grounding subject who confronts a world of objects. This subject–object relation is, in turn, central to the essence of modern technology.

On Heidegger's account, objectification and subjectivism developed historically in tandem, since the view of the world as fully knowable and controllable places the subject at the centre of the universe. He writes: 'The more extensively and the more effectively the world stands at man's disposal as conquered, and the more objectively the object appears, all the more subjectively, i.e. the more importantly, does the subjectum rise up' (WP: 133). However, modern technology entails a radicalization of subjectivism, whereby humanity's quest for mastering the external world is 'thrown back upon' the human subject itself, turning it into another resource to be mastered. Subjectivism is a dangerous pathway, cautions Heidegger, because when man becomes 'nothing but the orderer of the standing-reserve', he stands at 'the very brink of a precipitous fall' whereby he himself descends into the world of mere objects (QT: 26–27). In 'the technological age', humans have turned the *Gestell* upon themselves, codifying and scrutinizing their own species as exploitable and modifiable raw materials. By this turn, humans begin to take the same quantifying, exploitative attitude towards themselves as they take towards natural resources as mere *Bestand*. 'Has man not included himself in the standing reserve?', asks Heidegger (QT: 18). This diagnosis resonates in Foucault's analysis of discipline when he insists that the proliferating disciplinary objectification of the human body dovetailed with the birth of humanism, including the human subject, or 'the human of modern humanism' (DP: 140), a being endowed with an interiority such as consciousness, guilt, and determination, amenable to reform.

104 Foucault's Technologies

For modern technology brings humanity to a new stage in the historical transformation of disclosure, in which the *Gestell* is applied back onto the human subject, dissolving it into the undifferentiated stockpile of resources to be endlessly optimized. Subjectivism partakes in the forgetting of Being, argues Heidegger, because our essence as 'world-receivers', our primordial questioning relationship to Being, 'cannot be thought in terms of the subject–object relation. For the latter is precisely the necessary mistaken and ongoing concealment of both the relationship and the possibility of experiencing it' (NV3: 216). The double objectification of the external world and the objectification of the subject itself is for Heidegger bound to the same movement in Western thought—namely, the history of modern metaphysics.

Nietzsche: 'the last great metaphysician'

Modern metaphysics is, as Heidegger sees it, deeply implicated in humanity's oblivion of the question of Being. A common thread in metaphysical thought, he argues, is that the question of Being itself is never asked, since Western thinking at least since Plato and Aristotle has gradually foreclosed the interrelation of disclosure and concealment. Heidegger defines metaphysics as 'the truth of what is as such in its entirety, and not as the doctrine of any particular thinker' (WN: 54). Metaphysics, in other words, is a historical intelligibility, which unifies around a particular understanding of the being of entities but never exhausts Being as such. This is because no framework can ever catch the world's entities and hence be ultimately true of them. In Heidegger's history of philosophy, every major epoch, with their evolving modalities of Western metaphysics, entails a fundamental way in which reality presents itself. While this history may appear broadly comparable to Foucault's analysis of historical epistemes with their modalities of knowledge (Foucault, 1970 [1966]), Heidegger only speaks of *one metaphysics*, which evolves over the course of Western history. Heidegger did not see metaphysics as falling ready-made from the sky; instead, it comprises a set of passed-on concepts, doctrines, and assumptions that come to prevail as our framework of intelligibility. Our 'thrownness' means that we are caught in a metaphysical framework that occludes enquiry into its own modes of representation: 'Being itself remains unthought in metaphysics, not just incidentally, but in accord with metaphysics' own inquiry' (NV3: 211). In brief, for Heidegger, metaphysics is defined by closing itself around a set of pre-given categories that precludes recognition of Being as an event.

Heidegger buttresses his portrayal of modern technology by aligning it with modern metaphysics as described by Nietzsche, since the meaning of technology 'coincides with the term "completed metaphysics"' (Heidegger, 1973: 93). In particular, Nietzsche's detection of the nihilism of modern metaphysics acutely grasps, as Heidegger sees it, the predicament of thought that would dominate the twentieth century. Therefore Heidegger's comments on Nietzsche's diagnosis of European nihilism are interwoven with his portrayal of the technological age. With the advent of nihilism, the higher, 'super-sensory' values that previously gave direction and purpose to human life dissolves, as announced in Nietzsche's proclamation, 'God is dead'. Nietzsche shows that nihilism deprives humanity of ultimate values 'to which man can cling', God being the designator for such 'vitalizing and upbuilding power' (WN: 61). On Heidegger's account, Nietzsche uses the term 'the death of God' not merely to denote a state of 'Godlessness' but to describe the irreversible collapse of the transcendent, or the suprasensory world.

Deprived of such higher values, humanity now pursues the twin goals of 'preservation-enhancement', ceaselessly evaluating and ordering itself as a species in order to preserve, defend, and augment its vital capacities. Anticipating Foucault's (BP) analysis of the utilitarian aspects of biopolitics, Heidegger says: 'The flight from the world into the suprasensory is replaced by historical progress. The otherworldly goal of everlasting bliss is transformed into the earthly happiness of the greatest number' (WN: 64). Even if the belief in the Christian church has weakened, observes Heidegger with Nietzsche, its dominance has transformed rather than ceased: 'In place of the authority of God and Church looms the authority of conscience, or the domination of reason or the God of historical progress' (NV3: 203). To the forefront comes the 'apparent world' of human existence, which is valued according to the requirement of humanity's preservation-enhancement. Nihilism, defined as the collapse of higher values and loss of the transcendent, hence posits as the new ultimate value the actual life's infinite, technological augmentation. As Heidegger has Nietzsche inform his reader with a quote from *Will to Power*: 'Nihilism itself is thus transformed into "the ideal of superabundant life"' (WN: 67).

While Heidegger's rendering of nihilism and its implications appears essentially bleak, Nietzsche insisted that the collapse of higher values is not necessarily a loss, since it clears the space not simply for new values, but for a new way of valuing altogether. However, as Heidegger sees it, nihilism entails the fading of higher values, positions mankind as the unrivalled value-bestowing centre of the world, and eradicates the problem of human finitude

106   Foucault's Technologies

by celebrating life's infinite enhancement as well as history's progressive self-overcoming. We now see how Heidegger invokes Nietzsche in support of a history of the decline of Western thought, which began with the antique philosophers and culminates in the nihilism of modern metaphysics.

It must be noted that Heidegger's reading of Nietzsche is disputed, since Heidegger selectively interpreted elements from Nietzsche to support his own philosophical project. In reconstructing Nietzsche's thought and doctrines, Heidegger drew mainly on Nietzsche's posthumously published notebooks, compiled in *The Will to Power*. Hence Carman (2020: 106) asserts that Heidegger's treatment of Nietzsche 'is hardly convincing as scholarship', and Sluga (2007: 108–109) shows that Heidegger's reading of *The Will to Power* 'is highly selective', entirely ignoring major parts of this work. However, here we largely bracket these questions regarding the accuracy of Heidegger's readings of Nietzsche, since our core interest is the relationship between Foucault and Heidegger. Their contrasting inspirations from Nietzsche will be of key significance to our comparative discussion, which is why we need to look a bit closer at Heidegger's eclectic reconstruction of Nietzsche as 'the last great metaphysician'.

In Heidegger's reading, Nietzsche's metaphysics rests on two fundamental propositions, namely the will to power and the eternal recurrence of the same (NV2: 25). With the notion of 'will to power', Nietzsche assigns an irrefutable value to the perpetual striving of all life for self-preservation and self-enhancement, independently of organic form. Nietzsche writes in *Thus Spoke Zarathustra* that 'the will to power' is 'an unexhausted procreative will of life' (TSZ: 137). In *On the Genealogy of Morality*, he defines the will to power as a cosmological principle that drives all entities that exist, asserting that 'a power-will is acted out in all that happens' (GM: 52). Against transcendent values and Christian moral prescripts, which negate life, Nietzsche's will to power reaffirms forces that are 'beyond good and evil' and simply produce particular effects. Nietzsche's doctrine characterizes the totality of the world as will to power, since he portrays the universe as consisting of aggressive and formative forces that have no other end than self-perpetuation and self-overcoming by surpassing their current stage. Or, in Heidegger's words, 'life itself', which is essentially will to power, is 'surpassing itself towards itself by overpowering sundry stages of power to its zenith' (NV3: 214). It should be noted that since the notion appears sparsely in Nietzsche's published works, figuring mainly in his late aphorisms (WP), it is debatable whether the will to power constitutes the guiding principle of Nietzsche's overall thought.

For Heidegger, however, the will to power is one of the most important concepts in Nietzsche's philosophy (NV3: 193–201). Here, we should note that Heidegger believed that all great thinkers were metaphysicians, understood not as autonomous founders of metaphysical doctrines, but rather as spokespersons for their contemporary culture and its underlying metaphysics. Thus for Heidegger, explains Carman, Nietzsche is a 'sounding board' through whom the technological age speaks: 'Nietzsche thinks the meaning of [Being] not as it prevailed in antiquity, in the Middle Ages, or in early modernity, but as it has emerged in the understanding that holds sway in late modern technological culture' (Carman, 2020: 112). This is why Heidegger does not treat Nietzsche's central doctrines of the will to power and eternal recurrence as verifiable theories, 'but as oblique expressions of the modern "technological" understanding of [Being]' (Carman, 2020: 107). Understood as such expressions, Heidegger can declare that 'the essence of modern technology is identical with the essence of modern metaphysics (WP: 116). The will to power reveals modern technology's expansive indifference, since the will to power, as Heidegger sees it, is concerned not with Being but with emptiness; it 'originates out of a feeling of lack, as a striving after that which is not yet a possession' (WN: 76). This drive for expansion is inseparable from the will to power since, as Heidegger has Nietzsche tell us, 'every mere preservation of life is thus already a decline in life. Power is the command to more power' (NV3: 196). In brief, Heidegger equates the technological age with Nietzsche's portrayal of modern metaphysics, insofar as the will to power pushes humanity onto the path of ruthless objectification and self-overcoming through the endless optimization not just of natural resources but of humanity itself.

Nietzsche's doctrine of the eternal return has several layers of meaning. As an ethical principle, the eternal recurrence serves as an individual measure of life-affirmation, since it hypothetically asks one to reaffirm the events and choices immanent to one's life without reliance upon external justifications. This ethical principle thus asks us to confirm the present world in all its anguish and groundlessness, while precluding any final escape from it. Deleuze (2006: 68) specifies the eternal return as 'an ethical thought' by this condition: 'whatever you will, will it in such a way that you also will its eternal return'. We can perhaps take this to mean, in more prosaic terms, that one must not merely be able to live the historically received conditions of one's life, but one must embrace these conditions, create oneself from them, so that one's life becomes memorable and worthy of repetition.

More broadly, Nietzsche's eternal return elevates the forces of life as the ultimate essence of the world, proclaiming the possibility of a more abundant life whose value does not refer to any transcendent principles. As a critique of entrenched Christian values, Nietzsche's principle of the eternal return is well captured by Rose Pfeffer (1965: 276): 'the timeless eternity of a supernatural God is replaced by the eternity of the ever creating and destroying powers in nature and man'. The eternal return does not simply denote the return of the same, understood as a thing that returns or a past that is repeated. As Deleuze (2006: 48) writes: 'identity in the eternal return does not describe the nature of that which returns'. Deleuze reads Nietzsche as a thinker of becoming, who sees Being as unfolding through forces that create differences or multiplicities. Nietzsche's doctrine is central to his overall philosophy of becoming, as Deleuze sees it, since the eternal return denotes 'the fact of returning for that which differs' (Deleuze, 2006: 48). Interpreting the eternal return as an affirmation of the differences between forces and their ceaseless recreation of diversity, Deleuze can help in dislodging Nietzsche's doctrine from Heidegger, bringing it closer to Foucault's differential thinking on power and the *dispositifs* (as I will argue at the end of this chapter).

Heidegger, however, gives us a different Nietzsche, namely a metaphysical thinker who articulates techno-industrial modernity as an expression of the will to power and the eternal return. Although Nietzsche acutely diagnosed the metaphysics which unfolds through modern technology, Heidegger concludes that he failed in reopening the question of Being. This is because, argues Heidegger, despite Nietzsche's striving to overcome metaphysics, he 'remains in the unbroken line of the metaphysical tradition' (WN: 84). Like other great metaphysicians, argues Heidegger, Nietzsche must necessarily develop his doctrine on the will to power in the form of a 'metaphysical projection', which conceives the essence of entities as such and in their totality. Nietzsche's thought is metaphysical, Heidegger repeatedly declares, because Nietzsche characterizes 'the truth of beings as such and as a whole'. Heidegger writes: '"will to power" says what a being as such is', whereas '"[e]ternal return of the same" says how [Being] is as a whole' (NV3: 212). Put differently, the will to power is acted out in eternally recurring processes that 'impose upon' or stamp becoming with the character of Being (WP: 330). How this twofold projection entails the oblivion of Being is well explained by Taylor Carman (2020: 108): 'Nietzsche fell prey to a forgetting, an oblivion, indeed a "blindness" to the truth of [Being], in contrast to what he supposed was the meaning of [Being], namely will to power and eternal recurrence'. In brief, although Nietzsche breaks with the Platonic and Christian traditions, he nevertheless 'projects' the nature of Being and thus becomes the spokesman of a 'completed' metaphysics.

Heidegger appreciates how Nietzsche's axiom of *what* Being is, and *how* it is, seeks to approximate Being to becoming, insofar as it means the 'permanentizing' of becoming (NV2: 136). For Heidegger, modern technology entails such 'permanentizing' insofar as the standing reserve is what becomes permanent and constantly present. More importantly, the idea that becoming *is* what is permanent brings Nietzsche close to the key question of Being's unfolding. Indeed, Nietzsche himself declared: 'That everything recurs is the closest approximation of a world of becoming to a world of being' (WP: 617). Nevertheless, Heidegger insists that Nietzsche remains tied to metaphysics, since his distinction between 'the what' and 'the how' still presupposes that Being is ultimately conceived from within metaphysical categories and hence reified (Lundberg, 2018: 23–24). Caught up in metaphysical reification, Nietzsche cannot capture the evasive nature of Being, namely as that which *at the same time evokes and escapes* conceptualization. Heidegger thus writes in 'Letter on Humanism': 'From within metaphysics he [Nietzsche] was unable to find any other way out than a reversal of metaphysics' (LH: 95). In sum, despite Nietzsche's attempt to overcome the metaphysical tradition, he himself got trapped in metaphysics by positing permanently ordering principles, i.e. the will to power and eternal recurrence, which define entities as such and in their totality. By taking this route, argues Heidegger, Nietzsche completes the oblivion of the question of Being in its appearance and withdrawal.

Finally, on Heidegger's account, Nietzsche also fails to overcome subjectivism, insofar as his nihilism invokes the idea of a self-assertive will whose purest expression is the *Übermensch* ('Overman'), who posits new values. In Nietzsche's diagnosis of modernity, beings are assigned value according to the will to power as 'the principle of valuation' (NV3: 215), and this means that values must preserve and enhance the value-positing agent. Driven by this will to power, the value-positing agent does not recognize the worth of anything outside itself, hence manifesting a supreme will that essentially projects values *upon* the world, from its own viewpoint. For Heidegger (NV2: 215), Nietzsche's proclamation that the value-setting authority of the *Übermensch* is destined to take priority over Being ties Nietzsche to a metaphysical projection, which again forecloses the question of Being as event. In sum, Nietzsche's quest to fill the void left by nihilism with a supreme human self-affirmation means that we forget what Heidegger sees as our essential openness, namely our role as 'recipients' of Being's continual unfolding.

Heidegger's ethical response: *Gelassenheit*

Recall Heidegger's introductory statements in 'The Question Concerning Technology': 'We shall be questioning concerning technology, and in so doing we should like to prepare a free relationship to it' (QT: 3). His concluding comments in the essay are surprising and rather opaque, lending

110 Foucault's Technologies

themselves to different interpretations. He says, invoking Hölderlin's maxim, that in the greatest danger of technology lies the saving power: 'The closer we come to the danger, the more brightly do the ways into the saving power begin to shine and the more questioning we become' (QT: 35). In a first approximation, Heidegger seems to argue that only the fullest experience of the absolute predicament of our thought will prepare us for a future thinking that recognizes Being as an event.

In an interview with *Der Spiegel* from 1966, published posthumously a decade later, Heidegger declared: 'I am convinced that a change can only be prepared from the same place in the world where the modern technological world originated.' Here, Heidegger appears to posit that we cannot reach a freer relationship to modern technology by simply rejecting it, but rather by transcending it from within, as it were, as we relate to it differently. Such a view corresponds well with Heidegger's general assertion, developed in *Being and Time*, that we are always thrown into a historical context or 'tradition', which we did not choose and cannot master. Nevertheless, it is possible for us to confront Being, especially in terms of our own mortality, experiencing that something is beyond our limits as finite beings, and thereby modify how we relate to our historical condition. Heidegger argues that cultivating a freer relationship to modern technology starts from an acceptance of the prevailing mode of disclosure that we have inherited:

> Freedom is man's opening himself—his submitting himself in attentive awareness—to the summons addressed to him and to the way on which he is already being sent. It is to apprehend and accept the dominion of Being already holding sway, and so to be 'taken into a freeing claim'. (QT: 26)

Hence we must accept the reality of the history of metaphysics and so recognize that we are inevitably thrown into a metaphysical framework that we cannot make fully transparent. This means, in Heidegger's words, that affirming our role as 'receivers' paradoxically loosens technology's grip on us as our fundamental way of encountering the world. Dreyfus (1995: 29) observes that once we recognize 'that we receive our technological understanding of [Being], we have stepped out of the technological understanding of [Being]'. Put differently, our awareness that the disclosure of Being is a historical occurrence attunes us to how reality is produced for us by modern technology, precisely *as* a historical mode of disclosure, which constricts our openness towards what could matter and make demands on us.

Surprisingly, perhaps, Heidegger suggests that such a recognition requires that we 'look straight into' modern technology. He asks: 'Will we correspond

The 'Eye' of Technology **111**

to that insight, through a looking that looks into the essence of technology and becomes aware of Being itself within it?' (T: 49). To recover the question of Being, Heidegger seems to argue, requires another way of looking, but, surprisingly, this way of looking is found in modern technology itself. In other words, once we look into technology's greatest danger—i.e. that we disclose the world and ourselves as meaningless resources—we can recognize that this 'looking' *is* indeed a mode of disclosure that now discloses itself as such. The 'promise' is, then, that we can make a sudden shift and experience the ontological reduction, or 'flattening', of our reality, or, as Heidegger writes, 'encounter [Being] itself in its staying-away means to become aware of the promise' (NV4: 226). Against this backdrop, we can better understand Heidegger's declaration that the danger is 'the saving power', which holds the promise of affording us a freer relation to modern technology.

Because modern metaphysics places the human subject as the meaning and value-bestowing centre of the world, fostering 'a freer relation' entails a 'turning away from oneself', which in turn entails keeping our self-assertive will in suspense. Heidegger says: 'Only when man, in the disclosing coming-to-pass of the insight by which he himself is beheld, renounces human self-will and projects himself toward that insight, away from himself, does he correspond in his essence to the claim of that insight' (T: 47). Here, 'that insight' can be interpreted as the realization that modern technology in its 'danger' carries with it the turn towards *Gelassenheit* when perceived differently. Hence Heidegger argues that preparing ourselves for a shift in our way of seeing requires that we allow ourselves to be released from our deceptive projection of the subject as the centre of all meaning and the associated subject–object dualism.

Under modern technology, we approach the world in the mode of subjectivism which posits the subject as unified and confronted by discrete objects, whereas *Gelassenheit* allows us to relate to the world with our full human nature, i.e. as 'thrown', finite, and non-unified, recognizing that there is no subject of and by itself. For Heidegger, *Gelassenheit* serves as an effective counter-concept to subjectivism, since the passivity of 'receiving' is the antipode to active 'willing'. Passivity releases us from our modern will to dominate, which exerts itself as the will to represent everything in fixed categories in pursuit of a conceptual mastery. Conversely, therefore, *Gelassenheit* attunes us to 'the mystery' of Being's appearance and withdrawal. Heidegger says:

> That which shows itself and at the same time withdraws is the essential trait of what we call the mystery. I call the comportment which enables us to keep open to

112 Foucault's Technologies

> the meaning hidden in technology, openness to the mystery. Releasement toward
> things and openness to the mystery belong together. They grant us the possibility
> of dwelling in the world in a totally different way. (DT: 54)

Gelassenheit keeps us 'open to the mystery', which can be interpreted as a receptivity towards how the abundance of meaning is always concealed in the prevailing system of representation. For Heidegger, this kind of receptivity can be evoked by great works of art, insofar as he sees art as an autonomous domain that dislodges itself from society and prevailing norms. It often defies the subject-centred system of representation with its strict categories, allowing the world to reveal itself, if only in a glimpse, ambiguously and multidimensionally.

Ultimately, however, Heidegger believes that it is impossible for humans to actively induce a shift into a different mode of world-disclosure, since such shifts can only ensue from Being's historical unfolding itself. While we can prepare ourselves for a change by cultivating the attitude of *Gelassenheit*, we cannot overturn the prevailing mode of disclosure. And yet, through 'the courageous work of thinking' (DT: 56) we can change our relationship to disclosure, which nevertheless remains our unchangeable ontological condition. Here, we encounter a fundamental difference between Heidegger and Foucault, which we consider in more detail towards the end of this chapter. Whereas for Foucault the subject's practices of self-conduct can (and do) inflict changes in the prevailing *dispositifs*, Heidegger believes that we can only wrestle with the grip of modern technology by cultivating meditative thinking, or something like an inner contact with revelation.

However, a broad parallel can be established between the two thinkers in their attempt to redirect our attention from objects to that largely unnoticed light, 'the eye of technology', through which nature and humans appear. The next section explores the argument that Heidegger's and Foucault's thinking intersects around particular shared themes. We first examine their mutual focus on modernity's objectifying vision before discussing, in the last section, how Heidegger and Foucault ultimately diverge.

A shared obsession with visibility

We have already encountered notable parallels between Heidegger's and Foucault's works on the theme of modern technology. The most evident parallel perhaps runs between Heidegger's description of modern technology as the manipulative intrusion upon all things—including human beings—and Foucault's analysis of biopolitics as a set of far-reaching interventions into the population's productivity and vitality. A number of scholars have highlighted precisely this thematic intersection between the later Heidegger and Foucault's analyses of biopolitics in the 1970s (Dreyfus, 1996; Rayner, 2001; Sinnerbrink, 2005). Continuing the comparison, Foucault's detailed analysis of discipline as a major project for optimizing and normalizing the human body can be understood against the backdrop of Heidegger's diagnosis of humanity's self-objectification in the modern age. At the general level, Heidegger and Foucault share the premise that technology produces the world as particular objects, as implied in Heidegger's notion of ordering disclosure and in Foucault's attention to the visibilities produced by *dispositifs*. We can also identify similarities between Heidegger's notion of *Gestell* and Foucault's *dispositif* insofar as both terms denote modes of ordering that establish particular relations between humans and the world, and between humans themselves. First, we examine the theme of visibility in Heidegger and Foucault, and next we compare the notions of *Gestell* and *dispositif*. I take these themes to have great potential for digging deeper into Foucault's thoughts on technology in light of—and in comparison with—insights from Heidegger's philosophy.

Heidegger and Foucault shared a profuse interest in visibility, and they both identified in modernity something like a visual obsession. We have already seen that Heidegger describes modern technology in terms of the subject-centred attitude in which things become visible as calculable and manipulable objects. This is particularly the case in Heidegger's 'The Age of the World Picture' (WP), 'The Question Concerning Technology' (QT), and 'The Word of Nietzsche: "God is Dead"' (WN), which all describe modernity in what David Levin (1993: 194) has termed 'vision-saturated language'. It is not so much that Heidegger privileged vision in his overall philosophy, as that he launched critical inquiries into the historical character of our vision as it developed in Western culture since antiquity. One finds in Heidegger's work, argues Levin, 'a deeply critical examination of vision-based thinking and vision-centred discourse, situating this critique in relation to the vision distinctive of modernity and exposing the historical formation of this vision' (Levin, 1993: 194). Similarly connecting Heidegger and Foucault on the theme of visibility, Ijsseling (1986) asserts that they both viewed modernity as a time of radical objectification. Ijsseling suggests that the text by Heidegger that had the greatest impact on Foucault is 'The Age of the World Picture', from which we have quoted repeatedly in earlier sections:

> In that essay Heidegger describes the modern age as a period in which the world is re-presented. The modern age is the time of representation. Reality becomes an object; this goes hand in hand with the subjectifying and objectifying of man.

114 Foucault's Technologies

> Important in this respect is also Heidegger's claim that the modern sciences have taken on all the characteristics of institutions. (Ijsseling, 1986: 416)

Let us take our lead from these suggestions regarding visibility as a unifying theme in Heidegger and Foucault. We noted earlier that Heidegger described modern technology as marked by the pursuit of 'presence', which rests on the idea that human beings can fully represent all that exists by means of the adequate instruments. Using the term 'world picture', Heidegger makes clear that, in the modern age, to represent is not simply to copy or paint something—it is a matter of bringing everything to stand forth so that it becomes measurable and manipulable:

> But 'world picture' means more than this [a copy]. We mean by it the world itself, the world as such, what is, in its entirety, just as it is normative and binding for us. 'Picture' here does not mean some imitation, but rather what sounds forth in the colloquial expression, 'We get the picture' [literally, we are in the picture concerning something]. This means the matter stands before us exactly as it stands with it for us. (WP: 129)

Here, Heidegger and Foucault intersect in their parallel detection of a pervasive pursuit of limitless objectification characteristic of modernity. In particular, Heidegger's 'cognitivist picture' and Foucault's 'objectifying gaze' share certain similarities. These terms both define the modern quest for disclosing all entities, including inherent human capabilities, and the associated obsession with rendering nature and human beings fully visible. In Foucault's work, the objectifying gaze is particularly central in his studies of techniques of discipline, medical examination, and the 'pastoral' exposure of consciousness in the West, all of which he retrospectively termed 'the objectification of the subject' (SP: 777). *Discipline and Punish* has often been presented as Foucault's most Nietzschean work (e.g. Garland, 2014), but an alternative reading can also situate the book in continuity with Heidegger's diagnosis of modernity as pervaded by objectification. Indeed, it is possible to read Foucault's detailed descriptions of the numerous ways in which the disciplinary gaze probes into human bodies in parallel with Heidegger's claim that the modern subject turns 'ordering disclosure' back upon itself.

Extending the comparison, Foucault concluded in his genealogy of discipline that the normalizing techniques that he discovered in prisons, barracks, hospitals, schools, and factories had as their conditions of possibility a disciplinary *dispositif* (described in Chapter 1). Foucault said that discipline

The 'Eye' of Technology **115**

constitutes a general technology of power that invests different institutions, illuminating human bodies in a particular way, and he explained that his method entailed 'going behind the institution and trying to discover in a wider and more overall perspective what we can broadly call a technology of power' (STP: 117). By comparison, for Heidegger, the objects that are present to us appear as they do (e.g. as tools) in virtue of a more fundamental background mode of intelligibility, which constitutes the metaphysical world view of a particular epoch.

Clearly, for Foucault, the interconnection of power and knowledge is what makes objects appear in a particular 'light', for example as objects of normalization. While Foucault never invoked the notion of the ontological difference, it is as if, by carefully recovering the disciplinary project, he shows the light by the grace of which bodies and actions appear as objects of normalization. Pushing the integrative comparison, one might view 'the examining gaze' of discipline as a mode of disclosure. Reminiscent of Heidegger's notion of *Gestell*, a disclosure which places things in an ordering grip, Foucault says that disciplinary power holds subjects 'in a mechanism of objectification', and that it 'manifests its potency, essentially, by arranging objects' (DP: 187). By organizing institutional spaces and the location of bodies within these spaces, discipline produces a form of 'compulsory visibility' with innumerable points of application.

The Heideggerian echoes in *Discipline and Punish*

In *Discipline and Punish*, Foucault describes the *dispositif* of disciplinary normalization, which from the eighteenth century has come to define what Jacques Bidet (2016: 204) calls a 'general trait' of modern society. The book abundantly describes how human bodies are dissected, compared, and classified, hence becoming objectified by the disciplinary gaze. Foucault reaches rhetorical heights when portraying the disciplinary gaze with expressions like 'the normalizing gaze', 'permanent visibility', 'a compulsory visibility', 'a giant unblinking eye', and 'a perfect eye that nothing would escape'. If the propagators of discipline were obsessed with visualization, Foucault's writing displays to the fullest this relentless pursuit of visibility. Generally, Foucault might follow Heidegger, as Gary Shapiro (2003) suggests, in granting particular importance to the way in which vision makes objects present to us. Yet, more importantly, whereas Heidegger understands the overall history of Western thought as culminating in the modern pursuit of presence, Foucault's work evades notions like essence, culmination, or metaphysical epochs. Compared

116 Foucault's Technologies

to Heidegger, Foucault offers much more fine-grained genealogies of the modern quest for 'ordering disclosure', in particular human bodies and their dispositions and capacities.

Discipline and Punish unfolds through a series of contrasts in terms of visibility. There is the contrast between the sovereign's extraordinary visibility and the invisibility of disciplinary techniques, between the loud spectacle of public torture and the silent continuity of disciplinary correction, between the law that punishes acts and the 'micro-penality' that probes into multiple abnormalities, and between the sovereign power that excludes and the psy-expert gazes that normalize in order to integrate. Foucault says that discipline made use of its own type of ceremony: 'It was not the triumph, but the review, the "parade", an ostentatious form of the examination. In it the "subjects" were presented as "objects" to the observation of a power that was manifested only by its gaze' (DP: 188). Whereas judicial punishment finds the answer to the question of how to punish in legal texts, discipline undertakes detailed examinations of the offenders, uncovering abnormalities in order to apply 'the penalty of the norm'. Disciplinary power, writes Foucault, 'is opposed, therefore, term by term, to a judicial penality whose essential function is to refer, not to a set of observable phenomena, but to a corpus of laws and texts that must be remembered' (DP: 183). It is noteworthy that, for Foucault, discipline is about uncovering what is hidden in the depth of human bodies through detailed and permanent scrutiny, a project that, in Heidegger's terms, turns 'ordering disclosure' back upon the human subject itself. Furthermore, Foucault suggests that disciplinary normalization tends to become a mode of self-observation, whereby individuals turn others and themselves into disciplinary projects, which resonates with Heidegger's claim that the human subject had dissolved into the stockpile of meaningless resources, becoming part of the standing reserve.

Foucault makes two important contrasts when describing the emergence of discipline (DP: 224–225). First, he contrasts the growing web of minuscule disciplinary techniques with the law and juridical models of power. Whereas theories of power have focused on constitutions, great rulers, or the institutions of the state, they seldom discuss the actual exercise of power. Therefore it is to the specific mechanisms and techniques of power that Foucault wishes to turn: 'What generalizes the power to punish, then, is not the universal consciousness of the law in each juridical subject; it is the regular extension, the infinitely minute web of panoptic techniques' (DP: 224). In contrast to the exceptional spectacle of sovereign power, disciplinary power operates through a permanent micro-visibility. Foucault emphasizes the examination as one of those 'invisible techniques' characteristic of discipline, insofar as it 'imposes on those whom it subjects a principle of compulsory visibility. In discipline, it is the subjects who have to be seen' (DP: 187).

Second, Foucault sets disciplinary techniques in opposition to major technical inventions like industrial mining, the chemical industry, or national accountancy. He notes that historians have focused on grand mechanical innovations, while neglecting the minor techniques of panoptical discipline: 'compared with the blast furnaces or the steam engine, panopticism has received little attention' (DP: 224). This is a serious omission, says Foucault in an interview, since all the small disciplinary techniques constitute 'a veritable technological take-off in the productivity of power' (Foucault, 1980a: 119). From the perspective of a conventional history of technology, these techniques may seem of scant importance, and yet 'it would be unjust to compare the disciplinary techniques with such inventions as the steam engine or Amici's microscope. They are much less, and yet, in a way, they are much more' (DP: 225). While seemingly trivial and mundane, disciplinary micro-techniques are 'much more important' than the steam engine, argues Foucault, since they comprise a proliferating web that harnesses individuals as vehicles of disciplinary power.

For Heidegger, we recall, the modern age finds its most emblematic expression in major technical inventions such as the atomic bomb, the hydroelectrical dam, and the space telescope. At times, it is as if Foucault wants to invert the importance of minor, disciplinary techniques with those monumental innovations that so concerned Heidegger. Against the prominent acclaim of the large space telescope as the signpost of a new era of physical science, Foucault discovers a whole set of inconspicuous but no less important visualization techniques that sparked the new human sciences:

> Side by side with the major technology of the telescope, the lens and the light beam, which were an integral part of the new physics and cosmology, there were the minor techniques of multiple and intersecting observations, of eyes that must see without being seen; using techniques of subjection and methods of exploitation, an obscure art of light and the visible was secretly preparing a new knowledge of man. (DP: 171)

Foucault's mention of 'the major technology of the telescope' is striking, since it reads like an implicit reference that contrasts his approach with Heidegger's writing on modern technology. In the face of celebrated optical innovations, Foucault presents an insurrection of minor, largely overlooked visual techniques rooted in the spread of disciplinary power. Indeed, Foucault defines

118 Foucault's Technologies

the optical workings of disciplinary techniques as 'microscopic' (as opposed to 'telescopic'): 'The optical machinery of discipline is microscopic. It divides up space and movement, into smaller and smaller fragments, subjecting each to intense and extensive scrutiny' (DP: 174). Foucault makes other noteworthy contrasts between major technologies of visualization and minor, less salient techniques, for example when he describes the military camp as a means of visualization in opposition to 'the great science of optics': 'The camp was to the rather shameful art of surveillance what the dark room was to the great science of optics' (DP: 172). Clearly, it is not the major sources of light that Foucault wants to pay attention to.

Disciplinary technology produces an inversion of visibility, Foucault declares, insofar as the 'visibility of the monarch is turned into the unavoidable visibility of the subjects' (DP: 189). This inversion of visibility happened gradually through the proliferation of disciplinary techniques that invested the objectifying power of 'infinite examination' in the lowest regions of society (as described in Chapter 1). Instead of the modern age of representation, which Heidegger had announced in 'The Age of the World Picture', Foucault concludes: 'We are entering the age of the infinite examination and of compulsory objectification' (DP: 189). Hence, whereas for Heidegger, the philosopher, major technical innovations can emblematically express a metaphysical epoch, Foucault, the genealogist, must recover the continual transformations in minor techniques and practices that disobey the divisions between major historical epochs. Foucault's analysis of disciplinary techniques in their painstaking detail is far apart from Heidegger's sweeping philosophical critique.

Hence, while the theme of the objectification of the human being connects Heidegger and Foucault, they approach it differently. In his typical overarching tenor, Heidegger declares: 'Insofar as human representation readily sets up what presences as the orderable in the calculation of ordering, *the human being remains in its essence, whether consciously or not, set up as something to be ordered by ordering*' (Heidegger, quoted in Belu and Feenberg, 2010: 3, italics in original). By contrast, Foucault breaks down disciplinary technology into five modes of operation which all constitute distinct ways of visualizing the groups or individuals who are targeted for normalization (DP: 182–184). First, it situates individuals within a larger whole, or a space of comparison, which enables differentiation of actions in relation to a norm. In terms of visualization, the placement of individuals in a field of comparison makes gaps visible, and in turn these gaps visually manifest the distance between individual properties and the norm to be achieved. Accordingly, this differential partitioning of space renders visible an individual's failure

The 'Eye' of Technology 119

to reach the required standards, or the norm, which calls for the use of disciplinary techniques to reduce such gaps.

Second, the norm is established as either a minimum threshold, an average to be matched, or an optimum towards which individuals must strive. For this reason, disciplinary sanctions should not be repressive but function as 'essentially corrective', since they must bring the individual closer to the norm. Hence, discipline favours the use of exercises as a means to punish, or, in Foucault's words, preference is given to 'punishments that are exercise-intensified, multiplied forms of training, several times repeated' (DP: 179).

Third, normalization not only establishes hierarchical comparisons in quantitative terms, but also assigns value to those individual abilities and dispositions that become visible. Foucault emphasizes that this valuation 'is not one of acts, but of individuals themselves, of their nature, their potentialities, their level or their value. By assessing acts with precision, discipline judges individuals "in truth"; the penalty that it implements is integrated into the cycle of knowledge of individuals' (DP: 181). These normalizing assessments not only establish the fact of individual actions but the truth of each individual. Hereby an individual 'case' is established in which objective knowledge and individual subjectivity intersect.

Fourth, the norm specifies 'the constraint of conformity' that abnormal individuals must be subjected to as well as the corrections needed to secure their normalization. The core technique of visualization, notes Foucault, is 'the generalized examination', which is highly ritualized in all disciplinary institutions: 'It establishes over individuals a visibility through which one differentiates them and judges them' (DP: 184). As a means of selecting adequate disciplinary interventions, the examination combines 'the ceremony of power and the form of experiment, the deployment of force and the establishment of truth' (DP: 184).

Fifth, and finally, the norm establishes the exterior limit against which all other measurements of differences will be settled, 'the external frontier of the abnormal', and the group that falls outside the norm. This exterior limit allows a clear visualization of one group, which displays certain discrepancies from the norm, and another group, which falls entirely outside the norm. Foucault concludes that 'the perpetual penality that traverses all points and supervises every instant in the disciplinary institutions compares, differentiates, hierarchizes, homogenizes, and excludes. In short, it normalizes' (DP: 183). The penalty of the norm spreads across the social body, expanding into a range of institutions and practices. Yet, as noted in Chapter 1, this expansion is not a matter of simple 'diffusion' but of 'integration', since the disciplinary

120 Foucault's Technologies

diagram would intensify (rather than homogenise) the specific practices in the school, the factory, the barracks, the social services, and the hospital.

To conclude: at first glance, Foucault's disciplinary *dispositif* and Heidegger's *Gestell* display broad similarities. Whereas the disciplinary norm makes visible and sanctionable deviances from the norm, in a similar way the *Gestell* discloses everything by 'normalizing' and converting them from things in and of themselves into resources. Yet, on closer inspection, Foucault's acute attention to historical details and institutional context in his analysis of discipline places his genealogy at quite a distance from Heidegger's philosophy with its epochal approach to history. Whereas Heidegger's assertion of the 'destiny of Western thought' would appear to reaffirm his own possible observations, Foucault's immersion in the empirical world, down to minor techniques of normalization, steers him away from engaging in metaphysical thinking. And while Heidegger extrapolates his analysis of technology to 'the modern age' as such, presenting technical inventions as manifestations of the essence of modern technology, Foucault insists on studying techniques in their specificity. This is because, for Foucault, the genealogist cannot decipher the meaning and effect of a technique from a pre-established epochal category; instead, techniques are always ambiguous, as they produce their effects in mobile force relations. Chapter 4 will show that, for Foucault, techniques can both act as vehicles of domination *and* be used in the service of self-formation.

A shared 'capillary' view of power?

Some scholars believe that Heidegger and Foucault stand on common ground, since they both inquire into the historical conditions of the visualization of objects and work with a similar view of power. Here we could follow Dreyfus' (1996) influential reading, which posits that Heidegger and Foucault both view power as immanent, insofar as they rely on a similar 'capillary' understanding of power as radiating through the entire field of social relations. Parallel to *Gestell*, the disciplinary *dispositif* is a disposition for normalization, which is intrinsic to the network of institutional and social 'relays' through which power operates. In this immanentist view of power, the norm operates intrinsically in knowledge formation and in social practices, investing micro-relations and institutions. Dreyfus compares Heidegger's 'social clearing' with Foucault's notion of 'micro-power', suggesting that they both condition and restrict human beings in their historical existence: 'For Foucault, power, like Heidegger's [Being], is no fixed entity or institution, but

The 'Eye' of Technology   **121**

is incarnated in historical social practices' (Dreyfus, 1996: 3). The link that Dreyfus forges between Heidegger and Foucault rests on the premise that they both see social relations in modernity as imbued with a distinct objectifying and normalizing vision. Hence Dreyfus (1996: 14) argues that 'just as, for Heidegger, total mobilization cannot be understood by positing subjects and objects, so normalization bypasses the state and works directly through new sorts of invisible, precise, continuous practices of control that Foucault calls micro-practices'.

It should be noted that Dreyfus achieves his integration of Heidegger and Foucault by insisting on power as the intersection between them, a term that Heidegger rarely used but which Dreyfus inserts into the disclosure of Being. On such a reading, it would matter little whether we are in phenomenological or genealogical territory, insofar as both Heidegger and Foucault see historical vision as inherently invested with power. However, against Dreyfus' resolute integration, one could object that Heidegger thinks of power principally in terms of Nietzsche's doctrine of will to power. As noted earlier, this doctrine characterizes modern metaphysics and the *Gestell*, but not the disclosure of Being as such, at all times. By comparison, Foucault does assume that power is always immanent to discourse and social practices, and, as we noted in Chapter 1, power propels the *dispositif* in its emergence and proliferation.

Another difference between Heidegger and Foucault is the critical tenor of their respective analyses. As we have seen, Heidegger's account of 'the ordering disclosure' of modern technology is largely voiced in an explicitly critical register: this mode of disclosure drives humanity to endlessly categorize, calculate, and fixate, hence 'challenging forth' things for the purpose of control, exploitation, and circulation. Levin (1993: 212) captures this critical emphasis in Heidegger's writing by noting that vision 'assumed a certain uncontested hegemony over our culture and its philosophical discourse, establishing, in keeping with the instrumental rationality of our culture and the technological character of our society, an ocularcentric metaphysics of presence'. Shapiro similarly observes that Heidegger saw the prominence of the visual as integral to the culmination of modern metaphysics and its quest for making everything present. According to Shapiro, Heidegger 'understood the Western philosophical project as the pursuit of presence, a pursuit that typically clothed itself in the language of vision, supposing that vision makes things present to us in a way that no other sense does' (Shapiro, 2003: 293).

Levin and Shapiro capture well, I believe, the critical orientation of Heidegger's writing on modernity and modern technology. While our comparisons between Foucault's analysis of disciplinary visualization and Heidegger's

122   Foucault's Technologies

thesis on modern objectification could be said to extend Levin's and Shapiro's conclusions, the question is whether Foucault offers an analysis of discipline that concurs with Heidegger's critical tenor. Does Foucault assign to disciplinary technology an inherently 'evil eye', which confirms the dehumanizing claims that surface in Heidegger's portrayal of modern technology? Martin Jay believes that Foucault takes a critical position on the modern gaze in *Discipline and Punish*, in particular in his description of Bentham's panopticon, since vision is complicit in practices of domination: '(T)he occularism of those who praised the "nobility of sight" was not so much rejected as reversed in value: Vision was still the privileged sense, but what that privilege produced in the modern world was damned as almost entirely pernicious' (Jay, 1993: 384).

However, the discovery of such an unambiguous critique of disciplinary vision in Foucault's work is probably untenable, if we accept that Foucault practised analytical rather than normative critique (see Chapter 5). Shapiro takes the latter position, arguing that Foucault did not advance a critique of vision as generally dangerous. Hence Foucault, writes Shapiro (2003: 294), 'is an archaeologist of the visual, alert to the differential character of various visual regimes. And within the space of a certain epoch or culture, he is alert to disparate and possibly conflicting visual practices.' Even if we accept that some of the denunciatory tenor of Heidegger's overarching critique of modern technology resonates in *Discipline and Punish*, Foucault subsequently abandoned the rather bleak portrayal of disciplinarity conveyed by his 1975 book. In 1978, Foucault would present several technologies operating in dynamic interaction, a significant analytical move that circles us back to the *dispositif*. This move, I will now argue, ultimately brings Foucault's thinking to a greater distance from Heidegger.

Does *Gestell* 'correspond perfectly' to *dispositif*?

'Behind' modern innovations and the vast proliferation of all sorts of technical devices, another level preconditions their historical advancement. Heidegger and Foucault would agree that careful scholarly work is required to articulate this level. Their respective concepts of *Gestell* and *dispositif*, while reflecting a parallel in their thinking, take on their own distinct shapes as they articulate this level of reality. Foucault occasionally describes his genealogical tracing of the conditions of possibility of modern institutions and technologies as our 'historical ontology', a project that has been compared to Heidegger's history of how the disclosure of Being changes from one epoch to another (Dreyfus, 1996; Elden, 2001). Instead of making general claims regarding Heidegger and Foucault as like-minded writers of our 'historical ontology' (Foucault, 1984a: 49), we here zoom in on the concepts of *Gestell* and *dispositif*. This conceptual pair, I submit, offers a helpful vantage point for deepening our comparative discussion of Heidegger and Foucault on modern technology.

Scholars like Giorgio Agamben (2009, 2011) and Stuart Elden (2001) have suggested that Heidegger's and Foucault's thinking intersects clearly in their respective concepts of *Gestell* and *dispositif*. They argue that these concepts carry parallel significance, since they both designate how modern subjects came to objectify the natural world as well as themselves. Elden (2001: 79) argues that *Gestell* and *dispositif* are closely related. He instructively emphasizes that when Heidegger used *Gestell*, the term did not simply mean to 'frame something', since *Gestell* more accurately defines the presentation or production of things through the creation of a setting within which things will appear in a particular way. Similarly, Foucault's concept of *dispositif* denotes a configuration of discourse and practices, constituted in specific moments of history, which brings objects to emerge under a particular prescriptive light. François Fédier also seeks to align the two terms, suggesting *dispositif* as a translation for the *Gestell*, while giving *Gestell* a more all-encompassing meaning as 'dispositif unitaire de la consommation' (the overall consumption *dispositif*), which he further defines as 'all the prior measures by means of which everything is made available in advance in the framework of a putting in order' (Cassin et al., 2014: 188).

Agamben asserts that *Gestell* and *dispositif* are equivalent terms from an etymological point of view, since the notion of *Gestell* corresponds to the Latin terms *dispositio* (disposition) or *disponere* (arrange). For Agamben, both terms define how humans are brought to expose the world in the mode of ordering:

> When Heidegger, in *Die Technik* und die Kehre (The Question Concerning Technology), writes that *Ge-stell* means in ordinary usage an apparatus (*Gerät*), but that he intends by this term 'the gathering together of the (in)stallation [*Stellen*] that (in)stalls man, this is to say, challenges him to expose the real in the mode of ordering [*Bestellen*],' the proximity of this term to the theological *dispositio*, as well as to Foucault's apparatuses, is evident. (Agamben, 2009: 12)

However, Agamben extends the notion of *dispositif* to a much larger group of phenomena than Foucault himself did, and he assigns to it an almost universal scope by implying that human beings have been guided by *dispositifs*

124   Foucault's Technologies

ever since ancient times: 'I shall call a dispositive literally anything that has in some way the capacity to capture, orient, determine, intercept, model, control, or secure the gestures, behaviours, opinions, or discourses of living beings' (Agamben, 2009: 17). It quickly becomes clear that Agamben's conceptual intervention is tied to his own distinctive work on biopolitics and economy. Whereas Foucault uses the term *dispositif* as a tool in his genealogies of specific power/knowledge configurations, Agamben takes the notion to designate the primordial capture of human life by a very broad range of instruments, including language itself:

> Not only, therefore, prisons, madhouses, the panopticon, schools, confession, factories, disciplines, juridical measures, and so forth (whose connection with power is in a certain sense evident), but also the pen, writing, literature, philosophy, agriculture, cigarettes, navigation, computers, cellular telephones and—why not—language itself, which is perhaps the most ancient of apparatuses. (Agamben, 2009: 17)

Conceiving of the *dispositif* as more ubiquitous and pervasive than in Foucault's own definition, Agamben arguably brings the term close to Heidegger's *Gestell*. Reminiscent of Heidegger, Agamben broadens his definition of *dispositifs* to include the whole set of conceptual and technical devices which orders all that exists. This broadening can be referred to what Colin Koopman calls Agamben's 'style of looking', which, contends Koopman, 'has much to do with Agamben's intellectual roots in phenomenology' (Koopman, 2015: 574). Notably, then, in *Being and Time*, Heidegger argues that phenomena like tools can only be understood as part of a whole set-up of 'equipment' (Ger: *das Zeug*), since tools always exist in a network composed of other tools and institutions. In our everyday life, things tend to show up instrumentally, since 'useful things always are in terms of their belonging to other useful things: writing utensils, pen, ink, paper, desk blotter, table, lamp, furniture, windows, doors, room' (B&T: 68). This list reflects Heidegger's phenomenological emphasis on our immersive being in the world, in which we reveal things by using them and naming them, and simultaneously achieve a sense of who we are.

In his rendering of the *dispositif*, Agamben reiterates his basic division between living beings and *dispositifs*, whereby the latter ceaselessly capture the former. *Dispositifs*, in other words, turn living human beings into subjects. Or, more precisely, it is through the *dispositif* that the human being is at once transformed into a subject *and* an object of power relations (Esposito, 2012). We have, writes Agamben (2009: 19), 'two great classes: living beings (or substances) and dispositives, and between these two, as a third class, subjects. I call a subject that, which results from the relation and, so to speak, from the relentless fight between living beings and dispositives.' Agamben's interpretation contrasts starkly with Foucault in its ontological and universal character. In fact, Agamben goes as far as to advance the surprising claim that Foucault's *dispositif* serves as a substitute concept for universals: 'Apparatuses are, in point of fact, what takes the place of the universals in the Foucauldian strategy' (Agamben, 2009: 7). This claim is unexpected especially given that Foucault opened his *Birth of Biopolitics* with an unmistakeable critique of the traditions that deduce concrete phenomena from universals: 'instead of starting with universals as an obligatory grid of intelligibility for certain concrete practices, I would like to start with these concrete practices' (BP: 3). We can finally illuminate Agamben's idiosyncratic rendering of the concept by invoking Deleuze (1992), who sees Foucault's *dispositif* as an explicit 'repudiation of universals'. Indeed, Deleuze himself escapes the view of the *dispositif* as a stable entity, instead seeing it as a 'multiplicity' in perpetual movement (this is further discussed in Chapter 5). Unlike Agamben, Foucault evades ontological and universal premises, instead constructing his *dispositifs* 'from the ground up' by writing with painstaking attention to the particularities of the historical processes from which they emerge.

Ultimately, Agamben never actually achieves the promised 'equivalence' or integration of Heidegger's and Foucault's thinking around *Gestell/dispositif*, since he quickly leaves this task in pursuit of his own philosophical and philological project. In his later work, Agamben (2011) moves on to deploy the *dispositif* in a far-ranging genealogy of the doctrine of *oikonomia* that takes him back to the early church fathers and Greek antiquity. From this vantage point, Agamben shifts his comparative strategy by aligning *Gestell* and *dispositif* genealogically with the ancient Greek word 'oikonomia':

> The term *Ge-stell* corresponds perfectly (not only in its form: the German stellen is equivalent to ponere, that is, to place) to the Latin term dispositio, which translates the Greek *oikonomia*. The Ge-stell is the apparatus of the absolute and integral government of the world. (Agamben, 2011: 252)

In this context, we will leave aside this difficult pursuit (however, see Bussolini, 2010). Hence, while both Agamben and Elden note overall parallels between Heidegger's *Gestell* and Foucault's *dispositif*, they sidestep the challenge of undertaking a detailed comparison and integration of the two concepts. In fact, to the best of my knowledge, no detailed comparison of the two notions has yet been offered, which is the task we turn to now.

Foregrounding relationality and visibility

Let us recall Deleuze's (1992: 160) declaration that *dispositifs* are 'machines that make one see and speak'. The idea that the *dispositif* makes certain observations and evaluations more likely than others was anticipated in Heidegger's assertion that *Gestell* organizes our disclosure of the world, and in particular that things become meaningful to us in their relations to a totality of other things. In *Being and Time*, Heidegger had explained that tools form an overall setting in which objects appear in accordance with their meaningfulness and utility, since 'useful things always are *in terms of* their belonging to other useful things' (B&T: 68, italics in original). When a thing becomes useful to us, and is thus rendered meaningful principally in terms of its utility, it is always experienced as such within a totality of other useful things. Heidegger writes: 'Strictly speaking, there "is" no such thing as a useful thing. There always belongs to the being of a useful thing a totality of useful things in which this useful thing can be what it is' (B&T: 68). This phenomenological inquiry of everyday human experience means that the 'being' of a thing, that is, *how* and *as-what* the thing becomes meaningful, happens within an overall setting.

There are, of course, significant disjunctions between *Being and Time* and Heidegger's later work, of which the most central is that *Being and Time* sought to establish fundamental ontology in an ahistorical sense, which Heidegger later sought to correct. Nevertheless, the premise of things' interrelatedness in *Being and Time* anticipates Heidegger's later writings on modern technology, which assert that *Gestell*, 'that setting-upon which sets upon man' (QT: 20), disposes us to render our world meaningful precisely as a reserve of 'meaningless' objects awaiting exploitation.

The *Gestell* and the *dispositif* order elements such that they come to interrelate and appear in particular ways. For Heidegger, we noted, *Gestell* entails that relatedness—our ways of relating and the ways that things interrelate—unfold according to ordering disclosure, which charges us to perceive all entities as exploitable resources. This means that *modern technology is integral to modern relatedness as such*, and hence our reality is produced for us in relations that are intrinsically objectifying and calculative. Emphasizing this premise of relationality, Ziarek (1998: 183) explains that 'technology means here that forces occur in a manner that allows them to bear upon one another technologically, with a view to producing and conforming to a technology, to an array of the various, and interrelated, disciplines of calculability, efficiency, commodification, etc.' Notable in Ziarek's account is the resonance with Foucault's disciplinary *dispositif*, which institutes normalization as intrinsic to relations that span society in a 'capillary' manner. Indeed, as described in Chapter 1, the norm inscribes itself in institutions by means of adaptable techniques like the examination, hierarchical observation, and the normalizing sanction. Pertinent here is Ziarek's claim that, for both Heidegger and Foucault, calculation and normalization do not influence power relations externally, 'from the outside': 'In both accounts, technology is not something extraneous to force but works through and within forces, shaping and "normalising" them into technologies of power' (Ziarek, 1998: 180).

While Ziarek is right in arguing that Heidegger and Foucault both view power as integral to relations, he might go too far when he asserts that power determines 'the entire field of relations'. Ziarek (1998: 173–174) writes: 'They both rely on a similar, "capillary", as Foucault calls it, understanding of power as coursing through and determining the entire field of relations not only on macro but also on microscopic and local levels.' Foucault, however, develops an understanding of power as fluctuating, open-ended, and reversible, which would disallow any uniform notion of 'deterministic' power. Importantly, Foucault did not begin his analysis from the premise that the *dispositif* determines 'the entire field of relations' but from the question of how the *dispositif* organizes relations. In support of Foucault, Sverre Raffnsøe argues, to start from the assertion of technology's essential mode of functioning instead of analysing how a *dispositif* develops in historical context amounts to 'empirical laziness' (Raffnsøe, 2002: 81). Heidegger would probably have responded that avoiding a careful reading of the tradition of Western philosophy amounts to philosophical laziness.

It is true that *Gestell* and *dispositif* are both relational and 'insubstantial'— they are not substances, since they are defined by the effects they produce in our relations rather than what they are. With this mind, however, relationality or relatedness, I would insist, means something different in the two notions. Unlike the *Gestell*, the *dispositif* does not cast the world in a kind of general luminosity by way of its prevailing mode of disclosure. The *dispositif* emphasizes relationality as its fundamental premise, which means that it creates visibilities from within the relations established between its elements. As we concluded in Chapter 1, Foucault's approach brings into focus the immanent relations of each *dispositif* as well as the dynamic interplay through which *dispositifs* evolve in relation to each other. Foucault's fundamental premise of relationality becomes clearer, for example, in his analysis of how the object of grain transforms over time. As we saw in Chapter 1, Foucault (STP: 35–37) demonstrates that scarcity of grain becomes something entirely different when targeted by different *dispositifs*, hence becoming part of a specific set of relations (Villadsen, 2021a: 477–479). In a nutshell,

128   Foucault's Technologies

the example of grain scarcity shows that, whereas the *Gestell* casts things in a kind of general luminosity, the *dispositif* renders things visible through a set of specific relations that emerge and develop in particular historical contexts.

If disciplinarity in *Discipline and Punish* could be understood as a kind of ubiquitous modern visibility, comparable with Heidegger's *Gestell*, Foucault's subsequent work reveals different *dispositifs* in mutual interplay. We recall that several *dispositifs* surface in Foucault's analysis rather than one pervasive *Gestell*, particularly evident in the 1977–1978 lecture series, *Security, Territory, Population*. In these lectures, we find a range of different *dispositifs*, including not only the *dispositifs* of law, discipline, and security, but also the diplomatic-military *dispositif*, the police *dispositif*, the *dispositif* of European equilibrium, and more (STP: 524). In brief, whereas the *Gestell* defines *the* ubiquitous modern mode of disclosure through which natural resources and human capacities appear, Foucault lays out a multiplicity of *dispositifs*, each creating distinct visibilities.

The history of technologies or techniques

Foucault's distinction between 'the history of techniques' and 'the history of technologies' (STP: 8–9) is particularly instructive as a contrast to Heidegger's *Gestell*. At first glance, a parallel appears between Heidegger's discussions of specific technical innovations and 'the essence of technology', and Foucault's distinction between 'technique' and 'technology'. We could pursue this comparative path along Heidegger's and Foucault's respective use of technical inventions versus *Gestell* and techniques versus *dispositif*. In such a comparison, the latter side of the conceptual dyads, *Gestell* and *dispositif*, would constitute the historical conditions of possibility for the emergence and deployment of devices and technical innovations. On closer inspection, however, Heidegger does not actually draw a firm distinction between specific techniques and 'the essence of technology'.

It is here that Foucault's recovery of the emergence and transformation of techniques diverges markedly from Heidegger, since Foucault's Nietzschean genealogy foregrounds the transitory relationship between techniques and technologies. Foucault said that 'there is a history of the actual techniques themselves' that the genealogist explores:

> For example, you could perfectly well study the history of the disciplinary technique of putting someone in a cell, which goes back a long way. It was already

The 'Eye' of Technology **129**

> frequently employed in the juridico-legal age; you find it used for debtors and above all you find it in the religious domain. (STP: 8)

Thus, on Foucault's account, the genealogist must carefully trace how, for example, a specific technique of punishment was redeployed for different purposes over time. Such a study may also involve exploring how the use of a technique at some point becomes problematic, such that it needs to be invested with new justifications if it is not to recede. Foucault continues: 'So, you could study the history of this cell technique (that is to say, its shifts, its utilization), and you would see at what point the cell technique, cellular discipline, is employed in the common penal system, what conflicts it gives rise to, and how it recedes' (STP: 8).

In these passages, it is hard not to hear an echo of Nietzsche's *On the Genealogy of Morality*, where he advanced his genealogical principle of 'functional indeterminacy'. According to this principle, a custom may endure while its meaning and function are historically 'fluid', which means that the current function of a practice holds no clue to its origin. For Nietzsche, the genealogy of any given entity (concept, practice, technique) is the history of how it has been reinterpreted, or seized by different forces, and put to new functions which override previous functions: 'The whole history of a "thing", an organ, a tradition can to this extent be a continuous chain of signs, continually revealing new interpretations and adaptations' (GM: 51). This genealogical approach rules out ideas of history as logically progressive or evolutionary; instead, declares Nietzsche, 'it is a succession of more or less profound, more or less mutually independent processes of subjugation' (GM: 51). The meaning of punishment is indeed tied to a history of struggles around interpretations.

Bodies have been beaten and tortured for various reasons long before the meaning of 'punishment' was assigned to these practices. To prove his point, Nietzsche gives a long list of different functions of punishment throughout history, and asserts that the first function of punishment was to establish an 'equivalence' between the injury caused and the pain inflicted on the offender (GM: 53–54). The origin of this idea of equivalence, we note in passing, is in the contract between creditor and debtor, the 'uncanny and perhaps inextricable link-up between the ideas of "debt and suffering"' (GM: 41), which for Nietzsche constitutes a founding relationship for our modern morality. It is striking that Foucault, in his cursory comment on the historical uses of 'cellular punishment', mentions that the cell technique was used to punish debtors. Also noteworthy are the Nietzschean echoes in Foucault's remarks on punishment as creating a 'quasi-equivalence' in potential lawbreakers at

130 Foucault's Technologies

the level of interests, and that 'the memory of pain must prevent a repetition of the crime' (DP: 94–95). In brief, starting with punishment, Nietzsche advances his principle that the function of a 'thing' is never fixed or inherent but always malleable in a field of force relations, and reasserts his view of history as perpetual struggle between forces that intersect or come apart.

Foucault's analysis of different *dispositifs* in interplay (STP) bears these marks of Nietzsche's genealogy. Like Nietzsche, Foucault is sceptical of the generally accepted functionality assigned to what he studies, including institutions like the prison, the madhouse, and the psychiatric clinic. Broadly parallel to Nietzsche, Foucault insists on describing the past struggles and reappropriations that led to the birth of an institution. It seems, then, that Foucault took up the genealogical premise of 'functional indeterminacy' first coined by Nietzsche, and meticulously deployed it in his analysis of the evolving interplay between *dispositifs*. Recall that, according to Foucault, a specific technique can become 'reappropriated' by different *dispositifs* and invested with new purposes (see Chapter 1). Indeed, Foucault describes how, over time, the technique of imprisonment became invested with the imperatives of law, discipline, and security in processes of dynamic correlation. And consider Nietzsche's comment on how the usefulness of a 'thing' depends on its incorporation into 'a system of ends' that will transform and direct it to 'a new purpose':

> The origin of the emergence of a thing and its ultimate usefulness, its practical application and incorporation into a system of ends, are *toto coelo* separate; that anything in existence, having somehow come about, is continually interpreted anew, requisitioned anew, transformed and redirected to a new purpose by a power superior to it. (GM: 51)

Let us compare, then, the above quote with Foucault's explication of how a technique changes and becomes 'perfected' as it is taken up by *dispositifs*, which continually transform in a 'system of correlation':

> In reality you have a series of complex edifices in which, of course, the techniques themselves change and are perfected, or anyway become more complicated, but in which what above all changes is the dominant characteristic, or more exactly, the system of correlation between juridico-legal mechanisms, disciplinary mechanisms, and mechanisms of security. (STP: 8)

The parallels are evident, and yet Foucault breaks with the somewhat schematic sequentiality that often marks Nietzsche's genealogies. Foucault's use of genealogy allows for more complexity insofar as, at a given moment, several *dispositifs* coexist in a field of mutual interplay, support, and contestation. This kind of genealogy, insists Foucault, requires detailed studies that does not reduce the specificity of the developments in each social domain and each society to an overarching world view, because 'things do not necessarily develop in step in different sectors, at a given moment, in a given society, in a given country' (STP: 8). Hence one can study how 'a technology of security, for example, will be set up, taking up again and sometimes even multiplying juridical and disciplinary elements and redeploying them within its specific tactic' (STP: 8–9).

At this point, let us briefly return to Heidegger. I would argue that it is difficult to carry out the kind of genealogical analysis presented above within Heidegger's philosophy of technology. That there could be a series of *dispositifs* that appropriate and redeploy techniques according to specific strategies is ruled out by Heidegger's anticipation of how *Gestell*, the fundamental dispensation in modernity, already prefigures all techniques. We can here follow Andrew Feenberg (1999), who argues that Heidegger's 'one-dimensional technological essentialism' disallows a more fine-grained analysis of technologies, including their potentials and harmful effects. Dana Belu and Feenberg observe: 'The staggering implication [of Heidegger's thinking] is that machine technology is somehow superfluous for understanding the essence of technology' (Belu and Feenberg, 2010: 4). Whereas Foucault sets out to examine how techniques and their effects change as they are taken up by different *dispositifs*, Heidegger entirely precludes such an analysis, since technical devices serve as illustrations of the world view that prevails in modernity. This is the case since Heidegger, as we saw earlier, presents the fundamental traits of modern metaphysics that define our relation to all types of techniques. Heidegger declares: 'Western humanity, in all its comportment toward entities, and even toward itself, is in every respect sustained and guided by metaphysics' (NV4: 205). Foucault's genealogy, which examines *dispositifs* in their historical contexts and evolving social relations, contradicts Heidegger's typical usage of empirical material as mere illustrations of his philosophy of technology. For Heidegger, modern technology is not a phenomenon, or an imperative, that can have different effects depending on its contexts of emergence and social usage; instead, it always brings us to disclose the world in the mode of exploitative objectification.

We can now return to Agamben's claim and conclude that while the *dispositif* and *Gestell* display certain links between Foucault and Heidegger, they are neither equivalent nor 'perfectly corresponding' concepts. First, Foucault's analytical move to go 'behind' the institutions is not comparable with Heidegger's ontological difference, since, as Ziarek (1998: 173) notes, Foucault

132 Foucault's Technologies

does not situate technology at the 'ontological-historical' level. Although Foucault and Heidegger share the view that techniques of calculation, discipline, and optimization emerge from their historical conditions of possibility, those conditions are conceptualized very differently by the notions of *Gestell* and *dispositif*. Foucault's genealogical studies of *dispositifs* in their singular emergence, dynamic interplay, and ceaseless transformation confront Heidegger's philosophy, which situates all 'empirical' observations within his overall history of Western thought. Indeed, Heidegger argues that the *Gestell* refers what it designates back to the innermost history of metaphysics, which conditions our modern world view: 'The reign of the *Ge-stell* means: man is subject to the control, the demands, and the provocation of a power that is manifested in the essence of technology' (Heidegger, cited in Cassin et al., 2014: 188). In brief, Foucault, like Heidegger, diagnosed the ubiquitous objectification inherent in modernity, but he displayed how the historical and social production of technology evolves, not in any uniform fashion, but in complex dynamics and social struggles. Heidegger, by contrast, claims that humanity is inevitably and fundamentally subjected to the rule of *Gestell*, which again is rooted in modern metaphysics.

These significant underlying differences perhaps explain why those scholars who claim that *Gestell* and *dispositif* are equivalent terms (Elden, 2001; Agamben, 2009, 2011) have omitted the task of making a detailed comparison and integration of the two terms. Ziarek makes an observation regarding the challenge of integrating Heidegger's and Foucault's thought, which is highly pertinent, even if not directly addressed to the *Gestell* and *dispositif*. If one were to bring Foucault's thinking on power closer to Heidegger, argues Ziarek (1998: 169), one must see power 'as a modality of happening'. Such a shift of emphasis might be possible because Foucault already submits to a processual and relational notion of power. Yet one would need to dislodge power even more from materiality, conceiving of it as events that transpire among things and bodies:

> What would be required here is a rethinking of materiality away from substance and in terms of a poetic bringing forth and materialization. Materiality would be less solidity and substantiality and more an event of bodying, of taking place and shape within the world, both participating in the open context of relations and effected by it. (Ziarek, 1998: 169)

The integration of Heidegger and Foucault that Ziarek suggests around the *poiētic* quality of the event seems to me, however, to take place largely on Heideggerian territory. Relocating the encounter more on 'the middle

The 'Eye' of Technology **133**

ground' would require Heidegger's diagnosis of the prevailing disclosure of the modern age to be opened up much further by means of genealogical curiosity.

Where Heidegger and Foucault come apart

Foucault never offered any systematic assessment of Heidegger's philosophy or the phenomenological tradition more broadly. The above exposition has displayed significant ways in which Foucault's work echoes Heideggerian themes and perspectives. Nevertheless, as we are beginning to see, important differences separate the two thinkers, some of which Foucault indicates in comments scattered across his texts and interviews. Consider the following quote, which is one of the few comments that Foucault explicitly directed to Heidegger:

> For Heidegger, it was through an increasing obsession with *technē* as the only way to arrive at an understanding of objects that the West lost touch with Being. Let's turn the question around and ask which techniques and practices form the Western concept of the subject, giving it its characteristic split of truth and error, freedom and constraint. I think that it is here where we will find the real possibility of constructing a history of what we have done and, at the same time, a diagnosis of what we are. This would be a theoretical analysis which has, at the same time, a political dimension. By this word 'political dimension' I mean an analysis that relates to what we are willing to accept in our world, to accept, to refuse, and to change, both in ourselves and in our circumstances. (Foucault, 1999: 161)

This quote is a rich starting point for discussing the differences between Foucault's genealogy and Heidegger's philosophy. It contains four points that are essential for clarifying how their thinking diverges:

1. We note Foucault's scepticism of Heidegger's claim that the whole history of Western thought is its forgetfulness of Being, and the idea that it requires a privileged interpreter, i.e. a philosopher, to remind us of our oblivion of the ontological difference.
2. Foucault wants to replace the constitutive subject, including phenomenology's concern with consciousness, with studies of how the subject is crafted by techniques. Foucault's intention to write a 'history of what we have done', rather than of how we think, echoes Nietzsche, as does his invocation of the 'characteristic split' in Western thought of 'truth and error, freedom and constraint'.

134 Foucault's Technologies

3. Whereas Heidegger arguably kept his philosophy untouched by real-world social, political, and economic events, Foucault's genealogy carries a 'political dimension', often engaging with issues that he found socially, politically, or morally problematic. Heidegger's assumption of metaphysics as our unavoidable condition 'as receivers' contrasts with Foucault's recognition of our capacity to act upon the *dispositifs* that shape us.

4. Foucault concludes his commentary on Heidegger by relating genealogy to 'what we are willing to accept ... both in ourselves and in our circumstances'. While Heidegger's 'passage through' modern technology entails the cultivation of an inner relationship to disclosure, Foucault sees self-transformative work as inseparable from work upon 'our circumstances'. For Foucault, the undefined project of freedom, internally and externally, intersects in the self's work upon the self.

The remaining part of this chapter examines these four comparative themes. I take them to be fundamental for comparing Heidegger's and Foucault's thinking on modern technology as well as the related, broader themes of history, politics, and ethics which will be discussed in turn.

Does it take a philosopher to recover Being?

Let us turn to the first point, the difference between Foucault's genealogy and Heidegger's philosophical concern with the question of Being. The quote in the previous section makes clear that Foucault is sceptical of the idea that the key task of philosophy is to traverse the history of Western thought and recover an essential, yet forgotten question. He entirely eschews Heidegger's premise that the history of Western thought is one of forgetting, which Heidegger repeatedly states in unmistakeable terms: '(O)ur thought has not yet emerged from the division between the metaphysical question of Being, which asks about the Being of beings, and the question that inquires more primordially; that is, inquires into the truth of Being' (NV3: 217).

That the question of Being is alien to Foucault, especially from the early 1970s onwards, can be explained by his avoidance of metaphysics. While Foucault shares Heidegger's concern with the historically entrenched restrictions and reductions on what human beings can experience, it is true, as Charles Scott (1987: 95) notes, that Foucault displayed 'little interest in reshaping or denouncing metaphysics, or in countermanding metaphysical thinking'. The privilege given to metaphysics in Heidegger's thought, which Mark Wrathall

(2019) denotes 'The Universal and Total Grounds Thesis', entails that every age is grounded upon a particular metaphysics which universally conditions how all entities appear. Heidegger sometimes express this thesis in sweeping terms:

> Metaphysics grounds an age, in that through a specific interpretation of what is and through a specific comprehension of truth it gives to that age the basis upon which it is essentially formed. This basis holds complete dominion over all the phenomena that distinguish the age. (WP: 115)

We have noted that Foucault eschews Heidegger's account of how modern metaphysics completes the process of forgetting, whereby the pathway for exploring the conditions of disclosure *as such* narrows down. Heidegger's diagnosis asserts that we are so ensnared by the pervasive technological objectification in our everyday lives that the background intelligibility of entities slips out of sight: 'What is strange in the thinking of Being is its simplicity. Precisely, this keeps us from it' (LH: 107). This withdrawal means that our self, understood as a set of relations of meaning, is only accessible to us through a background intelligibility, our inherited 'tradition', which is never fully knowable: 'The tradition that hereby gains dominance makes what it "transmits" so little accessible that initially and for the most part it covers it over instead. What has been handed down is handed over to obviousness' (B&T: 20). For Heidegger, tradition, understood as a set of received categories and concepts, tends to become reified in the forgetting of its origin, since 'the tradition even makes us forget such a provenance altogether' (B&T: 21). Our background tradition and its provenance will always be partly ungraspable, and yet metaphysics displays the world as fully 'present' by way of fixed categories and causal relations.

Heidegger and Foucault would agree that it is difficult for us to interrogate the conditions of possibility for beings/objects, because the terms we use for that inquiry are themselves already embedded in the prevailing metaphysics/discourse. However, Foucault sharply departs from Heidegger on the idea that the elusive question of Being must be reclaimed by a privileged interpreter recovering the 'unthought' in the work of previous philosophers. Although Foucault does not mention Heidegger's name in the following quote, he undoubtedly addresses the latter's assumption about forgetting head-on:

> Nothing is more foreign to me than the idea that, at a certain moment, philosophy went astray and forgot something, that somewhere in its history there is a

136 Foucault's Technologies

principle, a foundation that must be rediscovered. I feel that all such forms of analysis, whether they take a radical form and claim that philosophy has from the outset been a forgetting, or whether they take a much more historical viewpoint and say, 'Such and such a philosopher forgot something'—neither of these approaches is particularly interesting or useful. Which does not mean that contact with such and such a philosopher may not produce something, but it must be emphasized that it would be something new. (Foucault, 1998a: 294–295)

As Foucault makes clear, he does not find 'useful' a strategy that claims to discover a truer meaning that thinkers before him could not themselves grasp. He thereby sets himself against Heidegger's idea of recovering openings to the question of Being in previous philosophers' thought. As Levin points out, Heidegger can be said to operate with two forms of vision, namely our habitual, objectifying vision versus another, potentially *poiētic*, form of vision:

Heidegger always attempts to articulate a difference (call it 'an ontological difference') between (1) the character of our habitual, 'normal' vision, a way of seeing that he regards as forgetful of the lighting by grace of which we are enabled to see, and which he therefore, in this sense, accuses of being degenerate and pathological, and (2) the character of a radically different way of seeing. (Levin, 1993: 194)

Foucault often opposed forms of analysis that require a privileged observer to rediscover a meaning, which supposedly remains hidden from the speaking subjects themselves (see Chapters 1 and 5). Consider, by comparison, Heidegger's statements in *Being and Time* regarding how Being's unfolding risks become concealed:

What remains concealed in an exceptional sense, or what falls back and is covered up [*Verdeckung*] again, or shows itself only in a 'disguised' ['*verstellt*'] way, is not this or that being but rather, as we have shown in our foregoing observations, the being of beings. It can be covered up to such a degree that it is forgotten and the question about it and its meaning altogether omitted. (B&T: 33)

Against the idea of elusive forms of background intelligibility or tacit premises that cover up their own origin, Foucault said that 'everything is said', implying that historical rationalities are directly observable in the textual archive and do not require any deeper interpretation (AK: 121). In taking this position, Foucault distanced himself from one of Heidegger's key axioms, which demands, explain Hubert Dreyfus and Paul Rabinow (1982: 56), that 'in order to study linguistic practices one must take into account the background of shared practices which make them intelligible'. Dreyfus' insistence on the compatibility of Heidegger and Foucault, discussed at the outset of this chapter, contradicts the position of his earlier book on Foucault co-authored with Rabinow (1982). This seminal book concludes that Foucault explicitly rejects Heidegger's phenomenology, since Foucault's archaeological preference for the exteriority of discourse contrasts sharply with the assumption of a background intelligibility. Indeed, Foucault's approach proceeds by isolating a group of statements 'in order to analyse them in an exteriority that may be paradoxical since it refers to no correlative form of interiority' (AK: 121). Against this background, we can conclude that Foucault, at least when theorizing his approach in *The Archaeology of Knowledge*, rejects the notion of background intelligibility, a 'clearing', never fully transparent to the speakers. Instead, he sets out to analyse discourse as a network of statements in which statements' signification depends *on the network itself*, not on any half-concealed 'background intelligibility'.

For Heidegger, to 'think', as noted earlier, is to recognize that one is caught up in historical traditions that condition disclosure and, on that basis, to become attuned to one's role as a recipient of Being in all its awe and mystery. Critics have argued that Heidegger's notion of Being invokes some kind of mysticism, a theology, or an illusory foundation of the world. Gianni Vattimo notes that Heidegger can give the impression that we could gain access to 'a different kind of Being, an alternative to the Being of metaphysics', but this overcoming of metaphysics 'would lead us to a sort of negative or mystical theology, a persistent illusion that Being has somehow been grasped in its difference and irreducibility vis-a-vis the principles and foundations imagined by the philosophy of the past' (Vattimo, 2006: 188). Although Vattimo wants to resist this 'mystical' interpretation of Being, he recognizes that it easily finds authorization in Heidegger himself, whose texts display the aspiration 'for a situation in which Being might once again speak to us "in person" as well as the "description" of Being in terms of event' (Vattimo, 2006: 188).

The alternative to mysticism would be to see the disclosure of Being as mere historical events; Vattimo calls this 'a Foucauldian outcome', which treats 'epistemes as pure effects of the play of forces' (Vattimo, 2006: 188). Ultimately, however, Vattimo argues for a 'postmetaphysical' interpretation of Being, which aligns with the one we have established in this chapter. Heidegger becomes postmetaphysical, argues Vattimo, by taking from Nietzsche the idea that Being 'evaporates' into events of becoming. There is, writes Vattimo, 'not just some false image of Being meant to be replaced by a solider, truer one. It is Being that, after Nietzsche, can "reveal itself", in postmetaphysical

138 Foucault's Technologies

thought, as not equatable to an object, arche, or foundation, but as a "sending"' (Vattimo, 2006: 189). The distinction between Heidegger's Being as a 'sending' and Foucault's *dispositifs* as products of social struggles provides a helpful contrast. We can add that in Foucault there is no 'sending' to humankind, which the *dispositifs* can either foreclose or be open towards, but, as the following chapters will demonstrate, different *dispositifs* can be more or less conducive for the self's reflexive work upon the self.

Foucault's Nietzschean passage out of phenomenology

Heidegger and Foucault both wished to escape the constitutive subject understood as a transcendental ego or self-identical entity, which persists over time, instead emphasizing the relational and processual character of the subject. They also shared the view that the frameworks and practices, through which our subjectivity is constituted, are historically changing and constitutive for knowledge. Insofar as the subject is conceived of not as a substance but as a *response* to its conditions (Being or the *dispositifs*), Heidegger's and Foucault's thinking could be said to intersect around a 'negative self', which characterizes strains of phenomenology that view the subject as 'a process without substratum', to use Michael Theunissen's (1981: 413) words. Perhaps, then, Heidegger and Foucault can be aligned in their parallel avoidance of assumptions of a positive self and in their preference for analysing the human subject through its negation—in terms of negativities common to us all such as illness, death, or unreason.

However, we soon reach the limits to our comparison, as Foucault indicates when he says that he wants to replace the primacy of the subject with an examination of how the subject is constructed through practices and techniques. In other words, unlike the early Heidegger, one finds in Foucault no attempt to establish a 'philosophical anthropology' (Theunissen, 1981: 392). What might be termed Heidegger's philosophical anthropology, presented in *Being and Time*, relies on the premise that it is through 'existential experiences' like angst, death, and boredom that we are confronted with the nothingness that underlies our world. The key significance of these experiences is to spur us to reflect on our relationship to Being, hence recovering our essence in terms of our questioning attitude into how our world becomes meaningful to us. Kieran Durkin (2022: 294) notes that through Heidegger's 'elaboration of his fundamental ontology, a concealed subjectivism breaks through, particularly in the second part of the book'. The questions of whether Heidegger, after *Being and Time*, found that his notion of *Dasein* lacked radicality, and whether he ultimately left his project of philosophical anthropology, remain debated.

There are also differences between Heidegger and Foucault regarding what modern subjectivism entails and when it emerged historically. Whereas Heidegger dates the emergence of the subject as foundation of all meaning to Descartes' philosophy from the mid-seventeenth century, Foucault locates the appearance of the modern subject in the nineteenth century. And, explains Elías Palti (2021: 25), instead of 'a same-self substance' as entailed in Heidegger's definition, Foucault identifies the modern subject with 'a duplicate of immanence and transcendence, subjectivity and objectivity, opening the doors to the emergence of the project of a human science'. In general terms, whereas the early Heidegger sought to establish the fundamental categories of *Dasein*, he later stressed that being-in-the-world, one's incessant 'becoming oneself', occurs historically. On this broad level, the later Heidegger's search for a radical contestation of subjectivism through a history of being finds a convergence in Foucault's genealogy, as Dreyfus (1996) has argued.

Foucault's work has sometimes been viewed as an extension of Heidegger's diagnosis of the prevailing objectification in the modern West, as noted early in this chapter. Yet, whereas Foucault would agree with the premise that the human subject is always historically situated, he believed that 'existential experiences' must themselves be examined in their historical contexts. As Robert Nichols notes, Heidegger sees the subject as 'thoroughly situated in the world' but neglects to explore the social and historical conditions of this situatedness. This is because, Nichols argues, 'claims to know this situatedness rest upon the presence of existential "experiences" whose historical and social situatedness are never themselves interrogated' (Nichols, 2014: 102). While Foucault and Heidegger both sought to overcome the constitutive subject, understood as a discrete, self-grounding, and sovereign agent, Foucault undertakes a more empirical historicizing of the forms of experience (illness, madness, sexuality, etc.) that are possible for the modern subject. Overall, Foucault avoided a priori anthropological assumptions and overarching historical models, preferring to explore a series of accidental trajectories in their historical contingency. 'So many things can be changed', he said, being as fragile as they are, 'tied more to contingencies than to necessities, more to what is arbitrary than to what is rationally established, more to complex but transitory historical contingencies than to inevitable anthropological constants' (Foucault, 2001a: 458). As this quote makes clear, the connection between Heidegger and Foucault hardly runs through philosophical anthropology.

140 Foucault's Technologies

Instead, Foucault's work can be said to extend Heidegger's diagnosis of the prevailing objectification in the modern West. However, as Nichols (2014: 221) notes, Foucault pursued this theme in 'specific, concrete cases in which human modes of subjectification congealed into rigid typological classifications—the mad, the delinquent, the abnormal, the sexual deviant'. For the genealogist, the emergence and transformation of these classifications are always inseparable from social struggles (recall the discussion of strategies in Chapter 1). Foucault's interest in these negative classifications is telling for his overall approach, which refuses to start from any positive conception of the human subject (the human being could be defined, e.g. as the only animal that reflects on its own mortality). Foucault instead takes his point of departure in negative conceptions of human existence, which brings him close to Heidegger but ultimately far removed from philosophical anthropology. He says that his enterprise is marked by 'a historicizing negativism', 'since it involves replacing a theory of knowledge, power, or the subject with the analysis of historically determinate practices' (GSO: 5). Foucault's genealogical approach entirely avoids the question of interiority, i.e. what the human subject is in its essence, and instead inquires into the exterior limits (madness, perversion, deviance) that tell us what the subject is not.

The differences between Heidegger and Foucault can be traced to their contrasting readings of Nietzsche. Foucault (1989b) himself said that it was Nietzsche who showed him the way out of phenomenology (which I take to include Heidegger), since Nietzsche paved the way for truly historicizing the subject and, specifically, escaping the phenomenological concern with consciousness. Recall that Foucault wished to 'turn the question around'—that is, presumably, the question of how the conscious subject bestows meaning upon the world—in order to study the historical practices and techniques through which subjects are constituted. In Foucault's words, Nietzsche posed the question, 'can a transhistorical subject of a phenomenological kind be accounted for by the history of reason? Here the writings of Nietzsche cause a break, a rupture [*coupure*] for me' (Foucault, 1989b: 351). Discussing Foucault's relationship to Heidegger, several scholars argue that Foucault ultimately relied upon Nietzsche in conceiving of history as evolving through continual struggles (Dreyfus, 1996; Rayner, 2001; Sluga, 2005). Hence Rayner posits that Foucault dislodged genealogy from Heidegger's overall philosophical framework, rearticulating it through a Nietzschean emphasis on power: 'Displacing this instrument from the world of Heideggerian concerns, and reinserting it within a Nietzschean realm of practices and struggles, Foucault turns Heidegger's way of thinking to a different end' (Rayner, 2001: 153). Foucault anticipated such an interpretation when he

The 'Eye' of Technology **141**

declared that reading Heidegger and Nietzsche together was his 'philosophical shock', and that despite his large and underestimated inspiration from Heidegger, ultimately 'Nietzsche prevailed over him' (Foucault, 1989b: 250).

Generally, Foucault foregrounds social struggle as opposed to the 'mildness' of Heidegger's appeal for cultivating receptive thinking. Invoking Nietzsche against phenomenology (often without specification), Foucault asserts that language is not a medium of meaning but a vehicle of domination. He said that Nietzsche showed a way to engage in interpretation without reference to consciousness and meaning: 'to speak of sign and interpretation, of their inseparability, without reference to a phenomenology' (WK: 213) and 'to connect up analyses of systems of signs with the analysis of forms of violence and domination' (WK: 214). Foucault would appear to embrace Nietzsche and escape Heidegger when he contrasts 'the mildness of a phenomenon' with the violence of infinite interpretation:

> Against the welcoming mildness of a phenomenon, it is necessary to set the murderous relentlessness of knowledge. But in this work this is never rewarded with access to being or the essence, but gives rise to new appearances, sets them against one another and beyond one another. (WK: 206)

Foucault's analysis, I submit, displays these Nietzschean premises. Hence, as discussed in Chapter 1, *dispositifs* emerge from social struggle and 'respond to urgent needs', and the particular visibilities that they create bear the imprint of these struggles and tactical responses. Like Heidegger, Foucault showed that the *dispositif* creates a general propensity in how objects and subjects can appear, but, unlike Heidegger, Foucault foregrounds social conflict as integral to *dispositifs*. Schematically, one can say that Foucault's genealogy substitutes Heidegger's double ontology (Being versus beings) with a Nietzschean surface field of interacting forces.

Deleuze (1988: 113) draws a similar conclusion when he declares that 'phenomenology is ultimately too pacifying and has blessed too many things. Foucault therefore discovers the element that comes from outside: force.' Notably, Deleuze gives an interpretation of force, or the will to power, that sharply diverges from Heidegger. Whereas Heidegger locates the will to power in the 'essence' of modern technology, which is marked by permanently self-surpassing progress, Deleuze describes the will to power in terms of ever-evolving tactics and strategies. For Deleuze, the problem with Heidegger's philosophy is that it neglects the play of forces that gives shape to modern technology as our historical ontology. This neglect in Heidegger, notes Deleuze (1988: 113), 'led to the deep ambiguity of his technical and

142 Foucault's Technologies

political ontology'. For Foucault, a 'political' strategy of 'receptive dwelling' by which one receives Being's unfolding will not do the job since, as Dreyfus (1996: 12) writes, things do not exist 'in their primitive vivacity'. Dreyfus also notes the absence in Foucault of a phenomenological 'background' which is not already pervaded by the play of power relations, since, for Foucault, 'the background practices reveal, as they do in Nietzsche, a constantly shifting struggle' (Dreyfus, 1996: 19). In sum, situated against the phenomenological tradition, Nietzsche not only showed Foucault the way out of the 'transhistorical subject', but pushed his thinking further away from Heideggerian themes such as the ontological difference, the appeal to 'receptive dwelling', and the quest for interrogating our tacit background practices.

Finally, we must contrast Heidegger's metaphysical *reconstruction* of Nietzsche with Foucault's genealogical *use* of Nietzsche. As noted at the outset of this chapter, the two thinkers both explored central themes in Nietzsche, including his approach to thought as historical and his identification of nihilism in modernity. Furthermore, in their respective readings of Nietzsche, Heidegger and Foucault both evade Nietzsche's attempts to link philosophical doctrines with physiological and psychological mechanisms, as well as assumptions about human beings' psychological nature. As Foucault would do later, Heidegger entirely ignored Nietzsche's biologism, that is, 'his preoccupation with life, blood, the metabolism, digestion' (Sluga, 2007: 107). However, the interpretative similarities between the two quickly cease, and instead significant contrasts come to the fore. Reading Nietzsche pre-eminently as a metaphysician, Heidegger largely ignored aspects of Nietzsche's thought that preoccupied Foucault, including Nietzsche's critique of nineteenth-century European culture, his analysis of Christian asceticism, his interest in ancient ethics, and of course his genealogical approach.

Recall Heidegger's critical conclusion that Nietzsche, despite his acute diagnosis of modernity, failed to escape from metaphysics, since his doctrines of will to power and eternal recurrence projected the nature of all beings. Hence 'Nietzsche's metaphysics is not an overcoming of nihilism', argues Heidegger, '(i)t is the ultimate entanglement in nihilism' (NV4: 203). By projecting the truth of beings as will to power, Nietzsche ends up in a metaphysics of the will, and, as Heidegger sees it, this metaphysical projection ultimately forecloses the question of Being. However, there are reasons to suggest that Heidegger himself, especially in his reading of Nietzsche, falls prey, if not to another metaphysics, then to his own version of historical teleology. This is because, in Heidegger's view, Nietzsche had exposed 'the inner logic of Western history', even if he failed to grasp the full implications of this logic. Indeed, Heidegger's choice of words at times convey the impression of history's predestination, since he presents nihilism as 'the fundamental movement of the history of the West', culminating in the modern age. Nihilism, writes Heidegger, 'moves history after the manner of a fundamental ongoing event that is scarcely recognized in the destining of the Western peoples' (WN: 62), and nihilism is 'above all the intrinsic law of that history' (WN: 67). Vattimo (2006: 189) aptly notes that 'Heidegger confers meaning on Nietzsche by showing that the will to power is, so to speak, "the destiny of Being"'. Extending this argument, one could suggest that Heidegger reads Nietzsche's doctrines of the will to power and eternal recurrence not only as metaphysical but also as a kind of historical teleology. Hence Robert Sinnerbrink notes that, contrary to Heidegger's *verfallsgeschichte* of the forgetting of Being which refers *Gestell* to an ontological condition unfolding teleologically in history, Foucault's genealogy 'explicitly rejects any teleological narrative of historical development' (Sinnerbrink, 2005: 247). This important difference, of course, places Heidegger at a great distance from Foucault's genealogy.

A core contrast between Heidegger and Foucault, then, is their irreconcilable readings of Nietzsche, which involve the question of what is to be understood by Nietzsche's notions of will to power and eternal return. Is the will to power a kind of unifying principle for how Being is disclosed in the modern age, or is it a principle of constant differentiation? Here, Deleuze's book *Nietzsche and Philosophy* (2006) provides an answer which frees Nietzsche's doctrines from Heidegger's philosophy and places them in close proximity to Foucault. Deleuze saw in Nietzsche, writes Michael Hardt (2006: ix), 'a profound betrayal of the primacy of identity and unity' and, on this account, the will to power is 'a machine of multiplicities'. Furthermore, Deleuze offers an interpretation of the eternal return which, at least implicitly, can help us distinguish Heidegger's rendering of the concept from Foucault's usage. This is when Deleuze suggests a twofold definition of the eternal return as a 'synthesis of diversity and its reproduction' (a Deleuzian emphasis) and as 'a synthesis of becoming and the being which is affirmed in becoming' (a Heideggerian emphasis) (Deleuze, 2006: 48). Contrary to a metaphysical reading, Nietzsche's differential thinking leads us to Foucault's technological thinking, which substitutes the question of Being with the analysis of unstable systems of relations, or, to be precise, how *dispositifs* emerge from multiple techniques, tactics, and practices. In a conversation between Foucault and Deleuze from 1972, Foucault recognized the influence of Deleuze's book about Nietzsche on his own thinking: 'underneath the ancient theme of meaning, of the signifier and the signified, etc., you [Deleuze] have developed the question of power, of the inequality of powers

144 Foucault's Technologies

and their struggles' (Foucault, 1977a: 213–214). It is plausible, then, that Deleuze's reading of Nietzsche helped Foucault in reaching a notion of power as differential forces.

Again, as I demonstrate in this book, the Nietzschean differential field of struggle is at centre stage in Foucault's analysis of *dispositifs* and their interplay. Sluga suggests that it is most productive to read Nietzsche with a Foucauldian emphasis: 'In contrast to Heidegger, we would look at Nietzsche not as the last metaphysician but as the first genealogist' (Sluga, 2007: 118). In this genealogical reading, the will to power becomes power's differential productivity. Its results cannot be anticipated or reflected upon in the form of 'Being's destiny', since power will produce manifold unexpected things. Reading Nietzsche's formula of the will to power in the opposite direction to Heidegger, concludes Sluga, brings us to a Foucauldian conception of power:

> Will to power will then come to mean to us as much as the power to power, that is, the power to have, manipulate, and, multiply power. Such a power, when considered genealogically, will prove not one thing but many. We will have to conclude that there is, strictly speaking, no such thing as power but only power relations. These will have different configurations. (Sluga, 2007: 118)

These 'different configurations', I would suggest, are analogous to the *dispositifs*. In broad terms, then, Foucault's genealogy evacuates the will to power both from its cosmological connotation in Nietzsche and its metaphysical rendering in Heidegger and puts it to work in historical analysis. Or put differently: Heidegger finds in Nietzsche a diagnosis of modernity wherein all human activities' manifest the value of 'preservation-enhancement', whereas Foucault uses Nietzsche to discover a series of *dispositifs*, propelled by diverse strategies that can never be captured with reference to modern technology's 'essence'. Whereas Heidegger succeeds in constantly reminding us of how modern thought carries the forgetfulness of Being, Foucault recovers how specific forms of thinking emerge in intricate connection with strategies and struggle. In short, instead of enlisting Nietzsche to reconstruct a metaphysics, Foucault puts the Nietzschean difference between forces to use in painstaking genealogical work.

Does philosophy carry a 'political dimension'?

The third important point in the long quote by Foucault at the start of this section concerns the practical and political significance of intellectual work— an issue which significantly distinguishes Foucault from Heidegger. Let us recall that in the quote Foucault spoke of the need to make a 'diagnosis of what we are'. He then continued: 'This would be a theoretical analysis which has, at the same time, a political dimension. By this word "political dimension" I mean an analysis that relates to what we are willing to accept in our world, to accept, to refuse, and to change' (Foucault, 1999: 161). Dreyfus speaks from his integrative position when he describes how the aim of diagnosing our historical conditions with the prospect of moving beyond them speaks to both Heidegger and Foucault: 'Thus an understanding of our historical condition weakens the hold our current understanding has on us and makes possible disengagement from the direction our practices are taking' (Dreyfus, 1996: 20). And, yet again, the integrative comparison between Heidegger's and Foucault's diagnosis of our contemporaneity quickly reaches its limit.

Whereas the very first point about diagnosing 'what we are' broadly resonates with both Heidegger's and Foucault's projects, Foucault emphasizes the necessary political implications of such diagnostics, as if he wished to contrast his approach with theoretical or speculative philosophical traditions. Bruno Latour (1993: 65) observes bluntly that Heidegger 'does assert the existence of an articulation between metaphysical purification and the work of meditation'. Indeed, Heidegger appears to shield his philosophical meditation on technology from 'contamination' by real-world social and political concerns. This point was even more forcefully argued by Gunter Anders, who declared that 'the real powers that be, are not worthwhile mentioning in Heidegger's philosophy' (Anders, 1948: 354). Whereas Heidegger read a select group of major philosophers to construct his history of Western metaphysics, Foucault pushed philosophy into engagement with real history. By 'real history' is meant the study of mundane and often marginalized texts that tell of struggles between social groups, institutional reforms, and the invention of new techniques in production, teaching, training, and curing, all of which necessarily constitute the analysis of *dispositifs*.

The contrast between Heidegger's and Foucault's relationships to their respective social and political contexts bears on the fundamental question of what it means to be an intellectual. It is no overstatement to say that Heidegger consistently ignored the political and economic factors involved in the advent of modern technological that he criticized so vividly. Albert Borgmann observes, not without irony, that Heidegger's writings from the 1940s and 1950s are marked by 'an eerie silence about the persecutions by the Nazis and the destruction and despair of the concluding war. Heidegger is concerned with what he must have considered more profound problems' (Borgmann, 2005: 425). On the central theme of technology, Borgmann

146 Foucault's Technologies

argues, Heidegger's work never explained how his appeal to a 'turning' in our relationship to technology could be carried into a social and political context: 'There is a large gap between the profundity of Heidegger's thoughts on the thing and technology and the ailments that trouble us in the broad daylight of contemporary politics and culture' (Borgmann, 2005: 431). From this assessment, it is easy to think of a series of political and social issues that concerned Foucault deeply but which received little, if any, attention from Heidegger, including psychiatry, punishment, state racism, and neoliberal thought.

Heidegger's style, which merges his tour de force of Western philosophy with an overarching critique of modernity, contrasts starkly in its form with Foucault's specific genealogies which seek to recover marginalized forms of knowledge without unifying the analyses into an overarching critique. This difference is evident at the moments where Heidegger's writing adopts its most all-encompassing, allegorical, or lyrical tenor. Consider, for example, this dystopian assessment of the consequences of modern technology:

> From this arises a completely new relation of man to the world and his place in it. The world now appears as an object open to the attacks of calculative thoughts, attacks that nothing is believed able any longer to resist. The world becomes a gigantic gasoline station, an energy source for modern technology and industry. (DT: 14)

The portrayal of the world as 'a gigantic gasoline station' that has become pure and unlimited *Bestand* is certainly both an overarching and a very bleak one. At his darkest moments, Heidegger seems to envisage 'a seamless web that wove together humanism, the Enlightenment, and modern technology as the hallmarks of a nihilistic world, one shaped by a "disempowering of the spirit"' (Milchman and Rosenberg, 2003: 17). Indeed, there is evidence in Heidegger's writing of such a 'seamless web' that aligns diverse evils of modernity, including mechanized food production, gas chambers, and the hydrogen bomb. Such a sweeping critique reappears in Heidegger's concluding comment in his Bremen Lecture delivered in 1949 (excluded from the later published lectures):

> Agriculture is now mechanized food industry, essentially the same thing as the production of corpses in gas chambers and annihilation camps, the same thing as the blockade and intentional starvation of countries, the same thing as the production of hydrogen bombs. (Heidegger, cited in Borgmann, 2005: 430)

The 'Eye' of Technology   **147**

Inviting critiques of agrarian nostalgia and romanticization of pre-modern times (Anders, 1948; Fuchs, 2017), Heidegger seems to hark back to a world without mass production and agribusiness, appealing to the value of marginal cultural practices often found in rural life and the country village. Allegedly, these practices were not yet saturated with the technological world view, and hence Heidegger gestured towards their potential for a more receptive attitude towards nature and other human beings.

Perhaps, a key explanation for Heidegger's neglect in properly addressing his social and political contexts is his reliance on the literary as the 'saving' foundation of his philosophy (e.g. LH: 83). This is Alain Badiou's conclusion in his critical commentary on Heidegger's philosophical heritage: 'What culminates with Heidegger is the anti-positivist and anti-Marxist effort to put philosophy in the hands of the poem' (Badiou, 1999: 66). According to Badiou, Heidegger stands at the peak of a pervasive tendency in twentieth-century German and French philosophy, 'the fetishism' of poetry: 'It so happens that the main stake, the supreme difficulty, is to de-suture philosophy from its poetic condition ... What has given potency to the poeticizing suture, thus to Heidegger, is far from having been undone, indeed has never been examined' (Badiou, 1999: 67). In this context, we leave aside the complex question of whether it is possible to further develop Heidegger's thinking in its political dimensions (see Shürmann, 1978). It suffices to say, however, that Heidegger's philosophical meditations on modern technology were largely detached from their economic, social, and political context. Hence Latour sarcastically depicts the Heideggerian attitude to empirical researchers: 'We don't know anything empirical, but that doesn't matter, since your world is empty of Being. We are keeping the little flame of Being safe from everything, and you, who have all the rest, have nothing' (Latour, 1993: 66). In Heidegger's defence, his writing on modern technology never pledged itself to historical or sociological analysis, and Heidegger wished instead to inquire into a phenomenon that he appears to have believed was the most significant in modernity. It is within these evident limitations, one might infer, that Heidegger's inquiry retains its validity.

We have already seen that, for Heidegger, modernity is characterized by a general kind of visibility in which objects appear as 'standing-reserve'. Objectification is intrinsic to our modern existence, because we are already predisposed, or 'attuned', to adopt such an attitude to whatever we encounter. We have also noted certain parallels to Foucault's analysis of the 'normalizing gaze' of generalized discipline, a propensity towards objectification which proliferated across modern institutions. Their fundamental difference perhaps lies in how the two thinkers conceive of our relationship to our historical

148   Foucault's Technologies

condition. David Webb (2014) points out this important difference in our possibility for transformative intervention into 'the conditions that make us what we are'. Webb highlights what we, in Chapter 4, will term Foucault's 'ethico-politics': 'the relations of power linking us to others, to institutions, and to forms of knowledge that feature in Foucault's account are in a process of continual change to which our own discourse and critical activities can contribute' (Webb, 2014: 637). Whereas, for Heidegger, we can only change our *reflexive relationship* to the framework we are 'thrown into', and not the essence of modern technology itself, Foucault assumes that our practices can induce minor displacements in the historical condition itself. Belu and Feenberg (2010) note Heidegger's emphasis on meditative thinking and his avoidance of strategies of change. This is because, they write, '[t]here can only be a different dispensation in the future, not alternatives in the present. Heidegger's theory is eschatological rather than practical, hence his claim that man is the being that waits' (Belu and Feenberg, 2010: 14). Eschewing Heidegger's assumption of metaphysics as our unavoidable foundation, Foucault sees our historical condition as constituted by *dispositifs*, which are in perpetual motion and transform through human activity.

This difference in optimism regarding our capacity for inducing change is reflected in the overall tenor of the two thinkers' writings. Foucault's genealogies never quite reach the lonely hour of the doomsday proclamations in Heidegger's portrayal of the modern age. Whereas, for Foucault, ethics and politics are inextricably linked, it is harder to establish this link in Heidegger—that is, the link between politics and *Gelassenheit*, the meditative attitude that Heidegger (T: 42) says belongs to 'the one who waits'.

Cultivating meditative thinking

Finally, the question remains of how ethical self-work relates to its historical and sociopolitical circumstances in Heidegger and Foucault. Let us begin this final comparison around Heidegger's notion of Being's unfolding and Foucault's concept of power (Dreyfus, 1996; Ziarek, 1998; Webb, 2014). We reiterate that Being is not a thing, just like power is not substance. Instead, in both cases, our reality is a process of becoming in which *Dasein*, or in Foucault's terms our ongoing subjectivation, is intricately involved. However, as noted earlier, it is in the possibility of ethics that the comparison between Heidegger and Foucault reaches its limit.

In Heidegger's view, we must cultivate our capacity to 'think', before we act. He argues that it is by learning how to think, or 'think courageously', that

The 'Eye' of Technology   **149**

we become attentive to the essence of technology. Heidegger thus cautions: 'before considering the question that is seemingly always the most immediate one and the only urgent one, "What shall we do?" we ponder this: "How must we think?" For thinking is authentic action' (Heidegger, cited in Wrathall, 2019: 22). Heidegger foregrounds reflection as the means to 'preparedness', announcing that 'the only possibility of salvation left to us is to prepare readiness, through thinking and poetry' (*Der Spiegel*). Hans Sluga drew a succinct contrast when he said that the fundamental difference between Foucault and Heidegger on the issue of technology is that while Heidegger urges us to reflect differently about technology, Foucault emphasizes how our thinking is embedded in material practices (personal conversation, UC Berkeley, May 2019), understood as practices through which we govern ourselves and others.

While both Heidegger and Foucault conceive of thinking as a practice in itself, Foucault paid much more attention to the specific tools and procedures—'the self-techniques'—through which thinking occurs (the subject of Chapter 4). Moreover, from Foucault's perspective, we need to be ardently attentive to not only how we shape ourselves in practices of self-formation, but also to the field of political and social force relations that confront us. Therefore, for Foucault, becoming receptive to the 'sending of Being' is hardly sufficient for confronting social and political conditions that he found 'intolerable' (Karlsen and Villadsen, 2015). Foucault said that he hoped his work would invigorate 'the undefined work of freedom' (Foucault, 1997: 316) by recovering, we can add, the *dispositifs* of power/knowledge that are integral to our practices. Webb (2014: 637) aptly describes Foucault's intention on writing in a way that makes a difference to our present: 'For Foucault, we are contemporaries with power in a way that, for Heidegger, we are never contemporaries with Being.' As I will argue in Chapter 4, the premise that we are 'contemporaries with power' allows for an active work of the self upon the self that can bend the forces of the *dispositifs*.

Jean Zoungrana (1998) suggests that Heidegger's influence on Foucault is more profound than has so far been recognized, but he cautions against turning Foucault into 'a disciple of Heidegger'. This chapter has discovered many Heideggerian themes in Foucault's work which he explores within his own genealogies. Similarly, Zoungrana asserts that for Foucault, Heidegger's work 'has functioned as an invitation to think with Heidegger, but beyond Heidegger' (Zoungrana, cited in Milchman and Rosenberg, 2003: 6). That Foucault himself subscribed to such an explorative use and rearticulation of Heidegger finds confirmation in the quote from a late interview with which our comparison of Heidegger and Foucault began. There, Foucault said that even if he did not find 'particularly interesting or useful' the claim that this or that philosopher forgot something, he could still take inspiration from the philosopher who claimed so, 'but it must be emphasized that it would be something new' (Foucault, 2000d: 295). While Foucault's work echoes many Heideggerian themes, we see that his genealogical approach, as well as his notion of the *dispositif*, ultimately departs from Heidegger in fundamental ways.

If one wants to express how our rapid devastation of our global ecosystem is rooted in an entrenched technological world view, Heidegger's philosophy is still highly pertinent. It articulates our limitless quest to impose ourselves on nature, shaping it according to our own needs and wants and yet find ourselves distressed by the technological understanding of Being. Even if Foucault could be pushed towards these themes, there is a difference both in terms of scale and matters of concern. Whereas Foucault explored the biopolitical optimization of humankind in detail, he never considered the possibility of the extinction of humankind or the global ecosystem. The fact that Foucault did not address the risk of the earth's extinction resulting from humans' exploitative activity, which Heidegger dramatically gestured towards, could be a serious omission. Hence, Ijsseling argues that 'Foucault misses a profound analysis of metaphysical thinking that, as representation, domination, verification and control, risks the danger of ending in a catastrophe', and, concludes Ijsseling, this is 'a catastrophe that as nuclear conflict will never be understood, because there will no longer be understanding beings' (Ijsseling, 1986: 424).

To draw a final, overall contrast, we conclude that Heidegger gives us the unilinear history of how manipulative objectification has become *the* generalized 'gaze' of our modern culture, thereby pushing our capacity to experience the ontological difference into oblivion. Foucault, instead, shows us the multiple historical trajectories through which 'the eye of technology' has come to operate in disparate ways, inextricably bound to our social and political reality.

Chapter Three
The Production of 'Normal' Citizens

How have we become inhabitants of an accelerating, growth-addicted capitalism, who freely reproduce the practices that underpin this system while being painfully aware of its personal, social, and environmental damage? Have we become faithful allies with a capitalism that naturalizes 'the free labour contract', 'sound household economics', and, recently, 'responsible consumption', while denouncing those people considered to be idle, irresponsible, apathetic, or addicted? If so, critical analysis is required to detach ourselves from the *ideology* that pervades the common sense of everyday life, obfuscating any full recognition of our current sociopolitical situation; a situation of growing inequality and impending climate catastrophe accelerated by contemporary techno-capitalism and its resource-plundering and mass-consumerist practices. Or rather, do we need to turn our attention to the *techniques* that ensure our commitment to these practices, shaping us as citizen-subjects who freely reproduce the infrastructure of the economic order? That would mean focusing on the web of rules, sanctions, performance assessments, credit score ratings, personality tests, consumer risk profiles, etc., that induces most people to lead lives that congeal around family, workplace, and mass consumption.

The techniques involved in the production of normal citizens in today's capitalist economies can broadly be distinguished as two types: 'hard' juridico-disciplinary techniques on the one hand, and 'softer' governance techniques on the other. The first group of techniques ties people to legal and administrative categories, turning individuals into 'cases' and imposing sanctions in response to diverse moral and economic infractions. These techniques include the criminal record, the social case file, psychiatric diagnosis, and employability assessment. Those who straddle, or fall outside of, the confines of wage-labour and consumer life will probably feel such juridico-disciplinary techniques exerted by institutions authorized to adjudicate and intervene through their juridico-disciplinary expertise. Of course, today juridico-disciplinary techniques are often also used by commercial agents, including potential employers, insurance companies, banks, estate agents, and pension funds. They use the health risk profile, the background

Foucault's Technologies. Kaspar Villadsen, Oxford University Press. © Kaspar Villadsen (2024).
DOI: 10.1093/oso/9780198819400.003.0004

consumer report, credit score, and rental history to profile ordinary citizens' riskiness, determining to what degree a certain profile is creditworthy or trustworthy, and hence whether a person merits access to services.

Worth noting is that the individual risk assessments provided by health profiles, background reports, and credit scores make possible not only 'sound business decisions' based on individuals' past risk behaviour. They also enable insurance companies, future employers, and potential landlords to make a moral representation of an applicant's propensity for misconduct versus productivity. Said otherwise, the juridico-disciplinary techniques put to use by state institutions or commercial actors claim to predict the probability of an individual's risk behaviour, for example predicting the likelihood of loan default. Ultimately, these techniques do not produce exhaustive knowledge about any particular individual and his or her inherent character, but provide a basis for acting on similar individuals or 'cases'.

The other kind of techniques apply a 'softer' modality of power, since they refrain from the use of prohibition, sanction, and exclusion. Instead, they seek to guide, motivate, encourage, or lift individuals' self-esteem, in order to induce changes in their attitudes and behaviours. We term these 'governance-techniques' to indicate that they aim to influence the conduct of individuals by working on their subjectivity and reorganizing the social contexts within which they make their choices. The premise of these techniques is that individuals are fundamentally free to act differently, and that they already hold their own rationalities, values, and ethical principles that any mode of governance must take into account. Examples of governance-techniques include motivational therapy, personal development plans, patient-centred medicine, culturally sensitive campaigns, and nudging. While they aim to bring individuals' own attitudes and aspirations into the practice of government, these techniques do not determine a person's character solely based on 'external data' like their criminal record, past evictions, or credit score. Instead, the individual's own discourse is a necessary and essential source that experts in criminology, motivational therapy, social work, and medicine require to make a representation of that individual's specific deviance, motivation, responsibility, and riskiness. These techniques require that the subjects reaffirm, in their own words, their risky individuality, such as their 'job-preparedness' or their inherent propensity as 'overspenders'— a representation that determines aspects of their moral attitude. Consequently, these 'softer' techniques often have a confessional character, since individuals must express in truth what they are, producing their inner self to the listeners. A better name for these techniques is therefore pastoral-governmental.

The Production of 'Normal' Citizens   **153**

It is important to note that the division between these two types of techniques of citizen-production is a heuristic one. Real social practices often connect up and create hybrids between juridico-disciplinary and pastoral-governmental techniques. Take, for example, the criminal justice system, which uses a range of intersecting techniques both to ensure that 'justice is served' and to minimize the risk of recidivism by targeting factors that might propel convicts back into criminal behaviour. A juridical sentence can determine that convicts, while serving time in prison, must participate in educational programmes, drug and alcohol treatment, parental counselling, or behavioural therapy. Furthermore, a sentence can stipulate that after being discharged from prison, ex-convicts must be subject to 'softer' governance techniques such as skills training, supervised jobseeking, outpatient alcohol or drug treatment, psychological therapy, or parenting classes. This expansion of the criminal justice system with a whole set of such justice-adjacent services has given rise to the North American 'prison-industrial complex'. In this complex, the interplay of clusters of juridico-disciplinary and governance techniques creates a conflation of illegality, misconduct, and abnormality. Such conflation is certainly not new to the history of industrial capitalism, which runs through perennial struggles around delineating the borderlines between worker misconduct needing moralization, legal infractions needing punishment, or manifestations of abnormality needing cure.

The matrix of juridico-disciplinary and pastoral-governmental techniques contradicts the image of a liberal state that leaves the economy to its own devices, and only intervenes when its legal codes are breached. Bernard Harcourt (2010) emphasizes the coexistence in the US of a hands-off ideology of economic liberty and a heavily moralizing, legal-punitive state, arguing that the public imagination of 'the well-ordered market' legitimizes both governmental non-intervention in the economy and criminalization of all deviations from market-based interaction. The vision of penality as the sphere par excellence where the state can legitimately intervene has driven the growth of the penal system since the 1970s. A mutually reinforcing relationship between the capitalist market economy and a growing penal system has emerged, propelling correctional facilities to become billion dollar corporations. Law-abiding citizens who in other ways fail to conform to the capitalist model of production and consumption are targeted through a series of 'softer' governance techniques, not only in the North American context, but across the globe. Foucault famously described the modern state's two poles of power, the juridico-disciplinary and the pastoral-governmental, as a 'tricky combination'.

***

154 Foucault's Technologies

In Foucault's authorship, the link between the formation of the capitalist state and 'techniques of subjectivation' took centre stage in the early to mid-1970s. Works from this period, including *Penal Theories and Institutions* (1971–1972), *The Punitive Society* (1972–1973), *Psychiatric Power* (1973–1974), and, of course, *Discipline and Punish* (1975), all offer rich resources for analysing the state's role in industrial capitalism, especially if one accentuates certain key themes in these sources. This chapter will thus offer a different emphasis from Foucault's influential 'decentring' of the state in his 1978 and 1979 lectures with his notion of 'governmentality', from which many scholars took inspiration, at the partial expense of lectures from the first half of the 1970s. In these early 1970s works, Foucault focused on a theme very pertinent to the current situation: the relationship between the state's juridico-disciplinary functions and the reproduction of subjects who serve the emerging capitalist economy. In continuous dialogue with the Marxist tradition, Foucault explored how in the eighteenth and nineteenth centuries the state's punitive and disciplinary institutions were established in response to the propertied groups' concerns for defending capitalist production. The state's regulation of the labouring classes, while first assigned to the penal system, was gradually extended to a web of other state agents, including the police, social work, mental health, and other authorities that supervised the lower social strata. In this process, declares Foucault in *The Punitive Society*, 'the laboring and lower classes become the point of application of the moralization of penality. The State sees itself called upon to become the instrument of the moralization of these classes' (PS: 108). In the early 1970s, Foucault thus traced how the state evolved as a punitive and moralizing agent in tandem with the rise of the capitalist economy.

In contrast, Foucault's late 1970s work displays a shift towards a genealogy of governmental and pastoral modes of power, which emphasizes the self-government of free subjects. In these years, Foucault shifted his attention to the theme of 'government', which is a modality of power exercised neither as command nor discipline, but one that 'conducts', 'guides', or 'directs'. He set out to study the history of government and how it relates to human beings not simply as subjects of right, but as living beings. Foucault thus opened his 1979–1980 lectures, *On the Government of the Living*, saying that he studied government 'in the broad sense, and old sense moreover, of mechanisms and procedures intended to conduct men, to direct their conduct, to conduct their conduct' (GL: 12). In *Security, Territory, Population* (STP), lectures delivered in 1977–1978, he gave attention to the meaning that the direction of 'souls' took in the Christian pastorate from the thirteenth to the sixteenth century, but also in the political government of the seventeenth and eighteenth centuries of men and women now understood as 'population'.

The theme of government also becomes central in Foucault's 1979 lectures, *The Birth of Biopolitics* (BP), where he analyses German liberalism and North American neoliberalism. There, Foucault also finds a mode of governance which is neither juridical nor disciplinary, but one which acts on 'the environment' in which subjects make their choices (BP: 271). Instead of the 'war-model' which Foucault had used to analyse the social struggles around penal law, discipline, and psychiatry, his late 1970s lectures introduce a notion of power which is not at all warlike, namely governance.

In broad strokes that sacrifice the complexities of Foucault's analysis, his work from the 1970s travels between two different forms of subjectifying power. First one encounters a juridical and disciplinary power propelled by social strategies of domination, whereas at the end of 1970s we find a notion of governance that takes the freedom of the governed as its precondition. Schematically, Foucault shifts from 'the internal subjugation' of disciplinary power to a neoliberal governance that dispenses with anthropological claims (as in *homo criminalis*) and introduces a 'flat' subject (as in *homo œconomicus*). I suggest that the implication of Foucault's concept of governance, which henceforth came to occupy the centre of his work, was that the link between subjectivation and state formation dissolved in his analysis, which also meant that the state's role in reproducing capitalism receded into the background of Foucauldian scholarship.

This chapter falls into four main sections. The first section considers Foucault's thesis that the modern state submits individuals to a 'matrix' of power at once judicial and pastoral, which he suggested in his influential essay 'The Subject and Power' (SP). The next section makes a series of connections to Althusser's text on ideological state apparatuses, demonstrating how Althusser's foundational text prefigures key themes in Foucault's work from the early 1970s—how the modern welfare state submits individuals to a combination of juridico-disciplinary and pastoral power. This section also points out similarities and differences between Althusser and Foucault. The third section traces Foucault's two trajectories in the 1970s: first, what I call the juridico-disciplinary trajectory, Foucault's genealogy of how the state became an agent of penality and discipline, and second, what I term the pastoral-governmental trajectory, his genealogy of government and pastoral power. Finally, the fourth section discusses how the link between subjectivation and the industrial capitalist state, central to Foucault's early 1970s work, largely disappeared from his focus in the 1980s as well as from most subsequent Foucauldian scholarship. In the concluding section, I return to Foucault's

156 Foucault's Technologies

'matrix' of individualizing and totalizing power, connecting it to today's techno-capitalistic technology. Specifically, I suggest applying this matrix to the recent rise of algorithmic decision-making and predictive profiling.

State power and subjectivation

The link between subjectivation and state formation reached an emblematic formulation in Foucault's most cited essay, 'The Subject and Power' (SP), published in 1982. The essay is important for our present discussion, because it merges the two main trajectories of Foucault's research in the 1970s: his genealogies of legal-disciplinary power on the one hand, and his studies of pastoral power and governance on the other. 'The Subject and Power' is a condensation, I suggest, of these two main trajectories, based on which Foucault makes his claim that the modern state combines two 'poles' of power—one 'totalizing', i.e. legal, administrative, and statistical, and the other 'individualizing', i.e. centred on guiding each individual's consciousness. Conceptualizing the state's twofold powers vis-à-vis the citizen brought Foucault close to his former teacher Louis Althusser's seminal thesis on 'the ideological state apparatuses' (ISA), which theorized the state's function in reproducing subjects who practise the ruling ideology. The following sections connect Foucault's analysis of state power to Althusser's thesis, demonstrating certain connections between Althusser's model of the ideological state apparatuses and Foucault's diagnosis of the welfare state as a 'matrix' of individualizing and totalizing power. Apart from the resonance between Foucault's two poles and Althusser's twin state apparatuses, one of the most interesting themes that connects Foucault and Althusser is the assumption of freedom in subjectivation. This theme resonates in Foucault's analysis of pastoral power and governance and in Althusser's claim that subjects are 'interpellated qua individuality', which ensures that they freely practise ideology.

'The Subject and Power' first appeared in January 1982 as an afterword to Hubert Dreyfus and Paul Rabinow's (1982) seminal book *Michel Foucault: Beyond Structuralism and Hermeneutics* and again in the journal *Critical Inquiry* (SP, also published 1982). Paul Rabinow (2003: 52) suggests that Foucault drafted significant portions of the essay during the mid-1970s. Similarly, Arnold Davidson (2011: 39 n4) notes that 'there is compelling internal evidence that parts of [the essay] were written several years earlier', but without providing this evidence. As such, the exact period in which Foucault wrote 'The Subject and Power' remains somewhat unclear, but the

The Production of 'Normal' Citizens   **157**

essay clearly summarizes key points from Foucault's work in the 1970s. It should thus not be surprising to hear echoes in the essay from the critical dialogues Foucault engaged in during the 1970s with his former teacher, Althusser. Indeed, throughout this decade Foucault's and Althusser's work displays both reciprocal conceptions and contradictory distinctions (Ryder, 2013; Balibar, 2014; Harcourt, 2015b). This dialogue centred on how to move beyond models of the state as repressive, how to reconceptualize ideology as integral to practice, and how to grasp subjectivation as not solely repressive but as working through individuals' voluntary submission to ideology.

'The Subject and Power' is probably best known for presenting Foucault's twofold concept of subjectivation, the form of power which turns individuals into subjects:

> There are two meanings of the word 'subject': subject to someone else by control and dependence; and tied to his own identity by a conscience or self-knowledge. Both meanings suggest a form of power which subjugates and makes subject to (SP: 781).

This definition emphasizes that subjectivation happens in social relations of dependency and control through which individuals come to submit to a particular truth about who they are. Thus subjected by others, the individuals will base their identity and self-interrogation upon the truth imposed on them, hence 'mastering' their own subjection. The power of subjectivation is not only exerted by experts or persons of authority (although the process is particularly visible in these cases); this power is inscribed in our everyday social relations where we categorize and tie each other to specific identities. Foucault wrote:

> This form of power applies itself to immediate everyday life which categorizes the individual, marks him by his own individuality, attaches him to his own identity, imposes a law of truth on him which he must recognize and which others have to recognize in him. It is a form of power which makes individuals subjects. (SP: 781)

It follows from Foucault's philosophical anti-humanism that his notion of subjectivation escapes reference to some 'human essence', which is constrained or suppressed in the process of subjectivation. Instead, subjectivation is what imbues the human subject with its 'essence', which both constrains *and* enables the subject to exert power in its own right. For Foucault, then, subjectivation defines a twofold process: the subordination to rules and the construction of a self-relationship. In practice, the two are

158 Foucault's Technologies

not opposed to each other but constitute two aspects of a single process of evolving self-identity. This is why Judith Butler notes that for Foucault, 'self-attachment is socially mediated', and hence: 'we will become attached to ourselves through mediating norms, norms which give us back a sense of who we are, norms which will cultivate our investment in ourselves' (Butler, 2002b: 17). Foucault's twofold conception recalls Althusser's (ISA) notion of 'interpellation', insofar as it identifies subjugation to power as the way one becomes a subject. Subjectivation identifies the contradiction between power as enabling (i.e. it *qualifies* the subject as a social actor), and power as *normalizing* (i.e. it subjugates the individual to the social order). Foucault points towards this fundamental ambivalence in the subject's constitution in submission to power, when saying that power 'attaches' the subject to its own identity. Similarly, Butler notes, 'subjects appear to require this self-attachment, this process by which one becomes attached to one's own subjecthood' (Butler, 2002b: 17), but she rightly observes that Foucault does not theorize further this deep ambiguity of subjectivation.

Foucault advanced these comments on subjectivation in the context of a broader argument, which was launched against what he felt were insufficient theoretical models for analysing state power. The dominant legal-constitutional theories with their concerns for legitimacy and the institutional models with their focus on delimitation of the state were both unsuited for capturing power as subjectivation (SP: 778). Foucault's essay can thus be seen as part of his provocations to conventional state theory, which rearticulates state power by emphasizing the subjectifying power of the state, which he also terms individualizing power. The modern state, argues Foucault, should not be conceived of as an agency that is uninterested in the subjectivity of citizens, 'ignoring what they are and even their very existence' (SP: 783). On the contrary, the state should be understood 'as a very sophisticated structure, in which individuals can be integrated, under one condition: that this individuality would be shaped in a new form and submitted to a set of very specific patterns' (SP: 783). The state has developed into an agent of subjectivation, suggests Foucault, because it has inherited a modality of power from the Christian tradition, which has intertwined with juridical and administrative power.

Specifically, it is the guidance of conscience, central to which is the production of individual truth in confession and self-examination, which has taken new modalities within modern welfare institutions. Foucault thus argues that the modern state has multiplied agencies that govern individuals in their individuality—'a new form of pastoral power'—including social work, medicine, psychiatry, and psychology (SP: 783). This portrayal of the

The Production of 'Normal' Citizens **159**

state as exerting not simply juridical and administrative power, but also individualizing power, was guided by what Foucault described as 'certain conceptual needs'. He added: 'We have to know the historical conditions which motivate our conceptualization' (SP: 778). The historical condition in question was a state that had developed around two poles: a *totalizing* pole constituted by population statistics and jurisprudence, and an *individualizing* pole constituted by techniques for the guidance of citizens' individual consciences.

Reconceptualizing the modern state was not merely Foucault's response to certain theoretical shortcomings, since he also referred to the recent emergence of everyday struggles against subjectivation. Taking as starting points contemporary struggles by groups who confront the totalizing and individualizing power in health, psychiatry, or education could serve as a catalyst for analysing power in the modern welfare state. In sum, instead of conceiving of the state as the centre of a power that is only and essentially juridical-punitive in its form, Foucault shifts the analytical coordinates by foregrounding the state's intrinsic involvement in the moulding of subjectivity.

Foucault's notion of the state's 'totalizing power' was prefigured in his studies from the early 1970s on how the strategy of moralization of the labouring classes got invested in the state's juridical and disciplinary institutions, which increasingly came to rely upon medical and sociological knowledge. On the other hand, Foucault's notion of the state's 'individualizing power' captures the analyses of government in the Christian tradition, or pastoral power, that he undertook in the late 1970s. More importantly, 'The Subject and Power' also displays how Foucault, at the end of the 1970s, made a shift in his thinking on subjectivation and power. Whereas the first part of the essay recapitulates his 1970s focus on the link between subjectivation and the state, this link disappears in the second part of Foucault's essay where he speaks of how to study power as governance, or 'conduct of conduct'. In effect, then, 'The Subject and Power' straddles two rather different notions of subjectivation that reflect Foucault's shift in emphasis from the early 1970s to the early 1980s. In the essay's first part, one finds a subject caught up between the individualizing/totalizing powers of the state. This subject is both the target of an intricate guidance of the soul and of juridico-administrative objectification. In the second part of the essay, Foucault shifts to consider governance: a form of power, which works as 'conduct of conduct'. The notion of governance echoes, I suggest, Foucault's analysis of neoliberalism, since governance avoids targeting individuals directly, intervening only in the environment in which free individuals make their rational, self-fashioning choices.

Althusser and Foucault on state power and subjectivation

Foucault's description of the state as an agent of subjectivation puts him in the close vicinity of Althusser's thesis in 'Ideology and Ideological State Apparatuses' from 1969 on the constitution of liberal-capitalist citizenship. In what follows, I will pursue several comparisons with Althusser's foundational text, thereby providing a deeper understanding of Foucault's analysis of the technologies of state power. My intention in comparing Althusser and Foucault is neither to demonstrate that Foucault's ideas were already pre-established by Althusser, hence creating the fiction of an 'Althusserian Foucault', nor to reduce Althusser to a predecessor, who prepared the ground for Foucault. Despite similarities, Althusser's concept of 'interpellation' is not equivalent to Foucault's 'subjectivation', just as 'apparatus' is not identical to '*dispositif*'. Nevertheless, a comparative reading can enrich our understanding of Foucault's thinking on technologies of state power for the benefit of the overall purpose of this book. Even if Foucault rarely refers to economic relations or to the capitalist order, his rendering of welfare institutions as involved in subjectivation brings him close to Althusser's (ISA) original thesis.

I here accept the claim that the differences between Althusser and Foucault are often exaggerated, since their works intersect in several ways (Montag, 1995; Ryder, 2013; Kelly, 2014). First of all, both men sought to extend the conventional model of the state's repressive power by including the productive power of cultural, educational, religious, and medical institutions. Second, we find in both Althusser's 'ideological state apparatuses' and in Foucault's 'individualizing' power of the welfare state a modality of power which operates by targeting the individual as subject. Interestingly, Althusser's thesis anticipates Foucault's notion of pastoral power, insofar as, we will see, Althusser compares the subjectifying voice of ideology with divine authority. Moreover, interpellation *qua individuality*, in Althusser's terms, entails that the person thus interpellated is addressed as a singular locus of free willpower. Third, the two thinkers both dissociate ideology or power/knowledge from any ideal or immaterial existence, 'the world of spirits', instead relocating ideology or power/knowledge into the material world. They also reject humanist notions of 'essence', insisting that the subject is produced by practices that must take centre stage when theorizing state power. Finally, an immanentist conception of ideology/power appears in both works, since Althusser and Foucault conceive of these forces not as ideational or abstract but solely as operative in institutions and social practices.

The Production of 'Normal' Citizens   **161**

Althusser taught Foucault at the École Normale Supérieure in 1948–1949, and they both engaged in discussions of Marxist theory around subjectivity, ideology, and the state. Andrew Ryder (2013: 136) notes that Foucault must have encountered the anti-humanist reading of Marx that Althusser undertook in those years. And Étienne Balibar (2014: xvi) observes that Althusser and Foucault both participated in the structuralist movement, whose essential goal was 'to conceptualize the constitution of the subject in place of "the constitutive subject" of the classic transcendental philosophies'. In accordance with their shared anti-humanism, the material production of the body took centre stage for both thinkers, while they excluded interiority and alienation from their frameworks. Balibar cautions against pitting Foucault univocally against Marxism, as his relationship to it evolved through a complex process in which Althusser was constantly present. Foucault's relationship with Althusser, Balibar explains, was 'at once personal, intellectual and institutional, [and] did not by itself determine this evolution, but certainly helped determine it from first to last' (Balibar, 2014: xi). In a seminal article, Warren Montag (1995) argues that Althusser and Foucault were united in their rejection of idealist notions of ideology, eliminating any essence from the subject in order to examine its purely material production. Montag (1995: 55–56) also notes that 'the most unforgivable question that Althusser and Foucault asked concerned the subject', because they both 'denied all that was distinctively human'. Comparing 'Ideology and Ideological State Apparatuses' and *Discipline and Punish*, Montag suggests that these works were not as opposed and external to each other as widely believed. From a historical distance, one can instead view Althusser and Foucault 'as reciprocal immanent causes, dynamic and inseparable' (Montag, 1995: 56), because in the French intellectual context of the 1960s and 1970s, they were questioning many of the same notions.

The best description of Foucault's relationship to Althusser is perhaps that of a constitutive negative dependency, with the qualification that Foucault did not simply struggle to *overcome* Althusser but often pursued Althusser's inventions as inspiration in his 1970s work. Bernard Harcourt (2015b) notes that Althusser's distinction between the repressive state apparatus and ideological state apparatuses served Foucault as a continuous theoretical contrast. Most importantly for our purposes, Althusser and Foucault shared the idea that subjectivation occurs when an individual freely submits to the prevailing ideology or power/knowledge, respectively. On Althusser's account, interpellation *qua individuality* happens when ideology 'hails' an individual as a singular locus of free will—a process that has affinities with Foucault's notion

162 Foucault's Technologies

of pastoral power. In this context, it is also important that Althusser, as we will see, models his theory of ideological interpellation on divine authority.

At the same time, it is well known that Foucault expressed scepticism of the term 'ideology' from early on in his career, and clearly his scepticism was often directed at Althusser's rendering of the term. Indeed, Montag (1995: 71) notes: 'It was as if Foucault followed with critical attention the successive definitions of ideology offered by Althusser and felt compelled to engage, often polemically, with them.' In particular, Foucault developed a conception of power in its dispersion and reversibility that clearly contrasted with Althusser's more delineated and centralized view of power. I believe, however, that Foucault's gesture of negation in relation to Althusser must be tempered by recognizing their significant parallels and points of intersection. I will do so by first examining Althusser's 'Ideology and Ideological State Apparatuses', supplemented with other key texts, and I will then proceed to Foucault's two trajectories from the 1970s. The following sections thus start from Althusser's seminal thesis, which is of lasting importance for theorizing subjectivation and the state's role in reproducing the capitalist economic order.

Althusser's twin apparatuses

The state's involvement in the shaping of citizens as subjects was central to Althusser's influential essay 'Ideology and Ideological State Apparatuses' (ISA). Althusser's essay has been greatly influential in social theory, and although Althusser's influence has diminished today, his original thesis remains highly suggestive (Jameson, 1981; Butler, 1997; Žižek, 1999). Althusser's signature concepts are still foundational for critical social theorizing on state power, ideology, and subjectivity, including 'ideological state apparatuses', 'ideological interpellation', and 'epistemological break'. Here, I will use Althusser's intervention into Marxist theory as a lucid starting point and dialogue partner in exploring Foucault's thinking on the state and its technologies of subjectivation. Althusser's essay (ISA) prefigures some of the key perspectives on state power which Foucault developed during the 1970s, a period in which Foucault frequently made comments directed at Althusser, or 'Freudo-Marxism' as he would often say.

The key premise for Althusser is that the reproduction of the capitalist economy requires the reproduction of a labour force that is not only adequately skilled but also voluntarily practises the ruling ideology: 'It is in the forms and under the forms of ideological subjection that provision is made

The Production of 'Normal' Citizens   **163**

for the reproduction of the skills of labour power' (ISA: 133). The state plays a crucial role of ensuring ideological subjugation by means of its twin apparatuses: the 'repressive state apparatus' operates through the use of force and sanctions, whereas 'ideological state apparatuses' operate by means of ideology. The repressive state apparatus comprises the bureaucracy, the courts, the prisons, the police, and the armed forces, while the ideological state apparatuses include schools, churches, as well as sports and cultural institutions, but also formally non-state actors such as family, political parties, trade unions, and the mass media (ISA: 142–143). It is particularly the role of the ideological state apparatuses in reproducing labour power in terms of subjectivity that Althusser wants to theorize.

Althusser begins his famous essay by invoking Marx's dictum that the basic requirement for the survival of any social formation is the reproduction of the conditions of production. Whereas Marxist theory has preoccupied itself immensely with the reproduction of the material means of production, it has neglected the other basic condition, the reproduction of labour power. The labour force must not only be reproduced in terms of its physical needs; it must also be diversely skilled to match the needs of the productive order at a given stage of its development, or 'according to the requirements of the socio-technical division of labour' (ISA: 131). However, apart from equipping the labour force with skills through education and training, another condition must be met: the reproduction of the worker's submission to 'the ruling ideology' (ISA: 133). Central for Althusser, therefore, is not the reproduction of labour power as commodity but *the reproduction of subjectivation*, that is, the formation of subjects that are immersed in and freely practise ideology.

After setting these basic premises regarding the reproduction of the social order, Althusser proceeds to the notion of the state in the classic Marxist tradition. He specifically refers to writings of Marx and Lenin, which essentially conceived of the state as a repressive apparatus. There, the state figures as a 'machine of repression', which has enabled 'the bourgeoisie and its allies' to dominate the working class. Viewing the state as an agency of constraint, this literature foregrounds the legal system, the police, and the army (ISA: 136–137). As the major vehicle of domination, the state becomes the centre around which class struggle evolves, which Althusser specifies as struggles for 'the possession, i.e. the seizure and conservation of State power by a certain class or by an alliance between classes or class fractions' (ISA: 140). From this premise follows the distinction between, on the one hand, 'state power' defined as the seizure and use of the state apparatus by a particular class and, on the other, 'state apparatus' defined as a set of material institutions. Acquiring control over the state apparatus is the central objective of class struggle

164 Foucault's Technologies

since, asserts Althusser, 'the proletariat must seize state power in order to destroy the existing bourgeois state apparatus' (ISA: 141), replacing it with a proletarian one, and ultimately dissolving the state apparatus altogether.

Worth noting is that Foucault made explicit comments on the tendency in Marxist thought to privilege the state as the ultimate centre of class struggle. Foucault had extensively studied, in his 1972–1973 lecture series, *The Punitive Society*, the ongoing rivalries between groups over the control of the legislative and punitive 'state apparatus'. Occasionally, he would make sarcastic comments regarding Marxists' obsession with seizing state power, since this obsession neglected the fact that the state apparatus rests on power relations that are 'capillary' and runs much deeper than they imagined. Therefore, said Foucault, 'neither control nor destruction of the State apparatus may suffice to transform or get rid of a certain type of power, the one in which it functions' (PS: 259). For Marxists, Foucault declared in 1978, the state was 'absolutely essential as the target to be attacked and, as you well know, as the privileged position to be occupied' (STP: 109). Foucault used the term 'revolutionary eschatology' (STP: 356) to designate the Marxist promise that history is endowed with a logic that culminates in the final unification of state and society.

Althusser's conceptual interventions renewed classic Marxist theory on the state, exceeding the image of the state as a strictly repressive tool of the ruling class as well as the dual model of society as infrastructure and superstructure (ISA: 134). The emphasis on the state as essentially repressive disguises, as Althusser argued, the multiple non-repressive ways that it sustains the capitalist order. Furthermore, the two-tier model of society assumes a one-way economic determination, obscuring the state's constitutive function in the reproduction of capitalist relations of production. In response, Althusser collapsed the base/superstructure model by dislodging ideology entirely from its conventional tie to the superstructure. In doing so, he advanced a materialist notion of ideology as a system of representations inherent to and reproduced by practices and institutions. Althusser's objective was not so much to eliminate the theory of determination, as to revise it by expanding the base/superstructure model with a number of semi-autonomous agencies that operate in reciprocity. He gives the example of the army and the police which 'also function by ideology both to ensure their own cohesion and reproduction, and in the "values" they propound externally' (ISA: 145). The twin state apparatuses supplement and intersect with each other, since there are no purely repressive or purely ideological state apparatuses.

Althusser asserts, in what looks like an anticipation of Foucault's work on discipline and pastoral power, that while schools and churches function primarily by ideology, they also 'use suitable methods of punishment, expulsion, selection, etc., to "discipline" not only their shepherds, but also their flocks' (ISA: 145). Although the original French term used by Althusser is not discipline but *'dresser'*—i.e. dressage (training)—the terminology remains very close to Foucault, who often used 'dressage' to describe the disciplinary training and moulding of the body. Althusser's revision of the distinction between repression and ideology is helpfully elaborated by Montag (1995: 72), who argues that the dichotomy of force and consent is not pure or absolute. In fact, says Montag (1995: 69), 'we are forced to acknowledge the "consubstantiality" of force and persuasion, that there is no persuasion (or activity at all) of minds, except insofar as it is immanent in force that may be overwhelming or subtle'. Hence, replacing the external/internal binary (i.e. repression exerted on the body versus ideology imposed upon the mind), *practice* merges force and persuasion in the subject's constitution. Most importantly, Althusser's revision of ideology as integral to practice resonates broadly in Foucault's dictum that power is inseparable from practice as well as the subject's constitution.

Ideology is material!

Althusser's most important contribution to Marxist theory was perhaps his introduction of the concept of 'epistemological break' (FM). He took the concept from the history of science, notably Georges Canguilhem and Gaston Bachelard, rearticulating it to designate the moment at which a theory breaks free from its ideological entanglements and becomes truly scientific. Althusser applied this idea of an epistemological break to Marx's authorship, arguing that a discontinuity separated the young from the mature Marx, with a number of theoretical concepts used by the young Marx disappearing after 1845, including human essence, alienation, and the continuity of history (Althusser and Balibar, 1970: 107–108). Instead, the mature Marx introduced a decentred history based on class struggle, economic determinism, and an exclusion of the transhistorical subject. Several scholars argue that Foucault and Althusser shared an endorsement of Marx's 'epistemological mutation of history' in their respective commentaries on Marx (Foucault, 1977a: 13; Smart, 1983: 75; Ryder, 2013: 134).

'Ideology and Ideological State Apparatuses' displays the anti-humanism that Althusser found in the later Marx, just as it reflects Althusser's project of overcoming the central contradiction in Marx's thought: the combination of materialism and Hegelian idealism (Kelly, 2014: 86). Althusser asserts resolutely that ideology does not have an ideal or spiritual existence, but only a material existence. In other words, ideology is present only in and through a network of material institutions, social practices, and rituals (ISA: 166–169). One must reject the view that the ideas that make up ideology are mental constructs residing in the realm of consciousness, which then prompt bodily effects and actions. Althusser thus rejects the conventional notion of ideology *as ideality* in the dual sense of the term: both a system of ideas that possesses an immaterial existence *and* an ideal that persuades the minds of individuals who then act in subjugation to this system (Montag, 2013: 143). Pierre Macherey explains that Althusser escaped the notion of ideology as illusionary representations in consciousness, endowing it with certain dispositions. Indeed, Althusser dismissed 'the reference to ideology, which purports to place between people, their natural dispositions, and the historical forms within which these are exploited, an intermediate layer occupied by ideal representations located in the spirit' (Macherey, 2015: 22). This revision of ideology reflects the theoretical anti-humanism that both Althusser and Foucault invoked. For Althusser (1976: 205), the mature Marx's anti-humanism 'means a refusal to root the explanation of social formations and their history in a concept of man with theoretical pretensions, that is, a concept of man as an originating subject'. This view entails rejecting a human essence upon which ideology imposes itself, guiding and deluding the mind. 'What we have here', says Macherey (2015: 21) regarding Althusser's anti-humanism, 'is a form of subjection that creates a corresponding subject by recreating it *ab initio* and entirely, denying it any prior, pre-constituted reality preceding its imposition.' Therefore, the constitution of a subject with particular beliefs and (mis)perceptions is derived from practices, including the order of language.

This hollowing out of the human subject, which leaves it entirely open for ideological fabrication, was unacceptable for some readers. Edward P. Thompson (1978: 174) calls Althusser's portrayal of individuals' subjective experiences as ideological 'the ugliest thing that he has ever done'. Like Althusser, Foucault rejected the view of power as an order that descends from the mind into bodily actions. We find instead an insistence on the irreducible materiality of practices and the body, since, asserts Foucault (1980d: 97), 'we should try to grasp subjection in its material instance as a constitution of subjects'. Montag (1995: 55–56) notes: 'The most unforgivable question that Althusser and Foucault asked concerned the subject', since they both 'denied all that was distinctively human'. If the notion of ideology remains idealist, observes Montag, it will divert attention 'from what is at stake in any form of subjection: the body, the body that works and whose power

The Production of 'Normal' Citizens   **167**

produces value, the body that obeys' (Montag, 2013: 162). Indeed, Montag (1995) sees Althusser and Foucault as united in eliminating from the subject any interiority in order to foreground its material production.

Disciplinary power thus exerts itself on the human body, and Foucault highlights all the minor practices and techniques aimed at subjugating the body to norms. Akin to Althusser's rejection of the spirit/action dualism, Foucault avoids the split between mind and body, often foregrounding techniques, which target bodies, gestures, and behaviours. We should ask, he says, 'how things work at the level of on-going subjugation, at the level of those continuous and uninterrupted processes which subject our bodies, govern our gestures, dictate our behaviours, etc.' (Foucault, 1980d: 97). For Althusser, the citizen-subject is immanent to material practices governed by the rituals of ideological state apparatuses, including 'a mass in a small church, a funeral, a minor match at a sports' club, a school day, a political party meeting, etc.' (ISA: 168). Similarly foregrounding practices, Foucault describes the disciplinary strategy's 'materialization' in schools, factories, and prisons, where the body becomes the target of quotidian techniques and institutional procedures.

The divine voice of ideology

Even if the human subject does not harbour any essence that must be subjugated by ideology, Althusser must still explain why we voluntarily submit to ideology. How, in other words, does ideology succeed in its fundamental operation of transforming individuals into freely self-subjugating subjects? Althusser's answer is 'interpellation', in which a subject is constituted by being addressed by the voice of ideology. The example of the policeman's call on the street: 'Hey, you there!', and one's subsequent 180-degree turn: 'Me?', illustrates how the anonymous voice of ideology interpellates, the policeman serving as the quintessential figure of state authority (ISA: 174). For Althusser, interpellation is the procedure of 'hailing', or recruiting us to the internal mechanisms of ideology, whereby ideology is encoded on the body. As a dual process of identification, interpellation ensures that one can give an account of oneself and that one becomes accountable to others (akin to Foucault's concept of subjectivation). The example of the policeman indicates, first, that we apparently identify with the premise of the interpellation, namely that we *are already* the subject being addressed, and, second, that we are predisposed to accept the accusation that we have violated the law or ideology. Althusser explains the first premise, that we are always-already

168 Foucault's Technologies

interpellated by ideology, even before birth, by invoking Freudian psycho-analysis: 'Before its birth, the child is therefore always-already a subject, appointed as a subject in and by the specific familial ideological configuration in which it is "expected" once it has been conceived', since it is in the family structure that 'the subject to-be will have to "find" "its" place, i.e. "become" the sexual subject (boy or girl) which it already is in advance' (ISA: 176). Althusser briefly recaptures Freud's theory of the unconscious as explanation for the child's 'pre-appointment' to ideology, which he discussed in an earlier essay on Freud and Lacan (Althusser, 1969b). On this account, the child is born into a world already saturated by ideology, mirroring itself in it while striving to form a coherent identity. Althusser (1969b: 60–61) writes: 'Lacan demonstrates the effectiveness of the Order, the Law, that has been lying in wait for each infant born since before his birth, and seizes him before his first cry, assigning to him his place and rôle, and hence his fixed destination.'

The theme of consciousness as the target of ideological interpellation remains somewhat underdeveloped in Althusser's thesis. Butler (1997) notes that Althusser's use of the term consciousness has received scant attention, although the notion is crucial for the compelling force of ideology. Leaving aside Althusser's (1969b) earlier essay on the unconscious in Freud and Lacan, Butler turns to Nietzsche's diagnosis of modern conscience as marked by self-negation. She then combines this diagnosis with Althusser's model of religious authority, since 'the doctrine of interpellation appears to presuppose an a priori and unelaborated doctrine of conscience, a turning back upon oneself' (Butler, 1997: 109). In Nietzsche's *On the Genealogy of Morality* (GM), we recall, modern man is plagued by constant self-negation caused by our unsatisfiable Good figure, providing the basis for bad conscience and guilt, which Nietzsche also defines as anger directed against the self or 'man's sickness of himself' (GM: 57). In Butler's (1997: 129–130) reconstruction of Althusser, self-negation is integral to being human insofar as becoming a subject requires such perpetual self-negation, and hence without exerting it, one would cease to be a subject at all.

Butler aptly suggests that in Althusser's 'example of religion' (ISA: 176–178), religion is not merely an 'example' but functions as *the template* for how ideological interpellation works irrespective of context. Hence, for Althusser, the constitution of the subject in Christian sacraments illustrates the force of the divine voice: 'I address myself to you ... in order to tell you that God exists and that you are answerable to Him' (ISA: 177). Put differently, interpellation functions because the voice of ideology constitutes the subject just like the almighty power of divine authority. Butler (1997:

The Production of 'Normal' Citizens   169

110–111) observes that 'the divine power of naming structures the theory of interpellation that accounts for the ideological constitution of the subject'. Of course, the God figure is also an authority to whom one confesses and is acquitted of guilt. Therefore, argues Butler (1997: 113), 'the very possibility of subject formation depends upon a passionate pursuit of a recognition which, within the terms of the religious example, is inseparable from a condemnation'. Being constituted by the God-like voice of ideology, the subject lives under the constant presumption of being guilty, needing to repeatedly be acquitted of guilt. To become a citizen-subject, concludes Butler (1997: 118), 'is to have become an emblem of lawfulness, a citizen in good standing, but one for whom that status is tenuous'. Butler's development of ideological interpellation through the religious theme of guilt, which brings us to turn back upon ourselves, is highly suggestive. However, whereas Althusser does invoke religious authority, the Nietzschean diagnosis of modern self-negation is rather foreign to his thesis on interpellation. Instead, he mentions, in another essay, Nietzsche together with Marx and Freud as 'the unexpected children' (Althusser, 1969b: 51) of the nineteenth century who revealed the human subject's decentredness.

Most importantly, the fact that Althusser and Foucault both invoke Christianity to explicate the mechanism of subjectivation should not lead us to neglect the divergence of their approaches. For Althusser, the divine voice of ideology serves as a purely theoretical model in his universal conception of ideology. By contrast, Foucault only arrives at his notion of pastoral power as the key technology of subjectivation in Western culture after genealogical explorations of the Christian tradition. Again, the difference between the philosopher and the genealogist comes to the fore.

The paradox of interpellation

There is a final important dimension in Althusser's thesis on ideology, namely the theme of freedom in interpellation. Althusser's insistence that ideology 'interpellates the individual as subject' entails that the individual is addressed as a locus of freedom, that is, an agent who chooses to freely submit to ideology. The demand to submit freely and entirely is paradoxical, notes Althusser, since it reveals the double meaning of the word subject: on the one hand 'a free subjectivity, author of and responsible for its actions', and on the other 'a subjected being, who submits to a higher authority, and is therefore stripped of all freedom except that of freely accepting his submission' (ISA: 182). Jacques Bidet suggests that Althusser's key contribution to theorizing

170 Foucault's Technologies

ideology was to coin this paradox of interpellation, the demand to freely submit to one's unfreedom. According to Bidet, Althusser 'set the stage for the paradox of a subject constituted as such through the injunction to conform to a law. A subject is only a subject at the cost of its voluntary submission' (Bidet, 2015: 63).

The idea that there is no ideology except if individuals practise it freely and continually, in voluntary servitude of ideology, is echoed in Althusser's rendering of the relationship between God and man: 'God needs men: the great Subject needs subjects' (ISA: 179). Continuing his religious analogy, Althusser suggests that ideology addresses the individual as free, just as God created man with a free will to choose to do either good or evil: 'interpellating the individual as subject means that he is free to obey or disobey the appeal, i.e. God's commandments' (ISA: 178). And just like the divine voice calls individuals by their names, hence recognizing them as subjects with a personal identity, ideology interpellates individuals as unique and irreplaceable. Indeed, ideology 'interpellates concrete individuals as concrete subjects' (ISA: 173). Althusser's assumption that freedom and individuality constitute ideology's medium of interpellation resonates in Foucault's (SP) claims that pastoral power is 'individualizing' and that liberal governance takes the subject's irreducible freedom as its premise. In brief, if ideology does not simply work through repression, but asserts the singularity of the individual, encouraging us to freely constitute ourselves, then Althusser is a theoretical ally of Foucault's dictum regarding power's production of subjectivity.

The philosopher versus the genealogist

Whereas significant approximations can thus be identified between Althusser's thesis and Foucault's analysis of state power, it is well known that Foucault was critical of Marxism's key doctrines, and that he held Marx in higher esteem than the theoretical variety of Marxism, which he often called 'Freudo-Marxism', typecasting contemporary Marxists such as Althusser and his collaborators. We must also recall that training in Marxism was next to mandatory for the generation of French academics to which Foucault belonged, and that Althusser was the key figure in Marxist theorizing at the time. Hence, Alan Sheridan (1980: 201) observes: 'For a whole generation of France's most gifted teachers, a knowledge of Marxism has been an indispensable part of their intellectual equipment. Althusser has done for Marxism what Lacan did for psychoanalysis at about the same time in the same place.' In this light, it is not surprising that Foucault found it necessary to

The Production of 'Normal' Citizens   **171**

continually address Althusser when discussing state power and technologies of subjectivation.

In terms of their differences, the most fundamental one lies in Althusser's and Foucault's respective pursuits as philosopher versus genealogist. While it is true, as Montag (1995) observes, that Althusser and Foucault both strived to make conceptual innovations in the same historical conjuncture, those innovations took place from within divergent intellectual and political projects. Perhaps Althusser is best described as *the philosopher* of Marxism who strived to rescue Marxist thought from the misguided bourgeois paths of humanism and economism. His major revision of Marxist theory took place essentially in philosophical terms with the goal of establishing its scientific validity. Althusser was therefore, as Sheridan (1980: 200) stresses, a philosopher dedicated strictly to the area of Marxist theory; he was not a historian or an economist. Althusser came to believe that philosophy is 'class struggle in the field of theory' (Althusser, 1976: 37), and it is only by producing results within itself, as it were, that philosophy can impact the interaction between science and politics. In contrast to Foucault's genealogical work, actual historical and social events are largely absent from Althusser's writings. To be sure, theoretical model-building was never Foucault's concern. Hence, Smart (1983: 74) aptly notes that 'in contrast to the excesses of Althusserian Marxism, theory is secondary to detailed historical analysis for Foucault'. Although Althusser and Foucault shared a number of similar concerns, central to which, as emphasized above, was power's grip on a subject devoid of human essence, their approaches and idioms diverged.

Althusser thus insisted on consistently using Marxist vocabulary, even if he was striving to fundamentally revise the very meaning of Marxism's key terms. Foucault, on the contrary, took pains to avoid employing Marxist idioms altogether, and he objected to notions like ideology, alienation, and consciousness (Foucault, 1980c: 58). To some extent, these contrasts can be understood in terms of Althusser's and Foucault's different trajectories in regard to the French Communist Party (PCF). Althusser joined the PCF in 1948 and Foucault followed in 1950. However, whereas Foucault left the PCF in 1952 after a mostly inactive membership, Althusser loyally stayed in the party even 'when many of his close disciples had become dissidents and demanded that he join them, before going on to accuse him of revisionism and treason' (Balibar, 2014: xi). Althusser's theoretical revisions often sat uneasily with the party doctrine, and his preservation of terms like ideology, consciousness, and base/superstructure can be seen as accommodations to orthodox Marxist thought. However, as Montag suggests, notions like consciousness and ideology do not actually survive Althusser's revisionism, since

172   Foucault's Technologies

he only preserves the language of interiority 'in order more effectively to sub-vert it' (Montag, 1995: 66). Having freed himself from the PCF, Foucault stayed clear of theoretical Marxism, and he made thinly veiled criticisms of the PCF, describing 'the political party' as 'totalizing', with its hierarchies, dogmatism, and monopolization of knowledge (SMD: 9–12).

We have noted that Althusser's reconception of ideology as immanent to practices is comparable to Foucault's emphasis on the body's embeddedness in power relations. Under the surface, however, Althusser's thesis depends on certain premises that set limits to the comparison. Even if ideology is material, given to individuals in everyday rituals and institutional practices, it remains largely unacknowledged as an entrenched consensus that obscures the reality of class antagonism. For Althusser, ideology defines individuals' 'imaginary relation' to their real conditions of existence. In *For Marx*, he writes: 'In ideology men do indeed express, not the relation between them and their condition of existence, but the way they live the relation between them and their conditions of existence: this presupposes both a real rela-tion and an "imaginary", "lived" relation' (FM: 233). Notably, Althusser's definition of ideology revises the classic Marxist distinction between delusive representations and real social antagonisms. Ideology, understood as indi-viduals' imaginary relation to their conditions of existence, brings about a misrecognition of these conditions, which, 'in the last resort', are constituted by the relations of production and the class relations derived from them (ISA: 183). It is debatable whether Althusser can successfully both dissolve the base/superstructure by giving ideas a material existence *and* maintain that the economic relations are, to a degree, fundamental (FM: 112–113). Fou-cault might have launched another jab at Althusser when he declared that power relations 'do not merely constitute the "terminal" of more fundamen-tal mechanisms' (SP: 782). Mark Kelly (2014: 90) notes that, in contrast to Althusser, Foucault 'is not concerned to make pronouncements about onto-logical priority', and he further suggests that a reason for this is that Foucault 'is not doing philosophy in its strict sense'. Furthermore, given Foucault's refusal of reductive and universal historical schemes, he was unable to accept a general model of social transformation.

For Althusser, ideology is an essential component of all human societies, and it is therefore tempting to assign to him a universal notion of ideology. However, his concept of ideology is at the same time universal and parti-cular, or, in Althusser's own terms, ideology is both 'eternal' and 'historically specific'. Hence, Althusser defines ideology as 'an organic part of every social totality', and as such it is 'not an aberration or contingent excrescence of his-tory [but] a structure essential to the historical life of society' (FM: 232–233).

The Production of 'Normal' Citizens   **173**

In any society, we acquire our identities by perceiving ourselves mirrored in the ruling ideology. Ideology is thus 'eternal', since, posits Althusser, individuals inevitably rely on ideology for their imaginary misrecognition of themselves as subjects. Althusser finds an immanent relation between ideology as 'eternal' and Freud's dictum that 'the unconscious is eternal'. The Oedipus complex, he writes, is 'imposed by the Law of Culture on every involuntary, conscripted candidate to humanity' (Althusser, 1969b: 63). Hence, before individuals engages in social-historical practice they already have a subconscious attachment to ideology. This 'double register' of Althusser's concept of ideology, observes Bidet, suggests a subject that is both 'generic' and produced in history:

> The anthropological, 'generic' register is indeed a question of the subject as such and its constitution in the social language game. The 'specific' register, that of so-called capitalist social relations, is also a question of a subject defined historically, emerging in the conditions of a particular social structure. (Bidet, 2015: 64)

Finally, there is Althusser's distinction between science and ideology, which Foucault found indefensible. Central to Althusser's theoretical project was his assumption that rigorous science possesses an 'autonomous' rationality, which holds the potential of drawing the dividing line between science and ideology. If ideology is a prevailing consensus which consistently blocks new ideas, then Marxist theory must break with this consensus, offering a knowledge whose adequacy can only, however, be tested in class struggle (FM: 239). In a defence of Althusser's scientificity, Paul Resch (1992: 246) suggests that Foucault's genealogies are marked by their opposition to Althusserian concepts, on which Foucault nevertheless displays his dependence. For Resch, Foucault owes his most groundbreaking inventions to Althusser, including the idea of the fabricated subject, but Foucault undermines the scientific and critical value of these innovations because of his anti-scientific reliance on Nietzsche's vitalism: 'all the positive attributes of genealogy derive from the recognition of subjectivity as a social production, an insight taken over completely from Althusser and then impregnated with a Nietzschean-Deleuzean vitalism' (Resch, 1992: 243). In sum, on Resch's account, Foucault's 'postmodernist' interventions are marked by their negative dependency on Althusser's modernist position.

For Foucault, however, Marxism could not become the science that Althusser assumed, since an autonomous scientific practice authorized by the Leninist party was an impossibility (Ryder, 2013: 153). Marxist theorizing was, Foucault believed, deeply involved in the social and political struggles of

174   Foucault's Technologies

its own time in the 1960s and 1970s. The claim to be truly scientific inscribed itself in a field of power relations, in particular around the PCF and their quest for a knowledge which was recognizable in the university institutions (Foucault, 1980a: 110). Althusser's increasing complication of the distinction between science and ideology (Goldstein, 1994) did not silence Foucault, who claimed that the 'university Marxism' was extra-scientific. Instead of striving to elevate Marxist theory by endowing it with the superiority of scientificity, Foucault insisted on allowing the real historical content of struggles to reverberate through his writing. This insistence is reflected in 'The Subject and Power', where Foucault states his preference for a non-substantial approach to power: 'I would say that to begin the analysis with a "how" is to suggest that power as such does not exist' (SP: 785). The little question, 'how is power exercised', he notes, is 'flat and empirical', but will arouse distrust in people who view power as a repressive substance.

Foucault had indeed followed the 'flat and empirical' question, in contradiction to Althusser's theoretical model, when exploring in great detail his juridico-disciplinary trajectory in the early 1970s. Whereas Althusser assigned the function of penality strictly to the repressive state apparatus, Foucault traced the development of law and punishment in a moving field of struggle between social groups. Discussing Foucault's genealogy of penality, Harcourt (2015b: 272) notes that Althusser's twin apparatuses 'do not offer Foucault the possibility of thinking about penality or the prison outside of State repression'. For Harcourt, Foucault breaks with Althusser by introducing a mobile conception of power, one that, unlike Althusser's centralized, binary model of the state, eschews a pre-established division between repressive and productive power. It is noteworthy, then, that Althusser always puts the 'Repressive State Apparatus' in the singular and in capital letters, as if it were a unified and centralized agency. Decisively transcending Althusser's theoretical model, Foucault (especially PS) analyses how moralization ('the ideological') intersects with penality ('the repressive') in struggles between social groups.

Our examination of Althusser's thesis on ideological state apparatuses has indicated a series of both positive and negative intersections with Foucault's work. These intersections will be helpful for exploring Foucault's juridico-disciplinary trajectory of the 1970s. To repeat the key point: Althusser's thesis principally aimed at dissociating ideology from the realm of consciousness and ideas. From this perspective, Althusser indicated the key theme in the work that Foucault carried out in the early 1970s: analyses of tactics and techniques centred on the body. Althusser theorized, but never actually studied the practices and rituals that constitute the ideological state apparatuses, just

The Production of 'Normal' Citizens **175**

as he did not describe the actual class struggles assumed to occur in or around the state apparatuses. Foucault, however, set out to do exactly that in his early 1970s lectures, which include *Penal Theories and Institutions* from 1971 to 1972, *The Punitive Society* from 1972 to 1973, as well as *Truth and Juridical Forms* from 1973. Hence, the following sections will attend to the first of the two major genealogies mentioned at the outset of this chapter—the juridico-disciplinary trajectory that Foucault developed in the early 1970s, and which his 1972–1973 lecture series, *The Punitive Society* (PS), explores particularly vividly.

The juridico-disciplinary trajectory

Foucault's *The Punitive Society* lectures will serve as the key source for the following exploration of the juridico-disciplinary trajectory for several reasons. First of all, this work brings Foucault closer than any other to the link between techniques of subjectivation and the reproduction of the industrial capitalist state. He approaches this problem in ongoing dialogue with Marxist thought, drawing upon Marxist vocabulary while simultaneously dislodging his analysis from that vocabulary. As Harcourt (2015b: 278) notes: 'Due to this silent dialog with Thompson, as well as with Althusser, the 1973 lectures are far more "Marxist"-sounding than other of Foucault's writings.' Indeed, *The Punitive Society* is arguably Foucault's most *Marxist* work, even if his analyses often break with or contradict Marxist concepts like state apparatus, ideology, repression, class struggle, and economic determination. Another reason for focusing on this lecture series is that it has received less attention than either *Discipline and Punish* (DP), Foucault's most widely read text, or his influential 'governmentality lectures' from the late 1970s (STP; BP). *The Punitive Society* forms part of Foucault's genealogy of what he sometimes termed 'the disciplinary society', which is also a key theme in *Discipline and Punish* (DP), *Penal Theories and Institutions* (PTI), 'Truth and Juridical Forms' (TJ), and *Psychiatric Power* (PP). However, the relationship between the proliferation of disciplinary techniques and the rise of the capitalist economy remains largely unaddressed in these related works. *The Punitive Society* approaches the relationship head-on, offering rich historical findings, many of which readily speak to our present, as well as analytical frameworks ripe for rearticulation in our contemporary context.

As is often the case in Foucault's work, his genealogies indirectly display part of our present, as implied in the term 'history of the present'. During

176 Foucault's Technologies

the genealogy presented in *The Punitive Society*, beginning in the seventeenth century, events appear that are strangely familiar to the present eye. We learn how the penal system is 'made by some for others' (PS: 24), meaning that laws and punishments are invented by the propertied groups with the aim of protecting production and wealth, tying the labourers to a regulated life of work, saving, and consumption. Indeed, the harshness applied to force the labouring classes into wage-labour is striking in Foucault's lectures. A key term used to denounce those individuals that refuse to take up their place in the nascent economic order is 'the social enemy'. The term not only designates individuals who break the law, but also names those who violate good morality by their idleness, drunkenness, and prodigality, all of which means that they 'steal' their own labour power and hence undermine the production process. Indeed, workers' refusal of work comes to be viewed as more dangerous to society than property-centred crimes like theft of goods.

The control of time becomes the crucial technique in the strategy for moralizing workers and linking them intricately to the capitalist order. We witness the invention of multiple techniques for detailed regulation of workers' time in the production line (stopwatch), the working week (contract), between workers and employers (workers' record book), and finally retirement (savings banks). At the end of Foucault's lectures, the reader is faced with the contours of a modern 'disciplinary society'. This is not so much a society in which one class exerts control over another through the penal system as one in which multiple agents apply 'para-penal mechanisms' to ensure that individuals fulfil their roles in the capitalist economic order.

Civil war as framework

At the outset, Foucault declares that he wants to study penal practices as tactical moves in the perpetual conflicts inherent to the social body (PS: 12–14). The framework he wishes to employ is 'civil war', which he gives a broader meaning, encompassing diverse forms of struggle between groups, conflicts over resources, and political protests. First, however, Foucault needs to clear the field of then-dominant frameworks, namely social contract theory, sociological functionalism, and Marxist critique. Social struggle should be viewed in its own specificity irreducible to judicial models, moral principles, or ideological frameworks. Foucault's aim to forge a research question of high generality, dislodged from prevailing theories, is expressed in this introductory statement:

> What will be in the forefront in this analysis are the forms of struggle between
> political power, as it is exercised in a society, and those—individuals or groups—
> who seek to escape this power, who challenge it locally or globally, who contravene
> its order or regulations. (PS: 12)

Against social contract theory (Hobbes and Rousseau), Foucault wants to reinsert perpetual struggle into societies where the monopoly of violence has supposedly been achieved by political sovereignty, and war has been expelled. Foucault further asserts that the process of civil war is constitutive for the formation of collectivities around kinship, religion, ethnicity, or class. Reversing Clausewitz's thesis, Foucault declares that 'politics is the continuation of civil war' (PS: 32), hence rendering civil war fundamental to the execution of political and bureaucratic power, including policymaking and legislative processes.

The civil war framework also displaces sociological functionalism of the Durkheimian variety. In this tradition, crimes as well as the instruments for their repression constitute social integrative mechanisms, which for Foucault entails an absolute neglect of power struggles around the very definition of offences and what is offended against. Hence, the idea that society secures its own cohesion by placing necessary constraints on its members conceals the immanent power at play in the social body, including penal tactics.

Finally, civil war substitutes Marxist theory in key aspects. Economism is replaced by an emphasis on working-class moralization, 'class struggle' is replaced by the open-ended category of 'civil war', ideology and hidden interests are replaced by 'cynical' tactics that are immediately visible, and the state is replaced as the privileged centre by mobile confrontations and alliances that cut across the social body.

Threats to the capitalist order

Foucault takes a technological emphasis, as he describes how new techniques of surveillance, control, and punishment emerged in the eighteenth and early nineteenth centuries in conjunction with the growth of capitalist production. In this process, a central concern of the bourgeoisie became how to protect their wealth at a time when goods as well as the productive apparatus itself were exposed to new threats. The capitalist mode of production was developing at a greater scale, the number of wage earners was multiplying, and population movements disrupted old enclosures such as market towns, parishes, and local magistrates. From these developments, two major

178 Foucault's Technologies

threats to capitalist production ensued which Foucault terms 'depredation' and 'dissipation'. In brief, depredation defined property-centred threats like plundering of goods and machine-breaking, while dissipation designated diverse kinds of working-class immorality which undermined wage-labour. The propertied groups waged war against both these enemies.

In terms of depredation, capital became exposed to a number of risks that were less controllable than previously since, explains Foucault, 'capital is exposed not only to armed robbery and plunder, as before, but to daily depredation by those who live on it, alongside it' (PS: 104). In the early nineteenth century, this fear intensified as more capital was invested in accessible materials like stocks, machines, and moveable commodities, and consequently the wage earner, i.e. 'the worker, stripped of all property', came into contact with this capital. Foucault says: 'The fear is connected to this physical presence of the worker's body, of his desire, on the body of wealth itself', and he adds, 'this fear is not a fantasy' (PS: 172). This was a real and growing fear of merchants and property owners in the industrializing centres of Europe.

The other threat to early capitalism, dissipation, did not attack capital or wealth directly. Instead, it entailed undermining the workers' own labour power through mismanagement of time and wasting of the body (PS: 191–192). Foucault recovers in the archive three forms of dissipation: intemperance in relation to one's body, improvidence in relation to one's time, and disorderly mobility in relation to family and work. The places of dissipation included festivity where workers wasted their wages, and the lottery where they sought an earning without working. Indeed, the lottery represented 'the sporadic time and luck ... which are opposed to earning money in the rational system of economy, that is to say by continuous work rewarded by an amount fixed in advance' (PS: 192). Although dissipation appeared milder and more trivial, it was considered more dangerous than depredation since the threat to industrial labour involved in dissipation was almost impossible to control and prohibit. The refusal of labour, says Foucault, is 'an illegalism that is not a breach of the law, but a way of stealing the condition of profit' (PS: 170).

How could one suppress idleness, absenteeism, gambling, and debauchery? These irregularities, Foucault notes, 'are not infractions and, given the freedom of the labor market necessary to this bourgeois economy, it is impossible to organize its juridical system so that they can all be constituted as infractions' (PS: 191). Dissipation posed two major challenges in terms of its suppression: first, it took spontaneous and mobile collective forms that did not require any organization, and second, it was not easily prohibitable since it constituted 'moral faults'—i.e. habits and manners rooted in psychological

The Production of 'Normal' Citizens **179**

propensities. Whereas depredation receded during the nineteenth century, dissipation would continue not only to confront bourgeois wealth but the capitalist order itself.

Foucault's analysis of early forms of resistance to capitalist wage-labour approximates Marxist key problematics. He retains a focus on class, exploitation, and the means of production, but he does not give any of them a privileged status. Foucault's strategy of analysis is captured well by Mark Kelly (2014: 86): 'he is effectively as close as one can be to being a Marxist without being a Marxist'. However, Foucault extends the Marxist concern with threats to property by focusing on workers' moral failures in contributing to capitalist production. As Mariana Valverde notes, 'Property-centred "illegalisms" were of course bread and butter for the Marxist historians of Foucault's time', whereas the challenge of dissipation to 'the ideal of the sober family-based working class, was not treated seriously or positively by mainstream Marxism' (Valverde, 2017: 43). The need to target the moral failures of the working class was voiced by commercial groups like merchants' and bankers' guilds and journeymen's associations promoting a 're-moralization' from below (PS: 105–106). Foucault describes such non-state agents as pressure groups and innovators of disciplinary and moralizing techniques, but he does not assign to them a uniform ideology. Yet, as Stuart Elden (2015: 155) correctly notes, there is a strong sense of whose interests and what purposes discipline and incarceration serve.

Importantly, Foucault does not perform a reading of the discourse on working-class morality that reveals the unsaid in the said. Explaining how he analyses the bourgeoisie's strategies for moralizing the workers, Foucault distances himself from Marxist theory of ideology. In a thinly veiled contrast to Althusser's notion of 'symptomatic reading' that fills out the empty spots in a text (Althusser and Balibar, 1970), Foucault insists on focusing the analysis not on 'the unsaid' but on what was actually said, reiterating his theoretical emphasis on treating discourse in its 'positivity' (AK: 25). One should, argues Foucault, view strategies as inseparable from discourse, analysing the discourse 'not through what it does not say, but at the level of the operation carried out through it, that is to say in its strategic function' (PS: 166). Against Freudo-Marxism, Foucault highlights 'the function of discourses in strategies and struggles' (PS: 165), which does not involve discovering the hidden interests or what was being repressed. The principle that 'everything is said' appears as both a specific historical point and a general analytical premise that Foucault repeats on later occasions (see Chapter 5).

Summing up his approach to penal tactics versus Marxism, Foucault says: 'I would like to approach these tactics as analyzers of power relations, and

180 Foucault's Technologies

not as revealers of an ideology.' This statement cautions against such abstract conceptualization as Althusser's 'state ideology' and insists on empirically describing how power and knowledge operate in specific processes. Whereas Althusser referred punishment to 'the Repressive State Apparatus' in which practices are invested with ideology, Foucault wants to analyse 'penal tactics' to reveal the play of shifting power relations in the social body. The notion of permanent civil war provides such an immanentist view of social struggle and the role of penality herein.

Foucault's 'Nietzscheo-Marxism'

The most important weapon in the bourgeoisie's remoralization strategy was the rearticulation of workers' dissipation in the register of moral and legal culpability: immoral acts demanded penance, delinquency required correction, and illegalities deserved punishment. In the second half of the eighteenth century, observes Foucault (PS: 45), there appears for the first time an analysis of delinquency conducted in relation to the mechanisms of production. The delinquents in question included wanderers and dubious elements such as vagabonds and men refusing to marry. Although marginalized, these individuals were viewed as a threat to the capitalist order of production and hence as enemies of society. Foucault declares: 'it is the delinquent's position in relation to production that defines him as a public enemy' (PS: 45). However, at the end of the eighteenth century, the objective and target of the commercial groups changed. They now campaigned for new laws that would extend the reach of judicial power into the level of moral failings, and at the same time the target was expanded significantly, since 'those designated as having to be the object of moral control are the "lower classes" as such' (PS: 106). The conversion in the late eighteenth century and early nineteenth century of dissipation, that is, workers' undermining of their own bodies (today termed 'human capital'), into moral failures and objects of penality is a crucial moment in *The Punitive Society*. It could also be called a Nietzschean moment, insofar as one group's struggle for dominance of another occurs by re-interpreting and tactically redirecting legal as well as moral categories.

In general, Foucault's genealogy dissolves metaphysical or theoretical foundations of knowledge, since the theoretical categories that define diverse forms of 'deviance' in psychiatry, the justice system, and social work are inseparable from power relations. An inspiration from Nietzsche's *On the Genealogy of Morality* is probably noticeable here, in that Nietzsche called for both our knowledge and moral categories to be viewed in terms of the difference between forces. In fact, Foucault invokes Nietzsche in a discussion of knowledge in the manuscript for the 1971–1972 lecture course, *Penal*

Theories and Institutions, delivered the year before *Punitive Society*. 'The Nietzschean analysis', he says, 'seeks [behind knowledge (*connaissance*)] something altogether different from knowledge. Something altogether different in relation to which the knowing subject and knowledge itself are effects' (PTI: 213). The relationship between knowledge and power, Foucault reminds us, is one of mutual reinforcement in which the capacity for exerting power and the corpus of knowledge is increased incessantly, resulting in 'power/knowledge': 'it is the bringing into play of forms of power that creates knowledge (*savoir*), which in turn enhances power' (PTI: 213). In 'Course Context' for *Penal Theories and Institutions*, Francois Ewald and Bernhard Harcourt (2019) describe Foucault's genealogy as an 'improbable marriage' between Marx and Nietzsche. The resultant 'Nietzscheo-Marxism' was an antidote to the prevailing 'Freudo-Marxism' of the time in which Althusser was the central figure.

Foucault's genealogy of penality and discipline retains class struggle, but frees the field of struggle from the Marxist binary model of contradiction and the historical teleology of the revolution. The Nietzschean inspiration gives to genealogy an insistence on the historical irreducibility of social struggle, as Ewald and Harcourt explain:

> not only is the result of the history always precarious, the outcome in suspense, the victory uncertain and vulnerable, but what matters is not where this or that struggle, battle, or confrontation is to be situated in the general law of the revolution, it is rather to grasp precisely the irreducibility of what emerges on each occasion. (Ewald and Harcourt, 2019: 256)

Foucault uses a Nietzschean-inspired genealogy that Ewald and Harcourt term 'an art of the detail', which is opposed to official art. Foucauldian genealogy seeks to 'rediscover the contingency of the event. Everything could have happened differently, yet everything had to happen, could only happen thus' (Ewald and Harcourt, 2019: 256). Foucault's juridico-disciplinary trajectory indeed traces the linking of a series of chance events. It is a genealogy of how minor techniques for the protection of wealth and moralization of workers gradually coalesced into a disciplinary *dispositif*: a history of singular events, always at risk of being abducted by the official historiographies.

'The social enemy' and time control

Perhaps the key category Foucault recovers from the bicentennial battle for moralizing the labouring classes is 'the social enemy'. He connects the emergence of this category with a fundamental change occurring in

182   Foucault's Technologies

eighteenth-century discourse on crime and punishment: henceforth, crime is not so much an offence causing injury to another individual, but rather an act which harms society, since crime is now 'an action by which the individual breaks the social pact' (PS: 32). Whereas earlier notions of crime located the infraction and its compensation in the relationship between an offender and the victim, the criminal now emerges 'as an individual "estranged from society", irreducible to laws and general norms' (PS: 35). The recodification of the criminal as 'social enemy' constitutes, Foucault argues, the condition of possibility for new knowledge of crime as social deviance, including 'discourses and institutions like those organized under the name of the psychopathology of deviance' (PS: 35). Furthermore, because the criminal now offends against society, it follows that society itself should sanction the criminal. The social enemy functions, in Foucault's term, as a 'connector' (PS: 36) which allows the privileged to transfer the power to judge to society, represented by the court and its associated psychiatric and sociological expertise. Foucault reminds us that this is a history of the present, since this early sociologization of the criminal is an event 'whose effects currently dominate penal practice, the psychopathology of delinquency, and the sociology of the criminal' (PS: 36). The reconstruction of the criminal as a threat to society will hence be of crucial importance for the modern state's approach to crime as deviance in the twentieth century.

In the eighteenth and nineteenth centuries, individuals perpetrating vagabondage and idleness were considered the worst kinds of social enemy. Against commercial groups' quest for transforming workers into labour power, the vagabond figured as an emblematic instance of 'anti-production'. Refusing territorial fixation and enjoying idleness were so detrimental to the social order that vagabondage figured as 'the general matrix of crime that contains eminently all other forms of delinquency' (PS: 45). Foucault asks why vagabondage came to constitute a crime against society, or better, against the economy, suggesting that the vagabond attacks the industrial production in several ways: 'that of the number of workers, of the quantity of labor provided, and of the quantity of money returning to the land for its exploitation. The vagabond is therefore someone who disrupts production and not just a sterile consumer' (PS: 47). Given that the vagabond figured as the source of all vices, several attempts to outlaw him were made, and in the seventeenth century the right to hunt him was proposed, so 'one could kill anyone who basically refused to be settled' (PS: 51). The criminalization of the vagabond corresponds to the rise of early capitalism with its imperative of primitive accumulation, demanding that productive bodies be tied to the productive apparatus. Foucault asserts:

The Production of 'Normal' Citizens **183**

> In fact, from the moment society is defined as the system of relationships between
> individuals that makes production possible and permits its maximization, one has
> a criterion that makes it possible to designate the enemy of society: any person
> hostile or opposed to the rule of the maximization of production (PS: 52).

There is a contemporaneity in the transformation of humans into productive labour power, the strategy of fixing all wandering elements to wage-labour, and the rise of the punitive technique of imprisonment. At the end of the eighteenth century, at the same time as the principle of the criminal-social enemy emerged in the penal system, the system of penalties came to be reorganized around incarceration (PS: 63–65). Of course, Foucault does not wish to assume economic determination by deriving the rise of correctional incarceration from the needs of capital. Instead, he gives attention to the arguments voiced by reformers for why imprisonment should be preferred over other types of punishment. Jacques Pierre Brissot (1754–1793), whom Foucault places among the great reformers, argues that if crime constitutes an attack on society, 'on social interest', punishment should neither aim for vengeance nor penance: 'what should the punishment be? Punishment then is not something [to do with] reparation or vengeance. Neither does it have anything to do with chastisement or penance. It is solely the defense and protection of society' (PS: 67). According to Brissot and like-minded reformers, the premise that crime offends against society renders unsuitable prior punishments modelled on infamy, talion, and slavery. Penality must not be an abuse of power. Instead, it should be measured and defend society in two ways: rendering the criminal incapable of doing harm or reinserting him into society.

Time becomes the new penal technique, because it has the advantage of being a variable, which can be endlessly modulated according to the severity of crimes: 'What society will appropriate to punish the individual is the time left to live' (PS: 72). Imprisonment determined by time and quantified wage-labour are 'historically twin forms', notes Foucault (PS: 70), without explaining their exact relationship. Nonetheless, Foucault does assert that the parallel between the 'prison-form' and the 'wage-form' is more than just metaphorical. In the same way that Marx emphasized the homology between military and civic training in harnessing productivity, there is, observes Foucault, 'a kind of continuity between workshop clock, production line stopwatch, and prison calendar' (PS: 72). First, time becomes a key measure of control in capitalist production and in the penal system alike, since in both domains power is essentially exercised on individuals' time. Second, time is akin to a universal equivalent of exchange. Whereas the wage supposedly

184   Foucault's Technologies

corresponds to the time of labour power purchased, the penality corresponds to an infraction via the extraction of time from the offender. Similarly, notes Foucault, 'when one cannot pay a fine, one goes to prison. The fine appears as substitute for the day's labor' (PS: 70). Third, the introduction of time as the privileged unit of control extends the hold of power on people's time throughout their lives and across work and leisure. In Foucault's words: 'From the workshop clock to the pension fund, capitalist power clings to time, seizes hold of it, makes it purchasable and utilizable' (PS: 72). And he concludes: 'The time of people's existence had to be fitted and subjected to the temporal system of the cycle of production' (PS: 211). There was time-management at the workshop, calculation of time by the wage, control of leisure time, and regulation of workers' life by savings schemes. Later on, the state would control the time determined for schooling, unemployment benefits, treatment for illness, maternity leave, and pensions.

At first glance, Foucault seems to place himself in Althusserian territory, confirming his materialist trope, insofar as the control of time can be seen as a 'material practice' of ideology. On closer inspection, however, Foucault's analysis of how time became a material unit of exchange appears rather as an implicit reference to Marx (and a critical comment on Althusser). Foucault says: 'power must have a hold on time, [not as an] ideological abstraction, but as a real extraction of time from people's lives: real condition of possibility of the functioning of the wages system and the system of imprisonment' (PS: 83). For Marx (1990), money functions as the universal equivalent, which allows commodity exchange abstracted from the quantity of labour embodied in commodities. In a similar vein, for Foucault, the judiciary begins to use time as the equivalent form to infractions, time being quantifiable and abstractable from particular individuals, motivations, and circumstances. In the penal system, time is exchanged against the gravity of the offence: 'time is exchanged against power' (PS: 72). Infractions can now be exchanged with time much like commodities exchanged on the market. Foucault did not comment on the US bail system, although the practice of temporarily regaining freedom in exchange for money obviously echoes his analysis.

When Foucault said '[not as an] ideological abstraction, but as a real extraction of time' (PS: 83), he probably wanted to contrast his approach against Althusser. What is under scrutiny is not ideology, understood as individuals' 'imaginary relationship to their real conditions', but it is a matter of real extraction of quantities of time from people's lives. It is the establishment of an instrument in power relations, a technique of exchange operative in penal practice as well as in employment relations. As Foucault insists, 'morality does not exist in people's heads; it is inscribed in power relations' (PS: 113). In this

The Production of 'Normal' Citizens **185**

way, he effectively dissolves ideology in the field of practices and techniques of power, just as he abandons the notion of false ideas misguiding people's consciences. Collapsing the division between bourgeois falsity and proletarian truth, Foucault takes the step that Althusser did not, or perhaps could not, take given his ties to the PCF.

The state as 'agent of moralization'

This chapter opened with a reference to Foucault's famous claim that the modern welfare state has inherited a technology of power from the Christian tradition: pastoral power. As a rule-governed and administrative structure, the modern state constitutes a 'tricky combination' of totalizing procedures and individualizing techniques (SP: 782)—tricky in the dual targeting of citizens both as a totality and qua their individuality. Hence the juridical or administrative case takes individuality into account: to counsel, the social worker must know who the client is, and to judge, the court must know the underlying individuality behind the offender's actions. The welfare state has, as Foucault would suggest, established an entire 'expert' apparatus that trades in subjectivation, or, as Althusser (ISA) argued, the ideological state apparatuses interpellate subjects qua individuality. *The Punitive Society* sheds new light on Foucault's claim that the welfare state has inherited pastoral power, a claim which is not well developed in 'The Subject and Power' or *Security, Territory, Population*, where he sketches out the transition from ecclesiastical to secular pastoral power (Dean and Villadsen, 2016: 141). What is missing from Foucault's accounts is the precise routes through which the technology of pastoral power became invested in welfare state institutions. Addressing this absence, our final observations on *The Punitive Society* will indicate places where Foucault does recover how the Christian tradition merges with the punitive-disciplinary arm of the modern state.

Foucault traces the genealogical root of the state's punitive-disciplinary wing back to the prison. Central to this claim is the belief held by seventeenth-century Protestant groups that only solitary confinement could ensure an inner conversion that would bring the sinner back to society. This merger of Protestant morality and punitive practice, argues Foucault, did not happen 'at the level of principles', but 'from the bottom, at the final stage of the penal process: prison, punishment' (PS: 89). Tracing the invention of the first correctional prison back to the Protestant Quaker sect and the notion of the penitentiary, Foucault suggests that the Quakers introduced the idea of penitence, the prison as a site of moral conversion, into penal discourse

186 Foucault's Technologies

(PS: 87–90). We should note that in this context Foucault undertakes the specific history of the cell, the technique of solitary confinement, which he later refers to in *Security, Territory, Population* (see the comparison of Heidegger's philosophy of technology and Foucault's genealogical method in Chapter 2).

Foucault explains that for the Quakers, political power should be nothing other than 'a force of coercion and morality' (PS: 87). This idea that political power should be a vehicle of moralization is exemplified by Edward Burrough (1634–1663), one of the founders of the Quaker movement, whom Foucault quotes: 'the government must "punish and suppress the malefactors", it must praise and reward "those who do good"; it must "protect the person and property of men against the violence and wrongdoing of the wicked"' (PS: 87). Hence, with the Quakers originated the idea that not only penal practice, but the exertion of government broadly, must advance moral betterment. In this way, the Quakers interlinked religion, morality, and governance.

Foucault believes that the prison—its techniques of punishment—says something important about how power operates in society generally. He notes that the Quakers saw confinement as a time for the examination of conscience, a technique later encapsulated in Foucault's 'pastoral technology' (SP), which will later diffuse into criminal psychiatry, psychological profiling, and criminal sociology. In the Quaker model, the cell was the site of penance, of 'soul-searching' in dialogue with God. However, Foucault specifies that the convent cell did not simply 'impose on' the prison cell its moral demands and its notion of penance (PS: 72–73). The prison cell rather emerges at the point of intersection between juridical confinement and Protestant morality of life: 'The penitentiary cell is the place of Calvinist, Quaker conscience, fixed by the tactic of internment' (PS: 73). And Foucault further concludes: 'So we cannot say that prison reproduces an old religious model of the monastery, but that a new form of juridical-religious connection is established through it' (PS: 92). Here, we notice an unexpected continuity of Christian morality from the eighteenth century onwards, a time supposedly undergoing a de-Christianization, and in the penal system there will henceforth operate a potential conflation of crime and sin. As if echoing Nietzsche's diagnosis of how 'Christian conscience' and its values were translated into scientific categories of normality and pathology (GS: 173), Foucault speaks of Christian conscience and a culpabilization of crime 'whose effects will be felt in other domains: psychiatry, criminology' (PS: 90). By treating labour unrest and crime as abnormalities, psychiatry manifests, in Nietzschean terms, the ultimate victory of the privileged, which is to cultivate in the oppressed a guilty conscience by enforcing on them one's own norms. In brief, the correctional prison lies at the root of how pastoral power became integrated in the state's juridico-disciplinary institutions.

From this process arose two elements of lasting importance in industrial capitalist societies: the technique of the individual case file and the persistent discourse on working-class degeneracy. The correctional prison needed to acquire knowledge of the prisoner and his character in order to prescribe the necessary moral corrections, and hence the need for the case file. Ensuring 'medical and religious transformation', says Foucault, required 'a judicial record, a dossier, of a biography, of an observation of the man's character, of inspectors whose attentions are supervisory' (PS: 91). Worth noting is that, on Foucault's account, the prison's case file merges formal judicial stipulations with the moral biography of the criminal, producing in a single technique what Foucault called a 'tricky combination' of 'individualization techniques and totalization procedures' (SP: 782). Foucault says that rendering the criminal an object of knowledge will 'have great historical importance', since it 'opens up a whole field of possible knowledge' such as psychopathology, criminology, and sociology' (PS: 91). The case file's integration of the juridical with the individual's biography and morality constituted a technique, which would become ubiquitous across state institutions like the police, the court, social work, education, and mental health. We can readily conclude that the technique of the case file-biography still functions as a key instrument of juridico-moral control of the labouring classes.

As Foucault's analysis unfolds, the penal tactics emerging under eighteenth- and nineteenth-century industrial capitalism gradually merge penality and moralization, establishing 'a range of everyday constraints that focus on behavior, manners, and habits, and the effect of which is not to sanction something like an infraction, but to act on individuals positively, to transform them morally' (PS: 110). In *Discipline and Punish*, Foucault explicates this point, writing that he refuses to 'concentrate the study of the punitive mechanisms on their "repressive" effects alone, but situate them in a whole series of their possible positive effects' (DP: 23). Apart from being productive, Foucauldian power is also dispersed, not localizable in the state apparatus or confiscated uniformly by one class. Launching a likely jab at Althusser, Foucault says that the installing of penal tactics 'is not just an ethical-juridical control, a State control to the advantage of a class' (PS: 110). On this backdrop, it is easier to understand why Foucault preferred the civil war model to analyse tactics of struggle, which are irreducible to the duality of class contradiction.

The second tactic of struggle recovered by Foucault, which is still part of our present reality, is the discourse on the 'immorality' and 'dangers' of the

188 Foucault's Technologies

labouring classes. Evidently, moral condemnation played a crucial role in strategies of control and criminalization of workers' misconduct throughout the seventeenth, eighteenth, and nineteenth centuries. Ian Hacking has explored the official statistics of the nineteenth century and finds one 'striking feature of the avalanche of numbers that begins around 1820', namely the obsession with numerical analyses of deviance: drunkenness, prostitution, vagrancy, suicide, madness, and crime (Hacking, 1999a: 161). The large masses of workers and underemployed who concentrated in the growing industrial centres were soon described as 'the dangerous class'. Foucault recounts vivid descriptions of the urban poor as simple, improvident, shameless, and extravagant. For example, a text by a physician described 'the proletarians' in Brest in 1830 as 'of a proportionally immense extent, which, apart from a few honourable exceptions, possesses profound ignorance, superstition, ignoble habits, and the moral depravity of wild children' (PS: 172). Other writers warned about a 'dissident class' foreign to society, a 'dark continent' of the poor, or a 'counter-nation' growing inside the nation, prompting demands that the state 'should master and correct this immorality' (PS: 171). It was in this context that the privileged groups intensified their pressure to inscribe diverse moral failings of 'the lower stratas' into the penal law.

Whereas the vagabond of the seventeenth century was the paradigmatic figure, or 'connector', in this penalization process, new figures take his place from nineteenth-century industrialization: 'shameless proletarians', 'undeserving poor', 'dysfunctional families', 'welfare queens', and 'young predators'. Foucault argues that life in the industrial capitalist state becomes pervaded by 'a kind of diffuse, everyday penality, with para-penal extensions introduced into the social body itself, prior to the judicial apparatus' (PS: 193). *The Punitive Society* lucidly traces the long-standing coupling of the judicial and the moral, suggesting its continual presence at every point of encounter between the labouring (or unemployed) poor and the modern state: prison, psychiatry, schooling, health care, and social services. Another continuity also emerges from Foucault's analysis. Whereas nineteenth-century penal law was organized around the worker's body in its relationship to wealth and profit, the modern welfare state now ensures the maintenance, discipline, and physical control of workers' physical being.

Althusser/Foucault again: ideology or disciplinary techniques

We note how Foucault's analysis proceeds in continual dialogue with Althusser, but also how it exceeds Althusser's framework in several ways.

Most importantly perhaps, Foucault does not analyse power as anchored in state apparatuses but as fluid, played out in tactical games across the social body and at the borders of the legal system. Focusing on the shifting moralized demarcations of tolerated 'illegalism' versus illegality, Foucault eschews a unified conception of the state as 'repressive machine'. His analysis shows how penal laws are invested with aims and moral values of privileged groups, many of which essentially concern the protection of capitalist relations. Describing dissidents of wage-labour as 'enemies of society' meant that moral notions could be recodified in penal categories. However, the civil war framework exceeds the dual class model, since collectivities are not given a priori or remain fixed through struggles, but are rather constituted and reconstituted in struggle. Assigning to penal tactics a productivity in creating individual and collective subjectivities, Foucault also transcends the binary of repression versus ideology (PS: 133), which guides Althusser's distinction between the repressive state apparatus and the ideological state apparatuses.

The final point of confrontation is Althusser's centralized state apparatuses versus Foucault's *dispositifs*. The attraction of Foucault's notion of *dispositifs* is perhaps that it allows 'cutting reality' in a different way than the divisions of base/superstructure, ideology/social reality, and sovereign/populace. Transgressing these categories, new relations of oppositions and alliances surface in Foucault's 1970s lectures. This does not mean, of course, that class struggle or capitalist relations disappear from the analysis, but they appear as much more mobile and transformable than Althusser's thesis assumes. The level of detail that Foucault unfolds means that the reader is faced with specific, emerging problems and tactical responses by specific actors in a moving field of connections. Towards the end of the *Punitive Society* course, Foucault begins to use 'discipline' as a substitute for penality and moralization. He portrays, as noted in Chapter 1, a diffusion of disciplinary techniques across different domains, not only those of production and punishment, but also schooling, medicine, psychiatry, social work, and more. Foregrounding these techniques, Foucault established a smaller unit of analysis than the ideological state apparatuses, but one that displays their constitution (Miller, 1994: 107). In terms of subjectivation, Foucault eschews Althusser's psychoanalytical model, or 'the psycho-sociological notion of authority' (PP: 40), avoiding any a priori theory which explains why individuals are ready to become interpellated by the voice of ideology. Instead, Foucault describes how techniques and practices are applied to bodies in a moving field of force relations.

Finally, whereas Althusser theorized ideology as material, Foucault described empirically the specific techniques through which the capitalist order is sustained. This focus on disciplinary techniques allowed for an immanentist view of power, as running through exchange relations and modes of production. Disciplinary power, on Foucault's account, is not a guarantee of the mode of production, but rather immanent to it. This point brings us back full circle to the liberal image of the free market versus the penal sphere, where the state legitimately intervenes in the latter (Harcourt, 2010). For example, Foucault's analysis of time control, the worker's savings book, and other disciplinary techniques cuts through the vision of a clear split between the free, self-organizing market and the punitive domain. Eroding this image of the market as a realm untouched by power, Foucault's analysis demonstrates numerous continuities and intersections merging penality with the allegedly free capitalist order.

The pastoral-governmental trajectory

We now shift attention to the other major genealogy of 'the welfare state matrix', the pastoral-governmental trajectory, which Foucault explored in the late 1970s. Pursuing this path, Foucault achieves a more multifaceted conception of state power, bringing into view power exercised through freedom, termed governance, and resistance against the totalizing and individualizing power of the state, termed counter-conduct. However, as I will argue, this pathway ultimately removed Foucault from the theme of the link between capitalist state formation and techniques of subjectivation.

Foucault gave his influential lectures on state formation and political governance in the late 1970s, today known as 'the governmentality lectures' (STP, BP). In those lectures, Foucault famously proposed a 'decentred' approach to the state, since, he proclaimed, the state does not possess the unity, the coherence, or the effective powers commonly assigned to it. He further argued that inasmuch as the state is not the ultimate centre of power, it should neither be the privileged object of analysis nor of political struggle. In taking a decentred view of the state, Foucault wished to extend the 'de-institutionalizing' approach he had pursued in his analysis of institutions like the prison, the psychiatric clinic, and the hospital (STP: 118–120). Foucault had 'gone behind', as he would say, these institutions by tracing the techniques and forms of knowledge that made their emergence possible: 'Can we talk of something like a "governmentality" that would be to the state what techniques of segregation were to psychiatry, what techniques of discipline were to the penal system, and what biopolitics was to medical institutions?' (STP: 120). Instead of accepting the state's self-evident identity as a constitutional and legal entity, Foucault discovered alternative sources in the technologies of biopolitics and pastoral power (Villadsen, 2015: 148). The strategy of 'going behind' the state took him back to nascent population statistics, early political economy, and Christian notions of care for the flock and the individual soul.

The pastoral-governmental trajectory also led to another analytical innovation, namely Foucault's influential definition of government as 'the conduct of conduct'. This notion served to free his analysis of power from the theme of knowledge-power around which his studies of penality, discipline, sexuality, and psychiatry had been organized in the early and mid-1970s. The concept of 'government', defined as the practice of conducting individuals' conduct, began to take centre stage in Foucault's analysis from the end of the 1970s onwards and would gradually replace the notions of 'power', 'discipline', and 'subjectivation'. Introducing this term, Foucault recovers the meaning of government in its sixteenth-century sense, which does not confine governance to political government but broadly designates the direction of individuals' or groups' conduct: '"Government" did not refer only to political structures or to the management of states', writes Foucault, but also to 'the government of children, of souls, of communities, of families, of the sick' (SP: 790). In *Security, Territory, Population*, Foucault had similarly reintroduced the notion of sixteenth-century governance, where the 'general problem of government' arises with particular intensity (STP: 89). There, he describes a major transition in Western Europe's political reasoning, running from princely territorial rule prevailing between medieval times and the seventeenth century to the rise of modern governance of the more complex reality of the population in the eighteenth century. Foucault echoes this transition in governmental reasoning in 'The Subject and Power', defining relationships of power as 'a mode of action which does not act directly and immediately on others. Instead, it acts upon their actions' (SP: 789). From the 1990s onwards, this 'formula' of power sparked a stream of studies, especially among Anglophone academics (e.g. Rose and Miller, 1992; Cruikshank, 1999; Garland, 2015), that explore how neoliberal governance works upon and through free individuals and their aspirations. We discuss this adoption of Foucault's work below, but let us first examine the component of pastoral power, or 'the technology of pastoral power' as Foucault sometimes said, in the pastoral-governmental trajectory.

Pastoral power

On several occasions, Foucault traces modern governmentality back to the Christian tradition or, in his terms, pastoral power. Hence, in *Security,*

192 Foucault's Technologies

Territory, Population, he says that the Christian pastorate is 'where we should look for the origin ... of the governmentality whose entry into politics, at the end of the sixteenth and in the seventeenth and eighteenth centuries, marks the threshold of the modern state' (STP: 165). Foucault further emphasizes that the pastoral 'art of governing men' is distinct from legal and disciplinary power, insofar as it cares for both the totality and the individual through a continuous and lifelong guidance:

> In Christianity the pastorate gave rise to an art of conducting, directing, leading, guiding, taking in hand, and manipulating men, an art of monitoring them and urging them on step by step, an art with the function of taking charge of men collectively and individually throughout their life and at every moment of their existence. (STP: 165)

It has been tempting to read Foucault's comments that pastoral power lies at the root of the modern state, as implying that pastoral guidance was renewed by the welfare state in terms of confessional techniques in health, psychiatry, crime prevention, and social work. In this reading, the shepherd's salvation of the flock stands in continuity with the security of the population under political governance, with pastoral care preceding the insurance of health in this life, the continual guidance of each citizen, and the pursuit of detailed knowledge on the population. Such an interpretation underlines the welfare state's involvement in producing subjectivity, as it interlinks confessional techniques with the objectifying knowledge of jurisprudence and statistics.

Describing the confessional technique, Foucault states: 'This form of power cannot be exercised without knowing the inside of people's minds, without exploring their souls, without making them reveal their innermost secrets. It implies a knowledge of conscience and an ability to direct it' (SP: 783). Foucault spends considerable time discussing the Christian technique of confession in different works from the late 1970s and early 1980s. While the confession is not the only technique that produces truth about an individual through a questioning of one's own conscience, Foucault sees it as 'the purest and also historically most important' (GL: 82). At times, Foucault describes the confession in rather general terms, as the prevailing mode of subjectivation in the modern West, dislodging it from the specific meaning and forms that it took in early and later Christianity: 'at the very heart of not only the Christian monastic institution, but of a whole series of practices, of apparatuses [*dispositifs*] that will inform what constitutes Christian and, as a result, Western subjectivity' (GL: 266). As such, the confession

The Production of 'Normal' Citizens **193**

is a verbal procedure in which the speaker is the guarantor of the truth of the discourse, while submitting to an authority who requires the revelation of what is hidden in the speaker's conscience. Foucault defines the confession as

> a ritual of discourse in which the speaking subject is also the subject of the statement; it is also a ritual that unfolds within a power relationship, for one does not confess without the presence (or virtual presence) of a partner who is not simply the interlocutor but the authority who requires the confession, prescribes and appreciates it, and intervenes in order to judge, punish, forgive, console, and reconcile. (HS1: 61)

In the modern welfare state, the confessional has become the generalized technique of subjectivation. Hence, to deploy juridico-administrative power, authorities must know about the subjectivity of citizens. The state comprises, because of its adoption of pastoral power, as Foucault suggests, a comprehensive system of welfare expertise that 'interpellates individuals as subjects', to use Althusser's terms (ISA: 170).

Pastoral guidance and the technique of confession clearly play a crucial role in Foucault's genealogies of governmentality, from the first centuries of European Christianity to the emergence of the modern state. However, if we examine Foucault's work in the late 1970s, while paying close attention to his comments on struggles around subjectivity, another important heritage from the Christian tradition comes to the fore. Notable in 'The Subject and Power', Foucault mentions the 'struggles against the "government of individualization"' (SP: 780), which unfold within the domains of sexuality, pedagogy, psychiatry, and medicine against the effects of administrative and pastoral subjectivation. Foucault specifies that they 'revolve around the question: Who are we? They are a refusal of these abstractions, of economic and ideological state violence, which ignore who we are individually, and also a refusal of a scientific or administrative inquisition which determines who one is' (SP: 780–782). Foucault's preferred term for these struggles is 'counter-conduct', a term he introduces in *Security, Territory, Population* when analysing belief-centred revolts against the Christian pastorate from the Middle Ages to the sixteenth century. As a base definition, he describes counter-conduct as 'struggle against the procedures implemented for conducting others' (STP: 201). Interestingly, in 'The Subject and Power', Foucault draws a sweeping parallel between contemporary struggles 'against the government of individualization' and anti-pastoral counter-conducts that aspired towards

194   Foucault's Technologies

an alternative (religious) subjectivity. This link emerges as Foucault moves seamlessly from present-day struggles back to the Reformation:

> I suspect that it is not the first time that our society has been confronted with this kind of struggle. All those movements which took place in the fifteenth and sixteenth centuries and which had the Reformation as their main expression and result should be analyzed as a great crisis of the Western experience of subjectivity and a revolt against the kind of religious and moral power which gave form, during the Middle Ages, to this subjectivity. (SP: 782)

What connects the struggles leading to the Reformation with present-day struggles in the welfare state is that they both challenge the pastoral aspect of power in Western societies. The theme of counter-conduct versus pastoral power occupies several lectures in *Security, Territory, Population* (STP: 191–255), where Foucault describes how diverse groups practised religious insubordination and challenged authority while invoking the Christian tradition itself. He notes that such counter-conduct can be found at a doctrinal level, in individual behaviour, and in organized groups (STP: 204). These groups reinterpreted asceticism, the ideal of self-sacrifice, and spiritual guidance, and in so doing 'certain themes of Christian theology or religious experience were utilized against these structures of power' (STP: 207). Foucault emphasizes how religious counter-movements evolved in tandem with the pastoral government imposed by the Christian church. In effect, Foucault describes the relationship between pastoral power and counter-conduct as an immanent relationship:

> The struggle was not conducted in the form of absolute exteriority, but rather in the form of the permanent use of tactical elements that are pertinent in the anti-pastoral struggle to the very extent that they are part, even in a marginal way, of the general horizon of Christianity. (STP: 125)

These movements at the church's margins challenged pastoral authority by readopting Christian doctrines, and some of these 'tactical elements' gradually pervaded the ecclesiastical institutions. Importantly, then, practices of counter-conduct inevitably carry political value. Arnold Davidson (2011: 29) explains: 'Even apparently personal or individual forms of counter-conduct such as the return to Scripture or the adherence to a certain set of eschatological beliefs have a political dimension, that is, modify force relations between individuals, acting on the possibilities of action.'

The Production of 'Normal' Citizens **195**

At stake in modern counter-conduct, as Foucault points out, is how to contest the subjugation of the juridico-pastoral state, or 'how to liberate us both from the state and from the type of individualization which is linked to the state' (STP: 785). By introducing the problem of how to liberate oneself from techniques of subjectivation linked to the state, Foucault emphasizes the twofold ethical and political scope of counter-conduct. The welfare state's power is hence irreducible to a juridical framework focused on power's legitimacy and limits, because the power of subjectivation 'passes through' subjects and their interrelationships. This insight elucidates why Foucault insists, in *The Hermeneutics of the Subject*, that elaborating an ethics of the self 'may be an urgent, fundamental, and politically indispensable task' (HES: 252). If modern state power productively constitutes and shapes subjects, it follows that 'there is no first or final point of resistance to political power other than in the relationship one has to oneself' (HES: 252). Because the modern state is pervaded by dispersed, productive, and reversible power relations, the citizen-subject becomes a point of dispersion, intensification, or reversion of power. As such, for Foucault, political power cannot be analysed in isolation from ethics, understood as the self's relationship to the self.

Foucault's portrayal of the state as involved in subjectivation raises the problem of expert knowledge in the governance of individuals' conduct. In the context of the modern state, conduct is ambiguous because it is both an activity of ethico-political value and a target of scientific and administrative scrutiny. Foucault would caution against the dominance of science as the exclusive framework through which human conduct is made intelligible: 'When a regime of scientific veridiction provides the framework of intelligibility for conduct, this concept completely changes register, losing its ethical and political dimensions and becoming the object of scientific explanation' (Davidson, 2011: 36). The diverse modern successors of pastoral power involve the scientific verification of psychology, psychiatry, and pedagogy with their character typifications and divisions of normality/abnormality, just as the security of the population involves health statistics and juridical knowledge.

The contemporary problem of subjectivity arises from within this compact of political power and juridico-scientific knowledge. Insofar as the welfare state's expertise is intricately involved in the shaping of subjectivity by tying us to particular identities, what kind of resistance would correlate with this individualizing power? Confronting this problem, Foucault famously posits that no 'positive self' has to be liberated, since today's main challenge is to develop a 'politics of ourselves' (Foucault, 1997: 230–231). Foucault's late work on self-conduct is an exploration of subjectivities very different from

196   Foucault's Technologies

those linked to modern pastoral power (with its quest to reveal inner truth), and of disciplinary power (with its reliance on anthropological characters like 'the criminal personality'). Given how central these truth-producing technologies are to state governance, the question guiding Foucault's early 1980s work concerns the relationship one can establish with oneself within different truth orders. Foucault's lectures from 1980 to 1984 examine the truth regime in early Christianity, while also tracing alternative constellations of self-conduct and truth production, such as *parrêsia* and *aphrodisia* in Roman and Greek antiquity. Against this backdrop, the pastoral-governmental trajectory takes Foucault from studies of penality and discipline in the 1970s, over his examination of pastoral power and liberal governance at the end of the 1970s, leading finally to ancient self-techniques in the early 1980s.

Liberal governance

We have witnessed how, in the early and mid-1970s, Foucault explored a series of *dispositifs* of power/knowledge, including the *dispositifs* of law, discipline, and sexuality, and that he was guided by the theme of social struggle in these inquiries, using the model of civil war as 'analyser of power relations'. We also noted that analysis of *dispositifs* was a means of eschewing the, at the time prevalent, notion of dominant ideology, or 'state ideology' as Althusser preferred. Above, we noticed how Foucault's genealogies revealed the state's juridico-disciplinary wing to be shaped by privileged groups' tactics of control in the eighteenth and nineteenth centuries. And in Chapter 1, we noted how Foucault, in his 1978 lectures, decentred the state into multiple *dispositifs*, which entailed that political governance is characterized by the evolving interplay between law, discipline, and security (STP). In 'The Subject and Power', Foucault reiterates this observation, describing the state as a very complex system 'endowed with multiple apparatuses' (SP: 792). Against the Marxist view of the state as a 'repressive machine', and specifically Althusser's twin apparatuses from where state ideology emanates, Foucault had decentred the state into a mobile set of power relations. A significant benefit of the *dispositifs* was that their heterogeneity precludes the notion of a centralized state imbued with a uniform ideology; instead, problems of governance and their technical solutions straddle divergent governmental rationalities.

However, around 1980 Foucault declared that he wanted to make a decisive revision of his own approach, shifting away from *dispositifs* and the theme of power/knowledge to the notion of governance. Foucault tells his audience, in his first lecture of the 1980 course, *On the Government of the Living*, that

The Production of 'Normal' Citizens **197**

he wants to distance himself from 'the now worn and hackneyed theme of knowledge-power', which merely served as a means to avoid a type of analysis 'that revolved around the notion of dominant ideology' (GL: 11). This entails two successive shifts in his approach, notes Foucault, where the first shift had helped him evade the abstract concept of ideology, performing instead a detailed analysis of the techniques whereby power/knowledge becomes operable. The notion of power, Foucault explains, had as its main function 'to replace the notion of system of dominant representations with the question or field of analysis of the procedures and techniques by which power relations are actually effectuated' (GL: 12). The second shift that Foucault now wants to make entails moving away from his notion of power/knowledge, replacing it with the concept of government by the truth. He even declared that this shift implies 'getting rid' of the notion of power/knowledge 'in order to try to develop the notion of government by the truth; getting rid of the notion of knowledge-power as we got rid of the notion of dominant ideology' (GL: 12).

Foucault proceeds by introducing what would become his influential definition of government as 'the conduct of conduct'. In doing so, as mentioned earlier, he recovers the meaning of government in its sixteenth-century sense, which does not confine governance to the political institutions of the state but broadly designates the direction of individuals' or groups' conduct. Government should be understood, Foucault says, 'not in the narrow and current sense of the supreme instance of executive and administrative decisions in State systems, but in the broad sense, and old sense moreover, of mechanisms and procedures intended to conduct men, to direct their conduct, to conduct their conduct' (GL: 12). In *Security, Territory, Population*, Foucault (SP: 89) had already reintroduced the notion of sixteenth-century governance, where the 'general problem of government' arises with particular intensity, since it was recognized that governing the state means governing a multiplicity of free individuals who themselves exercise government. Similarly, Foucault declares in 'The Subject and Power' that 'there is no face-to-face confrontation of power and freedom, which are mutually exclusive (freedom disappears everywhere power is exercised), but a much more complicated interplay. In this game freedom may well appear as the condition for the exercise of power' (SP: 790). Foucault's general idea that power runs through a network of mobile and reversible relations thus finds a compelling formulation in the concept of governance.

Around 1980, Foucault appears to have freed himself almost completely from his repeated dialogues with Althusser and the theoretical Marxism of the time that he routinely practised during the 1970s. Whereas Foucault's

198   Foucault's Technologies

description of *dispositifs* in motion and dynamic interplay were probably an antidote to Althusser's state apparatuses, Foucault leaves behind this concept in the early 1980s. In a 1982 seminar, 'Technologies of the Self', he corrected his previous work, declaring that he had overidentified subjectivation with the production of 'docile bodies' in disciplinary processes (Foucault, 1988a). Whereas Foucault's notions of discipline and pastoral power still displayed a concern with overcoming Althusser's psychoanalytical inspiration, which Foucault (PP: 40n) refers to as 'the psycho-sociological notion of authority', the idea of governance is free from such concerns. Most importantly, however, is that Foucault's newfound concept of governance is rather foreign to Althusser's and Foucault's unifying theme of how individuals are subjugated through material practices linked to the state.

Foucault emphasizes the centrality of freedom to modern governance, understood as the conduct of conduct, or to act upon others' actions. Patton perceptively notes that this understanding of power relations 'is significantly different from Foucault's earlier conception of power relations as a matter of conflict or struggle between opposing forces' (Patton, 2016: 71). Above, we noticed that Foucault applied 'the civil war model' as an analytical framework in *The Punitive Society*, but the model became prominent when Foucault reintroduced it in his 1976 lectures, *Society Must be Defended*. However, in 'The Subject and Power', published in 1982, Foucault explicitly rejects the civil war model: 'basically, power is less a confrontation between two adversaries or their mutual engagement than a question of "government"' (SP: 789). He continues: 'the relationship proper to power would therefore be sought not on the side of violence or of struggle ... but, rather, in the area of that singular mode of action, neither warlike nor juridical, which is government' (SP: 790). As Patton explains, Foucault's reorientation to power as government means, first, that those involved in power relations are reconceived of as 'agents endowed with a degree of freedom', and second, that the subject presupposed is 'a subject of interests and rationality' (Patton, 2016: 72). These points echo insights from Foucault's 1979 lectures, *The Birth of Biopolitics*, especially his analysis of American neoliberal economics.

During those lectures, Foucault examined the Chicago School, emphasizing how the liberal subject of interests, *homo œconomicus*, was assumed to act as an entrepreneur of itself. Endowed with a capacity to make self-enhancing investments and calculate trade-offs, this subject is the most efficient distributor of resources. This is why neoliberal economists insist that government activity—in every domain from education to punishment—should be based on the rationality of the governed. Moreover, government must always allow itself to be corrected by the rational choices of the governed, as Foucault explains at the end of his 1979 course: 'It is a matter of modelling government [on] the rationality of individuals', insofar as 'the rationality of the governed must serve as the regulating principle for the rationality of government' (BP: 312). The liberal assumption that rational actors serve as truth tellers in terms of government adequacy makes clear why government is predicated on freedom. Insofar as 'the internal rationality of human behavior' must inform governmental practice, freedom becomes 'a correlative' to government, produced from the interplay between government and those governed. The assumption of the *homo œconomicus* corresponds to a particular way of governing, which constantly exposes political governance to the test of the market. North American neoliberalism does not stipulate exactly what should be done (it does not posit that all public services should be turned over to commercial actors), but it demands that services, policies, and organizations are scrutinized and tested to reach the most efficient allocation of resources. This kind of optimization aspires to be 'free of morality'. Leading neoliberal economist Gary Becker hence wanted to exclude morality from society's reaction to crime by viewing the criminal subject as a *homo œconomicus*. Instead of moral doctrine, crime prevention should be based on tests of what means of deterrence exert the greatest impact in the market for crime at the lowest cost (BP: 256). The general techniques for such optimizing include outsourcing, the exposure of public services to market competition, and, generally, the (re)organization of all social affairs guided by individuals' rational choices.

Hence, in his analyses of neoliberal governance, Foucault gives emphasis to the view of the subject as capable of rational calculation and self-fashioning. In a debated passage in *The Birth of Biopolitics*, Foucault describes American neoliberalism as a nascent form of governance that does not target individuals directly, since it is not standardizing, identificatory, or individualizing:

> what appears on the horizon of this kind of analysis is not at all the ideal or project of an exhaustively disciplinary society in which the legal network hemming in individuals is taken over and extended internally by, let's say, normative mechanisms. Nor is it a society in which a mechanism of general normalization and the exclusion of those who cannot be normalized is needed. On the horizon of this analysis we see instead the image, idea, or theme-program of a society in which ... minority individuals and practices are tolerated, in which action is brought to bear on the rules of the game rather than on the players, and finally in which there is an environmental type of intervention instead of the internal subjugation of individuals. (BP: 259–260)

200 Foucault's Technologies

Initiated by Michael Behrent's (2009) provocative claim regarding Foucault's brief 'strategic endorsement' of neoliberalism in 1979, scholars have debated whether Foucault's analysis of American neoliberalism was critical, revealed fascination, or constituted a strategic endorsement guided by political motivations. This is not the place to evaluate the different arguments of this debate; I discuss Foucault's relationship to neoliberalism at length, with Mitchell Dean, in *State Phobia and Civil Society* (Dean and Villadsen, 2016: 145–165). Relevant for our present concerns, however, is the argument that Foucault discovers in neoliberal governance a non-disciplinary approach, which dispenses with the anthropological characters inherent to the psy-disciplinary expertise of the welfare state. Foucault could appreciate economic neoliberalism, argues Behrent, because 'he appreciated the thinness of its anthropological claims' (Behrent, 2009: 568), and with neoliberals' proposals for how to govern 'problem subjects' like drug addicts or criminals, these figures would undergo what Foucault terms 'an "anthropological erasure"' (Foucault, quoted in Behrent, 2009: 566). On Foucault's reading, North American economic liberalism dispenses with the philosophy of the subject, and this could perhaps explain why he might have found a certain compatibility between anti-humanism and economic liberalism. In place of the essentialist assumptions regarding the human subject that Foucault had identified in both disciplinary institutions and the catastrophic ideologies of the twentieth century (e.g. fascism and communism), Foucault discovered in his analysis of American neoliberalism a self-fashioning subject acting in a more 'tolerant' and open-ended environment.

Leaving aside many details in Foucault's 1970s itinerary, we can conclude that a significant shift took place in his analysis of techniques of subjectivation: in the early and mid-1970s, one encounters a subject 'interpellated' by punitive and disciplinary techniques of power, whereas at the end of the 1970s one finds a 'flat' subject of neoliberal governance—a form of governance, says Foucault, 'in which there is an environmental type of intervention instead of the internal subjugation of individuals' (BP: 259–260). Instead of the 'internal subjugation' of discipline, neoliberal governance incites individuals to undertake entrepreneurial self-work by means of various techniques of self-investment, self-development, and self-fulfilment. One can still read such governance through freedom as an 'ideological interpellation qua individuality', but there is no uniform ideology pervading all techniques. And against his own *dispositifs* of power/knowledge, Foucault declares in 1980 that he wants to allow for more differentiated relationships between knowledge and power. '[P]assing from the notion of knowledge-power to that of government by the truth', he says, 'essentially involves giving a positive and differentiated content to these two terms of knowledge and power' (GL: 12). The price to be paid for Foucault's newfound, more nuanced, framework for analysing governance is a weakening of the link between techniques of subjectivation and the formation of the state, which in turn meant that the question of the state's role in reproducing capitalism slipped out of focus.

Evacuating the state and capitalism

As Foucault's academic work, at the end of the 1970s, turns away from questions of social struggle and domination tied to capitalist relations, the link between the state and subjectivation also begins to disappear. Marxist scholars and other critics see this development in Foucault's academic orientation as a loss of critique proper, as issues of oppression, inequality, and degradations that result from the capitalist order are replaced by concerns with reflexive self-practices centred on sexual identity. For example, Michael Morris argues, in a general assessment of Foucault's 'collapse of critique', that

> for Foucault, the liberation of the oppressed has become incoherent. The degradations that come from poverty, the limitations that come from ignorance, and the deformations that come from alienated labor have all disappeared from view. More generally, questions of economic injustice and structural reform have been shelved, and we are now free to attend to our sexual interiorities and boundaries .... (Morris, 2016: 94)

In this trajectory, Foucault paralleled other French intellectuals who, from the mid-1970s, distanced themselves from Maoist and Marxist thinking and moved towards more moderate or liberal viewpoints (Dews, 1979). In this sense, Foucault himself paved the way for contemporary post-Foucauldian researchers, who have followed in his footsteps in evacuating the problem of the state's role in the reproduction of the capitalist order. Hence, in much Foucault-inspired scholarship from the last three decades, the focus on the state's involvement in sustaining capitalist relations, a parallel theme in Foucault's and Althusser's work from the 1970s, has slid into the background. As an acute observation, Jacques Bidet (2016: 169) notes that Foucault's discourse often inspired particularistic social struggles. From the 1970s onwards, scholars and activists recognized themselves in Foucault's writings as they engaged in issues of gender, homosexuality, race, postcolonialism, and health, yet largely divorced these questions from the overall

202 Foucault's Technologies

problem of the state's role in industrial capitalism. In other words, inspired by the themes of subjectivation and power/knowledge, they critically analyse marginalization, yet without connecting these themes to the capitalist economy:

> All these groups have their motives, their forms and their own urgencies, which are derivable not from relations of production (even if they are inseparable from them), but from the diverse management of their body by social power: management of the sexed body, of the healthy body, of the mortal body. (Bidet, 2016: 169)

In the early 1990s, Foucault's work on governmentality gained broader prominence as academics sought a new vocabulary with which to study neoliberal reforms of welfare states across the globe. Scholars inspired by Foucault in various disciplines began carrying out 'governmentality studies' that took a decentred approach to the state (Ewald, 1991; Mitchell, 1991; Rose and Miller, 1992). They pursued the methodological doctrine that analysis must be 'local' rather than 'global', focusing on the practices and technologies of governance instead of conceptualizing the state in juridical-constitutional models or as disseminator of ideology. Taking their lead from Foucault's cautionary comments regarding 'the overvaluation' of the problem of state (STP: 109), a stream of governmentality writers argued against overidentifying the exercise of power with the state. In contemporary liberal societies, they argued, power does not emanate from the state apparatus understood as a centre of repressive power. Instead, political power is produced in mobile networks, from the interaction between state and non-state actors. Power is not a force of constraints but is exercised in order to enhance subjects' self-governing capacities, taking the form of appeal, incitement, or counselling rather than command, restriction, or repression. In their seminal article, 'Political Power Beyond the State', Nikolas Rose and Peter Miller (1992: 173) explained that liberal forms of government depend on technologies for 'governing at a distance' that aim to create entities and persons capable of practising 'a regulated autonomy'. However, the analytical priorities of Foucault's inheritors are criticized by Resch, who cautions that Foucauldian analysis 'purchases its critique at a high cost—abandonment of any rational grounding of its own position, selective restriction of the scope of its analysis to the particular, the fragmentary, or the regional—thereby avoiding "totalitarian" global analysis' (Resch, 1989: 518). Critics correctly point out governmentality scholars' empirical overemphasis of the local and their tendency to identify power with the conduct of conduct, or 'governing through freedom'.

At the same time, the theme of capitalist state formation became a rarity in Foucauldian studies (Jessop, 2006), even when some scholars focused on how techniques of subjectivation are involved in the reproduction of capitalist state forms (for example, Cruikshank, 1999; Lazzaretto, 2012; Garland, 2015). Barbara Cruikshank (1999) explored the 'war on poverty' in the US in the 1960s. Focusing on the paradoxical notion of 'empowerment', she finds that anti-poverty programmes operate by 'turning inwards' problems related to poverty. In order to be empowered, the poor first had to be constructed as 'disempowered', which meant assigning to them a lack of agency, responsibility, and self-esteem. Cruikshank also notes the continuity of moralizing notions like 'welfare queens' in constructing the poor as in need of discipline. Judith Butler and Athena Athanasiou (2013) examine the question of what it means to be dispossessed, focusing on people who suffer enforced deprivation of their land, rights, livelihood, and belonging. They demonstrate with examples from across the globe that this dispossession often results from state-inflicted violence under the auspices of 'neoliberal governmentality'. Butler and Athanasiou also emphasize how people refuse to become disposable, assembling their bodies in protest against political and economic dispossession. Finally, David Garland (2015) considers the overall 'governmentality of welfare state' as a response to urban, industrial capitalism. The major sectors of the welfare state function to modify the economic effects and social problems that capitalism would otherwise create. The welfare state, argues Garland (2015: 346), 'is, in effect, an ancillary institution and not the primary one', and social welfare and economic security are thus designed to ensure, not challenge, the capitalist economy. These studies take up Foucault's lines of inquiry, critically exploring dimensions of the state's involvement in the constitution of subjectivities and in sustaining capitalist relations.

A few scholars insisted that liberal governance is not adequately defined by self-governance, since the liberal doctrine of 'maximizing self-rule' entails that the subject suppresses the allegedly irrational, impulsive, or passion-driven. Therefore, liberal governance is not foreign to constraint, but justifies particular kinds of subjects and human experiences being governed through practices that can be called 'despotic' (Valverde, 1996). Other scholars objected that the preferred vocabulary of governmentality scholars, including notions like self-government, autonomy, networks, and 'the conduct of conduct', corresponds too well with the discourse of liberalism to be able to analyse it critically (O'Malley et al., 1997). In hindsight, the initial reliance on merely one published lecture, lecture four in *Security, Territory, Population* (STP: 87–115), out of Foucault's extensive engagement with governance

204 Foucault's Technologies

and state power in the 1970s may also explain the emphasis governmentality scholars placed in their foundational work in the 1990s. The result was that the theme of the state's sovereign authority, as well as its role in reproducing the capitalist economy, became akin to a no-go for post-Foucauldians. One might argue that the 'state phobia' which Foucault critically diagnosed as a widespread feature of modern political ideologies (BP: 76) seems to reappear in the analytical state phobia of many of his inheritors (Dean and Villadsen, 2016). It is tempting to invoke Resch's description of 'dissident postmodernism' to account for the success of the governmentality tradition: 'the less it talked about economics, classes, and class struggle, the more influential it became' (Resch, 1989: 159). Governmentality scholars retained the political question of the governance of individuals but dislodged it from conventional notions of class, economy, and state apparatus.

Marxists have repeatedly criticized Foucault for neglecting the significance of the state in conditioning social relations. Nico Poulantzas claimed that Foucault underestimates the role of law, and that he 'fails to understand the function of the repressive apparatuses (army, police, judicial system, etc.) as means of exercising physical violence that are located at the heart of the modern state' (Poulantzas, 1978: 77). More recently, Slavoj Žižek (1999) has similarly criticized Foucault's analytical favouring of micro-powers over the state in a comparison of Foucault and Althusser. Žižek aptly notes that Foucault's counterpart to the ideological state apparatuses are disciplinary practices that always operate at the level of micro-power. In explaining the existence of sovereign power, writes Žižek (1994: 13), 'Foucault resorts to the extremely suspect rhetoric of complexity, evoking the intricate network of lateral links ... a clear case of patching up, since one can never arrive at Power this way.' Whereas Foucault thus dissolves power into webs of micro-power whose effects and value cannot be ascertained, Althusser insists on the state apparatuses as power's material embodiment. For Žižek, Althusser's advantage is that he assumes that the mechanism of interpellation, in order to function, presupposes the state as the unavoidable reference point. As we have noted throughout this chapter, Foucault does focus on the state in the 1970s in its relationship to subjectivation and the capitalist order. However, his genealogies eschew a pre-given binary model, a centrist view of power, and the premise of economic determinism. Using 'the civil war model', Foucault studied both penal techniques and social dominance, not as easily binarized phenomena, but rather as empirically discernible transformations.

A first step in rearticulating Foucault's earlier focus on the state's role in sustaining present-day techno-capitalism would be to re-emphasize the link between techniques of subjectivation and the reproduction of the economic

The Production of 'Normal' Citizens **205**

order. In particular, it would be necessary to consider two major developments in contemporary capitalism that have taken place since Foucault presented the state as a 'matrix of totalizing and individualizing power'. First, commercial actors have taken on increasingly important roles in shaping the web of rules, values, and restrictions that come to influence our attitudes and behaviours. Today, the 'matrix' includes a whole range of commercial actors who often determine the scope of acceptable behaviour, adjudicating and sanctioning those behaviours that they deem unacceptable. Key techniques for such interventions include the individual health profile, the credit score rating, and the consumer risk profile. These techniques interlink the totalizing pole of power (i.e. individuals objectified as data in health statistics, consumer credit markets, and loan default registries) with the individualizing pole (i.e. the need to recognize the specific individual produced by such statistics). This development calls for an analytical revision, which extends Foucault's focus on the state to the domain of private corporations and their use of techniques of subjectivation.

The second major development is, of course, the advent of big data and artificial intelligence, which buttress the expansive technique of predictive profiling. While private companies in the 1990s capitalized on the state's systematization of criminal records by selling consumer background reports on the market, we now witness the production of individuals as data points by machine-driven profiling and algorithmic decision-making. Patterns of user behaviour are detected and synthesized from huge data sets to generate predictive profiles, which can then be reapplied outside their original context in domains such as marketing, insurance, or employment screening. Traditional profiling used in the penal system or in evaluations of a person's credit eligibility relied on predefined criteria for criminal proclivity or economic trustworthiness. Whereas disciplinary techniques subjugated individuals through a predetermined 'case identity', present-day predictive profiles are derived from pattern recognition in our digital behaviour, generating a virtual identity, which is continually assigned to individuals. John Cheney-Lippold (2011: 165) notes that 'categories of identity are being inferred upon individuals based on their web use. Code and algorithm are the engines behind such inference.' These algorithmic processes erase the particular subject, as it were, and differ from Foucault's disciplinary and pastoral power. Nascent research into these processes add fresh knowledge to the shared theme between Althusser and Foucault of the link between techniques of subjectivation and the capitalist economic order.

Algorithmic profiling does not try to present a specific identity or to uncover an individual's intrinsic characteristics, since the aim is to predict potential future behaviour of individuals that share certain commonalities. Profiles are constructed from surveyed internet history in conjunction with other digital data, including searches, purchases, 'likes', posts, 'check-ins', etc. From this analysis arises a predictive profile which does not represent a real person, but instead a potential future person, such as a potential consumer, a credit default risk, or a carrier of bad health. Predictive profiling relies on detecting patterns and correlations in people's web-surfing behaviour. It does not entail a direct disciplinary subjectivation of an individual but instead confers a digital identity upon users through their continual interaction with categories like gender, age, and consumption preferences that compose and recompose their identity. As Richard Weiskopf explains: 'Predictions are derived from patterns in past behavior or they are derived from similar patterns of "groups" or "neighbors". Categorizations thus not only depend on individual actions, behaviors and histories, but on those of others who are similar to him or her' (Weiskopf, 2020: 16). From such data analysis emerges something like an aggregated individuality, since it represents no specific individual but rather a conglomerate of registered behavioural patterns.

Algorithmic profiling thus entails a mode of governance which resembles the *dispositif* of security, since profiling relies on statistics, predictions, and continual testing of categories in relation to user behaviour and the detection of unexpected patterns between categories. Mathematical algorithmic profiling serves to 'securitize' business sectors like marketing, recruitment, insurance, banking, and others, insofar as it predicts how a given profile can be expected to act, hence determining its value or riskiness. Companies like the one with the fitting name 'People Analytics' have advanced the use of statistical commonality models to predictively profile a person in terms of gender, class, religion, race, etc. They produce what Cheney-Lippold (2011) has termed a 'new algorithmic identity', one that both de-essentializes identity and re-essentializes it as a statistically verified object. For example, when the algorithm operates on the category of gender, writes Cheney-Lippold (2011: 170), it 'de-essentializes gender from its corporeal and societal forms and determinations while it also re-essentializes gender as a statistically-related, largely market research-driven category'. Importantly, he also notes that 'algorithms rarely, if ever, speak to the individual. Rather, individuals are seen by algorithm and surveillance networks as members of categories' (Cheney-Lippold, 2011: 176). The way that algorithmic identity works as a mechanism of subjectivation is to suggest streams of advertisements and web content to the user according to a perceived identity—a digital alter ego—which the user will confirm or modulate in their browsing choices. Perhaps, then, one could adapt Althusser's mechanism of interpellation to the present internet user, who is constantly faced with his digital alter ego: 'Hey, you, internet user! Are you not the digital profile that we have created for you?'

Like other ideologies, 'the computational truth' generated by algorithms has come to constitute a naturalized, everyday consensus imbued with its own truths and normativity. Hence, Weiskopf suggests viewing algorithmic profiling as a new mode of truth production whereby political and ethical debate is replaced by machine-driven calculations: 'I argue that (data-driven) profiling and algorithmic decision-making are new ways of producing truth by which (wo)men govern themselves and others'. And Weiskopf (2020: 4) further asserts that algorithmic profiling 'governs behavior by circumventing reflexivity, by grounding government in computational truth rather than ethical-political debate, and ultimately by substituting ethical-political decisions by calculations'. The growing reliance on algorithmic decision-making in marketing, finance, health, and policymaking could indeed be characterized as a substitution of ethics and politics by machine-driven calculations. Such calculations promise to ensure more efficient allocation of resources and to avoid human biases and errors. On the horizon, then, is a social order which is self-sustaining, evolving through infinite circulations of machine-optimized life (centred on consumption and production), without the need for any 'outside' intervention in terms of political or ethical decisions. Perhaps this order can be viewed as another modulation of the matrix of 'totalizing power' (i.e. legal, administrative, and statistical) and 'individualizing power' (i.e. guidance of each individual's consciousness) (SP). It is, then, at the intersection between the 'totalizing', computational truths and our 'individualizing' self-conduct in relation to our digital alter egos that corresponding forms of resistance and political inventiveness can take place. Foucault terms such practices, in which politics and ethics intersect, 'ethico-politics'. This concept assumes that our self-conduct inevitably involves a political dimension, and it will be a key theme in Chapter 4.

Chapter Four
Techniques of Self-Formation

How do we 'produce' ourselves in contemporary culture? By which technical means, with reference to what knowledge, and with the goal of becoming what kind of person? The appeal to actively produce yourself is evident in the widespread appeals to 'be yourself', 'act like a real person', and 'fulfil your potential' that sound from management, education, consumption, and popular culture. These appeals for self-fulfilment and the revelation of authenticity and personal emotions are perhaps most pronounced in the host of reality and talent shows that often celebrate not only creativity but also shrewd initiative and ruthless competitiveness. Today, disciplinary, external constraints are being replaced by the demand that one should overcome one's internal constraints through self-fulfilment. Hence Byung-Chul Han argues that we have passed from being subjugated subjects to seeing ourselves as 'projects' centred on self-optimization and individual achievement. This mode of subjectivation is integral to a 'neoliberal psychopolitics', which works through appeals to freedom, since it 'seeks to please and fulfil, not repress' (Han, 2017: 36). The neoliberal emphasis on compulsive achievement is epitomized by the verb 'can', writes Han (2017: 1–2): '*Should* has a limit. In contrast, *Can* has none. Thus, the compulsion entailed by Can is unlimited.' The assertive and self-fulfilling individual has been in the making for at least four decades now. In the late 1970s, sociologists discussed whether a new personality type had emerged in North America: 'the impulsive self' that was less bound by institutionalized norms and more driven by desire, impulse, and self-fulfilment.

Ralph Turner observed that a shift was occurring in young Americans' self-identification away from adherence to institutional morality towards the impulsive self which pursues 'the experience of impulse, such as undisciplined desire and the wish to make intimate revelations to other people' (Turner, 1976: 989). This new personality type, argues Turner, calls into question conventional sociological theories on social control, which are incompatible with the new pattern of self-identification. In response to Turner, Philip Wexler argued that impulsiveness need not be opposed to social control but can itself serve as a new mode of social control (Wexler

Foucault's Technologies. Kaspar Villadsen, Oxford University Press. © Kaspar Villadsen (2024).
DOI: 10.1093/oso/9780198819400.003.0005

and Turner, 1977: 181). The impulsive self, Wexler insisted, is not the break-out of an original, ahistorical self but is rather to be understood as a cultural creation. Instead of challenging the social order, the self which constantly strives for self-gratification signified a new form of moral consensus and insti-tutional loyalty compatible with consumerist capitalism. Wexler and Turner's exchanges on the impulsive self referred to Erving Goffman's seminal work on social morality and role-conformity. Almost presaging the coming to prominence of the recent 'just be yourself' doctrine, Goffman noted that, in modern society, many social roles require that one 'add one's personal character' to the performed role. Adding character to the role means perform-ing something 'that is characteristic not of the role but of the person—his personality, his perjuring moral character, his animal nature, and so forth' (Goffman, 1974: 573). The implication is that performing our roles in mod-ern society as 'authentic persons' often requires displays of role-distance, if not role-transgression. One may wonder how the cultural quest for authentic individuality intersects with the explosive growth of data-driven communi-cation technology in contemporary capitalism.

In diagnosing postmodernism as 'the cultural logic of capitalism', Frederick Jameson saw norm-transgressive practices as integral to the culture of advanced capitalist societies. Expressions of norm-defiance and transgres-sions of received morality hardly scandalize anyone, argues Jameson, in as much as such expressions 'have themselves become institutionalized and are at one with the official culture of Western society' (Jameson, 1991: 4). The cultural logic of capitalism assumes the absence of an originating subject as well as of fixed morality, merging still more intricately the capitalist eco-nomy and transformative cultural forces. Social theorists have argued, then, that creative individuality and contestation of received morality now dovetail with late modern capitalism (Jameson, 1991; Hardt and Negri, 2000). Cur-rently, the appeals to 'be yourself' and discover one's unique individuality are inscribed into commercial campaigning and consumer segment profil-ing. Similarly, the signs that express our authenticity and uniqueness tend to become stereotypified and put into the circuits of mass consumption. Under 'surveillance capitalism', observes Shoshana Zuboff (2019), rapidly expand-ing social media platforms thrive on our individual profiling and sell our data input. Relatedly, 'info-power' entails, suggests Colin Koopman (2019), that data have ceased to be external to our true selves, but now help consti-tute who we are. Or consider the growing industry of internet counselling by authors, musicians, and actors who offer to teach you (and thousands of others) how to find your 'own' unique style. As Han (2022: 12) notes: Products are charged with emotions by way of storytelling. What determines the value added is the distinguishing information that promises the consumer a special experience - or even the experience of specialness. Schools and universities have similarly seen the triumph of student-centred pedagogies like peer learning, creative writing, and making education 'personally relevant', all of which affirm the centrality of personal experience (Nealon, 2008: 88). These critical diagnoses challenge the idea that the subject constitutes a bulwark of human authenticity against capitalist consumerism, since authenticity has already been embraced and commodified by the capitalist economy.

***

In this context that celebrates the authentic self, how do we make sense of Foucault's famous proclamation that we should turn our life into 'a work of art' as well as his critical remarks on 'the Californian cult of the self' (GE: 261, 271). He also noted that an 'almost total absence of meaning' characterized certain 'very familiar expressions which continue to permeate our discourse—like getting back to oneself, freeing oneself, being oneself, being authentic, etcetera' (HES: 251). Foucault made both statements in the context of his genealogies of self-formation or self-techniques in Greco-Roman culture and in early Christianity, which he undertook towards the end of his life from 1980 to 1984. How to interpret Foucault's journey to the Greco-Roman world in the context of his overall project remains a debated issue. Some commentators find that in his late works Foucault escaped his earlier determinism and returned to the subject to establish something like an ethics of creative self-fashioning. Eric Paras, in his biographical work, *Foucault 2.0: Beyond Power and Knowledge*, argues that Foucault moved beyond his power obsession of the 1970s, embracing a humanist agenda in his work of the 1980s (Paras, 2006). Agreeing with this interpretation, Richard Wolin (2006) writes that 'under the sign of aesthetic self-realisation, Foucault rehabilitates and vindicates the rights of subjectivity'.

Other scholars insist, conversely, that the relationship between Foucault's mid-career and later work is marked not by rupture but by continuity. Instead of rediscovering an 'artistically self-fashioning' or 'solipsistic' subject, Foucault was still concerned with the subject's position in power relations. Alan Milchman and Alan Rosenberg (2011) thus argue that Foucault's 'ethical turn' in the early 1980s did not signify a departure from political issues, but rather a reconceptualization of politics as ethical politics. This is political in the sense that our self-fashioning involves what we are willing to accept or want to change, 'both in ourselves and in our circumstances' (Foucault quoted in Milchman and Rosenberg, 2011: 229). The scholarly division raises the questions: can an ethics of self-fashioning still be a critical response to the power structures of advanced capitalism, insofar as they increasingly operate through individualistic self-fashioning? And how does Foucault's analytical emphasis on positive self-fashioning pair with his earlier sustained attention to the normalizing power of discipline?

The specific task I will pursue in this chapter is to integrate the analysis of self-techniques with the concept of *dispositifs*, hence bridging the mid-career Foucault's 1970s analytics of power with the late Foucault's ethics. Notably, Foucault did not himself elaborate his concept of the *dispositif* in relation to the theme of self-formation through self-techniques. However, in 1982 he gestured towards an integration in the same framework of the *dispositif* and the analysis of self-formation, in his introduction to the lecture series *The Government of Self and Others* (GSO: 2–5). There Foucault looks back on his previous work, saying that he has tried to do 'a history of thought', which meant analysing how 'forms of a possible knowledge (savoir), normative frameworks of behavior for individuals, and potential modes of existence for possible subjects are linked together'. He adds that these three elements, 'or rather their joint articulation', can be called 'focal point of experience' (GSO: 3). This formulation could be understood as a rendering of how the *dispositifs* make modes of self-formation possible, or perhaps better, how the interlinking of power/knowledge with the subject's self-constitution makes possible our fundamental experiences. However, Foucault does not proceed to elaborate in detail his sketch for an integrative analytical framework. His comments rather constitute one of those intriguing moments where he describes his own work from a slightly different angle, reaping from it new insights.

The commentary literature typically divides Foucault's authorship into three overall phases to identify the main themes of his evolving work (Dreyfus and Rabinow, 1982). In brief, the early Foucault focused on discourse and knowledge (early 1950s–1970), the mid-career Foucault studied power and institutions (1970–1980), and the late Foucault explored ethics and self-conduct (1980–1984). In this interpretive model, the last phase is defined by Foucault's departure from subjugation, to his recovery of an active human agent who practises self-cultivation. However, this model has generally kept the analytics from Foucault's later project separate from his previous authorship. And the specific problem at hand here of integrating the study of self-techniques with the analysis of *dispositifs* remains, to the best of my knowledge, largely unexplored (Villadsen, 2021a). Foucault's late work has, as we will see, a number of fundamental continuities with his previous research that allow for an integration of the two.

212   Foucault's Technologies

Some scholars suggest that in the 1970s Foucault showed that subjects are historically constituted on the basis of particular *dispositifs*, whereas he shifted his focus to the subject itself in the 1980s. Milchman and Rosenberg (2007: 53) thus note that Foucault's late work evinces a search for the possibility that the subject could be constituted in autonomous fashion: 'Foucault seemed to be breaking new ground in his last years, inasmuch as the subject, and not the *dispositif* [networks] of knowledge-power, and their attendant social practices, had become the focus of his thinking.' I will suggest, however, that Foucault's late work should still be understood as analyses of *dispositifs* (and subjects' relation to them), just as the analysis of self-formation, especially in terms of 'counter-conduct', is already present in the 1970s.

Other authors have stressed the possibility of human agency in Foucault's work. Nealon forges a link between Foucault's late interest in self-formation and his work at the end of 1970s on neoliberalism and biopower, since these forms of power circulate through our very identities. Foucault's notion of self-fashioning should thus be understood in the context of biopower, which targets micro-relations and identities. This 'intensity of biopower' commits Foucault to analysing the self's work upon the self, insofar as it is in the self-relation that power operates most intensely (Nealon, 2008: 91). Recently, Karsten Schubert (2021) has argued that a space of freedom can be continually created from the subject's self-relation, because the self-relation can reach a degree of autonomy in relation to the outside that constitutes it: 'Freedom is an emergent level of operation vis-à-vis the subjectifications that constitute the subject' (Schubert, 2021: 644). Explicitly addressing the problematic of this chapter, Deleuze (1988) argues that the *dispositif* always constitutes possibilities for the subject to 'enfold' its relations to the outside world in irreducible ways. When one establishes a self-relation, writes Deleuze in his distinct vocabulary, 'it is as if the relations of the outside folded back to create a doubling, allow a relation to oneself to emerge, and constitute an inside which is hollowed out and develops its own unique dimension' (Deleuze, 1988: 100). Our integrative work begins with an assessment of the main claims regarding Foucault's mid-career exclusion of human agency, and ends with a reconstruction of the notion of technologies of the self. The critique of Foucault's alleged exclusion of human agency and freedom is still repeated in the classroom, at conferences, and on the pages of critical commentaries, and it is therefore important to address the stakes of this critique in some detail.

In this chapter, I pursue the key question of how to integrate Foucault's mid-career work on the *dispositif* with his late studies of self-techniques. My discussion falls into four main parts. The first part reviews the long-standing critical consensus regarding Foucault's missing agent, especially highlighting these critics' underlying assumptions about the human subject. The second part shows both how Foucault's work from the 1970s escapes the claims about an 'agentless' conception of power and how, beginning around 1980, his work on Greco-Roman antiquity explicitly counters such claims by his turn to self-techniques. Then the third part discusses Foucault's modest 'technical' notion of ethics as the self's work upon the self, starting from the question: what price do we pay when taking up a particular self-work? This Nietzschean question leads to a series of connections and differences between Foucault and Nietzsche around ancient self-cultivation, the subject's relationship to knowledge, and the goals of cultural critique. Finally, the fourth part returns to the overall challenge of merging the analysis of *dispositifs* with self-techniques, considering different possible relationships in which subjects can engage with the *dispositif*. This part also explores the neglected question of the sociopolitical conditions for self-formation, and gives an example of 'voice-hearers' who use self-techniques to transform themselves in opposition to the power/knowledge of institutional psychiatry.

Foucault's missing human subject

The exclusion of human agency from Foucault's analytical framework has long been a major interpretive tendency across a wide range of disciplines, including several generations of sociologists, political philosophers, anthropologists, ethnographers, organization scholars, historians, and gender scholars (Habermas, 1986; Honneth, 1991; Jameson, 1991; Fraser, 1995; Fox, 1998; McNay, 2000; Caldwell, 2007; Kioupkiolis, 2012; Wheatley, 2019). Many readers have criticized Foucault's subjectless position for its inability to observe, much less theorize, the ways in which human actors manoeuvre, negotiate, transform, or resist the discursive or social structures they are situated in. On a closer look, we can identify three related critiques in relation to Foucault's missing subject. The first critique holds that Foucault offers insufficient resources for exploring the complexities and dynamics of human subjects in their lived practices. A second critique argues that Foucault's position dissolves any platform for normativity and critique because it renders resistance—and the resisting subject—as entirely reactive to power. Finally, a third critique asserts that Foucault's analysis has the unfortunate 'ideological' effect on the reader of resignation and passivity in the face of power's omnipotent reach.

The first critique in particular pertains to issues related to empirical research. It concerns the analytical problem that Foucault's framework systematically rules out the agency of concrete agents in their lived context. It hence disallows an empirical analysis that examines the complexities of social reality since it remains at the level of programmatic ideals found in the textual archive. What Lois McNay (2000) terms Foucault's 'negative paradigm of subjectification' and Raymond Caldwell (2005: 102) calls 'surrogate determinism' implies that the subject is fundamentally constrained or produced by discursive and institutional constraints. In a formulation typical of this critical consensus, Caldwell (2007: 786) asserts: 'Foucault's most influential works tend to treat agency as an exogenous effect of discourse and power/knowledge.' This is the case, says Caldwell (2007: 786), since 'he does not provide a coherent theory of embodied agency or embodiment'. Lance Wheatley finds in Foucault's works 'views that were strongly structuralist', posing the question of whether his writing, in fact, reveals that agents have more influence than his quasi-structuralist approach can account for (Wheatley, 2019). The price that scholars inspired by Foucault pay for adopting his approach is empirical blindness with respect to how human subjects play out, manipulate, or resist the grip of discourse and power/knowledge. Scholars with an empirical focus are often appreciative of Foucault's framework for understanding power, while still finding a lack of tools for theorizing and describing human agency. What the critics of Foucault's alleged reduction of the complexities and dynamics of lived practice seem to be searching for is an originary, unconstrained, and individual act coming from beyond the web of the encroaching power that Foucault supposedly depicts.

The second variety of critique centres on the normative issue of how the subject can be a source of autonomous resistance and critique, if it is constituted by power. This assumption of power's constitutive efficacy allegedly hinders Foucault from developing a normative critique (Habermas, 1986). Critical scholars across disciplines stress the impossibility of referring to any normative foundation within Foucault's framework since he permits no position for the subject outside of the power/knowledge nexus. This critique reflects the broader debate on the ontological-political standing of the subject in Foucault voiced particularly by scholars inspired by the Marxist tradition (Callinicos, 1989; Eagleton, 1990; Resch, 1992). It claims that Foucault's concepts of power and subjectivity entail the dissolution of the subject as a locus of meaning, ethics, and reasoned dialogue, in effect providing no normative basis from which to resist the dominant order. Insofar as power constructs subjectivity, these critics argue, it becomes impossible to understand how individuals can resist their own subjectivation. On Foucault's account of power and subjectivity, acts of resistance become either a mere product of power or entirely reactive to it. According to this widely accepted critique,

Foucault foreclosed the space of informed social analysis, reasoned debate, and meaningful resistance (Habermas, 1986; Honneth, 1991). Some Marxists situate Foucault and Foucauldians within 'postmodern' thinking that supposedly dissolves all foundations for rational analysis in relativism and Nietzschean vitalism (Resch, 1989). As we saw in Chapter 3 this objection against Foucault forms part of a general critique of postmodern theorizing. Implicitly invoking Habermas' (1986) classic critique, Caldwell (2007: 787) insists that Foucault's position 'closes down ideals of agency founded on intentional action, knowledge, autonomy and reflexivity'. A precarious and atomistic position is assigned to the subject, which is deprived of any platform for collective activism informed by knowledge: 'We confront a world without structures, without "objective" knowledge, without "others", and without the possibilities of social or political action informed by reasoned discourse' (Caldwell, 2007: 787). This deprivation, continues Caldwell, has the effect of undermining 'a belief in the possibility that individuals or groups can affect social or organizational change' (Caldwell, 2005: 103). In sum, critics claim that the consequence of Foucault's 'empty', solipsistic subject is a withdrawal from the proper political domain into a nihilistic and aesthetic existence that lacks foundations for political engagement. Terry Eagleton (1990) defines the aesthetic as a particular realm in which values are set from apolitical and non-rational criteria of beauty and style. The long-standing 'aestheticizing tradition', argues Eagleton, transforms laws and ideological doctrine into personal 'taste', and Foucault even aestheticizes power itself when describing it as a complex system, a 'splendid aesthetic construct' (Eagleton, 1990: 380). Overall, Eagleton shares with other critics of Marxist orientation the view that post-structuralism performs an irresponsible gesture by which the structures of power become aestheticized and politics as such dissolves.

Following from the second, the third critique asserts that Foucault's work surrenders readers to a sensation of powerlessness under the all-pervasive regimes of power/knowledge depicted. This critique is concerned with the depoliticizing effects of resignation produced by the typical Foucauldian portrayal of power as omnipresent, network-like, expansive, and subtle. This systematic dismissal or negligence of the transformative capacity of human subjects allegedly surrenders the reader to resignation and disempowerment. Jameson gave this concern a concise formulation: "The more powerful the vision of some increasingly total system or logic ... the more powerless the reader comes to feel' (Jameson, 1991: 5). In the view of some neo-Marxists, Foucault has brought political analysis to a position that leaves no room for transformative, political agency within the tight nexus of institutional, disciplinary, and discursive constraints. The effect of this analysis

216 Foucault's Technologies

is to marginalize acts of resistance and to ride out any normative perspectives from which to articulate resistance of the status quo of contemporary (capitalist) arrangements (Callinicos, 1989; Eagleton, 1990).

In humanist varieties of this critique, the problem with Foucault's 'totalizing cage of power' is not only that it prevents researchers from observing collective resistance, but that it eliminates the uniquely human and subjective dimension of life. At the root of why so many critics view Foucault's influence in the social and human sciences as damaging is a critical mindset based on nineteenth-century ideas of humanism, human potential, and the promise of liberation. For example, in organization studies, representatives of this humanist legacy call for 'saving the human subject' in management practice and research (Bolton and Houlihan, 2007). In passing, it is a bit curious that organizational scholars invoke a notion of resistance underpinned by a universal humanism at a juncture where a thoroughgoing deconstruction of universalizing notions like gender, race, and class has been achieved across disciplines. On the 'neo-humanist' account, however, Foucault's privileging of power's efficacy not only has the effect of putting the reader into resignation; he also breaks up the political and ethical unity of autonomy, knowledge, and rational deliberation. Hence such critics of the resignation allegedly produced by Foucault not only quest for originary acts coming from outside of power/knowledge regimes; they equally call for the rehabilitation of an authentic, embodied, and biographical individual for whom the exercise of agency and reflection is anchored in their 'truly human', subjective core. On this note, it is unsurprising that Foucault continues to disappoint humanist critics, since humanism was indeed a key adversary throughout Foucault's career.

The scholarly critique of Foucault's neglect of human agency finds a curious parallel in the call for creative authenticity figuring centrally in contemporary consumerism and popular culture, as outlined above. The vocabulary of agency, freedom, personal initiative, autonomous self-fashioning, the creative moment, and resistant authenticity places the creative moment outside of, and in opposition to, the constraints of power, outmoded morality, the bureaucratic organization, etc. I would argue that the commonplace critique of Foucault's exclusion of agential freedom—and the related concern of preserving 'the genuinely human' in the face of the increasing rationalization of all areas of life—depends on two underlying premises. First, acts of genuine human agency and resistance must be essentially *external* to power structures to count as genuine. Acts that depend on the power structure itself—'immanent resistance'—do not fulfil the requirement of externality. This premise also rules out Foucault's notion of power's *productivity* taken to its full extent: the possibility that power can produce something extra, unexpected, or self-undermining (including resistant human agency). Second, insofar as Foucault's subject is fully determined by, or *internal* to, power, the subject's actions can only be entirely *reactive* to power. As such, the subject is eradicated as a source of critique and ethical practice. Put differently, if the subject's self-techniques are derived from the *dispositif*, there can be no irreducibility in the subject's reflexive practice. I suggest that the critique of Foucault's missing subject stands or falls by these two premises, and at the end of this chapter we will reassess whether the critique must stand or fall.

'Agency is all there is'

Admittedly, Foucault occasionally makes statements that lend themselves to the impression that power has an inescapable grip on the subject, especially when he speaks of discipline's production of individuals and 'docile bodies'. However, some basic facts pertaining to Foucault's work problematize such an impression. First of all, people who act are not a 'neglected' or rare phenomenon in Foucault's authorship, but actually fill the pages of his books and lectures. On those pages, one finds abundant descriptions of people who act, including hygienists, town planners, psychiatrists, industrialists, prison warders, 'infamous men', ancient truth-tellers, and more. One would have to accept that those diverse groups all act in the service of power, understood as a uniform and constraining force. In his study of discipline, as we noticed in Chapter 3, Foucault repeatedly emphasizes how discipline was created—and continually elaborated—by diverse privileged groups seeking solutions to workers' disobedience, threats to their properties, and other 'urgent needs'. Furthermore, descriptions of how aspirations for control are deflected, disappointed, or resisted can be found across Foucault's work. Recall, then, how the disciplinary project generates its own indiscipline in terms of crime, prostitution, and tolerated illegalities. Against this background, it is tempting to respond to the critics of Foucault's neglect of agency that his books are replete with actions, or, as Nealon (2008: 101) puts it, 'agency is virtually all there is'. These actions, as Foucault makes clear, do not 'originate' univocally from within a subject, but rather emerge in response to or as an arbitration of tactics within contexts already pervaded by strategies of power. In brief, power's immanence to practices replaces agent-centred power.

A second complication to the critique of Foucault's disciplinary determinism is that a strategy for creating a 'disciplinary society' does not guarantee

218 Foucault's Technologies

that people were actually disciplined. It is one thing to describe how, since the eighteenth century, a major project for disciplining the populations in Europe gradually emerged, but it is another to claim that these populations became more obedient as a result. Foucault's analysis takes place at the level of rationality, and on that level he could describe how 'an increasingly better invigilated process of adjustment has been sought after'—a disciplinary project which interconnects 'productive activities, resources of communication, and the play of power relations' (Foucault, SP: 788). Put simply, there is a major difference between a 'disciplined society' and a 'disciplinary society', as Foucault makes clear, since the project of creating a disciplinary society has constantly failed:

> When I speak of the diffusion of methods of discipline, this is not to maintain that 'the French are obedient'! In the analysis of normalizing procedures, there is no 'thesis of a massive normalization'. As if these developments weren't precisely the measure of a perpetual failure ... When I speak of a 'disciplinary' society, what is implied is not a 'disciplined society'. (Foucault, cited in Raffnsøe et al., 2015: 190)

A third challenge to the assumption of Foucault's determinism is that he substitutes the conventional human/material divide by what could be termed human-material hybridity. For Foucault, there is no question of (disciplinary) technology overturning the generic ethical quality of the human, since Foucault jettisons the 'ethical polarisation of the subject–object relationship' (Gordon, 1980: 238). His works contain many examples where humans interface with and shape themselves by means of technical devices and practices. For example, *Discipline and Punish* is rich with descriptions of practices that train and manipulate individuals by means of drills, equipment, and spatial arrangements. Here, repeated drills for correctly aiming, holding, firing, and reloading of rifles mean that the soldier and the device become fused into 'a body-weapon, body-tool, body-machine complex' (DP: 153). Although Foucault contests the idea of technical neutrality, since he sees even the most mundane techniques as agents of moral and political transformation (DP: 223), his view does not entail any technological suppression of the genuinely human. We recall that no individual or genuine human faculties exist before or outside of power relations. Accordingly, technical mediation denotes a more productive interaction with and investment of human thought into material devices and practices, which Foucault's work on self-techniques vividly explores. Corresponding to the premise that the subject does not harbour an essence but is shaped by diverse forces, Foucault finds a 'technical' conception of philosophy among the Stoics, for whom philosophical wisdom was a technique to forge the subject, a *technē* of life, akin to the expert knowledge of craftsmanship.

Finally, the critique of Foucault's 'missing subject' relies on the claim that acts of resistance against power are neglected or rare in Foucault. However, I would argue that resistance is relatively commonplace in Foucault's work. A likely reason why critics find a lack of resistance in Foucault is that he eschews the power/resistance binary, conceiving of resistance as integral to power relations, as implied by the term 'counter-conduct' (STP: 201–202). In his seminal redefinitions of power, Foucault thus described resistance as immanent to power, since power passes through 'innumerable points of confrontation, focuses of instability, each of which has its own risks of conflict, of struggles, and of an at least temporary inversion of the power relations' (DP: 27). One vivid example of such immanent resistance is psychiatric patients who resist medical authority by overproducing simulated symptoms. Foucault tells us that the eighteenth-century asylum is a 'tactical arrangement' and 'a battlefield', where the problem is primarily one of overturning the misguided will of the mad person (PP: 6–7). However, in the nineteenth century, the problem of symptom simulation began to confront psychiatric expertise since it put the very distinction between a true diagnosis and a false symptom in question. Psychiatry faced a crisis when, in the late nineteenth century, patients produced symptoms that were reactions to asylum discipline. In particular, hysteria constituted 'a typical asylum syndrome, or a syndrome correlative to asylum power or medical power', which Foucault qualifies, noting that he dislikes the term 'syndrome' since '[i]t was actually the process by which patients tried to evade psychiatric power' (PP: 137). In other words, more is at stake here than simple insubordination to the discipline at the asylum. Psychiatry became trapped by its own terms because its task of imposing 'reality' on patients was disrupted by simulators, who enacted symptoms from which it was impossible to deduce a univocal diagnosis. They put into play truth and falsehood by placing this indecipherable play of signs deep in themselves. We can hence reiterate that the *dispositif* is not a rigid deterministic structure but rather a 'battlefield' in movement, perpetually shaped by tactics and struggle.

Similarly, as discussed in Chapter 3, Foucault's lectures on pastoral power (STP: 191–255) describe how diverse groups practised religious insubordination, or 'counter-conduct', in ways closely linked to the pastorate, since they reconstructed their subjectivity within 'the general horizon of Christianity' (STP: 125). These groups reinterpreted the meaning of asceticism, the ideal of self-sacrifice and self-discipline, and in doing so 'certain themes of Christian theology or religious experience were utilised against these

220 Foucault's Technologies

structures of power' (STP: 207). Foucault describes how, from the Middle Ages to the sixteenth century, religious counter-movements evolved in close correlation with the power structures of the church. These movements at the margins of the church challenged pastoral authority by reappropriating Christian doctrines, and gradually some of these 'tactical' reappropriations became integrated in the ecclesiastical institutions. Generally, then, counter-conduct must be placed within the larger historical and social context where subjects respond to how they are governed, contesting the knowledge that underpins their government. At stake in these responses is the question of what relationship one can establish with oneself as a subject, which Foucault later denoted 'subjectivation'. This term pertains, Milchman and Rosenberg (2007: 55) explain, 'to the multiple ways in which a self can be constructed on the basis of what one takes to be the truth'.

Importantly, then, practices of counter-conduct or resistant self-formation are irreducible to aesthetics, since they inevitably carry political value. As noted in Chapter 3, in Foucault's work, the term 'counter-conduct' denotes subjects who invest their reflexive self-conduct with values of moral and political significance. In both these cases the truth, which underpins the exercise of power, is challenged, or more specifically there arises the question of what is truly expressed in symptoms in the asylum or the question of the true meaning of the scripture in Christian counter-conduct. Here we find, I suggest, the basic trademarks of Foucault's notion of 'resistance': first, resistance contests and negotiates the knowledge which supports practices of government; second, resistance involves forms of self-conduct, or reformatting of the self-relation, which aims at 'not being governed like that'. And third, resistance is immanent to the *dispositifs*.

Transposed onto Foucault's framework, the principle of the immanence of resistance means that counter-conduct gives shape to, and potentially modifies, the *dispositif*. As Davidson (2011: 28–29) explains: 'Force relations structure the possible field of actions of individuals', and yet 'resistance and counter-conduct modify these force relations, countering the locally stabilized organizations of power'. The principle of the 'effective' immanence of resistance and counter-conduct introduces new possibilities of subjects negotiating, subverting, and modifying the *dispositifs*, while never entirely breaking free of them. At this point, we can reconsider the critique that Foucault sees the subject and its 'agency' as an exogenous effect of power. From Foucault's notion of counter-conduct, we note that the 'agency' of subjects is not derivative of some original source existing 'before' or 'outside' the space, where the *dispositif* is already operating; instead, agency is exerted when the subject establishes a reflexive relation to the external world; 'agency', then, is immanent to the set of reflexive practices through which subjects relate to the *dispositif*, insofar as they perpetuate it, deflect it, or resist it in their self-conduct. Foucault gestures towards such a dynamic intermeshing between the *dispositif* and individuals' conduct by stating that 'schematically speaking, we have perpetual mobility, essential fragility or rather the complex interplay between what replicates the same process and what transforms it' (Foucault, 2007b: 58). In brief, then, as a particular inclination in social relations, the *dispositif* never determines human 'agency' or behaviour, but always maps out the immediate horizon upon which practices of freedom take place.

What price do we pay?

Around 1980, Foucault began to articulate what can be termed a politics of care of self, a project that was ongoing until the time of his death. Foucault's late works, from 1980 to 1984, explore, then, how individuals have produced themselves as subjects in relation to their discursive and material conditions, or what he terms 'the techniques of the self'. We have already seen that in the 1970s Foucault focused on how subjects were disciplined and governed by others through the use of tactics, moral categories, disciplinary techniques, legal prohibitions, and more. Foucault's new project, however, was to examine how individuals turn themselves into objects of self-fashioning techniques and practices. Now the goal is, as he writes, to examine the ways in which the subject is produced 'in the relationship of self with self and the forming of oneself as subject' (HS2: 6), and he gives special attention to the self-formation termed 'care of the self'. Foucault's project focuses on the Greco-Roman world, that is, the interlocking civilizations of ancient Greece (from the fourth century BC) and the Roman Empire (the first and second centuries AD), with frequent comparisons of this Greco-Roman period to early Christianity (the fourth and fifth centuries AD). The distant situatedness of these genealogies calls for a work of translation to make them relevant to other contexts (recall the discussion on 'disembedding' concepts in Chapter 1). The production of subjectivity is still strictly intertwined with the *dispositif*, but this premise is now accompanied by an insistence on the irreducibility of the subject's self-formation. Deleuze (1988: 101) helpfully explains: 'Foucault's fundamental idea is that of a dimension of subjectivity derived from power and knowledge without being dependent on them.' While this dimension of subjectivity is immanent to the dominant structures of the *dispositif*, it nevertheless holds a potential for creation, self-modification, and resistance to those very structures.

Let us again recall that Foucault's turn to the subject's formation through self-techniques in no way revives the constitutive subject. Particularly important in this regard, as discussed in Chapter 2, is that Foucault (2000c: 156) declared how he freed himself from phenomenology and its founding subject through Nietzsche. In place of a meaning-bestowing subject, Nietzsche introduced a subject existing in a field of force relations, including the forces brought to bear upon the subject as well as the forces that the subject applies upon itself. Hence Foucault's problem with the phenomenological tradition, especially Sartre and Merleau-Ponty, is that it elides the analysis of history in terms of singular events, since it centres on the founding subject, depth, and revelation. In Foucault's view, the subject cannot be the object of such revelation because it is in perpetual process, fractured by diverse forces or different *dispositifs*: 'Who fights against whom? We all fight each other. And there is always within each of us something that fights something else' (CF: 208).

For Foucault, the lack of essence as well the absence of foundational values constitutes the basic conditions of modernity, conditions that urge the subject to undertake the difficult task of self-elaboration: 'This modernity does not "liberate man in his own being"; it compels him to face the task of producing himself' (Foucault, 1984a: 42). Foucault describes 'the attitude of modernity' as firmly fixed on the present, without metaphysical beliefs and without a negation of the present in exchange for a better future. What the modern attitude takes aim at, writes Foucault, is 'not beyond the present instant, nor behind it, but within it', and hence there is a 'will to "heroize" the present' (Foucault, 1984a: 39). These proclamations on the present resonate with Nietzsche's disdain of the priest figure as a weak man of *ressentiment*, who awaits post-worldly triumph because he cannot achieve that world in the present. Indeed, the ascetic priest renounces our present life for the sake of the afterworld, since 'life counts as a bridge to that other existence' (GM: 85). The priest figure represents a Christian culture which, as Nietzsche sees it, consistently despises life as it is here and now, and the task for humanity is to overcome its need for consolation and explanation in the divine.

The attitude of modernity, by contrast, involves a transformative activity by confronting 'what is real', says Foucault, 'with the practice of a liberty that simultaneously respects this reality and violates it'. To be modern, continues Foucault, 'is also a mode of relationship that has to be established with oneself ... it is to take oneself as object of a complex and difficult elaboration' (Foucault, 1984a: 41). The activity of self-elaboration should not be understood as a frantic and deliberate transgression of all limits, since Foucault insists on a respect for what we are in our present, even as this present compels us to transform it. Taking a modern attitude to the present means not taking for granted those values that have been received as eternal, universal, and self-evident. Nietzsche's famous dictum on the need to consider 'the value of values' is a call to re-evaluate the entrenched hierarchy of moral values and create new values. If we pose the question, 'what is this or that table of values and "morals" worth?' we can then 'decide on the rank order of values' (GM: 34). Foucault echoes Nietzsche in combining the refusal of metaphysical grounds for action with the call for critical re-examination of the values imposed on us, taking an attitude that eschews good versus evil.

At times, Foucault condensed this dual task in the question: what price do we pay for adopting a particular value? This is the case in his 1978 lecture, 'What is Critique?', where he defines critique as an ethico-political attitude based on 'the will not to be governed thusly, like that, by these people, at this price' (Foucault, 2007b: 75). How are we to interpret this last notion of 'price'? Clearly, Foucault here invokes Nietzsche's key question in *On the Genealogy of Morality*: 'Have you ever asked yourselves properly how costly the setting up of *every* ideal on earth has been?' (GM: 65). And Nietzsche later concludes: 'Nothing has been purchased more dearly than that little bit of human reason and feeling of freedom that now constitutes our pride' (GM: 83). According to Nealon (2008: 17), Foucault's 'odd economics' asks the question 'what does it cost' to adopt any value, practice, or truth, which brings into view not its truthfulness but its social effects. The Nietzschean question about the 'cost' that we incur because of our fathers' belief in an afterlife reappears in Foucault's essay 'Nietzsche, Genealogy, History' (Foucault, 1984b: 82). For both Nietzsche and Foucault, the question of whether it is *true* to believe in an afterlife is foreign to genealogical critique. Instead, a central question they both ask is what a belief costs, both ethically and politically: 'what does it cost your relation to yourself, in terms of what you can do?' and 'what does it cost others, or others you're in a position to impact, if you believe in an afterlife?' (Nealon, 2008: 18). This double assessment of the price that one pays to oneself and the price that others pay reflects Foucault's exploration of politics-as-ethics. It articulates, in other words, the theme of the government of self in its relationship to others.

224 Foucault's Technologies

The question of 'costs' is a helpful way to understand Foucault's examination of governmental practices and different self-techniques. It is a modest diagnostic question, which asks about concrete effects while escaping assessments in terms of ideology, psychology, or morality. Notably, in Foucault's rendering of the question he sidesteps any reference to human instincts and psycho-physiological drives which Nietzsche often invoked to explain the belligerent construction of morality and social institutions. Michael Ure insists, nevertheless, that while Foucault reads Stoic and Nietzschean ethics of subjectivity 'in terms of aesthetic modernism's ideal of radical creativity', this ethics should actually be grasped from the perspective of 'the psycho-analytic problem of narcissism, its pathologies and cures' (Ure, 2007: 25). Foucault's somewhat sweeping gestures towards artful self-creation should not be understood as an insistence on an essentially aesthetic conception of self-conduct. As Ure (2007: 29) observes, a more differentiated set of practices of self-conduct emerge in Foucault's lectures, especially his 1981–1982 lectures, *The Hermeneutics of the Subject*. Like Nietzsche had done in his exploration of the Hellenistic archives, Foucault reveals practices that are more 'therapeutic' than aesthetic. I take the view, however, that Foucault effectively achieves a depsychologization of his approach, insofar as he relates tactics and self-conduct to the 'anonymous' *dispositifs*, not to innate psychological and physiological needs (Dreyfus and Rabinow, 1982: 109). Indeed, one can argue that Foucault's project in the early 1980s is deeply pervaded by a Nietzschean spirit, rather than strict adherence to Nietzsche's whole philosophy including its biologism and psychologism (Owen, 1994: 205; Schrift, 1995: 38). It is illuminating to view Foucault's inquiry into 'the conditions and the indefinite possibilities of transforming the subject' (HES: 24) in light of the many links to Nietzsche. Hence we will be tracing Nietzschean echoes in Foucault's analysis of ancient self-techniques, including the question of what price, or sacrifice, they entail for the subject.

It is not as easy to read Foucault's journey back to the Greco-Roman world as a 'history of the present' compared to his previous work on the more recent history of discipline, medicine, and psychiatry, since the excavations from antiquity may appear to us like museum pieces from a distant past. Gary Gutting notes: 'The ancient world is too far removed from ours for such a history to sustain sufficient connection to contemporary concerns; it cannot be what Foucault called a "history of the present". A key reason for Foucault's extensive interest in Greek antiquity, suggests Gutting, is that Foucault finds in this period 'a model for an ethics of self-creation that will be relatively independent of the power/knowledge structures of our society' (Gutting, 2014: 139). Similarly linking Foucault's journey to the present,

Colin Koopman (2013: 529) writes: 'Foucault was interested all along in developing an ethical response to the problems of modern subjectivity diagnosed by his genealogies.' In fact, Foucault insisted that his genealogies of techniques for self-conduct had a direct significance for the present problem of how to be a subject. At the outset of the lecture series, *The Hermeneutics of the Subject,* he says that 'the challenge for any history of thought, is precisely that of grasping when a cultural phenomenon of a determinate scale actually constitutes within the history of thought a decisive moment that is still significant for our modern mode of being subjects' (HES: 9). Seen from the perspective of the present, our modern mode of being subjects is shaped by the *dispositifs* that have been examined in detail in previous chapters.

We must also consider Foucault's journey to antiquity in the light of present problems of subjectivity, especially the problem of how individuals' reflexive self-government relates to the political government of the state. Let us recall that, in 'The Subject and Power' (SP), Foucault suggested that the modern welfare state is deeply involved in the production of individuals' subjectivity, insofar as it has interlinked the subjectivation involved in confessional techniques with the objectifying knowledge of statistics. Against this backdrop, we can understand Foucault's genealogical study of self-techniques as prompted by the following question: given that political power is intimately involved with our subjectivity, what kind of resistance would be the correlate to this individualizing power? Foucault appears to confront this very problem when he posits that there is no deep subjectivity to be renounced or liberated, but that our main challenge today is to develop a 'politics of ourselves':

> Maybe the problem of the self is not to discover … a positive self or the positive foundation for the self. Maybe our problem now is to discover that the self is nothing else than the historical correlation of the technology built in our history. Maybe the problem is to change those technologies, and then, to get rid of the sacrifice which is linked to those technologies. And in this case, one of the main political problems nowadays would be, in the strict sense of the word, the politics of ourselves. (Foucault, 1997: 230–231)

Foucault's conception of ethics goes against the grain of most mainstream definitions of ethics. Arnold Davidson explains that Foucault pursued 'an understanding of ethics that many Anglo-Americans will find extremely idiosyncratic', but his purpose was 'to isolate a distinctive stratum of analysis, typically overlooked by others' (Davidson, 1991: 228). Conventionally, ethics is taken to denote the moral principles that inform an individual's

226 Foucault's Technologies

actions and the inquiry into such moral principles. Foucault offers a different understanding of ethics as the reflexive and intentional work that subjects perform on themselves in order to submit to a set of moral principles. This distinct rendering of ethics as self-forming activity, as the way we forge our freedom, must be understood in relation to the problems that concerned Foucault when he studied self-techniques in ancient Greece and early Christianity. One of the key problems Foucault saw was the contemporary challenge of elaborating a new ethics that did not found itself on quasi-scientific claims of what constitutes the self, 'so-called scientific knowledge of what the self is, what desire is, what the unconscious is, and so on' (GE: 255–256).

In addition to this contemporary urgency, Foucault's tireless opposition to humanist notions of the subject in existentialism, Marxism, and humanism broadly, would motivate his search for another conception of ethics unfettered by the moral-scientific prescripts dominant in the modern West. For Foucault, humanism had come in such diverse guises, including Christianity, critiques of Christianity, Marxism, existentialism, National Socialism, and Stalinism, that it could neither offer a universal criterion of moral judgement nor provide a framework of philosophical analysis (Davidson, 2005: 139). A key problem in humanist thinking, on Foucault's account, is its division between truth and power and, as a corollary, its dictum that any liberating politics must be grounded in the truth of our humanity. Highly sceptical of this politics of truth, which Foucault identifies in twentieth-century ideologies like fascism and Stalinism, he turns instead to a Nietzschean view of truth and power as deeply entangled in the very production of the notion of our 'humanity'.

Nietzsche directs his genealogical gaze to the life-negating uses made of the principle of subjectivity in the service of a 'hangman's metaphysics', that invented the concept of the responsible subject in order to hold it accountable and judge it guilty (Nietzsche, 1990: 32). Although reconstituting an ethics of the self was an urgent necessity, Foucault did not see the celebration of the authentic self, occurring at that time, as a resource for this project. In his 1981–1982 lectures, he proclaims: 'I do not think we have anything to be proud of in our current efforts to reconstitute an ethic of the self', and he suspects that we may 'find it impossible today to constitute an ethic of the self' (HES: 251). In the same context, Foucault mentions Nietzsche among a selection of nineteenth-century authors who took up the necessary but difficult challenge of reconstituting an ethics of the self.

The parallel with Foucault is that Nietzsche diagnosed his own time as the advent of modern nihilism, and further explored what techniques of life should be prescribed as a response to this situation. In *The Gay Science* (GS), Nietzsche announces a way of living that must break with the universalism that he finds among the Stoics and instead seeks a life in non-conformity to a fixed set of rules. As Ure (2019: 200) explains: 'if Stoics are necessarily uniform and unvaried, Nietzscheans must be irregular and varied'. The aim of self-cultivation is to affirm and develop one's own singular self by setting laws for oneself in curiosity about what one might become. Without equating Foucault's project with Nietzsche (Ansell-Pearson, 1995), I believe that these Nietzschean principles for a non-juridical model of selfhood provide a helpful backdrop for exploring Foucault's distinct conception of ethics and self-technologies. One might propose, then, that Nietzsche helps Foucault in extending his thinking on the *dispositifs* of power/knowledge with a more agent-centred ethics, to use more mainstream parlance.

Foucault provides support for a Nietzschean reading of his overall project in 'Truth and Juridical Forms' (TJ), a lecture series delivered in Rio de Janeiro in 1973. At the beginning of these lectures, Foucault gives a set of comments on Nietzsche's attack on the unity of the human subject, which provide a helpful entrance to Foucault's later work on self-techniques. Notably, Foucault praises Nietzsche's work, which 'seems to me to be the best, the most effective, the most pertinent of the models that one can draw upon' (TJ: 5). What attracts Foucault to Nietzsche's approach is that it decentres the constitutive subject into an evolving historical process. In dissolving the subject of knowledge, Nietzsche ventures to see knowledge as essentially produced in a moving field of power relations. First, Foucault credits Nietzsche for problematizing the a priori existence of a constitutive subject of knowledge, thereby breaking with 'the oldest and most firmly established tradition of Western philosophy' (TJ: 10). Referring to Nietzsche's core views in *The Gay Science*, Foucault declares that we do not need to postulate the unity of the subject and that instead we should undertake 'a historical analysis of the formation of the subject itself ... without ever granting the pre-existence of a subject of knowledge' (TJ: 5–6). Nietzsche had given a similar warning against the idea of 'pure reason' and 'the dangerous old conceptual fairy-tale which has set up a "pure, will-less, painless, timeless, subject of knowledge"' (GM: 87). Foucault then asserts that if one follows Nietzsche in assuming that what makes up the human being is marked by 'discontinuity, relations of domination and servitude, power relations, then it's not God that disappears but the subject in its unity and its sovereignty' (TJ: 10). Indeed, on Foucault's account, corresponding to the dissolution of the constitutive subject is the collapse

228 Foucault's Technologies

of teleological history, endowed with a divine purpose and progressive rationality.

Foucault then invokes Nietzsche's (GM: 110) diagnosis of the sacred value of truth in Western culture when claiming that knowledge has no stable essence, since no universal conditions of knowledge can be given. Nietzsche had argued that even if 'God was dead', the Europeans kept intact the belief in ultimate truth, and hence their trust in modern science. Most important for Foucault is Nietzsche's claim that knowledge cannot be grounded in the human subject and its faculties, since 'knowledge is always the historical and circumstantial result of conditions outside the domain of knowledge'. Foucault also specifies that knowledge should be understood as event and activity, insofar as 'knowledge will only belong to the order of results, events, effects' (TJ: 13–14). In this context, then, Foucault presents an anti-humanist conception of subjectivity, echoing Nietzsche's dissolution of the human subject as the foundation of rationality, history, and knowledge. This anti-humanism, explains David Owen, 'locates the subject as a contingent historical product and claims that the answer to the question "What is Man?" is always already futural, that is, can never be finally given' (Owen, 1994: 219). In Nietzsche's writing, Foucault finds an effective remedy against attempts to derive truth claims and moral obligations from the presumption of human nature. Thus freed from transcendent determination and philosophical anthropology, the subject now emerges as a product of specific force relations and self-techniques.

Foucault particularly appreciates Nietzsche for his displacement of the correspondence model of truth with a power model of truth. This shift entails substituting the question of whether truth claims adequately represent reality, e.g. in logical positivism, with questions of how truth claims operate in relations of power. Notably, on Foucault's reading, Nietzsche's power model of knowledge means that the subject's knowledge of himself should also be understood as a relation of power. This conclusion invokes Nietzsche's rendering of knowledge as a product of actions by which, according to Foucault, 'the human being violently takes hold of a certain number of things, reacts to a certain number of situations, and subjects them to relations of force. This means that knowledge is always a certain strategic relation in which man is placed' (TJ: 14). In other words, there is always politics involved in any kind of knowledge production, a certain politics of truth, which is 'the very ground on which the subject, the domains of knowledge, and the relations with truth are formed' (TJ: 15). Of particular relevance for the concept of self-techniques is Foucault's remark that historical models of knowledge production are also constitutive of the subject who knows: 'Even in science one finds models of truth whose formation derives from political structures that are not imposed on the subject of knowledge from the outside but, rather, are themselves constitutive of the subject of knowledge' (TJ: 15–16).

Foucault thus denies knowledge any secure ground in the subject, instead relocating the knowing subject in the contingent flow of history with its evolving 'politics of truth'. To reiterate, any politics of truth, understood as the historical models through which one gains knowledge of the world and one-self, entails a certain 'price'. In his work on self-techniques in Greek antiquity and early Christianity, Foucault develops a distinct framework for analysing historical modes of self-formation and their 'costs'—to which we now return.

Self-formation along four dimensions

In Chapter 1, we noted that in the 1970s Foucault frequently used the term 'technology' to denote a system of knowledge and practices, which near the end of the 1970s he conceptualized as the *dispositif*. In his early 1980s works, *The Use of Pleasure* (HS2), *The Care of the Self* (HS3), and *The Hermeneu-tics of the Subject* (HES), Foucault often uses the term 'techniques', while the *dispositif* recedes into the background. An explanation of this shift might be that Foucault viewed the ancient modes of subject formation to be much more independent and shaped by individuals' choices than the systematic agglomeration of techniques of domination that characterize the modern *dispositifs*. Foucault's work on Greco-Roman antiquity recovers an array of self-techniques whose value cannot be understood independently from their context of application, reflecting an ethics which cannot be captured in uni-versal obligations or legislative moral codes. Kendall and Michael (2001) advance such an interpretation: 'Foucault's endeavour was not so much to describe antique forms of subjectivity as systematised, but as made up of a variety of independent and non-systematic procedures (or techniques).' They further suggest that the Anglophone academic community has almost entirely neglected the distinction that Foucault drew in French between '*tech-nologie*' and '*technique*'. The reason for this neglect is partly attributable to Foucault himself, since he largely skipped this distinction when com-municating in English: 'Although extremely careful in his native tongue to discriminate between instances and collections of actions upon the self, in English Foucault almost spurned "technique" altogether' (Kendall and Michael, 2001). Hence Foucault entitled the lectures he gave at the Uni-versity of Vermont in 1982 'Technologies of the Self', and in an oft-cited

230   Foucault's Technologies

passage, he described self-formation as a technical crafting. 'Technologies of the self', he said, permit 'individuals to effect by their own means or with the help of others a certain number of operations on their own bodies and souls, thoughts, conduct and way of being' (Foucault, 1988d: 18). Although the Anglophone academic community has largely translated '*technologie*' and '*technique*' as simply 'technology', due to the above concerns regarding Greco-Roman subject formation, the term 'techniques' is preferred in this chapter.

In the late interview, 'On the Genealogy of Ethics' (GE), Foucault says that the subject 'is constituted in real practices—historically analyzable practices'. As if wanting to expand his earlier analysis of the subject constituted in discourse, Foucault continues: 'There is a technology of the constitution of the self which cuts across symbolic systems while using them' (GE: 277). These practices of self-constitution, asserts Foucault, 'can be found in all cultures in different forms', and they should be studied, just as we have studied 'the techniques of the production of objects and the direction of men by men through government' (GE: 277). Foucault's emphasis on the constitution of the subject in 'real practices' resonates with Nietzsche's call for undertaking a 'real history of morality' in *On the Genealogy of Morality*:

> It is quite clear which colour is a hundred times more important for a genealogist than blue: namely grey, which is to say, that which can be documented, which can actually be confirmed and has actually existed, in short, the whole, long, hard-to-decipher hieroglyphic script of man's moral past! (GM: 8)

In order to perform this neglected genealogical analysis, Foucault introduces a four-dimensional framework for analysing the subject's self-constitution. Apart from the late interview, *History of Sexuality Volume 2: The Use of Pleasure* (HS2: chapter 3) contains elaborations of this framework. Whereas historians have predominantly focused on studying the codes of moral behaviour, Foucault instead undertakes a history of the forms of moral subjectivation. By moral codes, explains Davidson (1991: 228), 'Foucault understood, for example, the rules that determine which actions are forbidden, permitted, or required, as well as that aspect of the code that assigns different positive and negative values to different possible behaviours'.

While the sociology of morals has studied people's actual moral behaviour, and moral philosophy has strived to elaborate defensible moral codes, Foucault sets out to explore how the subject can relate to the moral codes, that is, how one reflexively constitutes oneself as a moral subject of one's own actions.

This exploration concerns what Foucault calls ethics, 'the kind of relationship you ought to have with yourself', or, put slightly differently, 'how the individual is supposed to constitute himself as a moral subject of his own actions' (GE: 263). By defining ethics as a reflexive practice, through which the self works upon itself, Foucault challenges the classic philosophical dualism of subject and object. In Greek ethics, Foucault finds an 'arts of existence' or 'artistic model' of self-formation (Smith, 2015) in which the self and the ethical work by which he acts upon himself was conceived of as immanent to one another. In this arts of existence, the moral value of one's actions was neither dependent on conformity to an external code originating in divine authority, nor structured as a persecutory 'hermeneutics of desire' as Foucault identified in Christianity. Foucault breaks down this processual and immanent self-formation into four dimensions:

1. *The ethical substance*: the part of oneself or one's behaviour that one submits to ethical reflection and judgement. Foucault notes: 'It's not always the same part of ourselves, or of our behavior, which is relevant for ethical judgement' (GE: 263). Such relevant ethical substances could be, for example, actions, 'the desiring flesh', or suppressed sexuality.
2. *The mode of subjection*: the way in which one establishes one's relation to the moral codes of society. Subjection, says Foucault, 'is the way in which people are invited or incited to recognize their moral obligations' (GE: 264). For example, one is required to rigidly follow universally binding rules rooted in divine law, or one is encouraged to actively take up an individual relationship to inspirational ideals regarding how to live.
3. *The mode of elaboration*: the self-forming activity that one performs on oneself in order to become an ethical subject. Here, the question is: 'what are the means by which we can change ourselves in order to become ethical subjects?' (GE: 265). This self-forming activity includes, for example, memorizing sacred texts, imitation of a mentor, scrutiny of desires, diary-keeping, and confessional practices.
4. *The telos*: the ultimate mode of being at which one aims when acting ethically. Foucault says: 'Which is the kind of being to which we aspire when we behave in a moral way? For instance, shall we become pure, or immortal, or free, or masters of ourselves, and so on?' (GE: 265). Such ultimate goals for one's being could be to live a beautiful life (Greek antiquity), salvation through self-renunciation (Christian morality), or self-realization in this life (contemporary culture of self-fulfilment).

232 Foucault's Technologies

Perhaps the reader will note that this framework reproduces Aristotle's doctrine of fourfold causality, which Heidegger also invoked in his philosophy of technology (see Chapter 2). But whereas Heidegger refers to this doctrine in his overall philosophical critique of modern technology, Foucault introduces the framework in a specific analysis of the shifting moral attitudes and techniques related to self-formation over the five or six centuries from the Greco-Roman world to the emergence of Christianity. Specifically, the analyses cover three periods: first, Greek antiquity, where Foucault foregrounds the Socratic care for the self; second, the Hellenistic and Roman period, 'a kind of golden age in the cultivation of the self' (HS3: 45); and third, early Christianity, where care for the self transforms into self-scrutiny and self-renunciation, a 'hermeneutics of the self'. The framework captures a series of contrasts that Foucault draws mainly between ancient Greece and early Christianity concerning the dominant ethical obligations in the two periods. The analyses foreground the obligations in regard to sexual conduct, but the theme of sex is interlinked with a series of other themes, including diet, sports, rhetoric, and politics, that all centred on the question of how to conduct oneself. Most importantly, in ancient asceticism, the obligations related to sexual practice were conceived of as a set of self-formative principles that lacked the aspiration to universality.

For the ancients, *the ethical substance*, 'the aspect or the part of myself or my behaviour which is concerned with moral conduct' (GE: 263), comprises sexual desires, acts, and pleasures. The Greeks thought of these acts of pleasure, '*aphrodisia*', as naturally benign, although they entailed some concerns and risks, principally because they were connected to the lower, animal nature and hence carried an extraordinary intensity. Therefore, extravagance should be resisted, and self-moderation should be strived for in one's sexual conduct. Foucault gives the example of the love of boys, where the ancient writers idealized the man who could express and maintain friendship or love for a boy while restraining his erotic desire: 'The problem was: Does he touch the boy or not? That's the ethical substance: the act linked with pleasure and desire' (GE: 264). For the Greeks, acts, pleasures, and desires were linked together in a dynamic relationship, but the act was prioritized over pleasure and desire.

For the Christians, by contrast, the ethical substance was no longer acts of pleasure, *aphrodisia*, 'but desire, concupiscence, flesh, and so on' (GE: 268). They did not see sex as in itself benign, but rather as a fallacy in its essence. Hence 'desires of the flesh' were the principal ethical substance, which linked up with very strict truth obligations. Foucault observes that the Christians were required to decipher their desires by exercising a 'permanent hermeneutics of oneself', which demanded telling the truth about oneself as a condition of one's salvation. In brief, the ethical substance changes from *aphrodisia*, the moderate use of pleasure, to desire, the suspicion of sexual desires.

Turning to *the mode of subjection*, Foucault describes the ancients' subjection to their ethical code pertaining to sexual behaviour as the careful and controlled use of pleasures. This careful relationship to pleasures was linked to the necessary cultivation of self-mastery required for exercising political power over others in the community. In Foucault's words: 'So political power, glory, immortality, and beauty are all linked at a certain moment' (GE: 265). This mode of subjection stands in contrast to the Christians' denial of sexual pleasure under the obligations of 'divine law', which settled the choice between either strict celibacy or restriction of sexual activity to procreation within the confines of monogamous marriage. 'The Christian "formula", declares Foucault, 'puts an accent on desire and tries to eradicate it. Acts have to become something neutral; you have to act only to produce children or to fulfil your conjugal duty. And pleasure is both practically and theoretically excluded' (GE: 269). For the ancient Greeks, by comparison, the ideal of self-mastery entailed that a man made autonomous and 'noble' choices that would fashion his life into a beautiful piece of art. In their mode of subjection, the value placed on the right use of pleasures concerned how a man managed pleasures in his life so that they did not jeopardize but rather enhanced his health and social standing. These goals served as a litmus test for appraising whether a man was crafting 'a life of beauty' with regard to his sexual conduct. Overall, concludes Foucault, the mode of subjection shifts from the use of pleasures to divine law (GE: 268).

Foucault draws another contrast between the ancients and the Christians in terms of *the mode of elaboration* or the self-forming activity that aims to either moderate one's acts, or to decipher what one is (GE: 265). Ancient Greek writers described the self's work upon the self as an antagonistic struggle with oneself, where victory is achieved when one is able to master the use of pleasures in a manner consistent with one's social status, one's needs, and the appropriate timing. This kind of self-mastery was to be obtained through regular training in practices of self-denial and the capacity to abstain from sexual fulfilment. Unlike Christian moral codes, however, the ancient mode of self-elaboration neither sought to eradicate desire nor to inculcate abstention as a moral ideal. Ancient techniques of self-formation rather revolved around exercising temperance and self-control, which left space for personal choice over the practices through which one 'gave style' to one's life. Foucault explains that the mode of elaboration

234   Foucault's Technologies

changes with Christianity, 'because now self-examination takes the form of self-deciphering' (GE: 268). Hence from Greco-Roman antiquity to early Christianity there was a gradual transformation from cultivation of the self through self-mastery towards a self-elaboration which Michael Mahon (1992: 171) terms 'elucidation-renunciation', emphasizing that the self was now to be deciphered and renounced.

Finally, with regard to *the telos*, Foucault recovers a change from the goal of a virtuous life in self-mastery to immortality through purity. For the ancient Greeks, the man who had achieved control over his passions also enjoyed freedom. A free self in complete self-mastery was the *telos* of the Greek's self-cultivation, which meant that the man who conquered himself had achieved the honourable state of a virtuous life. The contrast was a weak will, inclined to extravagance and dependency on others. The goal for the Greeks, says Foucault, was 'taking into account only oneself and not the other, because to be master of oneself meant that you were able to rule others' (GE: 267). Self-mastery was thus linked to a dissymmetrical and non-reciprocal relation to others. Ensuring his supremacy, and hence freedom, in relation to himself constituted a 'specific kind of civic freedom' required of free men in order to secure the welfare of the city-state (Raffnsøe et al., 2015: 386). With the advent of Christian culture, the telos changed so that self-mastery became disconnected from the rule of others in the polis: 'mastery of oneself is something that is not primarily related to power over others' since now, explains Foucault, 'you have to be master of yourself because you are a rational being' (GE: 267). A change in the *telos* for the self in its relationship to others took place, then, insofar as this new relationship was less one of self-to-self. The Christian who pursued the goal of maintaining his innocence and purity required the guidance of another: 'the subject who earns his salvation is, of course, the agent and effective instrument of his salvation, but in which someone else (an other, the Other) is always required' (HES: 181). In brief, the individual who sought freedom by escaping the impurity of this world depended on others for this freedom.

This schematic counter-positioning is too simplistic, however, which Foucault also emphasizes by recovering some important continuities in 'sexual ethics' between the ancient Greek and early Christian periods. Foucault argues, in fact, that the moral themes—the attention to certain desires and acts—did not actually change very much between the two periods that he compares, although prohibitions tended to be stricter and more rigorous under Christianity. What *did* change, however, was the *mode of subjection*, which we defined as the way in which one establishes one's relation to the moral codes of society. Foucault explains: 'So I think that the great changes that occurred between Greek society, Greek ethics, Greek morality, and how the Christians viewed themselves are not in the code but in what I call the "ethics", which is the relation to oneself' (GE: 265–266). For the Greeks, a rigorous elaboration or 'styling' of one's daily life in consistency with self-imposed principles of conduct served as the basis of moral approval, which meant that such approval was not limited to conformity to a moral code.

This means that the *telos*, the kind of being to which one aspires, also changed. For the ancients, moral valorization of conduct was primarily appraised according to the satisfaction of one's obligations to oneself, but such caring for oneself was, at the same time, a prerequisite for the government of others in the city-state. The social status of male aristocrats entailed that they would one day partake in the governance of the city-state, and this task ultimately linked the care of the self to the community (Raffnsøe et al., 2015: 390). With Christianity, however, valorization of conduct becomes primarily concerned with whether the single individual fulfils those moral obligations that constitute the Divine law.

Instead of a complete break in all four dimensions of his framework between Greek ethics and Christian morality, Foucault emphasizes that there can be discontinuity in one dimension and continuity in another, and hence it is only a matter of 'partial' change: 'I say "partially" because some of the parts of this ethics do not change: for instance, the aphrodisia. On the other hand, others do: for instance, the techniques.' Foucault then asserts: 'There is no complete and identical relation between the techniques and the tele. You can find the same techniques in different tele' (GE: 268). The impression of a 'clean break' between ancient Greek philosophy and Christian morality is also complicated by the fact that Foucault to some extent sees the Christian techniques of self-decipherment as a development of the ancient care of the self:

> The Greeks and Romans had a 'tekhne tou biou' in which the economy of pleasure played a very large role. In this 'art of life', the notion of exercising a perfect mastery over oneself soon became the main issue. And the Christian hermeneutics of the self constituted a new elaboration of this tekhne. (GE: 259)

According to Foucault, then, techniques of asceticism aimed at controlling one's desires did not begin with the Christians, since the Greeks already practised similar techniques as a means for their self-mastery. The Christians developed Hellenistic practices, says Foucault, since Christianity 'adapted, fashioned, and honed precisely ... those practices of the exegesis of the subject and self-renunciation' (HES: 258). However, Foucault gives nuance to

236 Foucault's Technologies

Nietzsche's assertion that the ancients' dictum 'know thyself' was simply a prior form of the Christian quest for uncovering the subject's deepest truths. Dreyfus and Rabinow (1982: 255) note that for Foucault, unlike Nietzsche, the demand to enunciate the truth of the self was 'a uniquely Christian perversion of Greek forms of self-examination.'

In ancient philosophy, on Foucault's interpretation, the injunction to 'know thyself' through self-questioning was inseparable from 'care for thyself', since the care of the self served as the justificatory premise for the injunction to know oneself. Taking this premise, Socrates 'was recommending an examination of one's concepts and their relation to one's acts, not a suspicious examination of one's fantasies, impulses, and intentions' (Dreyfus and Rabinow, 1982: 255). The key observation in Foucault's analysis is that the ancients' emphasis on caring for oneself gradually shifted with the Christians' 'new elaboration' of their doctrine of knowing oneself, and especially one's deceptive thoughts. In this analysis, Foucault drew a direct line to his earlier history of sexuality in which he claimed that 'Western man has become a confessing animal' (HS1: 59), obliged to tell the truth about himself to secure his afterworldly and secular salvation.

Foucault's Nietzschean tribute to the Greeks?

It is debatable whether Foucault's analysis of the transformation from Greek care of the self to the Christian scrutiny of the self is evaluative or merely a matter of historical excavation. Some scholars put the emphasis on the latter, such as Arnold Davidson, who asserts that Foucault's analysis of ethics as the self's relationship to itself opens for a deep exploration into ancient thinking, since he 'provides us with a framework of enormous depth and subtlety ... that allows us to grasp aspects of ancient thought that would otherwise remain occluded' (Davidson, 2005: 130). Other scholars believe that Foucault, like Nietzsche before him, writes in order to produce certain effects on the reader (rather than merely exploring the archive), and that they both found in ancient Greek philosophy sources for an alternative ethics of self-cultivation that contrasted with those dominant in modernity. Gutting represents this view:

> Although this schema allows for the operation of power, the way Foucault applies it to ancient sexual ethics emphasises ethical subjectification as something carried out by individuals who seem in control of their destiny ... Foucault speaks, with apparent admiration, of the Greeks' 'aesthetics of existence', in which a life is created like a work of art. (Gutting, 2005: 102)

There are at least three aspects of ancient care of the self that receive 'interest', or even something akin to positive evaluations in Foucault's late work: first, there is a valorization of self-cultivation rather than a demand of self-denial; second, the care of the self allows for an ethical work not strictly ruled by the dominant moral codes of society; and third, the ancient techniques of the self carry the potential to enhance individuals' capacities for self-creation and transformation. In all three aspects, parallels can be drawn between Foucault and Nietzsche, who was trained in classical philology and immersed himself deeply in Greek antiquity. Hence, consider this remarkable quote where Foucault both affirms a processual view of the subject and describes ancient practices of self as liberating. He asserts that

> there is no sovereign, founding subject, a universal form of subject to be found everywhere. I am very sceptical of this view of the subject and very hostile to it. I believe, on the contrary, that the subject is constituted through practices of subjection, or, in a more autonomous way, through practices of liberation, of liberty, as in Antiquity, on the basis, of course, of a number of rules, styles, inventions to be found in the cultural environment. (Foucault, 1988c: 50–51)

That the subject must derive its 'content' not from an inner essence but from its cultural environment, is of course consistent with Foucault's long-standing philosophical anti-humanism. As mentioned earlier, there is no reinstitution of a subject in humanist terms in Foucault's late work, but instead a genealogical recovery of self-techniques guided by a basic premise that Foucault shares with Nietzsche: the subject is a process rather than a substance. A few months before his death, Foucault declared about the subject: 'It is a form, and this form is not primarily or always identical to itself ... And it is precisely the historical constitution of these various forms of the subject in relation to the games of truth which interests me' (GE: 290–291). Deleuze similarly insists that, for Foucault, the subject is not an essence but a process: 'It's idiotic to say Foucault discovers or reintroduces a hidden subject after having rejected it. There's no subject, but a production of subjectivity.' Then Deleuze draws a link between Foucault and Nietzsche on the theme of self-creation:

> Subjectivity is in no sense a knowledge formation or power function that Foucault hadn't previously recognized; subjectification is an artistic activity distinct from, and lying outside, knowledge and power. In this respect Foucault's a Nietzschean, discovering an artistic will out on the final line. (Deleuze, 1995: 113–114)

Nietzsche had pronounced that the subject is nothing but a fictitious unity created by linguistic manipulation to explain the flow of forces and events.

238 Foucault's Technologies

It is 'only the seduction of language', Nietzsche declared, 'which construes and misconstrues all actions as conditional upon an agency, a "subject"' (GM: 26). As the basis of morality, our cultural misrepresentations indicate the subject as the origin from where action emanates, and as the arbiter who can choose to perform the action or not. As Nietzsche writes in the posthumously published (and controversial) *The Will to Power*: 'The "subject" is not something given, it is something added and invented and projected behind what there is' (WP: 267). Nietzsche's refusal of this subject is not only part of his critique of cognition and language, but more importantly of morality. Whereas our language induces us to name a subject who allegedly speaks and interprets, for Nietzsche the real question is what kind of power is active when someone speaks and interprets; or, in his terms, whether a 'life-affirming' or 'life-negating' will to power is at play. Nietzsche wants to teach 'no to all that makes weak' and 'yes to all that strengthens' (WP: 33). And, as Heidegger describes Nietzsche's quest, 'everything must be assessed in terms of the question of whether it enhances will to power or diminishes or hinders it' (NV3: 202). While Foucault did examine this dualism (WK: 208–214), this does not mean that he embraced it. However, it can be argued that at some moments Foucault incited his readers to struggle against a capture of the subject rooted in the Christian tradition. For Nietzsche, this struggle is against 'the self-enslavement' of subjectivity in Christian morality, and for Foucault it is against 'the individualization' embedded in scientific discourses and their normalizing techniques.

The second aspect that draws Foucault's interest is that ancient Greek ethics was much less connected to a legal and institutional moral codex than subsequent Christian notions of ethics. Hence Foucault says: 'What strikes me is that in Greek ethics people were concerned with their moral conduct, their ethics, their relations to themselves and to others', and, in contrast to Christianity, for the Greeks 'ethics was not related to any social—or at least to any legal—institutional system. For instance, the laws against sexual misbehavior were very few and not very compelling' (GE: 255). The ancient techniques of self-care have, in Foucault's view, a significant advantage, because they placed the emphasis on individual choice and adjustment to self-imposed codes instead of enforcing universally binding rules on how to live. Such an ethics of self-care, notes Gutting, centres on an individual's specific taste, which means that 'the ethical formation it guides allows for an existence that avoids the full force of social power structures by finding a location within the interstices of these structures where the individual as such can flourish' (Gutting, 2014: 140). Of course, adopting such self-care is not readily available to us moderns, since we have inherited a Christian morality which makes self-renunciation the requirement for salvation. Foucault

(1988d: 22) says: 'We find it difficult to base rigorous morality and austere principles on the precept that we should give ourselves more care than anything else in the world. We are more inclined to see taking care of ourselves as an immorality, as a means of escape from all possible rules.' In secularized modernity, we continue to invoke external principles inherited from the tradition of Christian morality, which means that using care of the self as the basis for our morality is almost an impossibility. It is in this context, then, that Foucault expresses his 'interest' and 'fascination' with how ancient Greek ethics was disconnected from a juridical system and premised on individual choices of an aesthetic nature:

> Greek ethics is centered on a problem of personal choice, of the aesthetics of existence. The idea of the bios as a material for an aesthetic piece of art is something that fascinates me. The idea also that ethics can be a very strong structure of existence, without relation with the juridical per se, with an authoritarian system, with a disciplinary structure. All that is very interesting. (GE: 235)

If we recall Foucault's discovery of the normalizing *dispositifs* of modern society, examined in Chapters 1 and 3, an ethics of self-cultivation would certainly provide an appealing mirror, since it contradicts the normalizing standards and 'types' derived from the psy-sciences, with the ideal of elaborating 'a beautiful life' (GE: 254). For Foucault, Greek ethics offers an interesting alternative to contemporary normalization—first, because it carves out a space in which self-formative work can be performed in relative independence from ruling political and social structures (GE: 261). Furthermore, the care of the self emphasizes the practical shaping of the self in contrast to the hermeneutics of suspicion that underpins the Christian guidance of the soul. It is tempting to contrast the Christian 'deep subject' of endless interpretation with the Greek 'surface subject' shaped through practical techniques, since for the ancients 'the problem was which techne do I have to use in order to live as well as I ought to live[?]' (GE: 235). At times, Nietzsche, in parallel with Foucault, praised the ancients for their 'superficiality' in terms of their admiration for the aesthetic play with forms. In *The Gay Science*, he wrote:

> Those Greeks were superficial—out of profundity. And is not this precisely what we are again coming back to, we daredevils of the spirit who have climbed the highest and most dangerous peak of present thought and looked around from up there— we who have looked down from there? Are we not, precisely in this respect, Greeks? Adorers of forms, of tones, of words? And therefore—artists? (GS: 38)

240 Foucault's Technologies

The aesthetic emphasis in the ancient Greek principle of self-cultivation offers, for Nietzsche, a remedy against the Christian hermeneutics of suspicion. Nietzsche also expressed admiration for the ancients' capacity to encounter life's suffering without the comfort sought by the Christian 'men of *ressentiment*'. However, Nietzsche's relationship to ancient Greek culture is complex and evolved during his authorship. In early works, such as *The Birth of Tragedy* (Nietzsche, 2008), Nietzsche would appreciate the interplay in Greek tragedy between Apollonian restraint and harmony and the Dionysian ecstasy of unbridled passion. Yet Nietzsche persistently scorned Platonic and Socratic rationalism, and his fascination with Dionysian vitalism takes precedence in his late works. While Foucault's contradistinction between ancient self-care and Christian self-suspicion are more analytical than normative, his description of self-cultivation as aesthetic was anticipated in Nietzsche's praises of ancient aesthetics: 'Oh, those Greeks! They knew how to live. What is required for that is to stop courageously at the surface, the fold, the skin, to adore appearance, to believe in forms, tones, words, in the whole Olympus of appearance' (GS: 38). At such moments, Nietzsche's declarations on the ancients are more explicitly evaluative compared to Foucault's cautious descriptions, and this must be understood in light of Nietzsche's interpretive framework in which phenomena are evaluated as healthy or decadent manifestations of will to power.

The third aspect of Greek ethics about which Foucault expressed his 'interest' was that it offers ideals for an art of living that gives space for the subject's self-transformation. In Foucault's contrasting description, the ancient care of the self comprises a set of ideals and practical techniques for wilful self-cultivation, whereas Christian morality shifts the emphasis to self-scrutiny, self-renunciation, and conversion. It is tempting to hear in Foucault's description an echo of Nietzsche's distinction between affirmative/healthy and reactive/decadent forms of will to power (Schrift, 1995: 42). Indeed, scholars such as Deleuze (1995), Mahon (1992), Schrift (1995), and Milchman and Rosenberg (2007, 2011) all draw parallels between Nietzsche's and Foucault's interest in ancient Greek aesthetics, self-cultivation, and care of the self. Central to these interpretations is the link between the polarities of affirmation versus *ressentiment* in Nietzsche and self-creation versus subjectification in Foucault.

Indeed, Milchman and Rosenberg (2007, 2011) point out that in his considerations on the care of the self and self-transformation Foucault makes a distinction between '*assujettissement*' and '*subjectivation*' as two separate modes of power. Unfortunately, this has largely been lost in English translations of Foucault, since the English language does not have such a distinction. Instead, most translators use 'subjectivation' for both forms of power, probably because they wish to convey Foucault's emphasis on the constraints upon the subject. (An option in English could be to distinguish between 'subjugation' and 'subjectivation', since '*assujettissement*' officially translates to 'subjugation' or 'submission'.) For Foucault, *assujettissement* is linked to *pouvoir*, understood as 'power over' or subjugation of a passive subject, whereas *subjectivation* is linked to *puissance*, understood as 'power to' or enabling power. Reducing these distinctions to subjection and power is unfortunate, since 'pouvoir is power over, while puissance is power to; the former is linked to relations of domination and subjection, the latter to capacities for self-creation and de-subjectification' (Milchman and Rosenberg, 2011: 232). In brief, notable parallels connect Nietzsche's detection of healthy and decadent forms of will to power, with Foucault's analysis of pastoral power's individualization as both subjugating *and* enabling.

Nietzsche's critical attention to the life-negating uses that the notion of the subject has served for humanity resonates in Foucault's genealogical efforts to challenge the primacy of the subject. The belief in the subject's sovereignty was, according to Nietzsche, a fictitious idea, which misconstrues the subject as the cause of action, instead of a multilayered process of becoming. In his appreciative essay on Nietzsche, Foucault declares that genealogy does not search for pure origins or immobile foundations such as the subject; instead, genealogical inquiry 'disturbs what was previously considered immobile; it fragments what was thought unified; it shows the heterogeneity of what was imagined consistent with itself' (Foucault, 1984b: 82). Foucault also credited Nietzsche for having analysed the ideal of depth, 'of depth of conscience' (Foucault, 1998b: 273), and Nietzsche's (GM: 84–86) portrayal of the ascetic priest who taught man guilt and self-denial resounds in Foucault's diagnosis that we moderns have inherited 'the tradition of Christian morality which makes self-renunciation the condition of salvation' (Foucault, 1988d: 22).

It is also a justifiable interpretation that Nietzsche and Foucault both found, in the ancient care of the self and its techniques, a revitalizing rejoinder to the modern problems of nihilism and self-negation. Deleuze notes that Foucault, like Nietzsche, looked to the ancients in search of another way of life, not in order to 'return to the Greeks' but to shed new light on the present: 'what are our processes of subjectification, irreducible to our moral codes?' (Deleuze, 1995: 114–115). Foucault's 'tribute to the Greeks' was that they invented subjectivation, understood as the force that the subject exerts upon itself: 'By bending force back on itself, by setting force in a relation to

242 Foucault's Technologies

itself, the Greeks invent subjectification' (Deleuze, 1995: 113). On Deleuze's account, Greek subjectification is about self-mastery. Instead of submitting to codified rules of knowledge or constraining power, the man who masters himself submits to rules in a more optional fashion (Deleuze, 1995: 113). It was not enough to exert force on others or submit to the force that others exert over oneself; the subject needed to exercise force upon the forces that run through the subject itself. In ancient Greece, this notion of subjectivation principally defined free men who existed in a social system of rivalry concerning rhetoric, sports, love, and so on. To become an admirable man, explains Deleuze (1995: 113), 'the best thing is to exert power over yourself', since for a man to be fit to govern his own household as well as his community, he must first achieve complete self-mastery.

However, there are important limits to the integrative reading of Nietzsche and Foucault that complicate the comparisons advanced by scholars like Mahon (1992), Deleuze (1995), and Milchman and Rosenberg (2007, 2011). First, Foucault dislodges his approach from Nietzsche's references to psycho-physiological drives and what has been termed Nietzsche's 'residual naturalism' (Owen, 1994: 205). We recall that Nietzsche asked whether actions and cultural creations were affirmative, serving life's enhancement, or whether they were reactive or life-negating. He diagnosed Judeo-Christian morality as essentially reactive, since it turned our drives against ourselves. At his most critical moments, Nietzsche argued that the Christian ideal of self-denial was invented by men of *ressentiment* who, because of lack of power, could not pursue their drives and aggression in outward actions, and hence they turned against themselves. However, 'the ascetic priest' did not merely ask man to suppress his sexual and aggressive drives but to admit that he should not possess those drives in the first place. This morality instils a permanent self-negation in our consciousness, insofar as the demand to repress our drives has fostered 'an animal soul turned against itself, taking sides against itself' (GM: 85). Nietzsche's diagnosis of modern man as the locus of permanent struggle between psycho-physiological drives and self-negation, split between his consciousness and instincts, can be assigned to 'the residual naturalism of Nietzsche's position' (Owen, 1994: 205).

We should recall that Nietzsche in fact understood himself as a 'moral psychologist', that is, someone who analyses and diagnoses the psychology of morality. In this role, he must necessarily 'psychologize'—and hence refer—all phenomena under examination to psychological mechanisms. The claim for 'naturalism' in Nietzsche is also weakened, if one sees the repression of the drives as being intricately linked to his diagnosis of the inherent meaninglessness of human life. The Christian values of piety, altruism, and self-negation is, for Nietzsche, but an attempt to fill this void in human life—that our life cannot rationally be given any ultimate meaning. The man of *ressentiment* seeks to avoid confronting this ineradicable condition which, for Nietzsche, is precisely what we must affirm (the affirmative will to life). In this reading, Nietzsche's alleged 'naturalism' and psychologism are merely aspects derived from this fundamental condition. Foucault recovers, like Nietzsche, the will to struggle as integral to the Greek ethics of self-cultivation, and he develops Nietzsche's critique of Christianity in terms of pastoral power, but he leaves behind the problem of *ressentiment* and its psychological effects. Overall, Foucault shared with Nietzsche the view of the human subject as a site of struggle, but he evaded theorizing the internal psychological mechanisms of the subject.

Second, Foucault did not, like Nietzsche, call for a permanent 're-evaluation' of all values, since he eschewed totalizing cultural and epochal evaluations, typically directing his work towards more specific questions. When Nietzsche spoke of the perspectival character of values and knowledge, he was postulating that values are not inherently good or bad, since they are merely human projections on the world (GM: 87; WP: 267). Therefore, according to Nietzsche, the real question is which values are at play in our 'imposition of meaning' on the world (WP: 301). Nietzsche used the term 'trans-valuation' to denote the necessary work of critically assessing the hierarchical ordering of values, such as the distinctions between good and evil, strong and weak, virtues and vices, truth and lies.

Trans-valuation is the movement through which one strives to overcome the boundaries of the existing system of values, and, on a deeper level, begins to change the very ways in which we assign values. This movement involves a suspicion against the moral distinctions that help identify 'the good man' who lives in comfortable conformity with the received morality. Fiercely Nietzsche writes: 'What if a regressive trait lurked in "the good man", likewise a danger, an enticement, a poison, a narcotic, so that the present lived at the expense of the future? Perhaps in more comfort and less danger, but also in a smaller-minded, meaner manner?' (GM: 8). Instead of taking the value of our values as given, Nietzsche declares, we must ask if the opposite is true, 'so that morality itself were to blame if man, as species, never reached his highest potential power and splendour? So that morality itself was the danger of dangers?' (GM: 8). This permanent practice of trans-valuation of values strives to free itself from the moral distinctions of our culture, argues Nietzsche, since it allows man to 'stand above morality' (GS: 164). Reconceptualizing philosophical practice in this way, Nietzsche wanted to avoid relying on transcendent, ahistorical categories. This was in

244 Foucault's Technologies

accordance with his detection of the advent of nihilism, which had removed the grounds on which to regard human life and activity as meaningful, a cultural decay with which Nietzsche and his contemporaries had to wrestle.

The history of ideas, in Nietzsche's view, was one of the devaluation of the highest traditional values, so that God, reason, moral law, and absolute truth had ceased to sustain Western culture. He argued, however, that the trans-valuation of values does not carry a value, being itself above evaluation. Trans-valuation denotes, writes Alain Badiou (2001: 2), 'the supreme act, the one that puts an end to Christian enslavement', while itself being 'subtracted from evaluation'. This is because, explains Badiou in an argument which recalls Heidegger's critique (discussed in Chapter 2), for Nietzsche, life itself is beyond evaluation. It works against the nothingness of nihilism, as Nietzsche's dictum says in *The Twilight of the Idols*: 'The value of life cannot be estimated' (quoted in Badiou, 2001: 21). This dictum can be linked to Nietzsche's view of the harsh realities of natural life, unfolding uncompromisingly and without moral judgement. Moreover, we should probably not understand trans-valuation, 'the supreme act', in any ultimate or transcendental sense but rather as the work of permanent critical, cultural inquiry. While Nietzsche and Foucault both used genealogy to diagnose urgent cultural problems, Nietzsche's diagnosis of Western culture differs from Foucault's in being more certain of the symptoms of the disease, what the infectious agent is, and what cure to prescribe.

Third, compared to Nietzsche's more explicit praises of 'those Greeks' and his occasional romanticism regarding their vitalism, Foucault repeatedly distanced himself from the idea of reinvigorating 'the golden days of self-cultivation' in the present. For all his interest and fascination with ancient Greek ethics and its self-techniques, Foucault refused the notion that returning to it presents a solution to present-day ethical problems. In a conversation in 1983, Hubert Dreyfus and Paul Rabinow asked Foucault if he thought that Greek ethics offer 'an attractive and plausible alternative'. 'No!', Foucault replied, 'I am not looking for an alternative; you can't find the solution of a problem in the solution of another problem raised at another moment by other people' (GE: 256–257). Greek ethics, Foucault made clear, had a number of problematic features that we would not want to imitate, such as their celebration of phallocentric virility, their depreciation of women, and their acceptance of slavery. All that is 'quite disgusting', Foucault said. Yet what he found interesting about the Greeks was how they problematized their own existence by making ethico-political choices on a daily basis 'to determine which is the main danger' (GE: 256). Hence, as we have already noted, Foucault was much more interested in the *form* of ancient ethics, i.e. the reflexive use of self-techniques, than in its *content*.

Nietzsche, in turn, expressed a more univocal enthusiasm for the contents of Greek ethics, since he found support in elements of it for his own struggle for the valorization of sense over the Christian suspiciousness of it (Badiou, 2001: 9). Indeed, Nietzsche posits that an emulation of Greek aesthetics is a possible remedy in a culture pervaded by the Christian opposition of spirit and flesh, which hence values reason and denigrates the body's affectivity: 'As an aesthetic phenomenon existence is still bearable for us, and art furnishes us with eyes and hands and above all the good conscience to be able to turn ourselves into such a phenomenon' (GS: 163–164). Finally, instead of a Christian God, who Nietzsche thinks Europeans invented to teach us self-denial and eternal guilt, the Greeks used their gods to affirm themselves. Whereas Foucault also emphasized how ancient self-techniques aimed at giving shape to a subject's lived, bodily experience, thus escaping the modern opposition of mind and body, I would resist Ure's (2007) interpretation, which unites Nietzsche and Foucault in viewing Greek ethics as 'therapy' that enables subjects to withstand the sufferings and losses of life. Again, it is quite difficult to find evidence in Foucault of 'a man sick of himself', who suffers from inherent contradictions, most important of which is the permanent self-negation of his psycho-physiological drives.

Finally, their respective national and historical contexts must be considered in comparing Nietzsche and Foucault on their explorations of Greek ethics. Nietzsche can be placed in a stream of romanticist German thought which, reacting to the decline of Christianity and its social and political institutions, invoked Greek antiquity as an identificatory myth. In their study of the intellectual prehistory of German Nazism, Philippe Lacoue-Labarthe and Jean-Luc Nancy (1990) examine the role of myths as instruments by which individuals, groups, or nations identify themselves. However, as Lacoue-Labarthe et al. explain, the myth can serve this function only if it is not fully adopted and, instead, a 'mimetic' relationship is established to it: '[T]he question posed by myth is that of mimetism, insofar as only mimetism is able to assure an identity' (Lacoue-Labarthe et al., 1990: 277). Early modern Europe was troubled by this problem of 'mimetism', or imitation, and took inspiration in Greek mythology and its principles of imitation. Hence, Lacoue-Labarthe et al. (1990: 299) note that 'since the collapse of Christianity a specter has haunted Europe: the specter of imitation—which means, above all, the imitation of the ancients'. In Germany, where Nietzsche had declared the death of God, the problem of imitation reached a particular urgency and came to constitute 'Nietzsche's central problematic' (Lacoue-Labarthe et al.,

246 Foucault's Technologies

1990: 298). The German intellectual traditions of classical philology, aesthetics, and historical anthropology understood the telling of myths as akin to works of art, which can serve as media of collective identification. This tradition developed the ancient Greek theory of mythic imitation, insisting that identification required not simply a return to ancient myths but an active construction, or 'fusion', of myths.

Nietzsche recognized the centrality of myths for any culture, and his works of the 1880s pursued the task of creating new myths for the future. Nietzsche's myths generally herald a remote future of elevated culture of creativity and vitality, personalized in the specific myth of the *Übermensch* as the sublime creator of new cultural values (TSZ). By way of comparison, Nietzsche's concern for reviving his contemporary culture by (re)constructing myths, often derived from Greek antiquity, appears foreign to Foucault's thought. Unlike Nietzsche's overall quest for new values, Foucault, the self-proclaimed 'specific intellectual' (Foucault, 1980c: 128–131), refused nostalgic imitation of the past in the name of cultural 'self-overcoming'. Although Foucault took significant inspiration from Nietzsche's genealogical inquiry into our moral values, as discussed in previous chapters, Foucault used genealogy to describe the emergence of specific *dispositifs* of power/knowledge, not to forge a mythology that could uplift a decadent culture.

Self-techniques and the *dispositif*

At this point, let us return to the discussion on the relationship between self-techniques and the *dispositif*, and specifically to the question of how to integrate them in an overall analytical framework. We have already seen how the analysis of self-techniques escapes the critical consensus, which portrays Foucault as a thinker of power's deterministic efficacy in relation to human subjects and their actions. And yet Foucault's late emphasis on the subject as both *constituted* and *self-constituting* complicates the dualism of power and the subject which so many critics of Foucault's 'lack of agency' rely on. In his studies of Greek antiquity and early Christianity, Foucault used the term 'self-techniques' to describe the practical and reflexive means by which subjects act to cultivate themselves. This move, as we have emphasized, did not entail any recovery of the constitutive human subject that opposed power on the basis of a violated or estranged human 'essence'. By analysing self-formation as 'technical', analogous to the expertise of craftsmen, Foucault eschewed two routes that he considered problematic: first, reducing the subject to an effect of power and, second, assuming a subject in modern scientific and humanist terms. This is probably why many critics could not be satisfied with Foucault's 'solution' and still circulate the critique of Foucault's 'negative paradigm of subjectification' (McNay, 2000), advanced by influential critical theorists like Habermas (1986), Honneth (1991), and Jameson (1991). The arguments of these critics invoke nineteenth-century ideas of humanism, human potential, and liberation in which the human subject confronts a modern world of sweeping fragmentation and increasing encroachment by techno-capitalism upon generic human qualities. In Foucault's late work, however, we find neither such an overall constraining system, nor a human agent or human 'life-world' that could be constrained by that system.

For Foucault, the subject is never totally determined by power or external conditions. To be clear, this is not because there is an 'essence' or a kernel of absolute freedom hidden deep within the subject that escapes complete subjugation to power. Foucault can advance a notion of freedom that the subject may forge *in relation to* the *dispositifs*, because his understanding of freedom does not rely on any human essence or sphere that exists 'outside' of the *dispositifs*. As Deleuze (1992: 164) writes: 'We belong to social apparatuses [*dispositifs*] and act within them', but he also stresses that a *dispositif* is not a structure of absolute determination, since subjects 'enfold' external forces in variable ways, creating 'variation of the fold or of subjectivation' (Deleuze, 1988: 95). Late in his career, Foucault understood subjects as historically conditioned by specific *dispositifs*, themselves emerging from contingent and transient practices, but he insisted on the irreducibility of the subject's reflexive self-constitution. In an interview from 1982, he said that his role was 'to show people that they are much freer than they feel, that people accept as truth, as evidence, some themes which have been built up at a certain moment during history, and that this so-called evidence can be criticized and destroyed' (Foucault, 1988b: 10). Hence there is no vacuous space or pure origin where self-formation begins. Koopman succinctly defines the situation in which the subject undertakes historically conditioned self-work: 'We all begin exactly where we find ourselves and with the weight of an enormous history bearing down upon us. The very space of possibilities in which we begin to imagine better forms of self hood is already conditioned by the past that constitutes us' (Koopman, 2013: 539). For subjects to begin reconstituting themselves, and hence redefine the freedom they can enjoy, they must undertake patient reflexive work on themselves in the face of what constitutes them. Self-techniques are the medium through which subjects are able to produce, as well as transform,

248 Foucault's Technologies

a conception of themselves and what they hold as truth in relation to the *dispositifs*.

It has become clear that, for all his fascination, Foucault does not assign a superior moral value to Greek ethics. Nevertheless, the experimental and transgressive potential that commentators often connect to Foucault's notion of ethics begs the question of the value of self-techniques. Is it possible to assign different values to distinct kinds of self-techniques? And is the use of self-techniques a necessary condition for the subject's capacity to engage with the *dispositifs*? Foucault's work from the 1970s and early 1980s reveals many ways in which the subject can relate to the *dispositifs* and their power/knowledge arrangements. We have examined a key contrast in Foucault's late work, which, very schematically, runs between ancient self-cultivation and self-mastery premised on principles of 'self-care' and early Christian self-scrutiny and self-renunciation under a corpus of binding moral codes. Or, put in terms of Foucault's technological approach: the ancients used a set of self-techniques propelled by a strategy of domination-cultivation of the self, while the Christians invented self-techniques, and developed existing ones, around a strategy of elucidation-renunciation of the self. Here, we must recall our definition of the *dispositif* from Chapter 1: it is not a solid and unified substance; instead, the *dispositif* constitutes a propensity for organizing practices and generating knowledge that is observable across the social body. Although Foucault had reached such a flexible notion of the *dispositif* in the late 1970s, he made self-critical statements in the 1980s on having insisted too much on domination in his earlier work. In the lecture 'Subjectivity and Truth', delivered in 1980, Foucault announced that his emphasis would now shift from 'techniques of domination' to 'techniques of the self', but also that government takes place at the point of interaction of the two. If one wants to write the genealogy of the subject, says Foucault,

> he has to take into account not only techniques of domination but also techniques of the self. Let's say: he has to take into account the interaction between those two types of techniques—techniques of domination and techniques of the self. He has to take into account the points where the technologies of domination of individuals over one another have recourse to processes by which the individual acts upon himself. And conversely, he has to take into account the points where the techniques of the self are integrated into structures of coercion and domination. (Foucault, 1999: 162)

If we supplement the analysis of *dispositifs* with the concept of self-techniques, we can consider how, in working on themselves, subjects replicate, extend, and intensify the *dispositif,* but also how they twist, reverse, and resist it. Hence Owen (1989: 116) explains that self-techniques 'offer possibilities for both the elaboration of power networks and the generating of modes of resisting the process of subjectification'. Directing analytical focus to techniques of the self, Owen (1989: 116) specifies that 'we can examine both the unwitting complicity of these techniques with the elaboration of techniques of subjectification but, also, the ways in which our modes of self-constitution resist subjectification'. Foucault's analysis of the bitter struggles to protect wealth and discipline workers during early industrial capitalism can be read along these lines (PS; DP). In Chapter 3, we discussed the tactics by which different social groups related to and inflected the legal *dispositif* and the emerging disciplinary *dispositif.* Instead of a fixed and deterministic structure, the *dispositif* appeared as a moving 'battlefield' shaped by perpetual struggle, unfolding through the tactics that individuals pursued in their self-constitutive practice. Below, we discuss a recent study of marginalized individuals' use of self-transformative techniques, focusing on how they engage with the *dispositif* and challenge its configuration of power/knowledge.

Commentators like Wolin (2006) have argued that Foucault's late work represents a turn away from politics and towards individual self-cultivation as an aesthetic practice. Conversely, Thomas Dumm (1996: 3) asserts that Foucault did not abandon politics in his work on ethics but redefined it as centred on the activity of self-constitution. Proponents of Foucault emphasize that the notion of 'the care of the self' entails an understanding of self-cultivation whereby the subject is always in a relation to others and the community towards which he holds certain responsibilities. Yet it must be admitted that Foucault's ethical subject specifically stands in a relation to itself. This reflexive self-relation is essentially what constitutes the subject, which Foucault makes clear in the dossier 'Culture of the Self': '[T]he self with which one has the relationship is nothing other than the relationship itself' (Foucault, cited in Gros, 2005: 533). Deleuze emphasizes that Foucault's subject is but a set of processual relations, since the subject exists in a field of interacting forces, and yet 'what comes about as a result is a relation which force has with itself, a power to affect itself, an affect of the self on the self' (Deleuze, 1988: 101). Hence ethics, in Deleuze's interpretation, is the reflexive process by which the self 'folds back' on itself external forces that constitute the individual as a subject, effectively reshaping and inflecting the forces of subjectivation in one's cultural environment. Ethics, in brief, is nothing

250 Foucault's Technologies

else than the reflexive work of the self upon self. This conception of ethics is strikingly simple or, as Smith (2015: 144) observes, 'surprisingly modest', but it should be understood in light of Foucault's search for a notion of ethics beyond the content derived from legalistic frameworks and universal imperatives.

Foucault's 'modest' conception of ethics is refreshing in terms of its analytical versatility and its escape from moral and legal models, and yet it has left some readers with the view that it turns away from politics as such. Perhaps the easiest and most pertinent way to connect Foucault's work on Greco-Roman antiquity to contemporary political analysis is to follow Foucault in his exploration of truth as integral to the subject's self-formation. Already in 1973, Foucault stressed the intricate connection between 'the subject of knowledge' and the political conditions for the production of knowledge: 'There cannot be particular types of subjects of knowledge, orders of truth, or domains of knowledge except on the basis of political conditions that are the very ground on which the subject, the domains of knowledge, and the relations with truth are formed' (TJ: 15). Central to Foucault from the early 1970s onwards was the interlinkage of knowledge and the *dispositif*: that is, the *dispositif*'s integration into knowledge production (see Chapter 1). We have already noted how the disciplinary *dispositif* intersected with new knowledge of deviance, producing individuals as 'cases' and 'types' through the normalizing categories of the rising psy-disciplines. The *dispositif* of sexuality also interlinked with normalizing knowledge produced by medicine, psychiatry, and psychology, but most notably it reappropriated the confessional technique, which turned the speaker into the object of his own true discourse.

In the early 1980s, Foucault shifted explicitly towards the subject's own production of truth and, more specifically, the historical conditions in which the subject can make true statements, including the self-techniques required to act as such a subject of knowledge. In this period, Foucault explores the position of the subject in different discursive domains, or 'orders of truth', and their related techniques, including pastoral care (the confession), jurisprudence (the avowal), and politics (*parrêsia*) (HES; Foucault, 2001b; 2014). Transposed into our framework of discussion, we can understand these different modes of truth-telling as techniques by which the subject can relate to the *dispositif*. Here, we shall focus on *parrêsia*, or 'frank-speaking', which Foucault (2001b: 11) described as nothing less than 'the roots of what we would call the "critical" tradition in the West'. He then set out to explore the limits, conditions, and consequences of this old philosophical practice of truth-telling.

Courageous truth-telling

The ancient Greek term *parrêsia* can be translated as 'frank-speaking', 'truth-telling', or 'fearless speech'. The term denotes the courageous telling of truth by which the speaker confronts others, particularly rulers, not merely to provoke or correct their injustices, but essentially to transform their ethos. Foucault's studies of *parrêsia* are pertinent to our discussion of the subject's relation to the *dispositif*, since they explore techniques of speaking truth to power, by which the subjects also constitute themselves. Indeed, *parrêsia* is, says Foucault, 'situated at the meeting point of the obligation to speak the truth, procedures and techniques of governmentality, and the constitution of the relationship to self' (CT: 8–9). Foucault's analyses of *parrêsia* and its self-techniques appear in *The Government of Self and Others* (1982–1983), *The Hermeneutics of the Subject* (1981–1982), and *The Courage of Truth* (1983–1984). These analyses particularly focus on texts from the fifth century BC by Euripides, Plato, and texts that report on the teachings of the Cynic school of philosophy. *Parrêsia* can denote very different situations, including the orator who addresses the assembled people, the educator who trains students, the philosopher who counsels the governor, and the confessional subject who reveals the truth about himself. Nevertheless, Foucault's analysis assigns to *parrêsia* a set of defining key characteristics. *Parrêsia* is: first, risky for the speaker; second, constitutive of the speaker's subjectivity; third, independent of social status; and fourth, addressed to the ethos of the listener (governor).

First of all, *parrêsia* is distinct from the performative speech act, which relies on predictability, routine, and institutional rules, whereas *parrêsia* entails unpredictability and exposes the speaker to a risk. The performative speech act, exemplified by the priest who declares a couple married, 'gives rise to a completely determined event as a function of the general code and institutional field in which the utterance is made' (GSO: 63). By contrast, the *parrhêsiast* does not rely on codified rules and routines but must speak from conviction regarding what the speaker believes to be true. *Parrêsia*, says Foucault, 'opens the situation and makes possible effects which are, precisely, not known. *Parrêsia* does not produce a codified effect; it opens up an unspecified risk' (GSO: 64). It is the speaker's uncompromising personal commitment to their public enunciations, despite whichever risks are entailed, that define *parrêsia*. Foucault thus identifies in *parrêsia* a forceful break with the institutional codes and received wisdom which always imperil the speaker. Roberto Brigati (2015) notes, while overlooking a brief comment (see below), that Foucault curiously fails to include Nietzsche in his

252   Foucault's Technologies

analyses of the tradition of *parrêsia*. In Nietzsche's writing, Brigati (2015: 81) suggests, one finds several figures, such as the character of Zarathustra, who are excellent personifications of the alternative truth-teller.

Second, like other self-techniques that surface in Foucault's later works, *parrêsia* is constitutive and transformative of subjectivity. In the act of asserting the truth, the speaker not only constitutes himself as a person who tells the truth, but he also recognizes himself, his very subjectivity, in the truth that he has told (GSO: 68). Foucault sees this as a double affirmation, or an 'affirmation of the affirmation', and by this *parrhêsiastic* pact the subject 'binds himself both to the content of the statement and to the act of making it: I am the person who will have said this' (GSO: 65). A certain equivalence is hence required of the *parrhêsiast*, and hence the educator can only be trusted to practise *parrêsia* if his character is fully perceptible in what he actually says (HES: 405). While Greco-Roman *parrêsia* entails a correspondence between the speaker's enunciations and his own conduct in general, this is not an obligation to tell a unique truth that reveals his subjectivity. Whereas the Christian confession requires that the one guided is the referent of his true discourse, in Greco-Roman *parrêsia*, the person who guides must be the one who is referent of the discourse. Foucault contrasts truth-telling in *parrêsia* with the Christian tradition, notably formulating the difference in terms of 'costs'. While the pastor needs to abide by a set of rules and obligations, the 'essential cost' is borne by the one whose soul is guided, since he can only be so guided 'at the cost of his enunciation of a true discourse about Himself' (HES: 408).

Third, *parrêsia* is independent of the speakers' social status. In comparison to the speech act, the *parrhêsiastic* utterance does not gain its value and effect because the speaking subject has a specific social status: 'He may be a philosopher, the tyrant's brother-in-law, a courtier, or anyone whomsoever' (GSO: 66). Instead, explains Foucault, what lies at the heart of *parrêsia* is freedom and courage, since the *parrhêsiast* breaks with the codes defining the situation and 'emphasizes his own freedom as an individual speaking' (GSO: 65). What gives the *parrhêsiast* the right to speak outside the institutional forms then? First, it is what today might be called the sincerity of the speaker, or specifically the 'perfect fit between the subject who speaks' (HES: 406) and his actual conduct. And second, there is the speaker's courage and perhaps his irrepressible conviction to enunciate the truth, making a 'transfer that does nothing other than put to work the truth of true discourse in all its naked force, without adornment' (HES: 382). Foucault makes a casual reference to Nietzsche, when he links the personal efforts and the acceptance of risks by the *parrhêsiast* with 'Nietzschean veridicity' (GSO: 66). Although Foucault does not explain his reference, one could suggest that the *parrhêsiast's* assertiveness works as a counter-image to the reluctance and self-negation of the man of *ressentiment*. Hence to negate what one desires to express constitutes, for Nietzsche and the *parrhêsiast* alike, a way of being which is neither sincere nor truthful. Conversely, the one who practises *parrêsia* will experience a circular effect whereby speaking the truth will confirm to him what subject he is, since 'the statement and the act of enunciation will produce some kind of "retroactive effects" on the subject himself' (GSO: 68). Nancy Luxon describes the subject's circular self-assertion in *parrêsia* as the development of 'a disposition to steadiness' (Luxon, 2008: 380). She suggests that *parrêsia* breaks with the image of the modern subject as divided against itself, since truth-telling does without the distinction between mind and body, emphasizing instead self-constitutive actions informed by the immediacy of one's experiences.

Fourth, *parrêsia* aims to transform the ethos of the person one is addressing. Although *parrêsia* practised in the realm of politics may aim to convince rulers or an assembly of injustices, the mode of affecting listeners differs from other modes of political advocacy and strategizing. Foucault contrasts *parrêsia* with two discursive tactics (HES: 373–386). The first of these is flattery, a tactic by which the flatterer takes advantage of the listener (often a political leader), exploiting the latter's lack of self-esteem and self-sufficiency, thereby placing him in a position of permanent dependency: 'The flatterer is the person who prevents you knowing yourself as you are' (HES: 376). The *parrhêsiast*, however, speaks not from self-serving motives but from an attitude of generosity, allowing his interlocutor to hear what flatterers conceal from him. Such truth-telling makes the listener aware of the state he is in, for example if he acts in rage, and the aim is to help him to form an independent relationship with himself. The other enemy of *parrêsia*, rhetoric, is not bound by an obligation to truth, since rhetoric is 'an art of persuading those to whom one is speaking, whether one wishes to convince them of a truth or a lie' (HES: 381). What is central in rhetoric is constructing the discourse according to the subject at hand, and the principles for doing so are independent of the specific occasion and the individuals present. In *parrêsia*, by contrast, the occasion—the particular situation that individuals have with regard to each other—is of key significance for how truth-telling should occur. The goal of *parrêsia*, explains Foucault, is not so much to persuade the listeners to take particular actions: 'Fundamentally it involves acting on them so that they come to build up a relationship of sovereignty to themselves' (HES: 385). In the case of the politician, observes Frederic Gros, *parrêsia* proposes 'structuring elements of a relation to self suited to arousing political commitment, adherence, or action' (Gros, 2005: 387). Hence,

254   Foucault's Technologies

in politics, *parrêsia* simultaneously confronts political power and transforms the political will of governors.

The distinction that Foucault recovers between a *parrhêsiastic* 'care of the soul' and a 'rhetorical art' fed by political ambition speaks to central aspects of modern politics. *Parrêsia* stands in stark opposition to the persuasive rhetoric of populist politics. It also diverges from the pragmatics of short-sighted political tactics as well as the demands for submission to party dogmas or universal ideologies. Instead, *parrêsia* both starts from and seeks to foster individuals' ethical capacities, and it explores arguments for different values in a community of interlocutors who proceed without blind adherence to doctrines. The difference induced by truth-telling in the political game, writes Gros (2010: 388), 'aims to disturb and transform the mode of being of subjects'. *Parrêsia*, argues Luxon (2008: 380), impels interlocutors 'towards the interpretive work that might allow individuals to discriminate between a multiplicity of ethical models and relationships'. She locates the singular voice of truth-telling in the tension between the formal equality of constitutionalism and the actual exercise of democratic power, noting that Foucault saw an ever-present risk of the procedures and doctrines of formal egalitarianism turning against the truth-teller. What Foucault finds in both ancient techniques of self-care and truth-telling is a concern with a problem which is also our modern problem: how to practise the courage to be one's own authority without obedience to another.

The conditions for self-elaboration

We can now define 'care of the self' and 'truth-telling' as modes of self-formation whereby subjects, in working on themselves, relate to the forces of their social and political worlds. They do so not by simply denying or resisting the dominant moralities, truth orders, and hierarchies of power, but by reflecting on them, rearticulating them, and perhaps exposing the hypocrisy of their political rulers. The subjects in Foucault's genealogies are not 'inherently autonomous' or 'resistant', but they can cultivate a conscience of the constraints imposed on them, undertaking a patient self-elaboration by means of historically contingent techniques. For Foucault, this self-work permits the subject a degree of freedom, insofar as the work of self-elaboration is informed by reflection. We here recapitulate Foucault's distinctive definition of ethics, which he explicated in one of his last interviews: 'what is ethics, if not the practice of freedom, the conscious [réfléchie] practice of freedom?'

Foucault then declared that 'ethics is the considered form that freedom takes when it is informed by reflection' (Foucault, 2000d: 281).

One must distinguish Foucault's emphasis on reflection from Jean-Paul Sartre's philosophy, in that Sartre typically worked from abstract ontological assumptions in explaining how meaning is produced, whereas Foucault situated reflexive practices in relation to *dispositifs* of power/knowledge within a specific social and historical milieu. Comparing Foucault and Sartre, Nik Farrell Fox (2003: 3) notes that 'meaning is produced by the Sartrean subject in ontological-individual rather than in socio-linguistic terms'—a conclusion that Fox subsequently moderates and complicates. For Foucault, the ethical self-relation arises, then, from the subject's own reflexive practice of freedom, which in the Greco-Roman world required attending to one's own thoughts and attitudes by techniques of self-reflection, self-testing, and meditation.

The circular, self-referential relation whereby the self works upon the self, along with the privilege given to practices of *reflection*, has led to critiques that Foucault neglects the material and sociopolitical conditions of self-formation (Callinicos, 1989; Eagleton, 1990; Fox, 1998). Nick Fox argues that while Foucault's work before 1980 implied determinism of the subject, his late 'notion of the "self"' moves to the other extreme, inadequately addressing the constraints which affect the fabrication of subjectivity' (Fox, 1998: 415). We might ask, then: was the freedom that Foucault describes as the 'condition of ethics' merely a privilege of an elite of 'free men'? And do we risk inheriting this (restricted) view of freedom, if we transpose this framework into contemporary analysis without due attention to the conditions that underpin or constrain the subject's self-formation? For example, Nikolas Rose's (1999) attempt to conceptualize a new ethics, an 'ethico-politics', in times of expanding potential for biogenetic self-modification can be criticized for its inattention to the sociopolitical conditions of such self-care (Dean and Villadsen, 2016: 40). Hence the inescapable question is whether the conceptual merging of ethics and politics in self-formation can escape 'tired' political issues like universal rights, struggles around distribution, and access to the innovations of biomedicine, surgery, and health care.

If we take Foucault's analysis of *parrêsia*, the production of a discourse of truth occurs principally in the relationship of the speaker and listeners. However, for Foucault, this relationship—i.e. 'the occasion' of truth-telling—does not depend on a juridical framework or the social position of the interlocutors, insofar as the scene is essentially achieved through the interlocutors' ethical work on themselves. Judith Butler makes this point when she highlights how Foucault's analysis of truth-telling ignores the speakers' habitus, their social context, and the sensorial dimension: 'Our narratives come up against an impasse when the conditions of possibility for speaking the truth cannot fully be thematized, where what we speak relies upon a formative history, a sociality, and a corporeality that cannot easily, if at all be reconstructed in narrative' (Butler, 2003: 132). Of course, it can be said in Foucault's defence that he never aimed to establish a universal *theory* of subjectivation or a political theory of ethics, and his journey back to the Greco-Roman world can hardly be evaluated as such a pursuit. If we want to extrapolate and synthesize a general formula of Foucault's ethics, it could be defined as the self's capacity to command the forces that target the self. Or, as Nealon (2008: 91) states: 'Foucaultian ethics concerns governing the forces that come to bear on the self.' In Nealon's interpretation, the subject's relationship to power is not reducible to mere refusal or resistance to power. Instead, 'we must always work *with* or *alongside*' the productivity of power, and, since Foucault's primary register for understanding power is 'intensification', argues Nealon, 'critique becomes a matter of attempting to extend, broaden, or saturate certain effects within a given field, while trying to constrict, limit, or downplay other effects' (Nealon, 2008: 95). This is a helpful interpretation which, in our terms, points to how the subject's self-formative techniques will intensify, deflect, or constrict the effects of the *dispositif*, insofar as these effects must 'pass through' the subject or, more specifically, the subject's self-relation and its relations to others.

Hence the problem is not, I contend, that the historical, political, and social context is left out of Foucault's work on ethical self-formation and its self-techniques. Instead, what is perhaps missing, or not sufficiently considered, in Foucault's late work is the problem of subjects' *capacity* to affect the forces that bear on them. In a rare contribution to this problem of the conditions for self-formation, Saul Tobias (2005) brings Foucault's thinking into a dialogue with the 'capability approach' of Martha Nussbaum. The starting point for Tobias is whether the Foucauldian notion of self-fashioning and self-transformation can stand alone, without a concern for the minimum conditions necessary to enable the subject to pursue such a project. It is thus not fully meaningful to talk about creating yourself 'as a work of art' in regard to severely deprived humans—those who are economically and politically deprived, like the millions of slum dwellers and refugees, who sustain life at its bare minimum and have no ability to bring about real changes in their lives. Foucault did occasionally mention his own felt need to confront 'the intolerable' in regard to prisoners and other disempowered groups, but he never theorized why these conditions should be resisted by 'political militancy' (Karlsen and Villadsen, 2015). Tobias (2005: 69) argues, however, that Foucault's oeuvre 'evinces a recognition of the basic conditions of human flourishing, which are themselves unavoidable and arguably primary objects of political activity'. This is where Nussbaum's (1993) theory of 'capability' and 'well-being freedom' provides a supplement by considering the basic conditions of agential self-determination. She argues that psychological and physical incapacity, as well as economic and political deprivation, must be included in any analysis of a human's capacity to pursue autonomy.

Foucault's (2000c: 248) thinking on the liberating potentials of 'limit-experience', whereby 'the subject escapes from itself', can also be developed by the theory of human capability. Reading avant-garde writers, especially George Bataille in the 1950s, Foucault had come to appreciate the idea of limit-experience as an experience that brings the subject to the limits of its own subjectivity and thus undermines it. In 'desubjectivation', one does not simply lose one's self but is rather returned to the problem of subjectivity, as one experiences that one can never completely get rid of—or ultimately arrive at—oneself. Such desubjectivation can be induced by illness, pain, and near-death experience, but it could also occur through the process of writing. At his inaugural lecture at Collège de France in 1970, Foucault mentions that the author can begin to lose himself by delving into the dispersion of language. Foucault would like, he says, to disappear in the discourse, 'to enmesh myself in it, taking up its cadence, and to lodge myself, when no one was looking, in its interstices ... All I want is to allow myself to be borne along, within it, and by it, a happy wreck' (Foucault, 1972b: 215–216). Through the experience of reading and writing, one could reach the border of rational language, thereby exposing the fragility of our knowledge and at the same time encountering the very limits of one's own subjectivity (Villadsen, 2020a: 288). In limit-experience, then, losing one's way in knowledge is the price of self-transformation.

Limit-experience is not, however, a secure route to liberating self-transformation, since it carries an inherent ambivalence, which Tobias identifies by considering Nussbaum's (1993) concern with both capability and fragility. The experience of self-loss, brought about by limit-experiences, can entail a destructive, crippling process whereby the human subject's capacity to merely function, let alone create change, effectively erodes: 'Pain, illness and extreme economic and social deprivation can all erode the capacity of the subject to function as an active agent within the networks of power' (Tobias, 2005: 79). Butler describes this problem as an ontological one, since once we begin questioning the norms on which our subjectivity depends, we risk becoming unrecognizable to ourselves: 'In order to be, we might say, we must become recognizable, but to challenge the norms by which recognition is conferred is, in some ways, to risk one's very being, to become questionable in one's ontology, to risk one's very recognizability as a subject' (Butler, 2002b: 18). A subject undergoing such 'desubjectivation' can hardly participate in the struggles around power/knowledge qua Foucault's ethical formula, i.e. reflexively affecting the forces brought to bear on it. Simply put, the *dispositifs* of power/knowledge in contemporary key domains of subjectivation, such as medicine, psychology, economics, and human resource management, demand quite a lot of capability on the part of the subjects who seek to exercise self-determination and change in these domains. Tobias concludes that, since Foucault's ethics is 'parasitic on the existing arrangements of knowledge and power' (Tobias, 2005: 77), critical, analytical, and political attention must be given to the basic conditions of human well-being and capacity for practising such ethics. Put in our terminology, subjects are in need of not only self-techniques that help them 'lose themselves', but also of those that enable them to engage with the power/knowledge formations, the *dispositifs*, which condition how subjects may transform themselves and work for social change.

The capability approach highlights a fundamental problem, namely the subject's capacity for self-formation, which is often neglected in the commentary literature on Foucault's ethics. Here, I proceed by examining this problem from within Foucault's own work on governmentality, which I develop by reflecting on the relationship between self-techniques and *dispositifs*. At the outset, let us note that the problem of self-formation and capability should be situated within Foucault's understanding of power as immanent to social relations, as reversible, and as passing through the subject. In *The Hermeneutics of the Subject*, Foucault recapitulates this view of power as immanent that he had earlier named governmentality:

> if we understand by governmentality a strategic field of power relations in their mobility, transformability, and reversibility, then I do not think that reflection on this notion of governmentality can avoid passing through, theoretically and practically, the element of a subject defined by the relationship of self to self. (HES: 252)

Governmentality, explains Foucault, distinguishes itself from the juridical conception of the subject of right in institutional political theory, since the analysis of power as a set of reversible relationships 'must refer to an ethics of the subject defined by the relationship of self to self' (HES: 252). At other places, Foucault tells us that the subject, understood as the point through which government must pass, is characterized by both techniques of subjugation and techniques through which the subject constructs or modifies himself (Foucault, 1999: 162). This analytical interlinking of ethics and politics and the Foucauldian injunction to govern the forces that bear on the self returns our attention to the positive conditions for such self-formation.

In our discussion of the welfare state and pastoral power in Chapter 3, we noted that Foucault's description of pastoral power as 'individualizing' implied a double-sided concept of subjectivation in which the subject is, at the same time, subjugated and enabled by power. It follows from our examination of Foucault's late work that the one subjectified is both object and agent in relation to the *dispositifs* (recall the duality of *assujettissement/subjectivation*). The ancient Greek man now resurfaces as the historical example of a subject that freely and reflexively subjects himself to 'the *dispositif* of *aphrodisia*', its moral knowledge, and its techniques. More generally, given that power, on Foucault's account, circulates in all relations, one can ask to what degree subjects are capable of utilizing, bending, or reversing the power circulating in their interrelations and self-relation. Wendy Brown (1995: 63) formulates this Foucauldian imbrication of power and freedom succinctly: '[I]nsofar as power always produces resistance, the disciplinary subject is perversely capable of resistance, and in practicing it, practices freedom.' It is possible, following this premise, to revisit Foucault's '*dispositifs* of domination' of the 1970s (law, discipline, and sexuality) while focusing on the self-techniques practised by those dominated. One must recognize, then, that those disciplined have a register of reactions, tactics, or enhanced capacities at their disposal by which they may induce diverse reverberations in disciplinary institutions and modalities of knowledge.

Self-elaboration as critique

We have already considered some challenges of transferring the framework of ancient self-care to the contemporary context, as well as its relative lack of attention to the sociopolitical conditions for such self-cultivation. Despite these concerns, it can be fruitful to deploy the framework of self-techniques for analysing present-day struggles around subjectivity and resistance to the modern *dispositifs* of power/knowledge. An illuminating

260 Foucault's Technologies

example of such a deployment is Lisa Blackman's (1998, 2000) work on the 'Hearing Voices Network' (HVN), which is a Foucault-inspired study of resistant self-formation through alternative self-techniques. The HVN is a self-help group which supports 'voice-hearers' (i.e. subjects who experience auditory hallucinations) in Britain, across Europe, and in Australia. Let us briefly consider Blackman's study of voice-hearing, while foregrounding the self-techniques that voice-hearers use to transform themselves as subjects.

In the Western world, the disciplines of psychiatry and psychology, the 'psy'-discourses, have played a key role in producing notions of health and abnormality, which continue to inform the way that individuals are induced to constitute their subjectivities. Within modern psychiatry, voice-hearing has been viewed as a pathological condition which inhibits the patient from having 'normal experience'. The phenomenon of hearing voices is used as one of the principal indicators of the presence of a specific psychiatric disease—schizophrenia—and the progressive deterioration of cerebral functions. This framework, notes Blackman, is rooted in Enlightenment notions of rationality and control, which explains why the 'psy'-disciplines have constructed voice-hearing as lack, deficit, and loss of normal rationality: 'The hearing of voices is a signifier of deficit, disease, pathology, and lack, indicating that a person has lost certain psychological propensities and is unable to function as a responsible citizen' (Blackman, 2000: 57). On this basis, psychiatry has generally sought to eliminate the voices in order to allow patients' reinsertion into society.

The HVN counsels and supports voice-hearers who reconceptualize voice-hearing in ways that diverge from and challenge the psychiatric system and its normalizing discourse. A key objective of the group is to loosen the grip of institutional psychiatric expertise on voice-hearers in order to open up new ways of relating to the voices. A self-help manual produced by members of the network says: 'It is important to see yourself as an individual rooted in society and not as a patient rooted in psychiatry' (Coleman and Smith, cited in Blackman, 1998). Exploring a set of alternative self-techniques, Blackman (2000: 63–69) describes how individuals constitute themselves in opposition to the psychiatric system, thus striving to become different subjects. This self-work requires that a different relation to the voices is established, one that reassigns a positive meaning to them: 'Within the modern "psy" ethical system a particular relation is engendered towards the voices or visions, where the voice-hearer is required to deny their existence and view them as meaningless epi-phenomena, having no other function than as signifiers of disease and illness' (Blackman, 2000: 59). Overall, the voice-hearers construct themselves in almost diametrical opposition to the pathological framework of the modern 'psy'-disciplines.

First, the HVN rearticulates voice-hearing as a 'gift', which equips the hearer with a special sensitivity, instead of conceiving of it as a mere lack and symptom of disease. In Foucault's terms, one might say that in this way the 'ethical substance' of the voice-hearer's self-formative work is transformed into 'positive voices' (Blackman, 2000: 70). Second, while modern psychiatry views the voices as an imminent threat to rational self-control—a threat that the one diagnosed must recognize—the HVN promotes a form of subjectiva-tion which integrates the voices into the hearer's life. With Foucault, we say that 'the mode of subjection', the way in which one establishes one's relation to the moral codes, shifts from one of fear and denial to one of acceptance of the voices' integral presence in one's life. Third, whereas the psychiatric expertise conceives of voices as random, uninvited assaults that must be sup-pressed by medical and custodial supervision, the HVN reconstructs voices as a capacity that, if handled carefully, can facilitate spiritual development. Again, in Foucault's words, 'the mode of elaboration' changes from medical normalization to individualized management of voices in terms of time, situ-ation, and the hearer's mood. Finally, whereas the psychiatric discourse turns the voice-hearer into a passive object of the disease, the telepathic discourse of the HVN constructs the hearer as an active person who carries a special potential for self-mastery and self-growth. In Foucault's framework, this is the difference in 'telos', i.e. the subject that one ultimately strives towards becom-ing. In sum, the self-help group supports a work of the self upon the self in which voice-hearers transform their relation to their voices, a work which is well captured by Deleuze's (1988: 101) notion of ethics as the reflexive process by which the self 'folds back' on itself the forces that constitute it.

Blackman's study shows that there exist very different ways of shaping subjectivity in opposition to the psychiatric regime, with its diagnostic exper-tise and custodial power of supervision and internment. She describes her research as 'a strategic attempt to de-naturalise and de-stabilise "psy" under-standings and show that they are historically contingent and not natural' (Blackman, 1998: 40). Her analysis of the voice-hearers' alternative self-techniques demonstrates that the 'psy'-disciplines and their institutionalized truths can be contested by novel ways of categorizing and giving meaning to 'pathological symptoms'. However, Blackman suggests that the implica-tions of her study reach further. It points to the possibility of negotiating or freeing oneself from the subject positions and their related 'self-mastery', which modern welfare institutions impose on citizens. Hence institutions such as medicine, schooling, and social work all normalize according to

262 Foucault's Technologies

'desired images of selfhood' (Blackman, 2000: 70). If we read Blackman's study through the lenses of Foucault's technological approach, as developed in this book, her discoveries attest to the evolving struggles around subjectivity and the entrenched knowledge of 'psy'-expertise. Given that institutional psychiatry and its disciplinary practices have been persistently criticized since the 1960s, and in response have undergone a series of reforms, the voice-hearing case also points to the historical transformability of the disciplinary *dispositif*. More broadly, we can locate in the 'voice-hearing experience' a profound concern with the problem of subjectivity in the modern welfare state and its institutions of 'psy'-expertise. One might wonder, however, if the relationship between the 'psy'-sciences and those individuals who straddle the institutionalized boundaries of 'normality' and 'abnormality' is more ambiguous than the discipline/resistance model suggests.

In analysing the voice hearers, Blackman showcases not only the evident analytical strengths of the Foucauldian framework, but also, I would contend, some of its key limitations. Consider our previous discussion of how individuals can exert active choices of self-creation without considering the role of public policy in ensuring access to a health care system that secures their well-being and capability. It appears that Blackman can only observe the psychiatric system with a critical emphasis, given the opposition she draws between, on the one hand, the 'psy'-disciplines that objectify, suppress, and restrict the potentials for experiencing voices and, on the other hand, the alternative self-techniques that enable and open up the possibilities of subject formation. The presence of negative dependency in which the voice-hearers depend on the very categories that they defy for their self-constitution is not mentioned (although such constitutive relationality is unsurprising for Blackman's post-structuralism). On the more tangible effects of institutional psychiatry, Blackman (2000: 60) writes: 'Most of the voice-hearers have been subjected to the "psy" ethical system and, indeed, may still be struggling with amounts of medication or living with the threat of compulsory admission to hospital.' Without denying either the constraints involved in psychiatric hospitalization or the 'somatic subjectivity' that it relies on, one may wonder if some voice-hearers do not indeed rely on the official psychiatric system in fundamental ways? This includes the right to treatment, diagnosis, counselling, and medicalization, which probably condition voice-hearers' capacity to experiment with alternative self-techniques for mastering their voices. Said otherwise, what does the premise that the *dispositif* operates both through subjugation and subjectivation mean in this context? For starters, researchers must not forget to ask how our institutions, in submitting those considered 'abnormal' to discipline, both constrain *and* enable them—perhaps stimulating their demands not to be normalized like that, not qua this knowledge, not 'at that price'.

Dispositifs and self-techniques today

This chapter began by charting a major critical consensus around human agency and freedom in Foucault's work. As a broad outline, Foucault is paradoxically criticized for portraying freedom and resistance as impossible in his 1970s work on discipline, sexuality, and biopower, and conversely for presenting the subject's freedom as too unconstrained in his late work on ancient self-care. I have shown that Foucault's approach escapes these critiques, insofar as his analyses of self-techniques—and his notions of power, knowledge, and subjectivity—transcend the critics' fundamental premises, including their divisions of agential freedom/structural determinism, and human essence/technological constraint. Centring on self-techniques, the chapter has shown that the subject's relationship to power is not reducible to the dualities of acceptance or refusal, submission or resistance, and 'internal or external' resistances to power. Analytically, I sought to bridge Foucault's 'power phase' of the 1970s with his 'ethical phase' of the 1980s. The resulting integration of self-techniques and the *dispositif* into a single analytical framework provides an effective remedy against Foucault's alleged exaggeration of power's efficacy. To use the terms of the critical consensus, our revisionist framework gives emphasis to the mutual interplay and intertwinement of 'agency' and 'structure', and it provides space for the relative freedom that subjects exert in the face of seemingly coherent and deterministic structures. This analytical revision does not insert into Foucault a notion of freedom as autonomous self-determination, just as it does not resurrect the self-identical, constitutive subject. Indeed, the subject is just as ambiguous and criss-crossed by contradictory forces as are the *dispositifs* and their attendant human and social sciences.

The question of what 'price' we pay when we submit to a particular subjectivity opens up a way of inquiring into the consequences of pursuing values without the normative foundations derived from humanism or modern science. Nietzsche already had an acute suspicion of the worth of values, what they cost humans, and how values are operative in social struggles for domination, and he fiercely set out to re-evaluate all existing values. Foucault rearticulates the question of what price subjects pay when they submit to particular orders of truth, but he was cautious to avoid overarching critiques of

264   Foucault's Technologies

our culture. In Foucault's genealogies, the question of 'the worth of values' becomes a matter of careful inquiry into the specific effects of values, that is, how values operate in historical contexts and in multifarious practices. By introducing the notions of the *dispositif* and self-techniques, Foucault frees this inquiry from Nietzsche's psycho-physiological theme and gives it a more open-ended, empirically sensitive formulation.

Foucault's analyses of Greco-Roman self-techniques, as well as his reflections on governmentality, show numerous ways in which subjects can relate to the *dispositifs* of their social worlds. Essential to these ways of relating is the reflexivity of the self upon the self, which grants the subject a degree of freedom in relation to the *dispositif*. Foucault finds in Greco-Roman antiquity a model of reflexive self-formation which is 'very interesting', and which becomes paradigmatic for subsequent Foucauldian notions of critique and resistance: the subject's reflection on the way one ought to conduct oneself in relation to the prescriptive elements of the *dispositif*. The relatively neglected issue of the subject's capacity for undertaking ethics—the work of the self upon the self—can be reconsidered by giving attention to human capability and fragility. Although much Foucault-inspired research has inherited Foucault's suspicion of the welfare state's insidious 'pastoral power' as well as his general silence concerning welfare provision and legislation, it is timely to shift the balance and, in light of rising inequality, consider the sociopolitical conditions for subjects' self-formation (and their engagement with the ruling power structures) as unavoidable issues in contemporary analysis.

Other recent developments might call for readjusting Foucault's framework to analyse self-techniques and their interrelation with our contemporary *dispositifs*. For starters, Foucault's emphasis in the 1970s on discipline's normalizing and pleasure-denying effects must be supplemented by a consideration of today's pleasure-permissive capitalism (Karlsen and Villadsen, 2016). Recall that Foucault described how, during early capitalism, people's time and life needed to be forged into continuous labour by moral coercion, petty sanctions, and sequestration. In his 1973 course, *The Punitive Society*, Foucault said: 'The time of life, which could be broken up by leisure, pleasure, chance, revelry had to be homogenized so as to be integrated into a time that is no longer the time of individuals, of their pleasures, desires, and bodies, but the time of the continuity of production, of profit' (PS: 211). It would seem that today this 'explosive energy', which is integral to life—namely 'pleasure, discontinuity, festivity, rest, need, moments, chance, violence' (PS: 213)— has itself been enrolled into the circuits of contemporary capitalism. This is an expansive capitalism, which works not simply by excluding or correcting abnormal individuals and their behaviours, but by accommodating different identities, lifestyles, and subcultures. The present globalized capitalism, observe Michael Hardt and Antonio Negri (2000), embraces difference and diversity, and it has even adopted the critical postmodern vocabulary against rigid binaries and hierarchies.

One consequence of the transformations in liberal-capitalist citizenship described above is that our ethics, understood as the reflexive work of the self upon the self, has become increasingly integrated in consumerist production. The recent explosion in social media technologies that facilitate and thrive on incorporeal, self-identificatory work through virtual profiles bears out this tendency. A parallel development is noticeable across institutions like health services, human resource management, and social work. There, experts do not so much determine and instruct subjects, but instead increasingly seek to initiate and supervise the self's work on the self towards objectives of improved health, professional development, or personal growth, which are defined in collaboration and dialogue (Karlsen and Villadsen, 2008). This development interlinks commercial standardization and 'psy'-normalization around calls to pursue self-improvement through consumers' and citizens' ethics, understood as their reflexive self-formation. We need to pay acute analytical attention to the novel techniques that emerge from the operation of contemporary *dispositifs* that increasingly incite individuals to carry out the autonomous work of self-improvement. Equally important, however, is the need to further explore how subjects intensify, 'bend', or resist such forces in their use of self-techniques—hence the term 'ethico-political' work.

Finally, let us briefly return to the chapter's opening discussion of the recent emergence of 'the impulsive self' that pursues self-fulfilment without regard to conventional moralities. This diagnosis indeed captures significant contemporary tendencies towards a generalized celebration of forms of self-conduct that express individual creativity, self-assertion, and uncompromising goal-pursuance. This cultural image of 'impulsive selves' that ceaselessly and ruthlessly seek their own self-enhancement would seem to broadly resonate with Nietzsche's *Übermensch*, who gives himself laws and develops his crafts of self-expansion around 'a single taste'. However, the key difference between the Nietzschean character—the creative wielder of the will to power—and 'the impulsive self' is that the latter is supposedly already akin to an institutionalized figure. The sociological diagnosis of the individual that strives for self-fulfilment at the borderlines and beyond received morality would appear to find support in certain moral messages from consumption, management, entertainment, arts, and perhaps politics. What this culture of self-enhancement cannot confront, and what the sociological diagnosis neglects, is the Nietzschean/Foucauldian premise regarding the subject as a site of struggle. From their perspective, we can assume neither a unified individual 'will' that can be fulfilled, nor a self that can find rest in harmony with itself. Instead, there is a permanent work of freedom in which subjects use self-techniques in crafting the necessary transformations on themselves in order to engage with the *dispositifs* of power/knowledge. This inherently political work of freedom must proceed not only in confrontation with others' moral judgements, but also in confrontation with oneself, i.e. the subject one takes oneself to be. In Foucault, one finds no final redemption or acquisition of subjectivity, but instead the indefinite unfolding of the history of the subject. In place of today's promises of ultimate self-fulfilment and self-knowledge, Foucault emphasizes the value of losing one's way.

Chapter Five
Critique and Questions of Method

This penultimate chapter will focus on two overall questions: what are the critical implications of Foucault's technological thought, and how does one carry out this kind of inquiry in concrete terms? I begin by recapitulating the key theoretical premises that underpin Foucault's concept of the *dispositif*, which Paul Rabinow and Nikolas Rose (2003: xv) endorse as 'one of the most powerful conceptual tools introduced by Foucault'. This involves differentiating the *dispositif* from major intellectual traditions that Foucault wanted to negotiate in order to pave the way for his own distinct approach, including ideology critique, structuralism, phenomenology, and sociological functionalism. This positioning leads to a discussion of Foucault's intellectual and critical aspirations, which can be signposted as genealogical 'showing' rather than 'telling', guided by a refusal of forms of critique that universalize, generalize, and denounce.

Against this backdrop, I proceed to the relatively underexplored problem of how to explicate the methods guiding Foucault's technological thought, and I suggest some methodological principles meant as inspiration for future studies that employ the *dispositif*. This chapter particularly draws on Foucault's lecture series *Security, Territory, Population* (1977–1978) and *The Birth of Biopolitics* (1978–1979), where he often gives clear and concise explanations of his mature view on power, critique, and methods, all of which are central to the following reconstructions.

'Cutting reality' in a different way

With the *dispositif*, Foucault found a concept that 'cut reality in a different way', to use the words of Rabinow and Rose (2003: xv). That is to say that, compared to other theoretical traditions, the *dispositif* allows new relations to come into view, thereby gaining analytical importance. Rabinow and Rose describe it as such:

> One of the most powerful conceptual tools introduced by Foucault is that of 'apparatus' or dispositif. Social theory had tended to work in terms of institutions,

Foucault's Technologies. Kaspar Villadsen, Oxford University Press. © Kaspar Villadsen (2024).
DOI: 10.1093/oso/9780198819400.003.0006

268 Foucault's Technologies

> classes, and cultures and, in a distinct register, in terms of ideas, ideologies, beliefs and prejudices. But in introducing the concept of apparatus [dispositif], Foucault cut reality in a different way. In cutting across these categories, new and rather different elements, associations and relations can be seen. This is not to say that class relations and the like disappear. (Rabinow and Rose, 2003: xv)

The *dispositif* is a helpful conceptual innovation because it allows detailed description of events and processes in their transformation. Hence Rabinow and Rose (2003: xv) conclude: 'The new problems and connections that come into view, precisely because of the level of detail at which they are described, seem to become more amenable to action and transformation.' This definition is a good starting point for digging deeper into how Foucault distinguishes the *dispositif* from major intellectual traditions, which will further help us 'sharpen the edges' of the concept that we have inherited. Recall that in Chapter 1 we defined the *dispositif* as a set of practices and techniques invested by an identifiable strategy. The disciplinary *dispositif*, for example, is a set of practices and techniques of training, punishing, and curing, which are all invested by a strategy of normalization. Foucault said that the *dispositif* denotes 'a thoroughly heterogeneous ensemble consisting of discourses, institutions, architectural forms, regulatory decisions, laws, administrative measures, scientific statements, philosophical, moral and philanthropic propositions—in short, the said as much as the unsaid' (CF: 194). We note that Foucault groups together a composition of elements that do indeed 'cut across' many conventional divisions such as discourse/materiality, science/morality, as well as the visible/sayable. We also recall that the *dispositif* is in permanent motion, especially because it produces effects in excess of what was planned and intended, some of which reverberate back at the *dispositif*, inflecting various transformations. As such, the *dispositif* can be described as a non-deterministic propensity in social relations broadly, one that traverses institutions, knowledge production, and governmental practices.

Apart from the concept's versatility and open-endedness in rearticulating the historical archive, Foucault's somewhat 'slippery' definition is designed to escape key limitations that he found in dominant intellectual traditions of his time. Schematically, the *dispositif*, understood as a system of evolving techniques and practices, is irreducible to larger and deeper logics such as Marx's logic of capital, Saussure's language system, Parsons' functionalism, or Heidegger's notion of Being. In Chapter 4, we saw how Foucault effectively dissolves the founding subject in a Nietzschean field of constitutive forces and self-techniques. We also noted (in Chapter 2) that, despite evident parallels between Foucault and Heidegger, Foucault insisted on exploring how techniques are assembled and reappropriated to form *dispositifs*, without totalizing this analysis into a technological world view, or modern attitude, in the manner of Heidegger. Foucault's emphasis on how local tactics form constellations of power/knowledge, which echoes Nietzsche's view of history as struggle between different forces, both provided an exit from phenomenology and became central to his evolving conception of power.

Without universals or transcendence

In his *Archaeology of Knowledge*, Foucault lays out a new way of writing history (AK: 3–16), which was already emerging among historians in the 1950s and 1960s. Hitherto, historians had often sought after underlying layers or models that could explain the succession of dispersed events. The key question of this 'traditional analysis', argues Foucault (AK: 3), was what continuity or overall significance do these events possess? There was a tendency to explain events and developments by means of explanatory schemas, the spirit of an epoch, the progress of consciousness, or historical teleology— i.e. assumptions about the inner necessity of history. These models shared the search for various forms of continuity under myriad events. Foucault notes, however, that a new approach to history was emerging that no longer sought to remove from history its discontinuity, that is, 'the raw material of history, which presented itself in the form of dispersed events' (AK: 8). Discontinuity, understood as interruptions, diversions, and chance happenings, was now becoming one of the basic elements of historical analysis. Historians could now describe these disparate events in their 'singularity', starting from the recognition that events are created from history itself in all its contingency. Indeed, discourse is, Foucault declared, 'from beginning to end, historical—a fragment of history, a unity and discontinuity in history itself' (AK: 117). Foucault wanted to explore this nascent view of history as a set of accidental, interrelating forces that have no natural direction, neat epochal divisions, or progressive evolution. When he endorsed Nietzsche in the early 1970s, Foucault now radicalized this premise of historical contingency, foregrounding strategies of power in his writing of history that he now called genealogy.

The path was hereby open to use the *dispositif* as a tool for describing how objects and subjects emerge in a history with no universals and no

270   Foucault's Technologies

transcendent subject. With this foundationless genealogical approach, however, Foucault did not argue for relativism. In other words, his goal was not to show that throughout history people have had different views of the same object. While a relativist approach might show that madness has been the object of different discursive representations or that madness as a problem has incited different reactions throughout history, Foucault did neither. What Foucault sought to show was how madness was constructed and reconstructed through a multifaceted process. For him, the issue with relativism is that it retains the object as a permanent or universal 'thing', which elides the object's constitutive correlation with the *dispositif*. Indeed, according to Paul Veyne (1997: 168), relativism relies on a 'false continuity' and a universalizing notion of madness. For Foucault, what we regard as madness in a given historical context is rooted in the prevailing knowledge of what madness is and, fundamentally, the divisions established between madness and reason. Foucault hence goes further than relativism, as Bernard Harcourt (2008: 155) argues: 'The idea is to explore how the concept was shaped and what work it performed—and his method was to start by supposing that the thing itself never existed.' Thus, relativism does not fully do the job of eliminating universalism. Foucault's analytical move is 'to reduce everything to events that cannot be universalized', since, explains Veyne, 'his genealogy traces everything back to an empirical occurrence' (Veyne, 2010: 107). In this way, Foucault has placed our lives in an absolute and endless historical contingency.

In 1983, Foucault called his own work 'a nominalist negativism', which 'involves replacing universals like madness, crime, and sexuality with the analysis of experiences which constitute singular historical forms' (GSO: 5). By invoking nominalism, Foucault thus rejected the existence of universals from the assumption that the use of a general concept, like madness or sexuality, does not prove the existence of such objects. The nominalist position denies the existence of universals, arguing that a general word such as 'humanity' does not represent a corresponding distinct entity named by it. However, in Foucault's version of nominalism, the correspondence between particular objects/subjects and the concept which encapsulates them, is forged by power relations. In brief, Foucault's genealogy operates against universals and abstract moral codex, instead analysing *dispositifs* as historical singularities, which emerge at particular junctures as a response to urgent problems.

One can understand these moves as part of Foucault's version of nominalism, or his 'nominalist anti-essentialism' (Protevi, 2016: 122), as he explains it at the beginning of his lecture series, *Birth of Biopolitics* (BP: 3–20). In this context, Foucault argues that although 'universals' like madness, delinquency, sexuality, or civil society do not exist as a singular whole, they are not 'pure ideas' or 'false constructs', which can be discarded through reasoning. This is because they are constituted by a whole set of material and concrete practices organized around a phenomenon which is supposed to exist: 'They are things that do not exist, and yet which are in reality and follow a regime of truth' (BP: 20). In other words, although these 'things' are constructs in discourse, they nevertheless possess a reality, in terms of real effects. It is in the belief that the discursive object 'X' exists that it exerts its effects, since practices have recourse to X, invoke the truth of X, and make a series of divisions with reference to X. Veyne lucidly explains the premise that universals only exist in terms of their effects: 'similarly, the functioning of an engine is not one of the parts of the machinery; it is the abstract idea that the engine functions' (Veyne, 2010: 29). In Foucault's analysis, then, objects like madness and sexuality are realities which do not 'exist in-themselves', but they nevertheless saturate or, as Deleuze would say, 'breathe life into' real social practices that invoke them.

Let us briefly consider the 'universal' concept of 'civil society' that is so central to modern political ideologies, which I analysed in my article 'Foucault and the Forces of Civil Society' (Villadsen, 2016). Foucault cautions against treating civil society as a natural given, a timeless reality that possesses certain inherent positive qualities. Towards the end of *Birth of Biopolitics* (BP), Foucault concludes that civil society 'is not an historical-natural given which functions in some way as both the foundation of and source of opposition to the state or the political institutions. Civil society is not a primary and immediate reality' (BP: 297). This cautioning does not mean, however, that civil society is an 'ideological construct' or an 'illusion' (BP: 20). Foucault eschews both the idea that civil society is a distinct object or sphere and the claim that civil society is an ideological effect, but it is nevertheless 'marked out in reality'. Like madness and sexuality, civil society is one of those universals that do not exist; instead, Foucault foregrounds the set of practices organized around this 'X', which supposedly exists.

Civil society emerged in liberal thinking as the correlate to the state, as a domain which always resists complete knowledge and effective governance. Since civil society was often assigned its own inherent 'naturalness', like individuals' 'natural motivations', 'organic solidarity', or 'the naturalness of the market', civil society showed the need for governmental self-limitation. This is why Foucault denotes civil society as part of a schematization, or 'a technology', for determining correct governance from the principle that government is always-already 'too much' or 'excessive', and hence its 'necessity and usefulness can and must always be questioned' (BP: 319). When a whole set of practices become linked with a regime of truth (as in early political

272 Foucault's Technologies

economy) then 'something which does not exist' (civil society) can become 'something', and yet, specifies Foucault, something 'that continues not to exist' (BP: 19). Civil society cannot be a universal, because of Foucault's epistemological premise that the term is bound to a set of practices from which it cannot be separated. Veyne explains: 'we cannot separate the thing in itself from the *dispositif* or "the set-up", in which it is bound up for us' (Veyne, 2010: 11), and this 'set-up' comprises both laws, actions, and words (Veyne, 2010: 31). Hence, instead of accepting the split between state and civil society as a universal, one must examine how the concept of civil society is immanent to *dispositifs* that model themselves upon it. The *dispositif* produces, as it were, a 'real fiction'.

What comes into view in the analysis of *dispositifs* are the power effects that arise when practices and actions are judged according to 'the truth' of object 'X'. Of course, many different notions of civil society have been constructed, spanning those diverse political ideologies that dream of a final unification of state and society where social contradictions are ultimately resolved—including the communist society, the fascist nation state, and perhaps the neoliberal 'competition state' (Villadsen, 2016: 13–15). From this perspective, civil society cannot fulfil the role often assigned to it in modern political discourse, i.e. an inherent source of progressive contestation of governments, since it is a 'false universal' pregnant with a range of incongruous political projects. The diverse parts that civil society has played in history and across different societies, often linked to political struggle, revolutionary bloodshed, and persecution, insert it into a history of continual reinterpretation and redirection that bend the concept to new purposes. Indeed, civil society appears as one of those universalizing concepts, the value of which must be questioned, as Nietzsche advocated.

We have already noticed how Foucault's genealogy involves a Nietzschean move that inserts a practice, technique, or concept into a historical process of new interpretations and adaptations. This processual view, proclaimed Nietzsche, removes doctrines about natural progression or historical teleology, as, for example, doctrines about society's progressive realization of a final unity:

> The 'development' of a thing, a tradition, an organ is therefore certainly not its progressus towards a goal, still less is it a logical progressus, taking the shortest route with least expenditure of energy and cost,— instead it is a succession of more or less profound, more or less mutually independent processes of subjugation. (GM: 51)

Nietzsche's view of history as a succession of 'more or less mutually independent processes of subjugation' resonates quite strongly with Foucault's analyses of how *dispositifs* emerge, gain ground, invest practices, and develop in mutual interplay. The term 'subjugation', here used by Nietzsche, will typically be substituted by words like government, conduction, or prescription in Foucault's work. Foucault's choice of terms can be understood from his attempt to convey the *dispositif*'s 'productive' effects, namely how it invests social relations, institutions, and knowledge creation with a particular propensity or a strategic imperative. As an analytical concept, the *dispositif* does not recover a determinant structure, but 'cuts reality' at what can be termed 'the prescriptive level'. In their recent article, Sverre Raffnsøe, Marius Gudmand-Høyer, and Morten Sørensen Thaning contend that this 'prescriptive level is a crucial aspect of social reality'. This is the case because

> it has a determining effect on what is taken for granted and considered real. Furthermore, it determines not only what is and can be considered possible but also what can even be imagined and anticipated as potentially realizable, as something one can hope for, or act to bring about. (Raffnsøe et al., 2016: 292)

When one analyses a *dispositif*, then, one is reconstructing a particular 'dispositionality' in how institutions, techniques, and practices may emerge, proliferate, and transform. The *dispositif* can therefore be conceived of as a productive network. This network interconnects strategies of power, production of knowledge, and formation of subjectivity, producing effects that cannot be renounced based on a fixed moral codex, as noted above. Rather, as discussed in Chapter 4, we can inquire into the concrete 'costs' to be paid regarding the possible relations we can establish to others and to ourselves; or, in brief, we can ask the price we pay for who we can be and imagine ourselves to become.

Genealogical showing

At the centre of Foucault's critical inquiries are not actions, policies, or even specific technologies, but evaluative frameworks. Foucault's thinking on critique and values echoes Nietzsche, insofar as his strategy is to open up the frameworks of evaluation themselves, provoking the reader to reflect on their adequacy and consider possible alternatives. Judith Butler (2002a: 214) describes this strategy lucidly: 'the primary task of critique will not be to evaluate whether its objects—social conditions, practices, forms of knowledge, power, and discourse—are good or bad, valued highly or demeaned, but to bring into relief the very framework of evaluation itself'. In this regard,

274 Foucault's Technologies

Foucault's approach resonates with Nietzsche, insofar as it explores 'the acceptance and transformation of systems of values' (GSO: 5). Foucault says that he works from '[a] negativism with a nihilistic tendency, if by this we understand a form of reflection which, instead of indexing practices to systems of values which allow them to be assessed, inserts these systems of values in the interplay of arbitrary but intelligible practices' (GSO: 5). Echoing Nietzsche's detection of the collapse of absolute moral values and truths in nineteenth-century Europe, Foucault says that genealogy does not evaluate practices from a given moral codex, but analyses how strategies of power operate by linking up practices and techniques in *dispositifs*. This work 'from below', which eschews a priori evaluative frameworks, is what we term genealogical 'showing' rather than 'telling'.

Foucault's expressed aspiration to write texts whose meaning and effects could not be derived from their author corresponds to this strategy of exposing the reader to the *dispositifs* without authorizing, a priori, their assessment. The same interpretation can be given as to why Foucault refused to write a preface to later editions of his *Madness and Civilization*, since he did not want to set the agenda for the book and submit the reader to 'a declaration of tyranny' (Canguilhem, 1997: 32). Nancy Luxon aptly characterizes Foucault's critical orientation when she argues that Foucault 'writes not to disable ethical impulses but instead to provoke reflection on the interpretive framework invoked and the adequacy of any attempted response' (Luxon, 2008: 381). To be sure, Heidegger also wrote in order to induce an ethical impulse, but in comparison to Heidegger's portrayal of modern technology's overwhelming cost to humanity as such, Foucault restricted himself to describing specific costs (discussed in Chapter 4). Indeed, a *dispositif* entails particular 'costs' by formatting institutions, theories, and subjectivities, and thereby foreclosing a plethora of alternatives.

A helpful way to delineate Foucault's critical orientation is by negative definition: it is opposed to all forms of critique which are universalizing and make general denunciations. Precisely these characteristics, argues Foucault (BP: 187–188), can be found in twentieth-century 'inflationary' critiques of the state, but we note that they also apply to totalizing critiques of modern technology as inherently instrumental and as constraining human potential. Foucault's critical assessment of the theme of 'state phobia' is illustrative of the form of critique that he strives to avoid. State-phobia can be identified in both left- and right-wing political ideologies, all of which assign to the state an inner expansive drive towards control that captures all social relations in a freezing grip. This critique, depicting the state as inherently malevolent, links together very different types of states, positing a continuity between the welfare state, the bureaucratic state, and the fascist state, all being 'the successive branches of one and the same great tree of state control in its continuous and unified expansion' (BP: 188). In this way, the necessary specificity of analysis is diluted, says Foucault, since the critic sweepingly jumps from the concentration camps to social security systems. In sum, Foucault has four issues with forms of critique that universalize, generalize, and denounce: first, they result in a loss of specificity instead of examining a distinct problem; second, they support non-specific and polemical denunciations; third, they fail to engage with the specific arrangements of power/knowledge in their own present; and fourth, they do not encourage critical ethical reflexivity.

Another important delineation of Foucault's critical attitude is that it opposes itself to 'imperative discourse', which from a position of authority tells people how to evaluate and distinguish what is good from what is bad. Instead, analytical critique can merely work from a 'conditional imperative', which entails showing to those who want to struggle what obstacles they face in a particular field, like psychiatry, sexuality, or pedagogy. At the outset of his 1978 course, *Security, Territory, Population* (STP), Foucault distances himself starkly from 'the imperative discourse'—one that 'consists in saying "love this, hate that, this is good, that is bad"', since such imperatives can only be based on an aesthetic discourse (STP: 3). Similarly, Foucault contends that the lecture podium is not the place from which to proclaim what people should fight against and how they should fight. If there has to be an imperative derived from genealogical analysis, Foucault prefers that it is 'simply a conditional imperative of the kind: If you want to struggle, here are some key points, here are some lines of force, here are some constrictions and blockages' (STP: 3). This would be a 'tactically effective analysis', one that explores the interplay between social struggle and truth production.

On other occasions, Foucault (1980a) dissociates his attitude from 'the universal intellectual', who conveys universal moral judgements, endorsing instead 'specific intellectuals', who engage with problems on the basis of their specialist knowledge. Foucault's scepticism of the intellectual-legislator parallels his critique of humanism, insofar as its propagators carry a 'double bind', that is, humanism's 'simultaneous commitment to, and undermining of, the space of freedom' (Owen, 1994: 204). The careful historical reconstruction of the emergence, transformation, and interplay of *dispositifs* involves such specialist knowledge, which can produce a 'tactically effective analysis' freed from the humanist 'double bind'.

Foucault's position, as he formulates it above, broadly parallels Max Weber's well-known stance on value-freedom in modernity, and in particular

276 Foucault's Technologies

the necessary refusal of legislating for others from the realm of science. Instead of a normative *telling* based on fixed normative foundations, Foucault's analytical strategy is one of *showing* in order to induce an impulse to autonomous re-evaluation. Critics of Foucault perhaps fail to understand this strategy, notes Owen (1994: 235), 'which leaves them confused by the relation between the richness of his empirical studies and the apparent lack of normative grounds'. In Chapter 4, we discussed a central Foucauldian strategy of asking 'how much does it cost?' During an interview, Foucault poses this question in relation to how the subject objectifies himself in knowledge: '(M)y question is this: How much does it cost the subject to be able to tell the truth about itself?' (Foucault, 1989b: 355). Notably, this question is not general or universal, but one that needs specification: in which domain? For which subjects? And which kind of costs do we talk about? It is thus telling that Foucault, in the same interview, immediately qualifies his question. The price that he considers is not the price of 'modern man' or of 'humanity' as such, but the specific price that the madman has to pay:

> How much does it cost the subject as madman to be able to tell the truth about itself? About the cost of constituting the madman as the absolute other and in that it not only pays this theoretical price, but also an institutional and even economic price as the organization of psychiatry allows it to be determined. (Foucault, 1989b: 355)

Genealogy must show, then, how it happened, for example, that modern psychiatry was established with specific 'prices' to be paid by those involved in the psychiatric institution, particularly the one considered to be mad. The question, however, is how one shows the coming-to-be of such prices in more concrete terms. Giving nuance to the genealogical strategy of showing these costs, Colin Koopman (2013) suggests that Foucault's approach is not simply to affirm that something is historically contingent but rather to describe precisely how it emerged from a process of complex composition. It is unfortunate, argues Koopman, that many of Foucault's commentators have submitted his genealogies to the rule of 'the anti-inevitability thesis', a thesis which 'holds that whatever we take to be inevitable about ourselves is in actual fact the process of contingent historical accretion' (Koopman, 2013: 258). For Foucault, a more important aim than simply establishing the fact of contingency, for example in relation to subjectivity, is what Koopman (2013: 258) describes as 'the composition thesis'. This thesis entails that genealogy proceeds by recovering how a phenomenon was gradually composed of a whole series of elements that contribute to its present identity.

In a nutshell, Koopman's argument can be said to endorse 'showing' rather than 'telling' that something is contingent. Emphasizing Foucault's attention to processes of composition, Koopman and Tomas Matza (2013) denote his approach as 'critical empiricism'. It asks, they say: 'Through what combinations of practices, subjectivities, relations of force, and rationalities has a particular practice been contingently assembled?' (Koopman and Matza, 2013: 834). If we extend the object of genealogy, i.e. 'a particular practice', to denote a system of interrelated techniques, we come close to the definition of the *dispositif* adopted in this book. The 'composition thesis' lucidly shows, then, that the genealogical recovery and delineation of a *dispositif* is always-already a 'critique', if by that term we mean an analysis which animates the ethical work of re-evaluation without firm normative foundations. In brief, the critical re-evaluation of a *dispositif* requires as its prerequisite a genealogy of how it came into being.

We can further specify Foucault's critical attitude by situating it within Ian Hacking's (1999b) discussion of different types of social constructionism. Common to the many varieties of thinking that can be termed social constructionist is that they have brought to all of those involved in debates on gender, race, sexuality, culture, and science the idea that 'X' phenomenon is a social construction. This idea is 'wonderfully liberating', writes Hacking, because it reminds us that 'X' phenomenon and its meanings 'are not fixed and inevitable'; instead, '[t]hey are the product of historical events, social forces, and ideology' (Hacking, 1999b: 2). Some constructionists advance from the description of how X was constructed to make normative claims asserting that not only is X contingent on history and culture, but that X is also bad and something to be done away with. Hacking characterizes social constructionists as being generally critical of the status quo, although only some conclude that the world would be a better place without X. He then suggests three grades of radicalism in constructionist stances towards X:

(1) X need not have existed, or need not be at all as it is. X, or X as it is at present, is not determined by the nature of things; it is not inevitable.

Very often they go further, and urge that:

(2) X is quite bad as it is.

(3) We would be much better off if X were done away with, or at least radically transformed. (Hacking, 1999b: 7)

Now, where does Foucault's genealogical critique fit into this schematic? While genealogy easily matches the constructivist default position (1), since it shows how X was brought into existence by a series of events, social struggles,

278 Foucault's Technologies

and chance happenings, it is harder to align genealogy's historicist constructivism with position (2). Of course, the obstacle is that Foucault is careful not to 'despise' our present and its *dispositifs*, and he does not offer stable normative criteria whereby one can conclude that X is 'quite bad'. Foucault does not figure in Hacking's discussion, but the genealogical approach best fits the constructivist stance which Hacking terms 'reformist constructionism': 'Agreed, we have no idea at present how to live our lives without X, but having seen that X was not inevitable, in the present state of things, we can at least modify some aspects of X, in order to make X less of a bad thing' (Hacking, 1999b: 20). Again, a qualification is that, while Foucault's work sometimes uses historical examples to display possible ways to 'live our lives without X', he refrains from telling people what they should change and how to do it.

Foucault's reluctance in passing from (1) (demonstration of contingency) to (2) (denunciation) and (3) (imperative discourse) appears to separate him from many contemporary social constructivists, who often articulate (1), (2), and (3) in almost the same breath. Drawing from a broad range of constructivist literature, Hacking (1999b: 7) thus observes: 'One may realize that something, which seems inevitable in the present state of things, was not inevitable, and yet is not thereby a bad thing. But most people who use the social construction idea enthusiastically want to criticize, change, or destroy some X that they dislike in the established order of things.' In comparison to such a radical constructionist critique, Foucault's genealogies examine the archive in search of patterns and transformations from a more curious attitude. At times he unearthed the brutality of successful domination, as in his work on discipline and all its tactics and techniques of subordination (Chapter 3), while at other times he explored more 'flexible' modes of self-constitution (Chapter 4), as in his exploration of self-care in Greco-Roman antiquity.

Foucault characterized his critical attitude as a vigilant effort to discern 'the main danger' (GE: 256), which Hubert Dreyfus and Paul Rabinow describe as 'paradigmatic' dangers: 'We maintain that [Foucault] is performing an interpretive act which focuses and articulates, from among the many distresses and dangers which abound in our society, those which can be seen as paradigmatic' (Dreyfus and Rabinow, 1982: 253). Owen (1994: 206) defines these dangers as 'those systems of constraint which most threaten to foreclose the possibilities of transgressive activity'. However, it is important that one cannot easily evaluate the *dispositifs* from a clear-cut dichotomy of freedom and constraint, since they constitute propensities in our social world that we inevitably must relate to and negotiate. Were we to accept the critical consensus on Foucault's 'deterministic view' of power (discussed in Chapter 4), which depicts power as a force external to the subject, constraining or distorting our humanity, we could more easily place Foucault among the radical constructionist critics. The constructed object 'X', the *dispositif*, would be a force of negative constraint, and as such one could denounce it as 'quite bad'. As we know, this neat simplicity is compromised in several ways. Notably, the *dispositif* is not a fixed or self-identical 'thing' but an arrangement under continual enactment. Individuals are involved in this enactment, participating and giving shape to it, rather than being simply determined or constrained by it. This is why the critical attitude cannot simply be one of denunciation.

Indeed, recall that Foucault's use of the compound term 'ethico-politics' indicates that our practices of self-formation are situated within relations to others, and these relations are invested by *dispositifs*. Insofar as modern subjectivity is inevitably interlinked with the *dispositifs*, the pertinent political question is how we forge a space to manoeuvre in relation to their modes of knowledge and practices of control. The writing of genealogy begins this task, since it produces what Foucault (1984a: 49) calls a 'critical ontology' of ourselves, which exposes the non-necessities in our present and in the subjectivities by which we have come to know ourselves. Or, as Owen (1994: 207) describes the genealogist's work: 'The space of the political is presented as the space of struggle in which the question "who are we?" remains perpetually open to negotiation and renegotiation.' More specifically, the analysis of *dispositifs* reconstructs a particular imperative, which carves out domains of speaking, thinking, and acting, and it therefore affects the ways that we relate to ourselves and others.

Hence the premise of Foucault's analysis is that such imperatives can be recovered, or 'read off', from social practices, and that individuals and societies organize themselves around these imperatives, while not necessarily being fully aware of them. Foucault (1984c: 388) says: 'Thought is not what inhabits a certain conduct and gives it its meaning; rather it is what allows one to step back from this way of acting or reacting, to present it to oneself as an object of thought and question it as to its meaning, its conditions, and its goals.' Acquiring greater freedom can happen, then, by cultivating our capacity to reflect upon how our practices and techniques are always-already predisposed and the question of how to carry out the open-ended ethical work of becoming slightly other than we are. An echo sounds here from Nietzsche's dictum that humanity must embrace life, as it is, with all its suffering and meaningless contingencies, and that such an embrace entails self-creation: 'We, however, want to become those we are—human beings who are new, unique, incomparable, who give themselves laws, who create themselves' (Nietzsche, GS1974: 266). As such, man is the animal yet to be determined. Leslie Paul Thiele stresses Foucault's Nietzschean inspiration in

280   Foucault's Technologies

precisely this vein: 'One's dignity is not that one is something, but that one may become many things' (Thiele, 1990: 919). Foucault's technological thinking offers us the possibility of taking one step back from the ways that our social world—and our conception of ourselves—has been 'formatted', and through this move we may re-evaluate the costs of how we think and give shape to our subjectivity.

Questions of method

The *dispositif* is an analytical tool that arises from a network of elements in social reality, which the tool at the same time describes. It is therefore both a discovery and an invention. We discussed this duality in Chapter 1, when we defined the *dispositif* as a concept in quest of 'historical content'. In other words, the concept can only materialize in the description of how practices, techniques, and institutions were interlinked and began to form the *dispositif* of 'X' (modern sexuality or discipline, for example). Foucault sometimes used the term 'grid of intelligibility' to denote how a concept, an institution, or an architecture has the effect of making objects visible. Using this metaphor of a grid, Rabinow and Dreyfus (1982: 121) explain the function of the *dispositif*: '(I)f we keep in mind that the "grid of intelligibility" is the method of the effective historian as well as the structure of the cultural practices he is examining, then we might approach a more adequate understanding of what Foucault is driving at with *dispositif*.' In this interpretation, Foucault's *dispositif* involves a double intelligibility: the kind of intelligibility that historical elements (institutions, practices) would have created when they interlinked in a particular 'set-up', but also the intelligibility that the *dispositif* creates as a conceptual tool when one deploys it in analysis. Owen, for example, defines the *dispositif* as a 'conceptual tool' constructed by the historian to grasp how power and knowledge are interrelated, since 'the construction of this grid of intelligibility allows Foucault to uncover the structure of the practices organized as an apparatus [*dispositif*] for constituting subjects and objects' (Owen, 1994: 220). Similarly, Dreyfus and Rabinow write:

> This dispositif is, of course, a grid of analysis constructed by the historian. But it is also the practices themselves, acting as an apparatus, a tool, constituting subjects and organizing them. Foucault is seeking to isolate and establish precisely the kind of intelligibility that practices have. (Dreyfus and Rabinow, 1982: 113)

To take a well-known example: the panoptic prison and its practices created a kind of intelligibility centred on normality and deviance. When scholars later use 'panopticism' as an analytical tool to study very different contexts, it provides a grid of intelligibility that needs to be embedded in those contexts. The concept does not define a material entity, and it is epistemological rather than ontological. Given the absence of an uninterpreted, objective perspective from which to observe 'social reality', the *dispositif* can only show practices, objects, and subjects in the light of its specific normativity. Gregg Lambert rightly argues that it is important to avoid giving the *dispositif* an ontological meaning, since 'what is called "a dispositif" can better be understood as a "conceptual device" that specifically causes something to begin to appear' (Lambert, 2020: 50). As such a conceptual device, we can heuristically distinguish between three forms of visibility-creation.

First, the visibility that the *dispositif* would have created as *a historical set-up*, causing, for example, objects of normalization to appear. This analytical emphasis is what I take Deleuze to mean when he says that the *dispositif*'s historicity can be found in its 'regimes of light' (Deleuze, 1992: 160). For example, Foucault showed in *The Punitive Society* (PS) how the penal system made the offender visible in a new way, namely as a morally decayed soul, once it had incorporated the Christian notion of penance. In analytical terms, this is the move whereby the researcher traces the assembling of an element into the *dispositif*. This assembling partakes in the creation of the penal system as an overall 'set-up', which creates a particular visibility—in the above case, of the criminal act, offender, and punishment.

Second, the visibility that the *dispositif* creates *for the researcher*, as the concept (the *dispositif* of 'X') is dislodged from its specific historical context and genealogical analysis. This function arises when researchers take inspiration from Foucault's more general statements on how the *dispositif* works, e.g. by means of panopticism and normalization. Now the concept begins to serve as a grid of intelligibility for analysing other institutions and practices (see some problems related to 'disembedding' of concepts in Chapter 1).

And third, the *dispositif*, recovered from history, displays its 'normative light', so that it also might illuminate *a dimension of our present and immediate future*. Deleuze (1992) emphasizes this function, since the *dispositif* displays both how an arrangement of power and knowledge has been sedimented, 'the lines of sedimentation', and how it is transfiguring and creating virtual possibilities, 'lines of 'breakage' and 'fracture' (Deleuze, 1992: 167). This means, asserts Deleuze, that the *dispositif* displays both our past, which we no longer are, and what we are in the process of becoming. The idea of focusing on 'fissures' and 'fractures' would entail, in my understanding, that the analysis directs attention to contradictions, inconsistencies, unintended results, counter-reactions, and resistant subjectivities,

282 Foucault's Technologies

all of which feed into and open up the *dispositif* for transformation and potentialities. However, Deleuze's original interpretation (to which we return shortly) essentially operates at the conceptual level and does not specify empirical focal points.

In the interview 'The Confessions of the Flesh' (CF), Foucault emphasizes that his description of the *dispositif* of sexuality involves a decisive act of construction. One of his interlocutors asks: 'You like to accentuate the artificial character of your procedure. Your results depend upon the choice of reference points ... Is it all a matter of appearances?' Foucault replies: 'Not a delusive appearance, but a fabrication' (CF: 212). Implied here is that the genealogist constructs the *dispositif* retrospectively by examining extensive historical material. There might be a dual meaning to the phrase 'delusive appearance'. First, it could mean that, even if the *dispositif* is the historian's 'fabrication', it is nevertheless 'not delusive'; it is real, insofar as it is constructed on the basis of real practices, institutions, and techniques. A second, probable meaning is that the *dispositif* does not produce something false, an ideology, and hence it cannot be 'unmasked' by ideology critique (recall Foucault's critical dialogue with Althusser and Marxist theory).

Let us for a moment return to the Foucault/Althusser relation (discussed extensively in Chapter 3). First, Althusser advanced what we termed an immanentist conception of ideology, which at first glance resonates with Foucault's *dispositif* in which power/knowledge is also immanent to social practices that require constant renewal. Warren Montag, we recall, argues for a material and immanentist notion of ideology in Althusser: 'Ideology is immanent in its apparatuses and their practices, it has no existence apart from these apparatuses and is entirely coincident with them. Ideas have thus disappeared into their material manifestations, absent causes that "exist" only in their effects' (Montag, 1995: 63). However, Althusser retains the opposition between science (Marxist theory) and ideology, since rigorous theorizing is required to step outside the reified distortions that constitute the common sense of everyday life. For Althusser, ideology is the set of material representations and practices whose distorting effect depends on people's imaginary relation to their real social conditions. By contrast, the productivity of the *dispositif* does not amount to an ideological distortion of social relations, since, asserts Deleuze (1997: 184), 'dispositifs of power operate neither through repression nor through ideology'. The *dispositif* composes a system of practices and techniques that escapes the schema of a determining mode of production as well as the knowledge/ideology division. It brings together elements in a relationality, and there is no constitutive base from which the elements emanate. For Foucault, modern capitalist society is not graspable from the doctrine of economic determination 'in the final instance', since no single *dispositif* could ever determine all social relations and thereby attain definitive closure.

One can perhaps compare the reconstruction of a *dispositif* with the drawing of a map, in that the map does not simply reflect the landscape but highlights some aspects of it rather than others. For Foucault, the choice of which 'map' to draw is a strategic one, motivated, partly at least, by his wish to open up for scrutiny the field of knowledge in question. It is thus telling that, in the roundtable conversation 'Questions of Method', Foucault said that he preferred writing texts that produce 'truth effects' to writing with the aim of producing the truth (Foucault, 1991: 82). Foucault's approach to the construction of the *dispositif* could be understood in light of his comments on Nietzsche's dictum on knowledge as 'perspectival' and forged by 'action' (ideas presented in *Will to Power*) (WP: 338–340). In 'Truth and Juridical Forms', Foucault said that for Nietzsche

> there is knowledge only in the form of a certain number of actions ...—actions by which the human being violently takes hold of a certain number of things, reacts to a certain number of situations, and subjects them to relations of force. This means that knowledge is always a certain strategic relation in which man is placed. (TJ: 14)

And in his McGill lecture from 1971 (WK), Foucault argued that Nietzsche induced an important break with the whole philosophical tradition by reconstructing the relationship between truth and the will. In Western philosophy, the truth–will relationship had hitherto been characterized by the idea that the will has to step aside, annulling itself, to let truth appear: 'Now in order to make way for the truth, the will had to erase from itself anything that might not be empty space for the truth. Erase all its individual characteristics, all its desires, and all its violence' (WK: 214). The basic premise is that only freedom from constraint allows truth to appear. Conversely, for Nietzsche, to state the truth is to enter into the game of struggle and domination, since truth exists only 'in the form of constraint and domination' (WK: 215). After Nietzsche's epistemological intervention, one can play this game of truth affirmatively by wilfully forging new interpretations upon existing ones, thus negotiating the rules that separate truth from falsity. Hence Foucault wrote in his essay on Nietzsche:

> if interpretation is the violent or surreptitious appropriation of a system of rules, which in itself has no essential meaning, in order to impose a direction, to bend it to a new will, to force its participation in a different game, and to subject it to secondary rules, then the development of humanity is a series of interpretations. The role of genealogy is to record its history. (Foucault, 1984b: 86)

284   Foucault's Technologies

At other places, Foucault explores the idea that writing history is like partaking in struggle, since the historian does not only *describe* war, bloodshed, and victories, but inevitably *partakes* in the battle around connecting blood with soil, race with territory. In other words, they tell the story of the righteous winners, the inheritors of a territory, and those who constitute 'the people' (SMD). It is tempting to push Foucault's analysis in this direction, which means that the description of the *dispositif* inevitably partakes in history, understood as the endless game of interpretation and reinterpretation. From this perspective, the *dispositif* is an analytical tool that displays a kinship to Nietzschean genealogy. Nietzsche at times advocated the idea that there is nothing accessible outside of our frameworks of interpretation (WP: 14, 264, 267). Foucault's approach shares the Nietzschean premise that what exists, including cultural phenomena, is, as Nietzsche writes, 'continually interpreted anew' and in the process 'transformed and redirected to a new purpose' (GM: 51). Tying together truth and the will, Nietzsche made an 'epistemological intervention' of great significance for Foucault's take-up of genealogy.

Foucault's invocation of the 'war-model' to describe social and discursive processes pits his work against sociological functionalism, which explains the endurance of specific practices and institutions in terms of their integrative effects on the larger social whole. Indeed, Foucault rejects the reduction of the institution to functions, or latent functions, that the institution may or may not fulfil (STP: 116). To be precise, a practice, an institution, or a technique (elements of the *dispositif*) do not possess any inherent function that it performs for the social body or the state. An important reason for refusing such functionality is that, for Foucault, the elements are not 'self-identical'; that is, they have no inherent nature but are unstable, since they can be reappropriated and reinvested by strategies of power. Foucault said that his genealogical method worked by 'de-institutionalizing and de-functionalizing' the institutions under scrutiny, like the prison, the hospital, or the army (STP: 119). He showed that such institutions do not hold any natural, inherent function by grasping their genealogy, i.e. 'the way they are formed, connect up with each other, develop, multiply, and are transformed on the basis of something other than themselves' (STP: 119n). Foucault gives the example of the army, which is irreducible to the function it serves for the state:

> We may say that the disciplinarization of the army is due to its control by the state (étatisation). However, when disciplinarization is connected, [not] with a concentration of state control, but with the problem of floating populations, the importance of commercial networks, technical inventions, models of ... community

management, a whole network of alliance, support, and communication constitutes the 'genealogy' of military discipline. (STP: 119)

Evoking Nietzsche to launch a jab at both functionalism and historical teleology, Foucault writes: 'The forces operating in history are not controlled
by destiny or regulative mechanisms, but respond to haphazard conflicts'
(Foucault, 1984b: 88). In brief, Foucault's institutions, practices, and techniques do not fulfil a purpose in a larger system, because they are embedded
in processes of struggle that will reach no overall equilibrium or ultimate
purpose.

How to construct and read one's archive

Despite the popularity of the term 'histories of the present', we do not need
to assert that writing the genealogy of *dispositifs* is solely and essentially
guided by concerns for contemporary problems and conflicts. I have elsewhere suggested (with Mitchell Dean) that Foucault's work often evinces a
multilayered set of interests: some of his statements were exegetical examinations of the archive, others were heuristic or methodological in character,
while others again explicitly addressed urgent problems at the time (Villadsen and Dean, 2012: 403). It is helpful to read Foucault's genealogical work
on *dispositifs* with these multilayered orientations in mind. Yet the key implication is this: genealogists must recognize that they inevitably partake in
(re)constructing history when, from complex and entangled processes, they
mark out a propensity that has become visible across a set of institutions and
practices, naming it a *dispositif*.

The task of reconstructing a more specific methodology for analysing *dispositifs* immediately faces a problem: Foucault rarely gave advice on how to
approach the historical archive, and when he did give explanations of how to
carry out an analysis, he typically tied his explanations closely to the specific
analysis in question, for example of sexuality or discipline (see CF). Michel de
Certeau suggests a reconstruction of Foucault's analysis of *dispositifs* based on
a reading of *Discipline and Punish*, which correctly stresses the vast amount
of historical material that Foucault used for his study. De Certeau also
emphasizes that in establishing the disciplinary *dispositif*, Foucault traced the
proliferation of specific practical procedures within the social body:

Drawing on an immense mass of historiographic materials (penal, military,
academic, medical), this method disengages the practical procedures which can

286   Foucault's Technologies

> increasingly be found to proliferate within our society, thereby identifying the disguised indices of [a *dispositif*] whose structure becomes more precise, complex, and determinate within the density of the social fabric or body as a whole. (De Certeau, 1986: 187)

Foucault accomplishes a kind of convergence between the disciplinary techniques and what de Certeau calls Foucault's own 'theoretical' discourse. Focusing on panopticism, de Certeau suggests a set of steps whereby Foucault builds his text from micro-techniques: 'the first step', writes de Certeau (1986: 190), 'isolates a design of some practices from a seamless web in order to constitute these practices as a distinct and separate corpus, a coherent whole, which is nonetheless alien to the place in which theory is produced'. Leaving aside that 'theory' is badly picked to describe his work, since Foucault preferred analytics, de Certeau highlights the basic analytical procedure for Foucault, namely the identification of a cluster of practices and techniques, which he then names a *dispositif*. 'In the second step, this unity thus isolated is reversed. What was obscure, unspoken, and culturally alien becomes the very element that throws light on the theory and upon which the discourse is founded' (de Certeau, 1986: 190). It is true that the *dispositif* becomes a conceptual tool which points out something ubiquitous and self-evident, but nevertheless little noticed. And whereas the *dispositif* can both elucidate new materials and partake in theoretical struggle, de Certeau's emphasis on 'the obscure' and 'unspoken' brings an obscurity to the method that he suggests. It is correct that Foucault often used little-noticed texts on disciplinary practices or 'the abnormals', but the practices are hardly 'unspoken'. How does one identify the obscure and unspoken in a textual archive, and does this identification not need to rely on a speculative interpretation?

Another route to reconstruct Foucault's analytics is to scrutinize his general statements on his approach and consider their methodological implications, such as the avoidance of universals, power as relational, the positivity of discourse, and history as singular. Foucault's critical comments directed at other traditions on how *not to read* texts are also a helpful source for reconstructing a set of tentative methodological principles. Let us first recapitulate and synthesize the key principles of Foucault's approach, as we have established them in previous chapters:

1. A principle of *empirical curiosity*: the *dispositif* is conceptualized as an unspecific and open-ended 'system of relations'. The concept is thus in quest of historical content.

2. A principle of *analytical procedure*: the analysis describes a prescriptive level of reality. It proceeds by recovering transversal patterns in the social body, extracting 'a strategic imperative' (e.g. normalization), which gradually invests institutions and practices.
3. A principle of *reappropriation and integration*: the *dispositif* interconnects multiple elements, often using and redeploying elements (e.g. a technique) previously belonging to other *dispositifs*.
4. A principle of *contingent effectivity*: the *dispositif* is not deterministic of all social forms, since the strategic imperative is always integrated into—and deflected by—multifarious contexts (e.g. institutions, social struggles, failures); 'things never work out as planned'.

For now, let us focus on the methodological questions of how to delineate one's archive and select specific texts (including plans, images, manuals, paintings), which Foucault left wide open for those who wish to follow him. His avoidance of discussing selection criteria can perhaps be seen as a safeguard against prematurely restricting one's analysis to specific institutions (e.g. only madhouses), distinct literary genres (e.g. only scientific texts), or predefined periods (e.g. only the last thirty years). Instead of relying on such pre-established entities, Foucault advocated for an explorative approach that did not define in advance which historical pathways (such as events and material) one would have to explore. Such openness was required because, as we know, the *dispositif* has no single origin but heterogeneous points of emergence.

Accordingly, Foucault (1991: 76) said that his genealogical inquiry starts from 'a sort of multiplication or pluralization of causes'. The emergence of practices, discourse, or a *dispositif* is a singular occurrence that should be analysed 'according to the multiple processes that constitute it' (Foucault, 1991: 76). Instead of identifying ultimate causalities behind an event, Foucault says that he proceeds by constructing a 'polyhedron' of intelligibility (a geometrical figure with many sides), 'the number of whose faces is not given in advance and can never properly be taken as finite' (Foucault, 1991: 77; see also BP: 33). These multiple 'faces' comprise a heterogeneous list of elements, including institutional reforms (e.g. new legal codes), the authorization of new knowledge (e.g. psychiatric definitions of deviance), technical innovations (e.g. surveillance architectures), and tactical responses to specific challenges like banditry and workplace disorder (e.g. campaigns by moralizing societies). Using correctional punishment as his example, Foucault says that the elements of his polyhedron included 'pedagogical practices, the formation of professional armies, British empirical philosophy, techniques of

288 Foucault's Technologies

use of firearms, [and] new methods of the division of labour' (Foucault, 1991: 77).

In *The Birth of Biopolitics*, Foucault makes a similar methodological point concerning how, in the eighteenth century, the market became 'a site of veridiction for governmental practice'. One has to establish, says Foucault, 'a polygonal or polyhedral relationship' (BP: 33) between a number of components, which together allow the market to emerge as a place of truth, telling the government whether it acted correctly or erroneously. Foucault's use of the term 'multiplication of causes' is, I would suggest, a gesture to Althusser's earlier notion of 'structural over-determination' (discussed in Chapter 1), but with the caveat that Foucault's analysis has no reliance upon a causal structure. Indeed, the *dispositif* is precisely conceived against such pre-established theoretical models. In any case, the main methodological lesson is that the analysis of *dispositifs* must be prepared to include a broad variety of historical materials and to examine the movement of techniques and concepts, whereby they integrate into new domains.

Foucault's metaphor of 'multiple causalities' is very inspirational for expanding the pathways of the genealogist's inquiry, but it does not bring us much closer to tangible criteria for the selection of historical material. For that, we can instead turn to *The Archaeology of Knowledge* (AK), where Foucault developed his programme for the analysis of discourse. Although the book is perhaps best described as a reflection on Foucault's approach in his prior studies of madness, medicine, and the human sciences, his reflections on discursive formations are nevertheless useful for reconstructing some principles for selecting archival material (Villadsen, 2020a). A key idea in *The Archaeology of Knowledge* is that discourse analysis cannot simply rely on the accepted discursive divisions and groupings (e.g. psychopathology, medicine, and political economy) that characterize a given period (AK: 25–26). Instead, Foucault advanced an approach that starts from these 'dubious unities' but begins anew, as it were, searching for formative principles of discourse across and underneath these accepted divisions.

Analysing a statement requires situating it within a field of texts, concepts, and propositions that together constitute a 'discursive formation'. Much like the analysis of *dispositifs*, Foucault at this point already privileged relations (discursive interdependencies) over entities (words, concepts, texts) in his discourse analysis. Hence it is the system of interdependencies, wrote Foucault, 'on the basis of which coherent (or incoherent) propositions are built up, more or less exact descriptions developed, verifications carried out, theories deployed' (AK: 182). This relational emphasis also applies to individual texts or an author's work, since the analysis must dispense with 'the self-evidence' of pre-given unities such as 'the book', the author's 'oeuvre', 'science', or 'literature' (AK: 23–24). Since no book exists in itself, one must reconstruct the system of references that the text contains and which it depends on for its existence. Foucault wrote:

> The frontiers of a book are never clear-cut: beyond the title, the first lines, and the last full stop, beyond its internal configuration and its autonomous form, it is caught up in a system of references to other books, other texts, other sentences: it is a node within a network. (AK: 23)

We have already discussed how interrelations come to the fore in the analysis of the *dispositif*'s emergence and development, including how elements from one *dispositif* can be enrolled by another *dispositif* and thus inserted into a new set of relations (e.g. the problem of grain supply discussed in Chapter 2). However, one can also use the principle of interdependence, which Foucault advances in *The Archaeology of Knowledge*, as a methodological principle for one's selection and analysis of archival material.

If a key task of Foucault's discourse analysis is to describe the dependencies that a text takes up with other texts, concepts, and statements, one can turn this task into a guideline for constructing one's archive. The approach involves, writes Foucault, 'not the interpretation of the document, nor the attempt to decide whether it is telling the truth or what is its expressive value, but to work on it from within and to develop it' (AK: 6). It is no longer a matter of seeing the document as a proof of what people have done or thought, but of trying to establish, from within the archive, new series, relations, and unities. One can start, then, from a text considered central within a particular field, for example nineteenth-century psychopathology, and begin mapping the system of references in the text. This mapping entails tracing *explicit* as well as *implicit* references in the text, understood as either references to other texts assigned with a source/author name as well as the text's use of implicit references such as concepts, theories, or assumptions, whose original sources one must track (Andersen, 1994; Villadsen, 2020a). By tracking explicit and implicit references one builds up an archive of texts, and when a circularity in the texts' references to each other begins to appear, one has established a good archive (Andersen, 1994: 32). From one's archive, one then selects a limited set of texts, defined as 'monuments', which one analyses in more depth. Such monuments may be texts that clearly display a significant discovery in one's analysis, such as the emergence of a new concept, the redrawing of divisions, the reinterpretation of an assumption, a radical discursive

290 Foucault's Technologies

rupture, or a surprising historical continuity (Villadsen, 2020a: 291). Good monuments are often texts that reflect on how to generate knowledge, e.g. how to know 'the economy', but also texts that reflect on how to govern adequately, manage better, punish rightly, or cure effectively. It can be particularly elucidating to study texts that contest existing theories, institutions, and practices, including, for example, reform proposals, committee reports, scientific discoveries, and administrative instructions. These are texts participating in struggles and reconstruction at 'the prescriptive level', which interlink what can be known with what should be done.

We already know that the *dispositif* cuts across the discursive and non-discursive; or, in Deleuze's words, it integrates 'the seeable and the sayable' (see Chapter 1). Foucault's turn to practices and institutions in the 1970s has been interpreted as his escape from a semi-structuralist framework in which he was allegedly caught in the 1960s (Dreyfus and Rabinow, 1982: 100). On this reading, the *dispositif* is the conceptual invention that allowed Foucault to study how discourse and practices intersect. I would submit, however, that Foucault already made efforts to study discourse as intertwined with institutions, practices, and techniques in his works from the 1960s, namely *Madness and Civilization*, *The Birth of the Clinic*, and *The Archaeology of Knowledge*. In *The Archaeology of Knowledge*, Foucault theorized this intertwinement by arguing that the discursive system in which an utterance becomes acceptable and meaningful consists of a whole set of discursive and non-discursive elements, including disciplinary divisions, rules of concept formation, principles of inclusion, and institutional procedures (for comparisons of discursive formation and *dispositif*, see Tepper, 2010; Hardy, 2015).

In this context, Foucault already sought to reconceive the relationship between the discursive and the non-discursive. He argued that statements must have material existence, on which they depend for their meaningfulness and tactical efficacy. The materiality of a statement falls under the rules of discourse formation, or 'the referential', which underpins assessments of the relevance of a statement at a particular time and in a particular context: 'The referential of the statement forms the place, the condition, the field of emergence, the authority to differentiate between individuals or objects, states of things and relations that are brought into play by the statement itself' (AK: 91). For example, the scientific journal is an 'effective' materiality for a scientific statement, whereas the church is an effective materiality for appeals to compassion, because of their respective 'referentials'. Foucault hence conceived of 'the statement' as that which integrates the discursive and non-discursive, parallel to how the *dispositif* integrates 'the sayable' and 'the seeable'.

Foucault's revisionist approach, which viewed discourse, social practices, and materials as 'strategically' connected, sits closely to actor–network theory (ANT). The 'flat' epistemology first adopted by Bruno Latour and Steve Woolgar in *Laboratory Life* (1979) broadly parallels Foucault's account of discursive practice, insofar as they both see knowledge production as supported by—and interwoven with—technical devices, institutions, and practices. ANT scholars stress that technical devices are far from being passive tools in the hands of human actors; instead, they extensively describe how tools and materials actively take part in creating realities (e.g. Latour, 2005). However, because of ANT's insistence on giving meticulous attention to empirical details, some scholars criticize its inability to chart the broader rationalities through which strategies and techniques are generalized (Higgins and Larner, 2010). Furthermore, a common critique of the ANT tradition is that it fails to give sufficient attention to asymmetries of social power—perhaps a consequence of its principle of generalized symmetry. I would contend that some ANT scholars (e.g. Callon, 1986) tend to evade the subtleties of the social and discursive dimensions of struggle in their eagerness to infer 'agency' to non-human agents. Compared to Foucault's analysis and its fundamental emphasis on reconstructing historical conditions of possibility, ANT would appear to subscribe to an 'inflated' concept of human and non-human actors' agency. We here leave aside the comparative discussion of Foucault's oeuvre and ANT, in order to briefly conclude on two implications that can be drawn for selecting material for the analysis of *dispositifs*.

First, instead of considering texts as disparate entities one must assess how they constitute points in a network, which one reconstructs by tracing its referentiality. This network not only consists of linguistic elements (such as utterances, concepts, texts), but also includes images, architecture, procedures, instruments, and techniques. Second, one cannot rely on pre-established divisions and hierarchies between texts (e.g. scientific versus non-scientific) or the conventional division between discursive and non-discursive elements. The choice of 'monuments' is, as mentioned, guided by the problematic that one is exploring, rather than consensus views that assert the status of texts, accepted disciplinary divisions, and conventions regarding the historical importance of specific authors.

Reading like a genealogist

In accordance with his Nietzschean-inspired genealogy, Foucault locates power as immanent to the *dispositif*. But how does one, in concrete terms,

292 Foucault's Technologies

read as a genealogist by viewing power as integral to the elements of the *dispositif* (discourse, institutions, practices, and techniques) that one studies? Helpful for addressing this question is Foucault's division between 'archaeological analysis' and 'the genealogical method', which he drew repeatedly in the 1970s. The key difference is that whereas archaeology analyses a text by reconstructing the rules of formation of its utterances, concepts, and exclusions, genealogy considers how the text is pervaded by tactics and hence serves certain political and social purposes. Schematically, archaeology locates the text in a 'theoretical field', whereas genealogy places the text in a 'sociopolitical field'. Foucault explains this difference in the context of how to read a text by the French physiocrat Louis Paul Abeille (1719–1807):

> [I]nstead of considering it [Abeille's text] in terms of an archaeology of knowledge, I would like to consider it from the perspective of a genealogy of technologies of power. I think we could reconstruct the function of the text, not according to the rules of formation of its concepts, but according to its objectives, the strategies that govern it, and the program of political action it presupposes. (STP: 35–36)

Reading as a genealogist expands the kind of intelligibility that the analysis brings to bear on the material under scrutiny. For instance, the technique of cellular imprisonment can be analysed from both an archaeological and a genealogical perspective, as Foucault makes clear in *Psychiatric Power*. In archaeological analysis, one examines texts by reformers of the penal system in the eighteenth and nineteenth centuries to reconstruct the rules of formation of their concepts and theories, as well as their transformation. Yet this analysis only brings us part of the way in tracing the proliferation of solitary confinement in the eighteenth century and this technique's enrolment into the disciplinary *dispositif*. As Bernard Harcourt explains, the archaeological method alone was inadequate for explaining how notions derived from Christian morality were tactically transferred onto the prison-form: 'For Foucault, the prison cannot be derived in an archaeological manner from the penal theories of the great eighteenth-century reformers' (Harcourt, 2015b: 290). Instead, the genealogical analysis of the emergence of the prison as a universal technique of punishment traced to the moral notion of 'penitence'. Harcourt (2015b: 291) continues: 'it is a genealogy from below of ascetic Quaker thought, that turns the unruly body (indocile) into labor-power, that deploys pervasively the idea of fault and sin, and that gives rise to the first mention of the term "penitentiary"'. This process, through which popular illegalities were moralized and the penitentiary was generalized, requires a genealogical analysis for its reconstruction. Foucault describes his tracing of the prison as a two-step process: 'After an archaeological type of analysis, it is a matter of undertaking a dynastic, genealogical type of analysis, focusing on filiations on the basis of power relations' (PS: 84). To repeat a key analytical point: in Foucault's technological framework, such 'filiations' can be described by tracing how specific techniques, programmes, and concepts travel from one *dispositif* to another, being reinvested with new purposes and strategies.

A lucid example of a technique's 'travelling' and reinvestment is the prison cell (STP: 8–9), which we discussed in Chapter 1. It was first used in the monastic system as a technique for salvation through purification of the soul, then in the legal system as a technique of incarceration, and finally in the modern prison system as a disciplinary technique of reintegration centred on work. To recapitulate a key point, this trajectory is not one of epochal succession where each 'system' replaces previous ones in a clean sequence, but rather one in which coexisting *dispositifs* reassemble and transfigure such techniques. In Foucault's analysis, we find the reappearance of Christian moral codes in the eighteenth-century disciplinary prison system, which constitutes an unexpected genealogical lineage. In such processes of reappropriation or rearticulation, the elements that are rearticulated transform as they are directed to new purposes and integrated into new *dispositifs*.

As I have argued, Foucault's technological approach is less focused on the elements in themselves (e.g. techniques), and rather looks for effects arising from their interrelation and mutual adjustment. For example, Foucault showed how ancient Greek techniques of asceticism that served the aim of self-mastery transformed in early Christianity into techniques for deciphering desire and purification of the soul. We noted (in Chapter 4) how the Christians took an ancient set of techniques of the self, which they invested with new moral content and new goals. In other cases, Foucault's analysis recovers how elements from one social domain travel into another, along with the *dispositif*'s proliferation in the social body. Here, the analysis establishes continuities across various spheres of the social space rather than continuities in history. For example, Foucault's study of the prison demonstrates how, in the nineteenth century, techniques foreign to penal law were incorporated into the prison: the timetable and the wage-form (PS: 186). He also shows how correctional punishment adopted a 'psycho-juridical discourse', which created the delinquent offender and recodified penal law in terms of correction and regeneration (PS: 178). In sum, Foucault's technological approach foregrounds the interplay between elements interlinked by a *dispositif*, but it also describes the reactions and strategic adjustments

294 Foucault's Technologies

occurring between different *dispositifs* over time and at a given historical juncture.

Importantly, the genealogical emphasis on power relations does not license explanations by reference to actors' concealed tactics, hidden meaning, or psychological motivation. In Foucault's analysis, force relations tend to work themselves out around 'urgent needs' and responding strategies, but the analysis of these pressing problems remains at the surface of events. Foucault (1989c: 57–58) declares: 'What I look for are not secret, hidden relations that are more silent or more profound than the consciousness of people. I try rather to define relations that are on the surface of discourse; I try to make visible what is invisible only because it is too much on the surface of things.' In fact, Foucault insists that the genealogist does not need to read for hidden content, since everything said is observable on the surface of the archive. There is no use for a reconstruction of 'the unspoken', repressed, or unconscious, since the strategies and rationalities which propel the *dispositif* are fully explicit. Hence Foucault describes how the bourgeoisie sought to discipline the working classes by morally condemning the idle able-bodied male as a 'social enemy' (see Chapter 3). There is nothing hidden in this strategy of moralization and criminalization, he says, but conversely 'it is said, and explicitly, in the texts, laws, and theories. It is presupposed in practices, decisions, and institutions. It is connoted in literary images. It is not the unsaid; it is the more-than-said. The excessively said' (PS: 289). Foucault repeatedly notes that the nineteenth-century bourgeoisie acted with lucid cynicism, since they said very precisely what they wanted and what they were going to do. In a theoretical *adieu* to Althusser, Foucault directs our gaze not to the imaginary structure of ideology underpinning the capitalist order but to the surface of words and things. This 'horizontal' reading, which characterizes the analysis of the *dispositif*, already prefigures in Foucault's *The Archaeology of Knowledge*: 'The statement is not haunted by the secret presence of the unsaid, of hidden meanings, of suppressions' (AK: 110). Similarly, for Foucault, the reconstruction of the *dispositif* of sexuality was not

> a reality below, difficult to grasp, but a large surface network in which the stimulation of bodies, the intensification of pleasures, the incitement to discourse, the formation of specialized knowledge, the strengthening of controls and resistances are linked together according to a few grand strategies of knowledge and power. (HS1: 106–107)

In terms of methods, the *dispositif* reiterates Foucault's basic approach to discourse analysis, which, as we know, set out to read texts transversally in search of observable regularities of discourse rather than to read in depth to recover the author's intention, meaning, or subconscious drive.

Emergence, sedimentation, and change

We have already noted how the analysis of a *dispositif*'s emergence involves identifying an 'urgent need'. Examples from Foucault's work that speak to our contemporary context include how to defend cities against epidemics, how to tie the workers' bodies to the productive apparatus, or how to compensate those struck by the 'social evils' of industrial capitalism. The *dispositif* does not emerge, as we have seen, as a direct and fully formed response to such pressing problems or crises. Rather, various responses arise at scattered locations, implementing an arsenal of techniques and inventions, including, for instance, revised poverty laws, partitioning of urban space, workers' record books, mandatory schooling, 'stop-watch production', and savings schemes. We will have to trace, then, how the *dispositif* arises in piecemeal fashion, 'from beneath', without identifying any ultimate origin or explicit decision of some central agency. Foucault had learnt from Nietzsche to refuse the postulate of the origin as 'the site of truth'. Indeed, Foucault wrote, 'history also teaches us how to laugh at the solemnities of the origin. The lofty origin is not more than "a metaphysical extension which arises from the belief that things are most precious and essential at the moment of birth"' (Foucault, 1984b: 372). One must trace the *dispositifs* back to relatively scattered responses and technical inventions, which gradually connect with each other, begin to converge, and operate in conjunction. The methodological point, then, is to start the analysis at a fine-grained level of tactics and techniques, or, as Foucault advises, 'begin with its infinitesimal mechanisms, which have their own history, their own trajectory, their own techniques and tactics' (SMD: 30). In brief, the genealogy of *dispositifs* must show how techniques and practices, initially formed for distinct and often mundane purposes, begin to converge in a general strategy for knowing and handling problems.

The next question is how one studies the process through which a *dispositif* is stabilized. Descriptions of how *dispositifs* expand in the social body and across different institutions are easy to find in Foucault's work, but explanations of *how* stabilization happens are sparse. In Chapter 1, we examined how the *dispositif* can expand by forming an abstract imperative, which lends itself to a wide range of institutions. The imperative of normalization, we recall, can integrate into institutions by intensifying their practices and knowledge production via the schematic of norm/deviance.

296 Foucault's Technologies

As the initial responses to an urgent problem are gradually routinized, forming a set of rationalized techniques, they become applicable to a range of other situations. This process of stabilization, then, is principally one of general applicability and successful adaptability. On this account, discipline could successfully expand and stabilize as a *dispositif* because: (a) it set in motion a distinct strategy for arranging bodies and spaces capable of extension beyond its initial points of emergence (specifically monasteries and plague-stricken cities); (b) as a general imperative of normalization, it could be adapted for prisons, barracks, schools, sweatshops, and hospitals; (c) it was continually adjusted, refined, and criticized, so that even failures drove new disciplinary knowledge and inventions; and, last but not least, (d) it was propelled forward by privileged social groups (e.g. doctors and psychiatrists in the asylums, merchants' guilds at the docks, and industrialists in the factories), because it had productive effects for their tactics of domination.

Jacques Bidet (2016: 140) synthesizes a similar methodological procedure while generalizing the example of discipline. The analysis begins with tactics of power in their specificity, which have no 'primary' or central point; then one arrives at a 'generalized' *dispositif*, which arises from the integration of specific tactics and techniques. The procedure is defined by the principle that 'nothing about the whole can be said before the elements of which it is the amalgamation are revealed' (Bidet, 2016: 140). This account, notes Bidet, imposes on the researcher a chronological schema of 'before' and 'after', which is somewhat artificial. It is an important analytical point, since genealogical work in reality often oscillates back and forth between the sequential steps assumed by such a chronological schema. With this qualification in mind, I suggest a set of guidelines for genealogical analysis of a particular *dispositif* (Chapter 1 discussed some modalities of interplay between several *dispositifs*):

1. Identify *the emergence* of similar techniques and practices across different social domains. This step also involves scrutinizing the problematizations and reasoning articulated by the agents who implement these inventions.
2. Reconstruct a *strategic imperative* which first emerged in response to an urgent problem but gradually begins to lend itself to problem-solving more broadly. This step also includes recovering the initial tactics and techniques that specific groups put to work in their struggle for reform or dominance.
3. Describe how similar techniques integrate into *diverse institutions* and begin to alter them, as techniques integrate into institutional practices

and their knowledge production. This step can describe both similarity and variation across contexts.

4. Trace how the *dispositif* (established in steps 1–3) gradually transforms under the influence of critique, resistance, and refinements. This step can consider how the *dispositif* endures, because it serves what privileged actors see as their needs and interests.

5. Recover how the *dispositif* might fail to accommodate various emergent challenges, disruptions, and conflicts, and hence loses ground to another *dispositif* or becomes infiltrated by it. This is normally a gradual process, since it is difficult to imagine that a *dispositif* completely dissolves in one single moment.

I suggest these guidelines merely as a heuristic device for inspiration. I do not posit that Foucault's own works always followed this list or that an analysis of *dispositifs* should rigorously proceed through all the steps. The last two questions concern how one studies the *dispositif*'s transformation. We have previously emphasized that diverse unexpected effects often result, and these can become new points of intervention and knowledge creation, and hence extend the *dispositif*. The well-known example of such an unexpected effect is the creation of a delinquent milieu inside the prison and the rise of illegal activities connected to it, which legal reformers certainly neither anticipated nor planned. As a result, the *dispositif* is perpetually in movement, which brings Rabinow (2003: 53) to suggest that Foucault relies on 'a type of dynamic systems approach'. I would add to Rabinow's exposition that all these unanticipated effects are material for genealogical analysis, along with the ensuing reactions. Furthermore, such unexpected results and feedback loops need not simply spur the extension of the particular *dispositif* whose operations initially caused them. Unintended results can also be taken up by other *dispositifs* and hence become points of their application and expansion. We noticed such a process in relation to discipline in Chapter 1, and we will discuss it again in a case study on immigration policy in Chapter 6.

It is analytically helpful to hold onto the assumption that the *dispositif* never fully stabilizes itself, just as it never fully saturates social relations (Dean and Villadsen, 2016: 110). Instead, the *dispositif* constitutes a particular prescriptive propensity (Raffnsøe et al., 2016), and as such one can explore how it establishes connections marked by inconsistency, failure, and contradiction that create conditions for change. The premise is that the relations that the *dispositif* orders can give rise to both sedimentation and transformation. Hence 'the state of a dispositif at a given moment', notes Stephen Legg, 'is the result of a number of past processes that are susceptible to being

298 Foucault's Technologies

transformed—traces and remnants from the past can be seeds and potential for the alternate state' (Legg, 2011: 129). This argument highlights that the analysis of *dispositifs* does not work with any pre-given antinomy between disruptive elements and stabilizing ones.

Here, Deleuze contributes with an important interpretative emphasis. For him, instability does not essentially arise from the interplay between several *dispositifs*, since he posits instability, change, and potential as inherent to any *dispositif*. In his essay *What is a Dispositif?*, Deleuze (1992) presents Foucault's *dispositif* as a set of immanent relations, formed in the past, existing in the present, and opening potential pathways into the future. First, Deleuze describes what we have already asserted throughout this book, that the *dispositif* evolves in processes that are always out of balance. This is because Deleuze does not see the *dispositif* as a structure or a unity, but as a set of 'lines' which dispose what can be seen and what can be said. Or, in Deleuze's words, each *dispositif* is 'a multiplicity' of operative processes that turn it into a perpetual becoming (Deleuze, 1992: 162). This multiplicity is highly unstable, since the lines of the *dispositif* carry transition, contradiction, and ongoing differentiation that create circumstances for change. For Deleuze, explains Lambert (2020: 43), the *dispositif* 'defines something that is in perpetual motion, in a constant state of disequilibrium or in a state of contraction or expansion'. This interpretation aligns with our assumption that Foucault's approach can diagnose changes in modes of organizing and subjectivation by tracing how particular *dispositifs* contract or expand in relation to each other.

Second, Deleuze asserts that, at a given conjuncture, the *dispositif* both carries the weight of past sedimentations and opens up lines of the future that allow us to seize the new. He writes:

> In every apparatus [*dispositif*] we must untangle the lines of the recent past from the lines of the near future: the archive from the current, the part of history and the part of becoming, the part of analysis and the part of diagnosis. If Foucault is a great philosopher, it is because he used history for something else: like Nietzsche said, to act against time and thus on time in favor, I hope, of a time to come. (Deleuze, 1992: 164–165)

Deleuze further suggests a general division in Foucault's oeuvre between his books, which display the lines of sedimentation, and his interviews, which are 'diagnostic', indicating the lines of the future. Some interviews with Foucault lend support to Deleuze's claim regarding 'diagnostic lines' to the future. In an interview from 1983, Foucault expressed the idea of detecting 'lines of fracture' that hold the potential for possible transformation:

> The function of any diagnosis concerning what today is ... does not consist in a simple characterization of what we are but, instead—by following lines of fragility in the present—in managing to grasp why and how that which is might no longer be that which is. In this sense, any description must always be made in accordance with these kinds of virtual fracture. (Foucault, 1998a: 449)

As suggestive as Deleuze's division between lines of sedimentation and lines of creativity is, I am not entirely convinced that a deeper scrutiny of Foucault's overall authorship would confirm it. Notably, Deleuze interprets Foucault's concept of power with inspiration from Baruch de Spinoza's theory of affect. Hence, for Foucault, Deleuze (1988: 71) notes 'each force has the power to affect (others) and to be affected (by others again), such that each force implies power relations ... Spontaneity and receptivity now take on a new meaning: to affect or to be affected.' I would agree with Stephen Legg (2011) that whereas the Deleuzian notion of assemblage gives preference to emergence and creation, Foucault's *dispositif* places emphasis on the processes of stabilization that connect heterogeneous elements. Although a *dispositif* is crossed by lines of fracture which might transform or disrupt it, it owes its lifespan to processes of stabilization that interlink its heterogeneous elements in systematic relations. More convincing is Deleuze's third key point about the subject constituting a 'line of flight', which finds broader support in Foucault's own elaborations.

Third, then, Deleuze suggests that Foucault felt trapped in his own analysis of the 1970s, and that he finds in ancient Greek subjectivation a line that might escape the sedimentation of power/knowledge (see Chapter 4). Foucault reacted to this impasse, asserts Deleuze, 'as if it had become necessary for him to redraw the map of social apparatuses [*dispositifs*], to find for them a new orientation in order to stop them from becoming locked into unbreakable lines of force which would impose definitive contours' (Deleuze, 1992: 160–161). When subjects begin to turn force back on themselves, acting on themselves, they can forge a new line of subjectivity: 'This dimension of the Self is not a preexisting determination that can be found ready-made', writes Deleuze, since it is, he adds, 'a sort of surplus-value. It is not certain that all social apparatuses [*dispositifs*] comprise these' (Deleuze, 1992: 161). In Chapter 4, we discussed in detail how Foucault discovered in Greco-Roman antiquity reflective practices, or self-techniques, by which subjects 'enfold', bend, or redirect the power/knowledge *dispositifs* in which they are entangled.

Whereas Foucault did distinguish between the ancient Greek self-techniques of subjectivation and the later pastoral power, scholars have

300 Foucault's Technologies

argued that Deleuze exaggerates their differences, construing a stark opposition between Greek self-government and Christian submission to a binding morality. Elias Palti argues that Deleuze depicts the ancient self-cultivation 'as the expression of a residue of original freedom that the pastoralist machinery sought to eliminate, locking it within the networks of knowledge/power' (Palti, 2021: 28). The notion of original freedom residing within a transcendent subject, which for Deleuze is a substance of vital impulse that precedes any subjectivation, was precisely a notion from which Foucault consistently tried to escape. What Foucault rejected and strived to refute, writes Palti, was 'the presence of some presumably eternal substance or vital principle underlying the different regimes of knowledge/power and the different historical formations' (Palti, 2021: 30). We here encounter a key difference between the philosopher Deleuze, and Foucault the genealogist, who eschews the question of ontology and instead explores the conditions of possibility of philosophical discourse itself.

Nevertheless, I suggest that Deleuze's brief essay harbours a distinct potential for developing a framework for analysing *dispositifs* which has general applicability. Pursuing this idea further probably requires 'reappropriating' the framework from Deleuze's own philosophy and putting it to work for more genealogical purposes. The motivation for such reappropriation is that when Deleuze wrote about other philosophers, artists, or writers, he often used these 'commentaries' to unfold his own thinking. Scholars are greatly divided on the question of the overall compatibility between Deleuze's and Foucault's thinking and on Deleuze's rendering of the *dispositif* specifically. Lambert notes that Deleuze approximates the concept of the *dispositif* into his own philosophy, since 'what Deleuze is actually providing is an analogue to his own concept of the "rhizome", which is described in exactly the same characteristics' (Lambert, 2020: 44). For this reason, Lambert finds it is necessary to leave Deleuze's notion and reconstruct Foucault's original meaning.

Conversely, John Protevi (2016) appreciates the Deleuzian nature of Foucault's analysis of *dispositifs* in the mid to late 1970s. On Protevi's account, Foucault applies a 'differential historical methodology', insofar as he makes use of the 'Deleuzian language of the linking together of differential elements and relations' (Protevi, 2016: 123). Instead of starting from a unity as the source of phenomena like the state, the prison, or the *dispositif*, Foucault starts from a differential field from which those phenomena emerge. As noted earlier in regard to the notion of the 'polyhedron', which signals the multiple elements and processes from which a *dispositif* emerges, Protevi asserts that Foucault's analysis is differential 'in the classic Deleuzian manner, in that the integration of a multiplicity produces an emergent effect' (Protevi, 2016: 123). As we have explored, particularly in Chapter 3, the integration of multiple elements is propelled by strategy. Foucault hence says: 'the function of strategic logic is to establish the possible connections between disparate terms which remain disparate. The logic of strategy is the logic of connections between the heterogeneous and not the logic of the homogenization of the contradictory' (BP: 43). The analytical point that follows from this assertion of heterogeneity is that the *dispositif* never resolves the disparity of its elements in a unity; instead, the task is to describe how elements that remain distinct interlink through the emergence of a *dispositif*.

In his overall comparison, Peter Hallward argues that Deleuze's philosophical affirmation of the world's immanent creativity differs fundamentally from Foucault's specific genealogies of institutionalized power/knowledge (Hallward, 2006: 161). Unlike Foucault, Deleuze's philosophy of immanent creativity moves his thinking 'towards a contemplative and immaterial abstraction' that fails to engage with the constraints of this world and ultimately seeks to escape it (Hallward, 2006: 7). Following Hallward, I would suggest that while Foucault introduced the *dispositif* to describe the very concrete tactics and techniques that condition our possible experiences, Deleuze articulates the concept so that it not only describes the sedimentation of power and knowledge relations but also affirms these relations as 'lines of flight' and as always-already creative, just like the world itself.

In extracting an analytical potential from Deleuze's concept, I do not seek to reconcile Foucault's genealogy with Deleuze's overall philosophy. For now, I merely wish to draw out a key point which Deleuze shares with Foucault—that the *dispositif* operates in multiple dimensions. Taking up this idea, Deleuze argues that the *dispositif* interconnects lines of visibility, lines of enunciation, lines of force, and lines of subjectification. If we emphasize the *dispositif*'s function as a 'conceptual device' (as opposed to verifiable structure or theoretical abstraction), Deleuze's concept thus provides four analytical entry points to be used for analysing the interplay of power and knowledge. The entry point offers distinct 'windows', or analytical dimensions, that specify this mode of inquiry (list adapted from Villadsen, 2021a: 480).

1. 'Lines of visibility': Visibilities are not produced by a general source of 'pure' light that falls upon pre-existing objects (Deleuze, 1992: 167). Instead, each *dispositif* has its own regime of light. It structures light in

a particular prescriptive way, creating objects which depend on it for their very existence.

2. 'Lines of enunciation': The *dispositif* effectuates rules of enunciation that establish specific relations between the object categorized and the speaking subject. Hence 'objects and subjects are immanent variables of the statement' (Deleuze, 1988: 95).

3. 'Lines of force': Ways of seeing and ways of saying integrate because of force or power. Power is integral to a *dispositif*; it passes through all its elements, imbuing it with a specific strategic imperative. The 'lines of force' are particularly visible in the calculated responses to sudden challenges and pressing problems.

4. 'Lines of subjectification': The subject is not determined by the *dispositifs*, but is rather 'dispositioned' in a process of becoming. The lines of subjectification involve studying how subjects constitute themselves by means of self-techniques, intensifying, bending, or redirecting the lines of force within which they act.

We note that for analytical purposes, Deleuze's most original contribution with this four-dimensional framework is his attention to visibilities. In his book, *Foucault*, Deleuze elaborates on how the *dispositif* directs the gaze by 'throwing light upon objects', making them shimmer under a particular normativity (Deleuze, 1988: 52). The effects of visualization are not simply that the gaze directs itself towards particular objects in the world rather than others. More fundamentally, Deleuze explains, the *dispositif* makes objects appear in a particular normative light (as noted in Chapter 2). This idea of a normative light was possibly anticipated in Nietzsche's claim that the will to power is 'perspectival' or has a 'perspective-setting force'. It is perspectivism, writes Nietzsche, 'by virtue of which every centre of force—and not only man—construes all the rest of the world from its own viewpoint, i.e. measures, feels, forms, according to its own force' (WP: 339). Foucault's *dispositif* entails a broadly similar relationship between power and knowledge, since there is no strict separation between power's obfuscation of reality and true knowledge. Transposed onto Foucault's framework, the 'perspective-setting force', to use Nietzsche's term, *produces* objects from a particular valuation—rather than simply illuminating pre-existing entities. This is because the *dispositif* assumes a dynamic interrelation of power/knowledge, where the strategic imperative, e.g. of normalization (see Chapter 1), constantly interlinks knowledge production with practices of discipline. In brief, ways of knowing abnormality open up fields of practice, while disciplinary tactics open up fields of knowledge.

In terms of concrete analysis, I suggest that the researcher can choose to give more or less emphasis to each of the four analytical entry points when undertaking genealogical or contemporary analyses (Villadsen, 2021a). Elsewhere, I employed Deleuze's four-dimensional framework in genealogical research on the knowledge production of modern social work (Villadsen, 2008, 2011) and in a study of a recent service reform of health care and professionals' reactions to it (Villadsen, 2021a). This latter study of a reform for disciplinary standardization of health services particularly focused on 'lines of visibility' and 'lines of subjectivation'. It showed that the employment relation, and the professionals' capacities were visualized differently when a new technology termed 'service packages' was introduced. This was an instrument designed to make nurses' visits predictable in terms of frequency and content by 'normalizing' the visits, determining the types of care assigned to each recipient and the time allocated for work tasks. The technology made visible a series of measurable objects (minute allocations, defined tasks, satisfaction levels), but it also probed 'deeper' into individual dispositions, insofar as the goal was to steer health care workers towards self-optimizing behaviour.

Traditionally, welfare professionals have invested their professional self-conduct with moral value, and health care workers often invoke a 'care-ethics' which defines care by its context, interactive relationships, and the recipient's vulnerability. They reacted to the service reform for standardizing care by employing non-compliant working practices. Some workers practised what they termed 'civil disobedience', arguing that violations of the new service regulation to preserve their care-ethics in effect defended the legal-universalist premises of care-giving. In the reform process, a 'line' of disciplinary visibility thus interlinked with a new 'line' of professional subjectivation, which care workers responded to by articulating the doctrine of civil disobedience, thereby 'bending' and redirecting this disciplinary *dispositif*. To repeat the key point, which Deleuze's interpretation emphasizes: the *dispositif* is not an entity or a unified system, but a propensity or 'formatting' immanent to social relations that allows specific programmes, techniques, and forms of subjectivation to emerge. Foucault's technological approach describes how our possible experiences—as citizens, professionals, and 'private selves'—are shaped by the *dispositifs*. But the approach can also explore how *dispositifs* evolve, as they spur forms of counter-conduct and perhaps the refashioning of subjectivities. It is to the empirical application of the *dispositif*—in historical as well as contemporary analysis—that the final chapter turns.

Chapter Six
Three Studies

This book has so far specified the *dispositif* in terms of theoretical traditions, critical effects, and questions of method. This final chapter will offer examples of how one can put the concept to work. It presents a set of main findings from three illustrative studies that apply Foucault's technological thinking with particular attention to the methods involved. The first example will be Foucault's own analysis of 'the *dispositif* of sexuality'. This analysis is particularly pertinent, because Foucault uses his notion of *dispositif* extensively in *The History of Sexuality, Volume 1* (116 occurrences, cf. Introduction). And it is on the basis of this study that Foucault explains the concept of the *dispositif* in the oft-cited interview, 'The Confession of the Flesh'. The other two studies come from my own research, which I have chosen not because they provide any finalized or superior way of applying these concepts, but because they offer material from which I can explicate the analysis of *dispositifs* in terms of the analytical and methodological choices I made. The second example, then, is a 'history of the present', which examines how recent Scandinavian social policy rearticulated nineteenth-century philanthropic doctrines of 'self-help', 'poverty of the soul', and 'advice is better than handouts'. My study traces how contemporary social work increasingly foregrounded the client's 'inner self-worth' over background structures, formal rights, and redistributional justice. And, finally, the third case example offers a brief genealogy of the discovery of 'the risky migrant' in Danish policy discourse—a thorny issue, which oscillates between the *dispositifs* of law, discipline, and security. The presentation of these studies results from my retrospective reading, which reconstructs these studies in the terms of the *dispositif* while making connections to general analytical and methodological points raised above.

Case 1: The *dispositif* of sexuality

It is worth noting that the interview in which Foucault gave his oft-cited definitions of the *dispositif*, 'The Confession of the Flesh' (CF), primarily

Foucault's Technologies. Kaspar Villadsen, Oxford University Press. © Kaspar Villadsen (2024).
DOI: 10.1093/oso/9780198819400.003.0007

centred on the theme of sexuality. Although one can draw some general analytical points regarding the *dispositif* from this interview, as many scholars have done, the fact that Foucault articulated the notion with close ties to his genealogy of sexuality is often ignored. In that context, the *dispositif* helped Foucault in 'playing a game' which turned the relationship between sex and sexuality upside down. Thus, Foucault's hypothesis was: 'couldn't it be that sex—which seems to be an instance having its own laws and constraints, on the basis of which the masculine and feminine sexes are defined—be something which on the contrary is produced by the apparatus [*dispositif*] of sexuality?' (CF: 210). Note that in this case *dispositif* is translated as 'apparatus', which designates an entity or institution that is too solid and neatly delimited compared to Foucault's use of the term *dispositif* (see Chapter 1). Foucault wanted to 'play a game' in order to challenge 'the repressive hypothesis' which alleged that natural sexual drives, desires, and practices had been suppressed during centuries of puritan moralization. What would happen, Foucault wondered, if instead one assumed that sex was produced by a *dispositif* of sexuality? One of Foucault's interviewers asked about his newfound object of sexuality:

> What is the nature of this new historical object which you term 'sexuality'? Evidently it isn't sexuality in the sense that botanists or biologists speak or have spoken of it, something which is more a matter for historians of science. Nor is it a question of sexuality in the sense that traditional histories of ideas or customs might have understood the term, the point of view which you are now contesting with your doubts about the 'repressive hypothesis'. Nor even, finally, do you seem to be talking about sexual practices such as historians study. (CF: 194)

Foucault's counter-move against the repressive hypothesis follows this route: instead of seeing sex as a natural property shared by all humans that is either suppressed or liberated, Foucault argued that 'sex' is a transient historical object. It was the advent of the *dispositif* of sexuality that created the possibilities for endless medical, juridical, and psychological deliberations on sex, as well as the discoveries of perversions and the introduction of prohibitions of certain sexual practices. In the twentieth century there arose the call for liberating sex and the promise that we may know ourselves by knowing our sexuality, both of which were inseparable from the *dispositif* of sexuality. Hence Foucault said that 'regarding everything that is currently being said about the liberation of sexuality, what I want to make apparent is precisely that the object "sexuality" is in reality an instrument formed a long while ago, and one which has constituted a centuries-long apparatus of subjection'

(CF: 219). Foucault's focal point, then, was the deep-seated existence in the West of regulated procedures for talking about sex, sexuality, and sexual pleasures, procedures that one must still submit to today when encountering a doctor, psychologist, psychiatrist, or therapist.

As in other cases, Foucault's story is not one of sudden appearance, but of a *dispositif* gradually infiltrating and gaining ground on top of another. The *dispositif* of sexuality emerged by overturning what Foucault terms the 'ancient system of alliance', while retaining elements of it, including the regulation of conjugal relations (HS1: 117). As an organizer of sexuality around 'alliance', this *dispositif* revolved around lineage and social control: 'a system of marriage, of fixation and development of kinship ties, of transmission of names and possessions' (HS1: 106). Instead of asserting whether a sexual relation was legitimate in this quasi-juridical sense of alliance, the emerging *dispositif* of sexuality was concerned with the truth of sex. Broadly parallel to Foucault's analysis of the disciplinarization of punishment, a series of techniques for uncovering the truth of sexuality begin to overturn the quasi-juridical relations of alliance. The *dispositif* of sexuality owed its key techniques to the Christian tradition and its centuries-old confessions that privileged sexual desires as a theme of penance. These techniques endured and yet transformed during the eighteenth century, when sex became an increasingly central matter of public hygiene, population statistics, economics, pedagogy, and psychiatry. As a result, a 'new technology of sex' emerged, writes Foucault, 'new in that for the most part it escaped the ecclesiastical institution without being truly independent of the theme of sin. Through pedagogy, medicine, and economics, it made sex not only a secular concern but a concern of the state as well' (HS1: 116). As sex became a key target across these major secular institutions, the *dispositif* of sexuality expanded along three axes (HS1: 104–116):

- Pedagogy, taking the specific sexuality of children as its object: 'the masturbating child'. A tactic of pedagogization of children's sex.
- Medicine, targeting the sexual physiology peculiar to women: 'the hysteric woman'. A tactic of pathologization of the woman's body.
- Demography, whose objective was the regulation of births: 'the Malthusian couple'. A tactics of socialization of procreative behaviour.

Foucault does not trace in detail the historical process through which the *dispositif* of sexuality emerged, because he intended volume one of *The History of Sexuality* as an outline of the subsequent volumes he had envisioned. While it is not Foucault's main concern to analyse the social group that propagates the *dispositif* of sexuality, he does identify the bourgeoisie as the initial instigators. As the bourgeoisie rose economically and politically in the latter half of the eighteenth century, they were concerned to distinguish themselves from other classes. They did so, Foucault notes, by constructing a particular 'sexualized' class body: 'This class must be seen rather as being occupied, from the mid-eighteenth century on, with creating its own sexuality and forming a specific body based on it, a "class" body with its health, hygiene, descent, and race' (HS1: 124). This concern with achieving class distinction constitutes 'the urgent need', as it were, to which the instigating group first responded. The idea that the propertied class simply dominated the lower classes' sexuality in order to extract maximum labour power must be refused, argues Foucault: 'On the contrary, the most rigorous techniques were formed and, more particularly, applied first, with the greatest intensity, in the economically privileged and politically dominant classes' (HS1: 120). Later, from the end of the nineteenth century, the juridical and medical techniques directed at abnormal sexuality and perversions expanded as the biopolitical concern for the health of the population intensified. This was the moment, recounts Foucault, when the *dispositif* of sexuality, which the privileged classes elaborated in its most complex forms, lost its ties to the bourgeoisie and expanded throughout the entire social body. We note, then, how a political strategy first emerges from a specific struggle around collective subjectivity, then departs from this specific tactic and becomes a general strategy, and begins to traverse social relations broadly.

As the modern welfare state intensified its biopolitical concerns for the entire population, the problem arose of connecting objectives at the level of the population (e.g. birth rates) with the regulation of the behaviours of families and individuals. The strategic imperative propelling the *dispositif* of sexuality was, I suggest, the task of aligning the protection of the population body with the disciplining of the individual body. Here, 'sexuality' became the register through which statistical concerns regarding the population's health were brought to bear on families and individuals while, conversely, disciplinary techniques could generate knowledge of individuals' abnormalities that fuelled and refined population statistics. In his genealogy, Foucault sidesteps the model of suppression and instead foregrounds 'perpetual inventiveness'—that is, the subsumption and alteration of diverse techniques as the *dispositif* of sexuality emerges:

> It is clear that the genealogy of all these techniques, with their mutations, their shifts, their continuities and ruptures, does not coincide with the hypothesis of a great repressive phase that was inaugurated in the course of the classical age and

308 Foucault's Technologies

> began to slowly decline in the twentieth. There was rather a perpetual inventive-
> ness, a steady growth of methods and procedures. (HS1: 119)

Foucault discusses a series of historical facts that contest accepted historical narratives, one of which posits that the object of sexuality emerged before Freud, since nineteenth-century medicine and psychiatry debated it extensively. Here, I will leave aside these historical details in order to recapture Foucault's overall procedure and conclusions. Taking as our point of departure the *dispositif* of sexuality as 'a fundamental historical given' (CF: 218), we can invert the relationship between 'sex', understood as repressed, and 'sexuality', understood as scientific knowledge and cultural prohibitions. It follows that sex is not intrinsic to the body, sexual organs, sexual drives, or certain stimuli; instead, sex is an object constituted by the *dispositif* of sexuality. Put differently, the modern object of sex exists 'in itself' (like the nominalist object 'X') only insofar as the knowledge claims of sexuality are accepted and continually invoked in diverse practices.

The object of sexuality entailed a specific mode of truth production premised on the idea that the truth about ourselves is to be found in our sexuality. This modality of truth production emerged, in part, because the confession, understood as scientific-administrative techniques of truth production, proliferated across diverse institutions, similar to the way panopticism had diffused in the social body. Foucault defines the confession broadly as 'all those procedures by which the subject is incited to produce a discourse of truth about his sexuality which is capable of having effects on the subject himself' (CF: 215–216). It would be necessary, suggests Foucault, to trace the process whereby the confessional techniques transformed so that their aim was no longer the denunciation of 'the desiring flesh' but the disclosure of one's sexuality through an essentially liberating speech.

This inversion accomplished by Foucault's 'game' did not reduce the historical significance of sex or disregard the intrinsic relation between sex and power/knowledge. Indeed, the object 'sex' emerged from within the matrix of regulatory techniques and scientific knowledge of sexual behaviours—i.e. from the *dispositif* of sexuality. Once invented, this object of sex allowed a fertile discourse to continuously evolve, as moral claims, medical distinctions, and political demands endlessly referenced 'our sexuality'. Along with the idea that the repression of sexuality caused various neuroses, the interlinking of truth and sex rooted itself in popular discourse and in psychoanalysis, which was particularly influential in 1960s and 1970s France. Hence Deleuze (1997: 186) observes that 'the dispositif of sexuality reduces sexuality to sex (to the difference between the sexes ... etc., and psychoanalysis is full of this reductionism)'. Against this reduction, Foucault asked 'how it comes about that people are told that the secret of their truth lies in the region of their sex' (CF: 214). This demand to extort the truth of one's sex is not only directed at the speaker but also at the listener, since 'this will to hear the other speak the truth of his sex, which today still hasn't ceased to exercise itself, is thus accompanied by a history of techniques of listening' (CF: 214). The modern attitude to sex became more like a transgressive attitude to a set of prohibitions. This demand for sexual liberation was able to further proliferate as it became entangled with commercial appeals for fulfilling one's desires in mass consumption and entertainment. In brief, constitutive of all the concerns, regulations, prohibitions, and recent promises for the liberation of sex was the *dispositif* of sexuality. Against this background, Foucault sees the critical task not as one of 'recuperating' sex by freeing us from constraining prohibitions and conventions, but rather as one of grasping the *dispositif*, which has institutionalized a particular understanding of sex and sexuality.

Case 2: The *dispositif* of social work

In a previous study I used the concept of the *dispositif* to explore historical transformations in the theories and techniques of social work. My study starts from the basic genealogical question: how did it happen that the client's 'inner willpower' became the privileged object of scrutiny and intervention in contemporary social work? (Villadsen, 2007, 2011). This inner source is variously termed 'willpower', 'inner motivation', or 'the positive core', and the study shows that today's social work increasingly uses theories and techniques that see the awakening of this source as the key avenue for ameliorating social problems from addiction to unemployment. This development has been described as a shift from 'depth to surface' in social work discourse (Howe, 1996), whereby previous theories which assumed a deeper order beneath manifest social behaviours have receded in importance. Since social work has a distinct knowledge-base and a set of interlinked techniques, I take it to constitute a *dispositif*, as it has been defined in this book.

The study traces the emergence of this *dispositif* back to late nineteenth-century philanthropy and proceeds through the twentieth century by describing a series of significant transformations that leads to the present. The archive consists of around sixty texts on poverty, social philanthropy, social work theory, textbooks, and instructions in social work techniques. The genealogy spans the period from 1870 to 2000, and while it centres on Denmark, influential texts from other national contexts are included, as

Danish developments were often influenced by events in other countries. I used the method described in Chapter 5, that builds up the textual archive by searching for explicit and implicit references, and I then selected a subset of 'monuments' from this extensive archive.

The genealogy of social work produces a kind of 'counter-memory' which provides a different intelligibility from the conventional history of social work and the welfare state more broadly. The welfare state, established in the early twentieth century, was supposed to end the stigma and indignity of the charity and poor laws that preceded that welfare state project. However, the rediscovery of philanthropic principles from the 1980s onwards meant that clients' inner self-worth once again took preference over formal rights and redistributional justice. 'Neo-philanthropy', I argue, turns social problems inwards, working for inner transformation, not social transformation. More specifically, my study traced techniques and concepts of modern social work back to the late nineteenth century, where philanthropists sought to overcome the growing class divide by 'visiting' the poor and representing their inner goodness to the more privileged classes.

This excavation of major social upheavals as 'breeding spots' for modern social work runs against the grain of conventional histories of the progressive development of social work and the welfare state. Politicians, planners, and historians have often contrasted the success of twentieth-century welfare provision based on universalism and scientific knowledge with prior centuries of philanthropic charity based on patronage and moralizing. In advancing a modern, rights-based social service system, welfare reformers distinguished their project from sentimental charity, which was portrayed as a reminiscence rooted in Christian morality, patronage, and particularism (in Denmark, e.g. Rold Andersen, 1970). Against the depiction of a fundamental historical break, my genealogy establishes a series of continuities between modern social work and philanthropic poor relief of the late nineteenth century (Villadsen, 2007: 314–316). At this time of rapid industrialization, philanthropic societies, which were mainly Protestant and located in the large cities, invented a set of methods for poor relief that became decisive for modern social work: home visiting, contractual agreements, criteria for distinguishing deserving from undeserving poor, and ways of revealing the pauper's degree of moral decay. Philanthropists advanced a new 'science of assistance' which began differentiating the poor into a system of subcategories. Subsequently, the nascent welfare bureaucracy in the early twentieth century adopted and refined this technology, applying it in social services with their eligibility criteria, divisions, and retraining programmes.

Philanthropic poor relief was a response to pressing social problems accompanying the disruptive industrialization of the nineteenth century, particularly 'the social evils' related to overpopulated urban centres, including infectious diseases, overcrowded housing, workers' uprising, the perceived class antagonism, and moral decay allegedly infecting 'the dark continent of the poor' (Villadsen, 2011: 1065). In other words, philanthropic work for the poor was an initial response to the severe predicaments arising from this complex of social evils. The philanthropists took up a strategic position between socialists who demanded that 'the social evils' became a state responsibility and liberalists who argued that these evils would dissolve through voluntary almsgiving and the free mechanisms of the market. In this debate, the philanthropic movement asserted that industrial society should avoid social fragmentation by means of moral cohesion and moral uplift. If one were to synthesize an 'urgent need', as articulated by the movement, it was the need to secure the social order by moralizing the masses of urban poor. This need was felt by members of the propertied classes who expressed their fear over the division of society and the unprecedented presence of urban poverty, a growing mass that was described as shameless, improvident, and barbarian, developing habits foreign to good morality. Priests, philanthropists, hygienists, journalists, and even poets all advanced this discourse on the urban poor's moral decay.

It was by circumventing the discourse on the dangerous working class that the philanthropists made a long-lasting invention. They argued that the poor were not inherently evil, but instead harboured an inner 'human nature' that could be salvaged in even the most miserable individuals (Villadsen, 2011: 1068). The philanthropist would thus speak for the essential human that allegedly dwelled within the poor, portraying them as less threatening for the privileged classes. This function of mediating the classes became essential to the modern social worker, who must also represent the client's inner potential to the rest of society. Mark Philp (1979: 99) argues that the mediation function, born out of the class divide in the late nineteenth century, was taken up by the modern social worker, who must also allude to an invisible, yet universal subjectivity in the client when dealing with a judge, a doctor, or the local community. This technique, which allowed the philanthropist to represent a potential subject in the poor, became key to the emerging social work *dispositif*, especially because it merged the production of knowledge with the governance of subjects. We find here the take-off of social work knowledge, namely the objectification of subjectivity, which, notes Philp (1979: 91), 'applies to all individuals and yet no one in particular'. Social work would henceforth apply an array of techniques that produce 'a subject in objective knowledge' (Philp, 1979: 91), that is, incite clients to speak of themselves in categories that define normal functioning, well-being, motivation, self-control, and more. The casework interview, clinical therapy, and motivational counselling are among such techniques of subject-production.

Genealogical analysis typically proceeds by tracing the historical emergence of dispersed techniques and practices that gradually become rationalized and interconnected. We also recall that specific social groups often initiate and engender this process, and that these innovators gradually recede out of sight. Indeed, the significance of the philanthropists' response to 'the social evils' lies particularly in the movement's technical inventiveness. One key technique was home visiting, which carved out a space for observing visible signs of the state of morality in the poor family and passing a verdict on their eligibility for assistance (Villadsen, 2007: 315). If the poor were prudent and of good character, their housekeeping, clothes, child rearing, even their postures would reveal this, which in turn warranted donation of household relief. If the inspection of these visible signs proved an 'absolute moral decay', the poor were referred to the public poorhouses and forced labour, since they were allegedly impervious to moral uplift. In this dual role as loving counsellor and firm judge, declares Giovanni Procacci (1991: 165), the philanthropist was 'a figure with a great future'. In privileging the working-class home as a domain of moral judgement, the technique of home visiting embodied an emergent strategic imperative. Philanthropists could redirect political demands raised by the working class back to the poor homes, arguing that even in deep poverty good people will maintain a 'decent cleanliness'.

As a technique for detailed character study, the home visit became a vehicle for defending the social order through moralization of the lower strata of society. Hence, as social philanthropy reached its peak in the late nineteenth century, the visitors of the poor cultivated a number of techniques that became constitutive for modern social work. Perhaps the technique of visiting the poor constitutes one of those 'lowly origins' that genealogy recovers. The character study and the quest for inner improvement, so central to modern social work, can possibly be traced back to this early technique—a technique that cannot be dissociated from a strategic imperative, born in the late nineteenth century, which shifts the critical attention from the social order to the order of the subject.

My genealogy of the modern social work *dispositif* explored a series of decisive inventions that emerged from late nineteenth-century philanthropy. Most importantly, perhaps, this movement gave twentieth-century social work a client who is not simply a subject of the law who possesses a series of formal rights and responsibilities. By inventing techniques that cast light on the recipient's moral character and fostered moral uplift, philanthropy opened up a domain of 'client-centred' social work that greatly supersedes a liberal constitutional form of state (Villadsen, 2011: 1071). This early social work also instituted the paradoxical figure of the client-subject as simultaneously particular and universal. In time, the social services of the modern welfare state adopted this figure. Today, the client figures as a particular subject, whom social workers must meet in his irreducible individuality, and yet the client embodies certain universal features that must and should be realized. In conclusion, the significance of late nineteenth-century philanthropists reaches beyond the techniques and concepts that they invented in their immediate historical context. Genealogy shows how the philanthropists forged a distinct strategy and made a series of decisive inventions that, after a process of rearticulation and readjustment, came to constitute the modern social work *dispositif.*

Case 3: The discovery of 'the risky immigrant'

The affluent parts of the world have witnessed a dramatic shift in the political discourse on immigrants and immigration during the last three to four decades. Immigrants are often portrayed as carriers of a complex set of risks, including the risks of radical political and religious views, lower motivation to work, 'outmoded' attitudes towards democracy, gender, sexuality, and child-rearing, and 'a culture of dependency' that allegedly destines them to strain public budgets. In Europe and across the Atlantic, nationalist arguments for the defence of borders and governments' irrefutable right to sovereign decision-making are sounding increasingly loudly. The recent measures to restrict migrants' access to affluent countries, such as the tightening of border controls, diminishing of quotas for refugees, and stricter criteria for family unification, have been described as the 'restrictionist policy paradigm' (CLANDESTINO, 2009: 112). This development is often explained with reference to a general political shift to the right in many countries, whereby nationalist parties have taken up office or become decisive for securing majority government. I do not contest the significance of this overall change in political sensibilities and parliamentary compositions. However, in a recent study (Villadsen, 2020b), I sought to situate the emergence of the 'risky immigrant' in a broader perspective, first by relating it to the modern state as simultaneously open and enclosed, and second by

314   Foucault's Technologies

tracing the discursive and technical elements involved in the making of this new category.

The analytical approach of my study follows one variant of Foucault's technological thought discussed earlier, namely the use of the *dispositif* as a 'conceptual device' to make something visible. Rather than constructing how a *dispositif* gradually comes into being, the analysis explores how the concept of 'the risky immigrant' emerged in the interplay between the *dispositifs* of law, discipline, and security. The reader will recall that Foucault in his 1978 series introduced the three major *dispositifs* of law, discipline, and security (STP: 5–24), and that he showed, on the basis of eighteenth-century debates on the government of cities, how these *dispositifs* each produced problems like crime, illness, or grain supply in incomparable ways. Very pertinent to the current theme of immigration, Foucault suggested that one of the key concerns of eighteenth-century city governance was to open up cities that were enclosed spatially, judicially, and economically, in light of the new imperative of freeing circulations. I thus follow Foucault's analytical appeal to 'move behind the institution', i.e. the restrictive migration regime, in order to chart the prior historical transformations from which the institution emerged. The analysis does not so much ascertain how the three major *dispositifs* were at play in these transformations, as it asks, first how the strategy for restricting 'risky immigrants' emerged, and second how it evolved at the intersections of law, discipline, and security (in terms of its knowledge-base and its specific techniques). In brief, I wanted to extract the notion of the risky immigrant from the present political discourse and relocate the concept in its genealogical trajectory.

My genealogical analysis places the emergence of the risky immigrant in a complex of national and international developments that, in Foucault's terms, constitute its 'conditions of historical emergence' (STP: 110). It shows how the concept, in all its ambiguity, became a central reference point for the stream of restrictive techniques implemented to impede risky immigrants' entrance into 'fort Europe'. Some of these restrictions now impede and slow down the circulation of labour power, goods, and travellers that the European Union (EU) project intended to facilitate. Quite clearly, the thorny question of how to control border-crossers straddles the fundamental contradiction between the economic logic of free circulation and the national logic of sovereign territoriality. I derive this contradiction from Foucault, who did not see the modern state as a unity, but instead as the evolving integration of sovereign power, territorial borders, and the security of the population's life processes, including its movements. He describes the modern state as 'the superimposition of the state of sovereignty, the territorial state, and the commercial state' (STP: 15). On this account, entrance and inclusion into European states is rooted in both sovereign control of territories (the legal *dispositif*) and the securitization of good circulations within 'the single market' (the security *dispositif*). Against this background we may understand the invention of diverse filtering techniques, such as 'fast-mover', green card arrangements, and schemes for attracting highly skilled labour, since they align territorial enclosure with an openness for beneficial circulations.

The tension between national territoriality and expansive market transactions appears to be intensifying. Étienne Balibar argues that Europe has reached a turning point where global networks of ideas, goods, capital, and information are reconfiguring the spatiality of the member states as well as the European Union itself. Throughout the twentieth century, notes Balibar, the European states have undergone a detachment of borders from traditional sovereign control, and their borders have continually transformed,

> some being steadily reinforced (particularly the police function, controlling the flows of immigrants, etc.), others being weakened and separated from the borderline (e.g. the monetary independence, the fiscal control). As a consequence, the constitutive relationship between territory, population and sovereignty is no longer taken for granted. (Balibar, 2009: 193)

This dissolution and reconfiguration of conventional borders can be identified in the infrastructure within the European Union and in the techniques invented to control them. Hence, as a central element in the 'single market' project, the trans-European routeways have been improved and opened up in order to facilitate integration, transport, and trade. In recent decades, however, this enhanced infrastructure has been identified as offering passages for uncontrolled, unwanted migration. As a response to this 'urgent need', techniques of surveillance, detection, and arrest now dominate the trans-European infrastructures, and instead of open passages, a new network of control and filtering is now in place. Some countries have reintroduced the conventional border controls, typically with reference to terrorist threats (in 2020–2021 in Norway, Austria, Germany, Sweden, Denmark, and France). In the terms of our technological approach, the security *dispositif* that underpinned the EU single market strategy is being increasingly infiltrated by the 'old' *dispositifs* of sovereign law and discipline.

316 Foucault's Technologies

Theoretically, this is an example of how techniques and practices that belonged to one *dispositif* have been reappropriated by other *dispositifs*, creating effects that negate or support each other. Hence, today, European routeways are pervaded by both law and security, becoming a network of controlled and 'filtered' circulation. In the case of the internal EU borders, these borders appear as the object of continual controversy and redefinition of what beneficial mobility is. It becomes clear that the border is not a permanent object, but transforms as it is targeted by the different *dispositifs*; hence the sovereign-territorial border is not the same as the disciplinary border, which again is not the same as the security border.

In Denmark, the last four decades have witnessed an increasingly harsh public debate on immigration, accompanied by continual restrictions to the Alien Act, resulting in one of the strictest immigration regulations on the globe. The nationalist political party, 'The Danish People's Party', has campaigned for reviving 'the original welfare state', understood as controlled by 'the Danes' themselves and as rooted in the country's history and cultural heritage. The view that immigration to Denmark must be kept at a minimum is today shared by most political parties, although some of them, notably the Social Democrats currently in government (as of August 2021), emphasize economic arguments regarding the risks that immigrants pose to the welfare state project. One does not need to move further back than the 1960s and 1970s to find a radically different discourse as well as vastly different techniques for handling immigrants, who were then called 'guest workers'.

The early 1970s were characterized by optimism regarding the welfare state as a major economic and socially integrative project, which was sometimes termed 'welfare planning'. When the topic of guest workers was discussed, it was with reference to an accelerating industrial-economic process that underpinned the project of welfare planning. Industry required more labour power, and guest workers—mainly from Turkey, Poland, and Yugoslavia—were considered a temporary labour supply. As politicians and planners realized that the majority of the workers were likely to stay permanently, debates ensued on how to prevent the risks entailed in this unforeseen immigration. Notably, in contrast to the current discussion, 'risks' were seen as pertaining both to the Danes, who might 'not be ready' to adjust to the newcomers, as it was often said, and to the newcomers themselves, who might risk suffering from poor working contracts or living conditions and did not fully enjoy the welfare state's educational and health services. These concerns about including the guest workers in the universalist aspirations of the welfare state would sit awkwardly with today's political sensibilities. However, they must be understood from within the policy framework of welfare planning, which took levelling of class differences as a main target, addressing low social mobility and the hereditary transmission of marginalization. Welfare planners believed that some citizens held higher probabilities of suboptimal social and economic development, and they were categorized as groups 'at risk'. When various problems arose among some guest workers, this group was conceptualized by the already existing risk concept:

> There was a tendency to identify minorities as 'groups at risk' and consider them especially prone to developing social problems. In this context, the idea of 'minimizing the risks' that guest workers allegedly faced—and posed to the rest of society—resonated with the political reasoning of the time. (Villadsen, 2020b: 159)

The political discussions of the early 1970s regarding guest workers extended this welfarist strategy of risk prevention to the newcomers to Denmark, identifying them as a new at-risk group. In fact, it was considered not merely beneficial for immigrants to be submitted to 'normalizing' integration, but something like a right. Notably, the political-administrative discussions of the time did not consider hindering or minimizing the influx of guest workers; instead, they focused on how to manage the risks and potential problems arising from this 'circulation' of labourers, which echoes the *dispositif* of security (see Chapter 1). Extending the welfare systems of mandatory schooling, health care, social insurance, and labour protection to the newly arrived was the central risk-preventing strategy. This welfarist strategy soon comprised efforts to identify, predict, and carry out preventive interventions in relation to those groups who displayed patterns of dysfunctionality. The combination of risk-prevention through normalizing interventions and inclusion into the welfare systems' protection was soon challenged, however, by nationalist demands for the territory to be protected from immigrants, who were said to carry a series of endemic risks.

During the 1980s and 1990s, successive governments implemented a series of legal restrictions to reduce the number of immigrants coming to Denmark. These changes broadly targeted refugees, labour migrants, and foreigners seeking family unification. Targeting the last group, a new technique, termed the 'attachment requirement', was implemented in 2000 with the goal of hindering 'forced marriages' that unified young residents with immigrant backgrounds with a spouse from their original region. However, this requirement covered a broad set of criteria and came to affect a larger group than the intended one: young people allegedly forced into marriage. It meant that applicants for spousal unification needed to prove that they had a greater attachment to Denmark than to other nations. It also examined the applicants' willingness and capacity to exert efforts at integrating themselves in Danish society in terms of duration of prior stays in Denmark, learning

318 Foucault's Technologies

Danish, jobseeking efforts, and 'willingness to integrate', for example by participating in civil society associations like sports or voluntary work. Critics like Mons Bissenbakker (2019) have noted that this requirement gave the immigration authorities great discretionary powers, because it entailed rather vague definitions of what efforts would satisfy the new attachment criteria.

In 2018, the attachment requirement was removed from the Danish Alien Act, and instead another legal technique was invented to restrict family reunifications, particularly from the Middle East and African countries. This was the much debated 'ghetto clause', which stipulated that sponsors are not permitted to apply for spousal reunification if they live in a neighbourhood that figures on the official list of 'vulnerable' neighbourhoods. The ghetto clause is a legal-spatial technique which reconfigures the sovereign border inside the national territory. Indeed, the segmentation of the urban space into ghettos where specific rules redefine the inhabitants' social and civil rights entails a certain 'ubiquity of borders'. Instead of simply demarcating the state from its exterior, the border becomes movable. It becomes, as Balibar (2002: 184) suggests, more like a grid partitioning the entire social body. Commentators have often explained these restrictions in the Danish Alien Act as due to the growing electoral support for the nationalist party, the Danish People's Party, which since its inception in 1995 has successfully influenced presiding governments. I suggest, however, that, irrespective of the play of political strategies and party alliances, a broad consensus regarding immigrants as 'dangerous' could be formed, because this notion invokes a deep-seated discourse on dysfunctional population segments that are assumed to pose risks for the welfare state.

Genealogically, an oblique link runs from the discovery of 'the dangerous immigrants' of the ghetto back to the welfare planning of the 1960s and early 1970s, which invented techniques for profiling segments that were predisposed to become dysfunctional and burdensome to the welfare project. This oblique link makes up an unexpected continuity between the recent preventive discriminatory profiling of immigrant groups and the welfarist techniques for detecting groups that hold a higher probability of endangering the welfare state. A lesson from genealogical analysis is that such continuities hardly ever form a straightforward lineage. In this case, the difference between the heyday of welfare planning and the recent restrictionist immigration paradigm is that the first was characterized by optimism and the hope of integrating all groups at risk, whereas an emergent strategy of enclosure propels the second. In terms of the analysis of *dispositifs*, the overall development evinces a shift in Danish immigration policies from the securitization of circulations while minimizing risks, to a resurrection of legal sovereignty which emerges 'on top of' and redirects the previous techniques of discipline and security. In brief, then, sovereign intervention now finds support in security calculations of unacceptable levels of 'bad circulation' as well as disciplinary profiling based on norm deviations.

The Covid-19 pandemic

Finally, I wish to briefly consider the recent Covid-19 pandemic, which entirely dominated the world just a few years ago. In this context, I will merely offer a few tentative and preliminary thoughts that require deeper analysis and reflection on the dramatic events. The Covid-19 pandemic could readily be termed an 'urgent need', comparable to those acute problems that gave rise to Foucault's *dispositifs*. These problems include, we recall, the need to turn masses of unruly bodies into effective labour power during nineteenth-century industrialism, the need to secure grain supplies in eighteenth-century France, the need to protect European cities against the deadly plague in the fourteenth century, and the need to control the circulation of smallpox in the sixteenth century. The global pandemic posed an acute problem that prompted extensive governmental reactions such as the closure of international borders, lockdowns of entire countries, unprecedented government stimulus packages, and the invention of a range of tracking devices that allowed authorities to monitor infection rates and the movements of infected individuals, while also inciting individuals to exert self-surveillance via mobile apps.

Some commentators argue that Covid-19 exacerbated existing problems in the neoliberal economic order, such as growing populist nationalism, xenophobia, and the shaming on social media of certain ethnic groups for allegedly causing the pandemic. Judith Butler observes that Covid-19 did not strike individuals equally in capitalist societies such as the USA—not because a virus itself discriminates, but because the interlocking social and economic inequalities ensure that it does. The recent surge in nationalism, racism, and xenophobia in the USA demonstrates, writes Butler, how fast 'radical inequality, nationalism, and capitalist exploitation find ways to reproduce and strengthen themselves within the pandemic zones' (Butler, 2020: n.p.). Seen from the perspective of the technological framework, as developed in this book, the pandemic incited responses from within our existing *dispositifs*, just as it provoked transformations, contradictions, and realignments between them. A pandemic could thus be understood as a catalyst, as suggested by Anders Fogh Jensen (2012), which reactivates modes of organizing and knowing infectious diseases that are part of the heritage of European history. Particularly noteworthy was the return of the disciplinary strategy for fighting epidemics, namely the detailed structuring of space from a central position (Fogh Jensen, 2012: 31). From the perspective of our analytical approach, Covid-19 incited responses that recombined the *dispositifs* of law, discipline, and security, and one could explore whether the pandemic will act as a catalyst for the formation of new *dispositifs*.

An interesting way to approach pandemics is via Deleuze's (1992) assertion that each *dispositif* carries both 'lines of sedimentation' and 'lines to the future'. We recall that Deleuze incites the researcher to 'untangle the lines of the recent past from the lines of the near future' (Deleuze, 1992: 164). It is relatively easy to find lines of sedimentation in Foucault's analyses of the *dispositifs* that emerged in response to epidemics throughout European history. Foucault contrasts the model of the exclusion of lepers with that of the inclusion of plague victims. He suggests that in the Middle Ages the incarceration of lepers was mainly achieved using a series of legal laws based on a binary division between lepers and the healthy. Foucault says that 'exclusion essentially took place through a juridical combination of laws and regulations, as well as a set of religious rituals, which anyway brought about a division, and a binary type of division, between those who were lepers and those who were not' (STP: 9). By comparison, the handling of plague victims in the seventeenth century combined the techniques of discipline, including a minute partitioning and surveillance of the city. This regulation involved, says Foucault, 'a prohibition to leave the town on pain of death, the killing of all stray animals; the division of the town into distinct quarters' (DP: 195). The strict division of spaces and the creation of enclosures constitutes, according to Foucault, the trademarks of the disciplinary *dispositif*, since the space of discipline is usually cellular.

Turning our attention to the range of anti-epidemic measures that governments recently implemented against Covid-19 worldwide, we can possibly extract some 'lines to the future' (in Deleuze's sense) from these measures. Analytically, I take such 'lines to the future' to constitute both the transformations that a particular *dispositif* undergoes, as well as modifications in how the *dispositifs* are interrelated. First, in response to the pandemic's exceptionality, there is the global resurrection of state sovereignty evident in governmental interventions like border closure, general lockdown by ordinance, and the use of police and military to enforce curfews, disperse crowds, and deter individuals from entering public spaces. This deployment of sovereignty takes the nation state's own population as the principal object of legalistic and protective measures. The appeal by authorities to assume solidarity with 'our nation', or 'the people' parallels this reaffirmation of national sovereignty. We may speak of a recomposition in which the legal *dispositif* expands, becomes increasingly predominant, and begins to make use of disciplinary techniques and security calculations. Foucault described how the fight against the plague in seventeenth-century Western Europe gave rise to an intensification of disciplinary interventions:

> Rather than the massive, binary division between one set of people and another, it called for multiple separations, individualizing distributions, an organization in depth of surveillance and control, an intensification and a ramification of power. (DP: 198)

Disciplinary techniques were indeed prevalent in contemporary preventive and anti-epidemic measures, as many commentators have noted (Couch et al., 2020; Bigo et al., 2021; Villadsen, 2021b). As discussed in previous chapters, discipline aims at continuous control, improvement, and correction of individual bodies in accordance with norms. In 2020–2022, we witnessed anti-epidemic strategies based on the recognition that human-related interfaces and social relays of circulation cannot be entirely shut down by legal command. Hence authorities across the world implemented disciplinary techniques for restricting the movement of the pandemic's human carriers in public spaces, such as access restrictions, partitions of cities, and surveillance of public spaces, along with appeals for generalized peer-to-peer surveillance and self-discipline. One might say that discipline reaches further into the social body than the law. Indeed, Foucault describes discipline as an 'infra-law', or a 'counter-law', which extends 'the general forms defined by law to the infinitesimal level of individual lives' (DP: 222–223). Some scholars argue that the introduction of these renewed disciplinary techniques establishes unprecedented levels of surveillance, which operates through the awareness of citizens' visibility to others and the authorities, a development whereby the loci of power become inexorably diffused across society (Couch et al., 2020). To be sure, disciplinary techniques are not new in medicine and health promotion. However, Covid-19 sparked a multitude of novel surveillance techniques that use new digital technology such as smartphone apps for contact tracing, drone surveillance, automatic data collection through mobile apps, and ankle bracelets for people who violated quarantine or self-isolation requirements.

Intersecting with law and discipline, we saw a set of tools that can be termed 'anticipatory governance', that is, predictive models based on mathematical projections, which are increasingly indispensable for decision-making in financial markets, climate change, and global health (Rhodes et al., 2020). The predictive measures that governments adopted in response to the pandemic can be elucidated by Foucault's notion of security and securitization. Security calculates the acceptable level of infections by weighing the costs of intervention against the risks of allowing the disease to circulate. If law and disciplinary techniques aim to constrain the circulation of epidemics, isolating the infected from the healthy, securitization accepts that viruses will inevitably circulate, while seeking to predict, control, and minimize damage at the population level. We recall that Foucault said that the *dispositif* of security inserts the phenomenon of interest into a series of probable events, aiming for acceptable levels of incidence, while considering the costs of reacting to it: 'instead of a binary division between the permitted and the prohibited, one establishes an average considered as optimal on the one hand, and on the other, a bandwidth of the acceptable that must not be exceeded' (STP: 6). Securitization of epidemics entails projecting the spread of infections over an exposed population, while weighing the costs of intervention against the consequences of letting the disease circulate.

Security instruments came into effect in a systematic fashion during the breakout of smallpox in eighteenth-century Europe. The problem posed by the major smallpox epidemic was handled very differently from previous epidemics, says Foucault, insofar as the response only partly relied on disciplinary techniques. Now, seen from the emerging security perspective, the problem was 'knowing how many people are infected with smallpox, at what age, with what effects, with what mortality rate, lesions or after-effects, the risks of inoculation' (STP: 10). In this new approach to epidemics, says Foucault, there is an acute attention to 'the statistical effects on the population in general' (STP: 10). Instead of the strategy of exclusion of those infected by leprosy, or of quarantining those struck by the plague, the response to smallpox took the form of medical campaigns that aimed to stop or slow the epidemic. These medical campaigns involved techniques, first of variolization, then of vaccination, that were decisive for programmes of mass immunization in Western Europe, as well as the statistical calculation of contagion risks and predictions of infection rates so crucial for today's governmental strategies. Foucault says that 'thanks to the statistical instruments available, the certain and generally applicable character of vaccination and variolization made it possible to think of the phenomena [of contagion] in terms of the calculus of probabilities' (STP: 58–59).

We see here the emergence of the recognition that epidemics will circulate, and that interventions must centre on minimizing the risks of such inevitable circulation. This rationality of tempering interventions against epidemics broadly parallels the securitization of grain supply in the eighteenth century that focused on acceptable levels of fluctuation in grain supply (discussed in Chapter 1). Security entails tempered governmental aspirations that seek to mitigate and prepare for epidemics rather than eradicating them. Informed by statistical data of disease patterns, securitization seeks to control the spread of epidemics and minimize their damage by calculating the costs and benefits of interventions on the population, the health care system, and the economy at different infection rates. In brief, securitization entails projections of pandemic futures.

Recent governmental responses to Covid-19 raise significant questions regarding the appropriate balance between protecting the population's health and respecting individuals' privacy. Take, for example, the use of mobile contact-tracing apps to trace citizens' movements and interactions with others in order to monitor the spread of the virus. Essentially, this strategy functions by mobilizing people's smartphones for public health ends, repurposing digital technologies that are fully integral in the everyday life of most people. In a recent essay, Didier Bigo, Elspeth Guild, and Elif Kuskonmaz (2021) argue that when individuals comply with the use of contact-tracing apps, it is not so much because they fear state sanctions, but rather because they are concerned about exposing themselves and their close ones to the virus. They use the term 'governmentality of unease' to designate governmental policies that are 'articulated upon the concerns of the individuals themselves' and involve 'a less coercive and intimidating perspective than the one of a politics of fear organized by the state' (Bigo et al., 2021: 3). Even if ostensibly less coercive, these measures for curbing infection rates raise serious concerns regarding state authorities' access, storage, and limitless use of personal data obtained through quasi-mandatory mobile apps. It is probably because the declared purpose of collecting such data is to protect the population that we discuss much less issues regarding access, circulation, and elimination of personal data. Overall, the exceptionality of the Covid-19 crises entailed a blurring of the limits to governmental infringement of citizens' privacy rights. A key question is whether these transformations in the *dispositifs* will outlive the pandemic and leave long-lasting effects on democratic structures. Surveillance through personal data accumulation is certainly foreign to modern medicine and health promotion. However, Covid-19 led to unprecedented levels of surveillance that caused a new form of generalized discipline or 'unease', which operated through individuals' constant awareness of their visibility to others and to the authorities.

Most people obey the authorities' demand to use tracing apps and to have their personal data registered, either because they feel compelled to do so, or possibly because they are struck by 'unease'. How should we negotiate or resist the development whereby sovereign state power and digital

324   Foucault's Technologies

surveillance technology encroach upon personal privacy? Perhaps the problem with dichotomous discussions of governments versus citizens, private versus public, and obedience versus disobedience is that the imperative to fight public threats by means of sovereign power and disciplinary surveillance is deeply ingrained in our historical heritage—one that can be termed 'biopolitical'. Hence, in a recent commentary, Danielle Lorenzini (2021) doubts that an effective strategy of resistance to such dangerous aspects of the recent anti-pandemic strategies can come in the form of global refusal. Lorenzini writes: 'Biopolitical power is not (only) exercised on our lives from the "outside", as it were, but has been a part of what we are, of our historical form of subjectivity, for at least the past two centuries.' If we listen to Foucault, there can be no overall refusal of modern biopolitics, 'since it is the very fabric of our being that we should be ready to question' (Lorenzini, 2021). The model citizens constituted by the *dispositifs* of law, discipline, and security are not simply 'out there', conceptualized in legal ordinances, social distance campaigns, and statistical projections. They are also part of our subjectivity: how we constitute ourselves and what we expect from others in times of pandemic crises.

In these tentative considerations and analyses, we notice how elements of sovereignty, discipline, and biopower combine in new and swiftly evolving constellations. Yet the above studies of social work, risky immigrants, and anti-pandemic interventions did not so much confirm that these *dispositifs* were identifiable in the material scrutinized. Foucault's concepts are in quest of historical content, as we noted at the outset of this book. Indeed, by using concepts like discipline and security we do not intend to predetermine the field of possible empirical observations, as if the goal was to identify phenomena that correspond to Foucault's original descriptions. As we reach the end of the book, it is worth recalling that the *dispositifs* should serve as guiding lenses which direct our attention to particular kinds of normativity ingrained in the modern West, while they require of us the careful description of the contradictory developments as they appear in the archive. Such careful studies can also give us crucial indications of 'lines to the future', or what we are about to become. A task for future Foucault-inspired research is to explore how practices of categorizing, normalizing, and segregating citizens articulate broader *dispositifs* of power/knowledge as well as techniques and ways of reasoning that belong to each nation's political and cultural heritage. I hope this book will serve as inspiration and an invitation to carry out such work. As Foucault (1971: 162) said: 'I don't write a book so that it will be the final one; I write a book so that other books will be possible, not necessarily written by me'.

Bibliography

Agamben, G. 2009. *What is an Apparatus?* Stanford, CA: Stanford University Press.

Agamben, G. 2011. *The Kingdom and the Glory: For a Theological Genealogy of Economy and Government.* Stanford, CA: Stanford University Press.

Althusser, L. 1969a. 'Contradiction and Over-Determination'. In *For Marx*, by Louis Althusser, pp. 87–129. London: Allen Lane.

Althusser, L. 1969b. 'Freud and Lacan'. *New Left Review 55* (May–June): pp. 49–65.

Althusser, L. 1976. *Essays in Self-Criticism.* London: New Left Books.

Althusser, L. and É. Balibar. 1970. *Reading Capital.* London: New Left Books.

Anders, G. 1948. 'On the Pseudo-Concreteness of Heidegger's Philosophy'. *Philosophy and Phenomenological Research 8* (3): pp. 337–371.

Anders, G. 2016. 'On Promethean Shame'. In *Prometheanism: Technology, Digital Culture and Human Obsolescence*, edited by Christopher J. Müller, pp. 29–95. London: Rowman & Littlefield International.

Andersen, N. Å. 1994. *Institutionel historie: En introduktion til diskurs- og institutionsanalyse, COS-rapport, 10/94.* København: Handelshøjskolen i København.

Andreasen, T. A. C. 2016. Foucault som tænker af teknologien. *Agora 34* (1): pp. 83–100.

Ansell-Pearson, K. 1995. 'The Significance of Michel Foucault's Reading of Nietzsche: Power, the Subject, and Political Theory'. In *Nietzsche: A Critical Reader*, edited by Peter Sedgwick, pp. 13–30. Oxford: Blackwell.

Badiou, A. 1999. *Manifesto for Philosophy.* Albany: State University of New York Press.

Badiou, A. 2001. 'Who is Nietzsche?' *Pli: The Warwick Journal of Philosophy 11*: pp. 1–11.

Balibar, É. 2002. *Politics and the Other Scene.* London: Verso.

Balibar, É. 2009. 'Europe as Borderland'. *Environment and Planning D: Society and Space 27* (2): pp. 190–215.

Balibar, É. 2014. 'Foreword: Althusser and the Ideological State Apparatuses'. In *On the Reproduction of Capitalism: Ideology and Ideological State Apparatuses*, by Louis Althusser, pp. vii–xix. New York: Verso.

Behrent, M. 2009. 'Liberalism without Humanism: Michel Foucault and the Free Market Creed 1976–1979'. *Modern Intellectual History 6* (3): pp. 539–568.

Behrent, M. 2013. 'Foucault and Technology'. *History and Technology: An International Journal 29* (1): pp. 54–104.

Belu, D. and A. Feenberg. 2010. 'Heidegger's Aporetic Ontology of Technology'. *Inquiry 53* (1): pp. 1–19.

Benton, T. 1984. *The Rise and Fall of Structural Marxism: Althusser and His Influence.* New York: St Martin's Press.

Bidet, J. 2015. 'The Interpellated Subject: Beyond Althusser and Butler'. *Crisis and Critique 2* (2): pp. 63–85.

Bidet, J. 2016. *Foucault with Marx.* London: Zed Press.

Bigo, D., E. Guild, and E. Kuskonmaz. 2021. 'Obedience in Times of COVID-19 Pandemics: A Renewed Governmentality of Unease?' *Global Discourse: An Interdisciplinary Journal of Current Affairs 11* (3): pp. 471–489.

Bissenbakker, M. 2019. 'Attachment Required: The Affective Governmentality of Marriage Migration in the Danish Aliens Act, 2000–2018'. *International Political Sociology 13* (2): pp. 181–189.

326 Bibliography

Blackman, L. 1998. 'The Voice-Hearing Experience'. *Nordiske Udkast 1*: pp. 39–50.

Blackman, L. 2000. 'Ethics, Embodiment, and the Voice-Hearing Experience'. *Theory, Culture & Society 17* (5): pp. 55–74.

Bolton, S. and M. Houlihan (eds). 2007. *Searching for the Human in Human Resource Management*. London: Palgrave.

Borgmann, A. 2005. 'Technology'. In *A Companion to Heidegger*, edited by Hubert Dreyfus and Mark Wrathall, pp. 420–432. Malden, MA: Blackwell.

Brigati, R. 2015. 'Veracity and Pragmatism in Nietzsche's on Truth and Lies'. *Parrhesia 23*: pp. 78–102.

Brown, W. 1995. *States of Injury: Power and Freedom in Late Modernity*. Princeton, NJ: Princeton University Press.

Bussolini, J. 2010. 'What is a Dispositive?' *Foucault Studies 10*: pp. 85–107.

Butler, J. 1997. *The Psychic Life of Power: Theories in Subjection*. Stanford, CA: Stanford University Press.

Butler, J. 2002a. 'What is Critique? An Essay on Foucault's Virtue'. In *The Political: Readings in Continental Philosophy*, edited by David Ingram, pp. 212–226. London: Basil Blackwell.

Butler, J. 2002b. 'Bodies and Power Revisited'. *Radical Philosophy 114* (July–August): pp. 13–19.

Butler, J. 2003. *Giving an Account of Oneself: A Critique of Ethical Violence*. Amsterdam: Uitgeverij Van Gorcum.

Butler, J. 2020. 'Capitalism has its Limits'. Verso Books blog, 30 March 2020. Available at: https://www.versobooks.com/blogs/4603-capitalism-has-its-limits (accessed 3 May 2024).

Butler, J. and A. Athanasiou. 2013. *Dispossession: The Performative in the Political*. Cambridge: Polity.

Caldwell, R. 2005. 'Things Fall Apart? Discourses on Agency'. *Human Relations 58* (1): pp. 83–114.

Caldwell, R. 2007. 'Agency and Change: Re-evaluating Foucault's Legacy'. *Organization 14* (6): pp. 769–791.

Callinicos, A. 1989. *Against Postmodernism*. Cambridge: Polity Press.

Callon, M. 1986. 'The Sociology of an Actor-Network: The Case of the Electric Vehicle'. In *Mapping the Dynamics of Science and Technology*, edited by M. Callon, J. Law, and A. Rip, pp. 19–34. London: Palgrave Macmillan.

Canguilhem, G. 1991. *The Normal and the Pathological*. New York: Zone Books.

Canguilhem, G. 1997. 'On Histoire de la folie as an Event'. In *Foucault and His Interlocutors*, edited by Arnold Davidson, pp. 28–33. Chicago, IL: University of Chicago Press.

Canguilhem, G. 2008. 'Machine and Organism'. In *Knowledge of Life*, by Georges Canguilhem, pp. 75–97. New York: Fordham University Press.

Carman, T. 2020. 'Heidegger's Nietzsche'. *Inquiry 63* (1): pp. 104–116.

Cassin, B., J. Apter, and M. Wood. 2014. *Dictionary of Untranslatables: A Philosophical Lexicon*. Princeton, NJ: Princeton University Press.

Certeau, M. de 1986. 'Micro-Techniques and Panoptic Discourse'. In *Heterologies: Discourse on the Other*, by Michel de Certeau, pp. 185–193. Minneapolis: University of Minnesota Press.

Cheney-Lippold, J. 2011. 'A New Algorithmic Identity: Soft Biopolitics and the Modulation of Control'. *Theory, Culture & Society 28* (6): pp. 164–181.

CLANDESTINO. 2009. *Undocumented Migration: Counting the Uncountable. Data and Trends across Europe*. CLANDESTINO Project, Final Report, 23 November.

Collier, S. J. 2009. 'Topologies of Power: Foucault's Analysis of Political Government beyond Governmentality'. *Theory, Culture & Society 26* (6): pp. 78–108.

Bibliography 327

Cooper, R. 2020. 'Pastoral Power and Algorithmic Governmentality'. *Theory, Culture & Society* 37 (1): pp. 29–52.

Coté, M. E. 2007. *The Italian Foucault: Communication, Networks, and the Dispositif*. Burnaby: Simon Fraser University.

Couch, D. L., P. Robinson, and P. A. Komesaroff. 2020. 'COVID-19: Extending Surveillance and the Panopticon'. *Bioethical Inquiry* 17 (4): pp. 809–814. https://doi.org/10.1007/s11673-020-10036-5

Cruikshank, B. 1999. *The Will to Empower*. Ithaca, NY: Cornell University Press.

Davidson, A. I. 1991. 'Archaeology, Genealogy, Ethics'. In *Foucault: A Critical Reader*, edited by David Couzens Hoy, pp. 221–233. Oxford: Oxford University Press.

Davidson, A. I. 2004. *The Emergence of Sexuality: Historical Epistemology and the Formation of Concepts*. Cambridge, MA: Harvard University Press.

Davidson, A. I. 2005. 'Ethics as Ascetics: Foucault, the History of Ethics, and Ancient Thought'. In *The Cambridge Companion to Foucault*, edited by Gary Gutting, pp. 123–148. Cambridge: Cambridge University Press.

Davidson, A. I. 2011. 'In Praise of Counter-Conduct'. *History of the Human Sciences* 24 (4): pp. 25–41.

Dean, M. 1996. 'Putting the Technological into Government'. *History of the Human Sciences* 9 (3): pp. 47–68.

Dean, M. and K. Villadsen. 2016. *State Phobia and Civil Society: The Political Heritage of Michel Foucault*. Palo Alto, CA: Stanford University Press.

Deleuze, G. 1988. *Foucault*. Madison: University of Wisconsin Press.

Deleuze, G. 1991. *Bergsonism*. New York: Zone Books.

Deleuze, G. 1992. 'What is a Dispositif?' In *Michel Foucault Philosopher*, edited by Timothy J. Armstrong, pp. 159–168. London and Chicago: Harvester Wheatsheaf and University of Chicago Press.

Deleuze, G. 1995. *Negotiations, 1972–1990*. New York: Columbia University Press.

Deleuze, G. 1997. 'Desire and Pleasure'. In *Foucault and His Interlocutors*, edited by Arnold I. Davidson, pp. 183–195. Chicago, IL: Chicago University Press.

Deleuze, G. 2006. *Nietzsche and Philosophy*. New York: Columbia University Press.

Deleuze, G. and F. Guattari. 1994. *What is Philosophy?* New York: Columbia University Press.

Dews, P. 1979. 'The Nouvelle Philosophie and Foucault'. *Economy and Society* 8 (2): pp. 127–171.

Dillon, M. 2007. 'Governing Through Contingency: The Security of Biopolitical Governance'. *Political Geography* 26 (1): pp. 41–47.

Donzelot, J. 1979. *Policing of Families*. New York: Pantheon Books.

Dorrestijn, S. 2012. 'Technical Mediation and Subjectivation: Tracing and Extending Foucault's Philosophy of Technology'. *Philosophy & Technology* 25 (2): pp. 197–201.

Dreyfus, H. 1995. 'Heidegger on Gaining a Free Relation to Technology'. In *Technology and the Politics of Knowledge*, edited by Andrew Feenburg and Alastair Hannay, pp. 25–34. Bloomington: Indiana University Press.

Dreyfus, H. 1996. 'Being and Power: Heidegger and Foucault'. *International Journal of Philosophical Studies* 4 (1): pp. 1–16.

Dreyfus, H. L. and P. Rabinow. 1982. *Michel Foucault: Beyond Structuralism and Hermeneutics*. London and Chicago: Harvester Wheatsheaf and University of Chicago Press.

Dumm, T. L. 1996. *Michel Foucault and the Politics of Freedom*. London: Sage.

Durkin, K. 2022. 'Adventures in the Anti-Humanist Dialectic: Towards the Reappropriation of Humanism'. *European Journal of Social Theory* 25 (2): pp. 292–311.

Eagleton, T. 1990. *The Ideology of the Aesthetic*. New York: Basil Blackwell.

328   Bibliography

Elden, S. 2001. *Mapping the Present: Heidegger, Foucault and the Project of a Spatial History*. New York: Continuum.

Elden, S. 2015. 'A More Marxist Foucault: Reading La société punitive'. *Historical Materialism* 23 (4): pp. 149–168.

Elden, S. 2021. *The Early Foucault*. Cambridge: Polity.

Ellul, J. 1980. *The Technological Society*. New York: Continuum.

Esposito, R. 2012. 'The Dispositif of the Person'. *Law, Culture and the Humanities 8* (1): pp. 17–30.

Ewald, F. 1991. 'Insurance and Risk'. In *The Foucault Effect: Studies in Governmentality*, edited by Graham Burchell, Colin Gordon, and Peter Miller, pp. 197–210. London and Chicago: Harvester Wheatsheaf and University of Chicago Press.

Ewald, F. and B. E. Harcourt. 2019. 'Course Context'. In *Penal Theories and Institutions: Lectures at the Collège de France, 1971–1972*, by Michel Foucault, pp. 242–269. New York: Palgrave.

Falcon, A. 2015. 'Aristotle on Causality'. In *The Stanford Encyclopaedia of Philosophy* (Spring 2015 edition). Available at: http://plato.stanford.edu/archives/spr2015/entries/aristotle-causality/ (accessed 3 May 2024).

Feenberg, A. 1999. *Questioning Technology*. London: Routledge.

Flynn, T. R. 2010. *Sartre, Foucault, and Historical Reason, Volume Two: A Poststructuralist Mapping of History*. Chicago, IL: University of Chicago Press.

Fogh Jensen, A. 2012. *The Project Society*. Aarhus: Aarhus University Press.

Foucault, M. 1970 [1966]. *The Order of Things: An Archaeology of the Human Sciences*. London: Tavistock Publications.

Foucault, M. 1971. 'Entretien avec Foucault'. In Dits et Ecrits II, edited by Daniel Defert and Francois Ewald, pp. 157–174. Paris: Gallimard.

Foucault, M. 1972b. 'The Discourse on Language'. In *The Archaeology of Knowledge*, by Michel Foucault, pp. 212–238. New York: Pantheon.

Foucault, M. 1976 [1954]. *Mental Illness and Psychology*. New York: Harper & Row.

Foucault, M. 1977a. 'Intellectuals and Power: A Conversation between Michel Foucault and Gilles Deleuze'. In *Language, Counter-Memory, Practice*, edited by Donald F. Bouchard, pp. 205–218. Ithaca, NY: Cornell University Press.

Foucault, M. 1977b. 'What is an Author?' In *Language, Counter-Memory, Practice*, edited by Donald F. Bouchard, pp. 113–138. Ithaca, NY: Cornell University Press.

Foucault, M. 1980a. 'Truth and Power'. In *Power/Knowledge: Selected Interviews and Other Writings 1972–1977*, by Michel Foucault, pp. 119–134. New York: Pantheon.

Foucault, M. 1980b. 'The Eye of Power'. In *Power/Knowledge: Selected Interviews and Other Writings*, by Michel Foucault, pp. 146–166. New York: Pantheon.

Foucault, M. 1980c. 'Body/Power'. In *Power/Knowledge: Selected Interviews and Other Writings 1972–1977*, by Michel Foucault, pp. 55–62. New York: Pantheon.

Foucault, M. 1980d. 'Two Lectures'. In *Power/Knowledge: Selected Interviews and Other Writings 1972–1977*, by Michel Foucault, pp. 78–102. New York: Pantheon.

Foucault, M. 1980e. 'The History of Sexuality'. In *Power/Knowledge: Selected Interviews and Other Writings 1972–1977*, by Michel Foucault, pp. 183–194. New York: Pantheon.

Foucault, M. 1984a. 'What is Enlightenment?' In *The Foucault Reader*, edited by Paul Rabinow, pp. 32–51. London: Penguin Books.

Foucault, M. 1984b. 'Nietzsche, Genealogy, History'. In *The Foucault Reader*, edited by Paul Rabinow, pp. 76–101. London: Penguin Books.

Foucault, M. 1984c. 'Polemics, Politics, and Problematizations: An Interview'. In *The Foucault Reader*, edited by Paul Rabinow, pp. 381–390. London: Penguin Books.

Foucault, M. 1988a. *Technologies of the Self: A Seminar with Michel Foucault*. Boston, MA: University of Massachusetts Press.

Foucault, M. 1988b. 'Truth, Power, Self'. In *Technologies of the Self*, edited by Luther H. Martin, Huck Gutman, and Patrick H. Hutton, pp. 9–15. Amherst: University of Massachusetts Press.

Foucault, M. 1988c. 'An Aesthetics of Existence'. In *Michel Foucault: Politics, Philosophy, Culture: Interviews and Other Writings 1977–1984*, edited by Lawrence D. Kritzman, pp. 47–57. New York: Routledge.

Foucault, M. 1988d. 'Technologies of the Self'. In *Technologies of the Self*, edited by Luther H. Martin, Huck Gutman, and Patrick H. Hutton, pp. 16–49. Amherst: University of Massachusetts Press.

Foucault, M. 1989a. 'The Return of Morality?' In *Foucault Live: Interviews, 1966–84*, edited by Sylvère Lotringer, pp. 465–474. New York: Columbia University Press.

Foucault, M. 1989b. 'How Much does it Cost to Tell the Truth?' In *Foucault Live: Interviews, 1966–84*, edited by Sylvère Lotringer, pp. 233–257. New York: Columbia University Press.

Foucault, M. 1989c. 'The Archaeology of Knowledge'. In *Foucault Live: Interviews, 1966–84*, edited by Sylvère Lotringer, pp. 57–65. New York: Columbia University Press.

Foucault, M. 1991. 'Questions of Method'. In *The Foucault Effect: Studies in Governmentality*, edited by Graham Burchell, Colin Gordon, and Peter Miller, pp. 73–86. Chicago, IL: University of Chicago Press.

Foucault, M. 1993. 'Dream, Imagination, and Existence'. In *Dream and Existence*, by Ludwig Binswanger, pp. 31–78. Atlantic Highlands, NJ: Humanities Press International.

Foucault, M. 1997. *The Politics of Truth*, edited by Sylvère Lotringer. New York: Semiotext(e).

Foucault, M. 1998a. 'The Ethics of the Concern of the Self as a Practice of Freedom'. In *Ethics, Subjectivity and Truth: The Essential Works of Foucault, 1954–1984, Volume 1*, edited by James D. Faubion, pp. 281–303. New York: New Press.

Foucault, M. 1998b. 'Nietzsche, Freud, Marx'. In *Aesthetics, Methods, and Epistemology: The Essential Works of Foucault, 1954–1984, Volume 2*, edited by James D. Faubion, pp. 261–269. New York: New Press.

Foucault, M. 1998c. 'Structuralism and Poststructuralism'. In *Aesthetics, Methods, and Epistemology: The Essential Works of Foucault, 1954–1984, Volume 2*, edited by James D. Faubion, pp. 433–459. New York: New Press.

Foucault, M. 1998d. 'Life: Experience and Science'. In *Aesthetics, Method, and Epistemology: The Essential Works of Foucault, 1954–1984, Volume 2*, edited by James D. Faubion, pp. 465–78. New York: New Press.

Foucault, M. 1998e. 'On the Ways of Writing History'. In *Aesthetics, Method, and Epistemology: The Essential Works of Foucault, 1954–1984, Volume 2*, edited by James D. Faubion, pp. 269–279. New York: New Press.

Foucault, M. 1999. 'About the Beginning of the Hermeneutics of the Self'. In *Religion and Culture Michel Foucault*, edited by Jeremy R. Carrette, pp. 158–182. New York: Routledge.

Foucault, M. 2000a. 'Space, Knowledge, Power'. In *Power: Essential Works of Foucault 1954–1984, Volume 3*, edited by James D. Faubion, pp. 349–364. London: Penguin.

Foucault, M. 2000b. 'About the Concept of the Dangerous Individual'. In *Power: Essential Works of Foucault 1954–1984, Volume 3*, edited by James D. Faubion, pp. 176 201. London: Penguin.

Foucault, M. 2000c. 'Interview with Foucault'. In *Power: Essential Works of Foucault 1954–1984, Volume 3*, edited by James D. Faubion, pp. 239–298. New York: New Press.

Foucault, M. 2000d. 'The Ethics of the Concern for Self as a Practice of Freedom'. In *Ethics, Subjectivity and Truth: Essential Works of Foucault 1954–1984, Volume 1*, edited by James D. Faubion, pp. 281–302. New York: New Press.

330 Bibliography

Foucault, M. 2001a. 'So is it Important to Think'. In *Power: Essential Works of Foucault 1954–1984, Volume 3*, edited by James D. Faubion, pp. 454–458. New York: New Press.

Foucault, M. 2001b. *Fearless Speech*. Los Angeles, CA: Semiotexte.

Foucault, M. 2007a. 'The Meshes of Power'. In *Space, Knowledge and Power: Foucault and Geography*, edited by Jeremy W. Crampton and Stuart Elden, pp. 153–163. Aldershot: Ashgate.

Foucault, M. 2007b. 'What is Critique?' In *The Politics of Truth*, edited by Sylvère Lotringer, pp. 23–83. Los Angeles, CA: Semiotext(e).

Foucault, M. 2008 [1964]. *Introduction to Kant's Anthropology*. Los Angeles, CA: Semiotext(e).

Foucault, M. 2014. *Wrong-Doing, Truth-Telling: The Function of Avowal in Justice*. Chicago, IL: University of Chicago Press.

Fox, N. F. 2003. *The New Sartre: Explorations in Postmodernism*. London: Continuum.

Fox, N. J. 1998. 'Foucault, Foucauldians and Sociology'. *British Journal of Sociology 49* (3): pp. 415–433.

Fraser, N. 1981. 'Foucault on Modern Power: Empirical insights and normative confusions'. *Praxis International 1* (3): pp. 272–287.

Freud, S. 2010 [1899]. *The Interpretation of Dreams*. New York: Basic Books.

Fuchs, C. 2017. 'Günther Anders' Undiscovered Critical Theory of Technology in the Age of Big Data Capitalism'. *TripleC 15* (2): pp. 582–611.

Garland, D. 2014. 'What is a History of the Present? On Foucault's Genealogies and Their Critical Preconditions'. *Punishment & Society 16* (4): pp. 365–384.

Garland, D. 2015. 'The Welfare State: A Fundamental Dimension of Modern Government'. *European Journal of Sociology 55* (3): pp. 327–364.

Gerrie, J. 2003. 'Was Foucault a Philosopher of Technology?' *Techné 7* (2): pp. 14–26.

Goffman, E. 1974. *Frame-Analysis: An Essay on the Organization of Experience*. New York: Harper & Row.

Goldstein, P. 1994. 'Althusserian Theory: From Scientific Truth to Institutional History'. *Studies in 20th Century Literature 18* (1): pp. 15–26.

Gordon, C. 1980. 'Afterword'. In *Power/Knowledge*, edited by Colin Gordon, pp. 229–260. New York: Pantheon Books.

Gros, F. 2005. 'Course Content'. In *The Hermeneutics of the Subject: Lectures at the Collège de France, 1981–1982*, by Michel Foucault, pp. 507–551. New York: Palgrave Macmillan.

Gros, F. 2010. 'Course Context'. In *The Government of Self and Others: Lectures at the Collège de France 1982–1983*, by Michel Foucault, pp. 377–393. London: Palgrave Macmillan.

Gudmand-Høyer, M. and T. Lopdrup-Hjorth. 2009. 'Liberal Biopolitics Reborn'. *Foucault Studies 7*: pp. 99–130.

Gutting, G. 2005. *Foucault: A Very Short Introduction*. Oxford: Oxford University Press.

Gutting, G. 2014. 'Ethics'. In *The Cambridge Foucault Lexicon*, edited by Leonard Lawlor and John Nale, pp. 136–143. Cambridge: Cambridge University Press.

Habermas, J. 1986. 'Taking Aim at the Heart of the Present'. In *Foucault: A Critical Reader*, edited by David C. Hoy, pp. 103–108. Oxford: Basil Blackwell.

Hacking, I. 1999a. 'Making Up People'. In *The Science Studies Reader*, edited by Mario Biagioli, pp. 161–171. New York: Routledge.

Hacking, I. 1999b. *The Social Construction of What?* Cambridge, MA: Harvard University Press.

Hallward, P. 2006. *Out of This World: Deleuze and the Philosophy of Creation*. London: Verso.

Han, B. C. 2017. *Psychopolitics: Neoliberalism and New Technologies of Power*. London: Verso Books.

Han, B. C. 2022. *Upheaval in the Lifeworld*. Cambridge: Polity Press.

Harcourt, B. E. 2008. *Supposons que la discipline et la securite n'existent pas: Rereading Foucault's Collège de France Lectures (with Paul Veyne) (October 3, 2008).* University of Chicago, Public Law Working Paper No. 240, pp. 1–18.

Harcourt, B. E. 2010. 'Neoliberal Penality: A Brief Genealogy'. *Theoretical Criminology 14* (1): pp. 74–92.

Harcourt, B. E. 2015a. *Exposed: Desire and Disobedience in the Digital Age.* Cambridge, MA: Harvard University Press.

Harcourt, B. E. 2015b. 'Course Context'. In *The Punitive Society: Lectures at the Collège de France 1972–1973*, by Michel Foucault, pp. 265–310. Houndmills: Palgrave.

Hardt, M. 2006. 'Foreword'. In *Nietzsche and Philosophy*, by Gilles Deleuze, pp. ix–xv. New York: Columbia University Press.

Hardt, M. and A. Negri. 2000. *Empire.* Cambridge, MA: Harvard University Press.

Hardy, N. 2015. 'Alea Capta Est: Foucault's Dispositif and Capturing Chance'. *Foucault Studies 19*: pp. 191–216.

Heidegger, M. 1950. *Holzwege.* Frankfurt: Vittorio Klostermann.

Heidegger, M. 1973. 'Overcoming Metaphysics'. In *The End of Philosophy*, by Martin Heidegger, pp. 84–110. New York: Harper & Row.

Heidegger, M. 1992 [1921–1922]. 'Phenomenological Interpretations with Respect to Aristotle: Indication of the Hermeneutical Situation'. *Man and World 25* (3): pp. 355–393.

Heidegger, M. 1998. *Pathmarks.* Cambridge: Cambridge University Press.

Higgins, V. and W. Larner. 2010. 'Standards and Standardisation as a Social Science Problem'. In *Calculating the Social: Standards and the Reconfiguration of Governing*, edited by Vaughan Higgins and Wendy Larne, pp. 1–17. New York: Palgrave Macmillan.

Himick, D. 2023. 'When Aging and Climate Change are Brought Together: Fossil Fuel Divestment and a Changing Dispositive of Security'. *Sustainability 15* (5): p. 4581.

Honneth, A. 1991. *A Critique of Power.* Boston, MA: MIT Press.

Hopwood, A. G. and P. Miller. 1994. *Accounting as Social and Institutional Practice.* Cambridge: Cambridge University Press.

Howe, D. 1996. 'Surface and Depth in Social-Work Practice'. In *Social Theory, Social Change, and Social Work*, edited by Nigel Parton, pp. 77–97. Routledge: London.

Ijsseling, S. 1986. 'Foucault with Heidegger'. *Man and World 19* (4): pp. 413–424.

Jameson, F. 1981. *The Political Unconscious: Narrative as a Socially Symbolic Act.* Ithaca, NY: Cornell University Press.

Jameson, F. 1991. *Postmodernism, or the Cultural Logic of Late Capitalism.* Durham, NC: Duke University Press.

Jay, M. 1993. *Downcast Eyes: The Denigration of Vision in Twentieth-Century French Thought.* Berkeley: University of California Press.

Jessop, B. 2006. 'From Micro-Powers to Governmentality: Foucault's Work on Statehood, State Formation, Statecraft and State Power'. *Political Geography 26* (1): pp. 34–40.

Karlsen, M. P. and K. Villadsen. 2008. 'Who Should Do the Talking: The Proliferation of Dialogue as Governmental Technology'. *Culture and Organization 14* (4): pp. 345–363.

Karlsen, M. P. and K. Villadsen. 2015. 'Foucault, Maoism, Genealogy: The Influence of Political Militancy in Michel Foucault's Thought'. *New Political Science 37* (1): pp. 91–117.

Karlsen, M. P. and K. Villadsen. 2016. 'Health Promotion, Governmentality and the Challenges of Theorizing Pleasure and Desire'. *Body & Society 22* (3): pp. 3–30.

Kelly, M. 2014. 'Foucault Against Marxism: Althusser beyond Althusser'. In *(Mis)readings of Marx in Continental Philosophy*, edited by Jernej Habjan and Jessica Whyte, pp. 83–99. Houndmills: Palgrave.

Kendall, G. 2001. 'From Foucault to Latour and Back Again: Technological, Historical Nonhumans'. *In-Between: Essays & Studies in Literary Criticism 1*: pp. 53–64.

332 Bibliography

Kendall, G. and M. Michael. 2001. 'Order and Disorder: Time, Technology and the Self'. *Culture Machine 1* (1). Available at: https://culturemachine.net/interzone/order-and-disorder-kendall-michael/ (accessed 9 April 2024).

Kioupkiolis, A. 2012. 'The Agonistic Turn of Critical Reason: Critique and Freedom in Foucault and Castoriadis'. *European Journal of Social Theory* 15 (3): pp. 385–402.

Koopman, C. 2013. 'The Formation and Self-Transformation of the Subject in Foucault's Ethics'. In *A Companion to Foucault*, edited by Chris Falzon, Timothy O'Leary, and Jana Sawick, pp. 526–544. Oxford: Wiley-Blackwell.

Koopman, C. 2015. 'Two Uses of Michel Foucault in Political Theory: Concepts and Methods in Giorgio Agamben and Ian Hacking'. *Constellations* 22 (4): pp. 571–585.

Koopman, C. 2019. *How We Became Our Data: A Genealogy of the Informational Person*. Chicago, IL: University of Chicago Press.

Koopman, C. and T. Matza. 2013. 'Putting Foucault to Work: Analytic and Concept in Foucaultian Inquiry'. *Critical Inquiry* 39 (4): pp. 817–840.

Lacoue-Labarthe, P., J.-L. Nancy, and B. Holmes. 1990. 'The Nazi Myth'. *Critical Inquiry 16* (2): pp. 291–312.

Lambert, G. 2020. *The Elements of Foucault*. Minneapolis: University of Minnesota Press.

Latour, B. 1993. *We Have Never Been Modern*. Cambridge, MA: Harvard University Press.

Latour, B. 2005. *Reassembling the Social: An Introduction to Actor-Network Theory*. Oxford: Oxford University Press.

Latour, B. and S. Woolgar. 1979. *Laboratory Life: The Construction of Scientific Facts*. Beverly Hills, CA: Sage Publications.

Lazzaretto, M. 2012. *The Making of the Indebted Man*. Los Angeles, CA: Semiotext(e).

Legg, S. 2011. 'Assemblage/Apparatus: Using Deleuze and Foucault'. *Area* 43 (2): pp. 128–133.

Levin, D. M. 1993. 'Decline and Fall: Ocularcentrism in Heidegger's Reading of the History of Metaphysics'. In *Modernity and the Hegemony of Vision*, edited by David Kleinberg-Levin, pp. 186–218. Berkeley and Los Angeles: University of California Press.

Lindberg, S. 2015. 'Lost in the World of Technology with and after Heidegger'. *Epoché 20* (1): pp. 1085–1968.

Lorenzini, D. 2021. 'Biopolitics in the Time of Coronavirus'. *Critical Inquiry 47* (2): pp. 40–45.

Lundberg, J. 2018. *Allermest undrer det mig at vi kan glemme*. Speciale Afhandling, Filosofi & Videnskabsteori. Roskilde: Roskilde Universitet.

Luxon, N. 2008. 'Ethics and Subjectivity: Practices of Self-Governance in the Late Lectures of Michel Foucault'. *Political Theory 36* (3): pp. 377–402.

Macherey, P. 2015. 'The Productive Subject'. *Viewpointmag.com*, 1 November, pp. 1–36.

Mahon, M. 1992. *Foucault's Nietzschean Genealogy: Truth, Power, and the Subject*. Albany: State University of New York Press.

Marx, K. 1990. *Capital, Volume 1: A Critique of Political Economy*. London: Penguin Books.

Matthewman, M. 2014. 'Michel Foucault, Technology, and Actor-Network Theory'. *Techne: Research in Philosophy & Technology 17* (2): pp. 274–292.

McNay, L. 2000. *Gender and Agency: Reconfiguring the Subject in Feminist and Social Theory*. London: Polity Press.

McQuillan, C. J. 2016. 'Beyond the Analytic of Finitude: Kant, Heidegger, Foucault'. *Foucault Studies 21*: pp. 184–199.

Milchman, A. and A. Rosenberg. 2003. *Foucault and Heidegger: Critical Encounters*. Mineapolis: University of Minnesota Press.

Milchman, A. and A. Rosenberg. 2007. 'The Aesthetic and Ascetic Dimensions of an Ethics of Self-Fashioning: Nietzsche and Foucault'. *Parrhesia 2*: pp. 44–65.

Milchman, A. and A. Rosenberg. 2011. 'Michel Foucault: An Ethical Politics of Care of the Self and Others'. In *Political Philosophy in the Twentieth Century: Authors and Arguments*, edited by Catherine Zuckert, pp. 228–239. Cambridge: Cambridge University Press.

Miller, T. 1994. 'Althusser, Foucault, and the Subject of Civility'. *Studies in 20th Century Literature 18* (1): pp. 97–118.

Mitchell, T. 1991. 'The Limits of the State: Beyond Statist Approaches and Their Critics'. *American Political Science Review 85* (1): pp. 77–96.

Montag, W. 1995. 'The Soul is the Prison of the Body: Althusser and Foucault, 1970–1975'. *Yale French Studies 88*: pp. 53–77.

Montag, W. 2013. *Althusser and His Contemporaries: Philosophy's Perpetual War*. Durham, NC: Duke University Press.

Morgan, W. R. 2023. 'Finance Must Be Defended: Cybernetics, Neoliberalism and Environmental, Social, and Governance (ESG)'. *Sustainability 15* (4): p. 3707.

Morris, M. 2016. *Knowledge and Ideology: The Epistemology of Social and Political Critique*. Cambridge: Cambridge University Press.

Nealon, J. T. 2008. *Foucault beyond Foucault: Power and its Intensifications since 1984*. Stanford, CA: Stanford University Press.

Nichols, R. 2014. *The World of Freedom: Heidegger, Foucault, and the Politics of Historical Ontology*. Stanford, CA: Stanford University Press.

Nietzsche, F. 1990. *Twilight of Idols and Anti-Christ*. London: Penguin Books.

Nietzsche, F. 2008. *The Birth of Tragedy*. Oxford: Oxford University Press.

Nussbaum, M. 1993. 'Non-Relative Virtues: An Aristotelian Approach'. In *The Quality of Life*, edited by Martha Nussbaum and Amartya Sen, pp. 242–269. Oxford: Clarendon Press.

O'Farrell, C. 2005. *Michel Foucault*. London: Sage.

O'Malley, P. 2010. *Crime and Risk*. London: Sage.

O'Malley, P., L. Weir, and C. Shearing. 1997. 'Governmentality, Criticism, Politics'. *Economy and Society 26* (4): pp. 501–517.

Owen, D. 1989. 'Review: Luther H. Martin, Huck Gutman, and Patrick H. Hutton (eds), *Technologies of the Self: A Seminar with Michel Foucault*, London: Tavistock, 1988'. *History of the Human Sciences 2* (1): pp. 113–116.

Owen, D. 1994. *Maturity and Modernity: Nietzsche, Weber, Foucault and the Ambivalence of Reason*. London: Routledge.

Palti, E. J. 2021. 'Deleuze's Foucault: On the Possibility of an Outside of Knowledge/Power'. *History and Theory 60* (4): pp. 20–35.

Panagia, D. 2019. 'On the Political Ontology of the Dispositif'. *Critical Inquiry 45* (3): pp. 714–746.

Paras, E. 2006. *Foucault 2.0: Beyond Power and Knowledge*. New York: Other Press.

Pasquinelli, M. 2015. 'What an Apparatus is Not: On the Archaeology of the Norm in Foucault, Canguilhem, and Goldstein'. *Parrhesia 22*: pp. 79–89.

Patton, P. 2016. 'Foucault on Power and Government'. *Sociological Problems 3* (4): pp. 57–76. Available at: https://www.ceeol.com/search/journal-detail?id=760 (accessed 3 May 2024).

Pfeffer, R. 1965. 'Eternal Recurrence in Nietzsche's Philosophy'. *Review of Metaphysics 19* (2): pp. 276–300.

Philp, M. 1979. 'Notes on the Form of Knowledge in Social Work'. *Sociological Review 27* (1): pp. 83–111.

Poulantzas, N. A. 1978. *State, Power, Socialism*. London: NLB.

Procacci, G. 1991. 'Social Economy and the Government of Poverty'. In *The Foucault Effect: Studies in Governmentality*, edited by Graham Burchell, Colin Gordon, and Peter Miller, pp. 151–169. Chicago, IL: University of Chicago Press.

334 Bibliography

Protevi, J. 2016. 'Foucault's Deleuzian Methodology of the Late 1970s'. In *Between Deleuze and Foucault*, edited by Nicolae Morar, Thomas Nail, and Daniel Smith, pp. 156–160. Edinburgh: Edinburgh University Press.

Rabinow, P. 2003. *Anthropos Today: Reflections on Modern Equipment*. Oxford: Princeton University Press.

Rabinow P. and N. Rose. 2003. 'Foucault Today'. In *The Essential Foucault: Selections from the Essential Works of Foucault, 1954–1984*, by Michel Foucault, pp. vii–xxxv. New York: New Press.

Raffnsøe, S. 2002. *Sameksistens uden common sense: En elliptisk arabesk* [Co-Existence without Common Sense: An Elliptical Arabesque]. København: Akademisk forlag.

Raffnsøe, S., M. Gudmand-Høyer, and M. S. Thaning. 2014. *What is a Dispositive?: Foucault's Historical Mappings of the Networks of Social Reality*. Copenhagen Business School, Working Paper.

Raffnsøe, S., M. Gudmand-Høyer, and M. S. Thaning. 2015. *Michel Foucault: A Research Companion*. New York: Palgrave Macmillan.

Raffnsøe, S., M. Gudmand-Høyer, and M. S. Thaning. 2016. 'Foucault's Dispositive: The Perspicacity of Dispositive Analytics in Organizational Research'. *Organization 23* (2): pp. 272–298.

Rayner, T. 2001. 'Biopower and Technology: Foucault and Heidegger's Way of Thinking'. *Contretemps 2*: pp. 142–156.

Read, J. 2003. *The Micro-Politics of Capital: Marx and the Prehistory of the Present*. Albany: State University of New York Press.

Resch, R. P. 1989. 'Modernism, Postmodernism, and Social Theory: A Comparison of Althusser and Foucault'. *Poetics Today 10* (3): pp. 511–549.

Resch, R. P. 1992. *Althusser and the Renewal of Marxist Social Theory*. Berkeley, CA: University of California Press.

Rhodes, T.,K. Lancaster, and M. Rosengarten. 2020. 'A Model Society: Maths, Models and Expertise in Viral Outbreaks'. *Critical Public Health 30* (3): pp. 253–256.

Rold Andersen, B. 1970. *Borgeren og Tryghedssystemet, Socialreformundersøgelserne, Bind II, Socialforskningsinstituttet*. [The Citizen and the Security System: The Social Reform Studies, Vol II]. København: Teknisk Forlag.

Rose, N. 1999. *Powers of Freedom: Reframing Political Thought*. Cambridge: Cambridge University Press.

Rose, N. and P. Miller 1992. 'Political Power beyond the State: Problematics of Government'. *British Journal of Sociology 43* (2): pp. 173–205.

Rose, N. and M. Valverde. 1998. 'Governed by Law?' *Social and Legal Studies 7* (4): pp. 569–579.

Ryder, A. 2013. 'Foucault and Althusser: Epistemological Differences with Political Effects'. *Foucault Studies 16*: pp. 134–153.

Saar, M. 2011. 'Relocating the Modern State: Governmentality and the History of Political Ideas'. In *Governmentality: Current Issues and Future Challenges*, edited by Ulrich Bröckling, Susanne Krasmann, and Thomas Lemke, pp. 34–55. London: Routledge.

Sawicki, J. 1987. 'Heidegger and Foucault: Escaping Technological Nihilism'. *Philosophy and Social Criticism 13* (2): pp. 155–173.

Schatzberg, E. 2006. 'Technik Comes to America: Changing Meanings of Technology before 1930'. *Technology and Culture 47* (3): pp. 486–512.

Schrift, A. D. 1995. *Nietzsche's French Legacy: A Genealogy of Poststructuralism*. London: Routledge.

Schubert, K. 2021. 'Freedom as Critique: Foucault beyond Anarchism'. *Philosophy and Social Criticism 47* (5): pp. 634–659.

Scott, C. E. 1987. *The Language of Difference*. Atlantic Highlands, NJ: Humanities Press International.

Shapiro, G. 2003. *Archaeologies of Vision: Foucault and Nietzsche on Seeing and Saying*. Chicago, IL: University of Chicago Press.

Sheridan, A. 1980. *Michel Foucault: The Will to Truth*. London: Tavistock.

Shürmann, R. 1978. 'Political Thinking in Heidegger'. *Social Research 45* (1): pp. 191–221.

Silva-Castañeda, L. and N. Trussart. 2016. 'Sustainability Standards and Certification: Looking through the lens of Foucault's dispositif'. *Global Networks 16* (4): pp. 490–510.

Sinnerbrink, R. 2005. 'From Machenschaft to Biopolitics: A Genealogical Critique of Biopower'. *Critical Horizons 6* (1): pp. 239–265.

Skinner, Q. 2023. 'Political Philosophy and the Uses of History'. In *History in the Humanities and Social Sciences*, edited by Richard Bourke and Quentin Skinner, pp. 194–210. Cambridge: Cambridge University Press.

Sluga, H. 2005. 'Foucault's Encounter with Heidegger and Nietzsche'. In *The Cambridge Companion to Foucault, Second Edition*, edited by Gary Gutting, pp. 210–240. Cambridge: Cambridge University Press.

Sluga, H. 2007. 'Heidegger's Nietzsche'. In *A Companion to Heidegger*, edited by Hubert L. Dreyfus and Mark A. Wrathall, pp. 102–121. Malden, MA: Blackwell Publishing.

Smart, B. 1983. *Foucault, Marxism and Critique*. London: Routledge and Kegan Paul.

Smith, D. 2015. 'Foucault on Ethics and Subjectivity: "Care of the Self" and "Aesthetics of Existence"'. *Foucault Studies 19*: pp. 135–150.

Tauzer, J. 2023. 'CSR and the Hermeneutical Renovation of Foucault's Toolbox'. *Sustainability 15* (5): pp. 1–22.

Tepper, R. 2010. *Michel Foucault: Toward a Philosophy and Politics of the Event: Continuity in Discontinuity*. Saarbrücken: Lambert Academic Publishing.

Theunissen, M. 1981. *Kirkegaard's Truth: The Disclosure of the Self*. New Haven, CT: Yale University Press.

Thiele, L. 1990. 'The Agony of Politics: The Nietzschean Roots of Foucault's Thought'. *American Political Sciences Review 84* (3): pp. 907–925.

Thompson, E. P. 1978. *The Poverty of Theory and Other Essays*. New York: Monthly Review.

Thompson, K. 2008. 'Historicity and Transcendentality: Foucault, Cavaillès, and the Phenomenology of the Concept'. *History and Theory 47* (1): pp. 1–18.

Thomson, I. 2014. *Heidegger, Art and Postmodernity*. Cambridge and New York: Cambridge University Press.

Thomson, I. 2018. 'Technology, Ontotheology, Education'. In *Heidegger on Technology*, edited by Aaron Wendland, Christos Hadjioannou, and Chris Merwin, pp. 174–193. New York: Routledge.

Tobias, S. 2005. 'Foucault on Freedom and Capabilities'. *Theory, Culture & Society 22* (4): pp. 65–85.

Turner, R. 1976. 'The Real Self: From Institution to Impulse'. *American Journal of Sociology 81* (5): pp. 989–1016.

Ure, M. 2007. 'Senecan Moods: Foucault and Nietzsche on the Art of the Self'. *Foucault Studies 4*: pp. 19–52.

Ure, M. 2019. *Nietzsche's The Gay Science: An Introduction*. Cambridge: Cambridge University Press.

Valverde, M. 1996. 'Despotism and the Ethical Liberal Subject'. *Economy and Society 25* (3): pp. 357–372.

Valverde, M. 2017. 'Review: The Punitive Society: Lectures at the Collège de France 1972–73 by Michel Foucault'. *British Journal of Criminology 57* (1): pp. 238–246.

336 Bibliography

Vattimo, G. 2006. 'Nietzsche, Heidegger's Interpreter'. In *Dialogue with Nietzsche*, by Gianni Vattimo, pp. 181–190. New York: Columbia University Press.

Veyne, P. 1997. 'Foucault Revolutionizes History'. In *Foucault and His Interlocutors*, edited by Arnold Davidson, pp. 146–182. Chicago, IL: University of Chicago Press.

Veyne, P. 2010. *Foucault: His Thought, His Character*. Cambridge: Polity Press.

Villadsen, K. 2007. 'The Emergence of "Neo-Philanthropy": A New Discursive Space in Welfare Policy?' *Acta Sociologica 3* (50): pp. 309–323.

Villadsen, K. 2008. 'Doing Without State and Civil Society as Universals: "Dispositifs" of Care beyond the Classic Sector Divide'. *Journal of Civil Society 4* (3): pp. 171–191.

Villadsen, K. 2011. 'Modern Welfare and "Good Old" Philanthropy'. *Public Management Review 13* (8): pp. 1057–1075.

Villadsen, K. 2015. 'Governmentality: Foucault's Concept for our Modern Political Reasoning'. In *Education Policy and Contemporary Theory: Implications for Research*, edited by Kalervo N. Gulson, Matthew Clarke, and Eva B. Petersen, pp. 147–159. London: Routledge.

Villadsen, K. 2016. 'Foucault and the Forces of Civil Society'. *Theory, Culture & Society 33* (3): pp. 3–26.

Villadsen, K. 2020a. 'Michel Foucault's Discourse Analysis'. In *Qualitative Analysis: Eight Approaches for the Social Sciences*, edited by Margaretha Järvinen and Nanna Mik-Meyer, pp. 283–305. London: Sage.

Villadsen, K. 2020b. 'I Assure You, We Have the Strictest Alien Act Possible! The Emergence of the Concept of Risky Immigrants in Denmark'. *Qui Parle 29* (1): pp. 145–179.

Villadsen, K. 2021a. '"The Dispositive": Foucault's Concept for Organizational Analysis?' *Organization Studies 42* (3): pp. 473–494.

Villadsen, K. 2021b. 'What is the New Governmentality of the COVID-19 Pandemic? A Reply to Didier Bigo, Elspeth Guild and Elif Mendos Kuşkonmaz'. *Global Discourse 11* (3): pp. 491–496.

Villadsen, K. and M. Dean. 2012. 'State Phobia, Civil Society, and a Certain Vitalism'. *Constellations 19* (3): pp. 401–420.

Villadsen, K. and J. Lundberg. 2023. 'Guest Editors' Introduction to Special Issue: Foucault, Corporate Social Responsibility, and Corporate Sustainability'. *Sustainability 15* (6): pp. 1–11.

Villadsen, K. and A. Wahlberg. 2015. 'The Government of Life: Managing Populations, Health and Scarcity'. *Economy and Society 44* (1): pp. 1–17.

Webb, D. 2014. 'Martin Heidegger (1889–1976)'. In *The Cambridge Foucault Lexicon*, edited by Leonard Lawlor and John Nale, pp. 630–639. New York: Cambridge University Press.

Weir, L. 1996. 'Recent Developments in the Government of Pregnancy'. *Economy and Society 25* (3): pp. 373–392.

Weiskopf, R. 2020. 'Algorithmic Decision-Making, Spectrogenic Profiling, and Hyper-Facticity in the Age of Post-Truth'. *Le foucaldien 6* (1): pp. 1–37.

Wexler, P. and R. H. Turner. 1977. 'Comment on Ralph Turner's The Real Self: From Institution to Impulse'. *American Journal of Sociology 83* (1): pp. 178–186.

Wheatley, L. 2019. 'Foucault's Concepts of Structure ... and Agency?: A Critical Realist Critique'. *Journal of Critical Realism 18* (1): pp. 18–30.

Wolin, R. 2006. 'Foucault the Neohumanist?' *Chronicle of Higher Education*, 31 August 2006.

Wrathall, M. 2019. 'The Task of Thinking in a Technological Age'. In *Heidegger on Technology*, edited by Aaron James Wendland, Christopher Merwin, and Christos Hadjioannou, pp. 13–39. New York: Routledge.

Zdebik, J. 2012. *Deleuze and the Diagram: Aesthetic Threads in Visual Organization*. New York: Continuum.

Ziarek, K. 1998. 'Powers to Be: Art and Technology in Heidegger and Foucault'. *Research in Phenomenology 28* (1): pp. 162–194.

Zimmerman, M. E. 2021. 'Technology (Technik)'. In *The Cambridge Heidegger Lexicon*, edited by Mark Wrathall, pp. 721–727. Cambridge: Cambridge University Press.

Žižek, S. 1994. 'The Spectre of Ideology'. In *Mapping Ideology*, edited by Slavoj Žižek, pp. 1–33. London: Verso.

Žižek, S. 1999. *The Ticklish Subject: The Absent Centre of Political Ontology*. New York: Verso.

Žižek, S. 2008. *In Defence of Lost Causes*. London: Verso.

Zoungrana, J. 1998. *Michel Foucault: Un Parcours Croisé: Lévi-Strauss, Heidegger*. Paris: L'Harmattan.

Zuboff, S. 2019. *The Age of Surveillance Capitalism: The Fight for a Human Future at the New Frontier of Power*. London: Profile Books.

Index

For the benefit of digital users, indexed terms that span two pages (e.g., 52–53) may, on occasion, appear on only one of those pages.

Actor–network theory (ANT), 20–21, 291
Agamben, Giorgio, 123–125, 131–132
Algorithm, 6–9, 88, 205–207
  Algorithmic profiling, 66–67, 205–207
  Algorithmic identity, 8–9, 206–207
Althusser, Louis, 17–18, 46, 77–79, 83, 85, 156–157, 160–175, 179–180, 184–185, 188–190, 196, 197–198, 204, 282–283
Analytics, 9–14, 18–20, 33–38
  Analytical category, 29–31, 33, 34–36, 41–42, 48–49
Ancient ethics, 142, 244–245
Ancient self-care, 240, 259–260, 263
Anders, Günther, 88, 145, 147
Archaeology, 47, 288, 291–292
  Archaeological analysis, 291–293
Architecture, 11–12, 15, 47, 56, 280
Archive, 10, 31, 136–137, 236, 278, 285–291, 294, 309–310
Aristotle, 97–98, 104, 232
  Aristotle's theory of causation, 97–98, 232
Art, 112, 238–239, 244–245
Asylum, 55, 62, 78, 219, 295–296
Authenticity, 148–149, 208–210, 216–217
  Authentic self, 210, 226
Author, 24–28, 93–94, 257, 274, 288–289
  Author function, 26–27

Badiou, Alain, 147, 244
Balibar, Étienne, 67–68, 161, 315
Behrent, Michael, 22–25, 44, 200
Being/beings, 15–16, 91–92, 100–104, 106–111, 120–121, 124–126, 133, 134–138, 141, 142–144, 147, 148
  The Question of Being, 100–101, 108–111, 134–136, 142–144
  Oblivion of the question of Being, 101–102, 104, 108–109
Bestand, standing reserve, 88–89, 97–99, 103, 108–109, 116, 146
Bidet, Jacques, 52–53, 115–116, 169–170, 172–173, 201–202, 296
Big data, 6, 9, 205
Biopolitics, 34–35, 89, 105, 112–113, 123–124, 190–191, 323–324
Biopower, 212, 263, 324
Blackman, Lisa, 259–263

Body, 22, 38–40, 89, 114–115, 161, 164–167, 178, 201–202, 218–219, 306–307
Border(s), 313–321
  Territorial border(s), 314–315
Brown, Wendy, 259
Butler, Judith, 157–158, 168–169, 203, 255–258, 273–274, 319–320

Canguilhem, Georges, 83–86, 165, 274
Capability, 7, 256–258, 262–264
  Capability approach, 256–258
Capitalism, 6–9, 60, 151–156, 162–164, 175–190, 201–210, 264–265
  Capitalist economy, 51, 81, 151–152, 154, 162–163, 201–202, 205, 209–210
Certeau, Michel de, 17–18, 21, 285–286
Christianity, 40, 70–71, 169, 191–196, 219–220, 225–226, 230–232, 234–235, 238–239
  Christian asceticism, 41, 142
  Christian morality, 69–71, 186–187, 230, 235, 237–241, 292–293, 310
  Early Christianity, 40, 221–222, 228–229, 232, 233–234, 293–294
Circulation, 65, 72–73, 121, 207, 314–315, 317, 318–319, 321–323
Citizens, 6, 19–20, 151, 261–262, 265, 323–324
  Citizen-subjects, 151, 167, 168–169, 195
Civil society, 27, 271–272
Civil war, 176–177, 179–180
  Civil war model, 16–17, 187, 196, 198, 204
Class, 51–53, 82, 163–164, 172, 174–177, 179, 187–188, 306–307
  Class antagonism, 79, 172, 311
  Working class, 51–52, 163–164, 179, 294, 311–312
Commodity, 73–74, 89, 97–98, 178, 184
  Commodification, 6, 97–98, 126–127
Concept(s), 29–37
Confession, 74, 152, 158–159, 192–194, 250–252, 308
  Confessional technique(s), 192–193, 225, 250, 308
Consciousness, 15, 26–27, 116–117, 133, 141, 165–166, 168, 242, 294
Consumer profile(s), 6, 151, 204–206, 209–210
Counter-conduct, 190, 193–195, 212, 219–221, 303
  Resistance, 51–52, 61, 179, 195–196, 213–217, 219–221, 255–256, 259

Index 339

Covid-19, 319–324
   Pandemic(s), 19–20, 66, 319–324
Credit score, 6, 151–152, 204–205
Critique, 3, 23, 34, 213–217, 223, 264, 267, 273–280
   Normative critique, 122, 214–215
   Analytical critique, 13–14, 122, 275

Dasein, being-in-the-world, 138–139, 148
Data, 6–9, 29–31, 66–67, 88, 204–207, 321, 322–324
   Digital data, 205–206
   Personal data, 323–324
Davidson, Arnold, 33–34, 36–37, 156–157, 194, 195, 220–221, 225–226, 230, 236
Dean, Mitchell, 10–11, 200, 285
Deleuze, Gilles, 31, 33–34, 37, 54–63, 92–93, 107–108, 124–126, 141–144, 212, 237, 241, 247–250, 281–282, 298–303, 308–309, 320–321
Diagram, 54–63, 72, 85–86, 119–120
   Panoptic diagram, 57–60
Digital exposure, 7
   Digital society, 6–9
   Digital technology, 6–9, 321
Discipline, 3, 41–42, 49–54, 64–65, 71, 114–118, 217–220, 259–263, 314, 319–322
   Disciplinary techniques, 3, 5, 21, 38, 52, 64–66, 71, 89, 116–119, 151–152, 188–190, 200–201, 205, 286, 293, 320–322
   Disciplinary society, 17, 50, 63, 175, 176, 199, 217–218
Disclosure, 96–102, 109–122, 126–128
   Disclosure/concealment, 97–98, 100–101, 104
   Mode of disclosure, 95–102, 109–112, 115, 121
Discourse, 27, 46–49, 136–137, 179, 269, 285–291, 294–295
   Discourse analysis, 32, 288–290, 294–295
   Discursive formation, 288–290
Divine, 84, 167–169, 222, 227–228, 230, 233–235
   Divine voice, 17, 167–170
   Divine authority, 160–162, 168–169, 230
Documents, 20, 24, 27
Dreyfus, Hubert, 16, 91–93, 110, 120–121, 136–137, 139, 141–142, 144–145, 235–236, 278–280

Economy, 6, 30–31, 72–74, 81, 153–154, 162–163, 178, 182, 201–204, 209–210
   Economic relations, 79, 160, 172
   Economic determination, 164, 175, 183, 282–283
Elden, Stuart, 25–26, 90, 91–92, 122–123, 125, 132, 179
Ellul, Jacques, 12–14
Epidemics, 19–20, 66, 319–324
   Infectious diseases, 38, 311, 319–320
Eternal recurrence, 106–109, 142–143
   Eternal return, 107–108, 143–144
Ethics, 210–211, 218–219, 223–239, 244–245, 248–250, 254–259, 261, 274–275
   Ethical phase, 40, 263
   Ethico-politics, 147–148, 279

Ewald, François, 8–9, 180–181

Feenberg, Andrew, 131, 147–148
Freedom, 5–6, 155, 169–170, 197–199, 208, 212, 216–217, 234, 247–248, 263–266, 279–280, 299
   Practice of freedom, 254–255, 259
Freud, Sigmund, 37, 77, 167–169, 172–173, 179, 180–181
Functional indeterminacy, 68, 129–130

Garland, David, 114, 191, 203
Gaze, 15, 88–90, 114–116, 147–148, 226, 302
   Objectifying gaze, 88, 114
   Disciplinary gaze, 15, 31–32, 71, 89, 114, 115–116
Gelassenheit, 109–112, 148
   Meditative thinking, 147–150
   Receptive thinking, 141
Genealogy, 15–16, 18, 48–49, 120, 129–131, 133, 141–143, 180–181, 241, 269–285, 291–295
   Genealogical method, 284, 291–295
   Genealogical showing, 273–280
Gestell, enframing, 94–104, 112–113, 120, 122–133, 142–143, 269
   Ordering disclosure, 99–100, 112–116, 121, 126–127
Goffman, Erving, 29, 208–209
Gordon, Colin, 218–219
Governance, 151–156, 159, 190–192, 195–201, 203–204
   Liberal governance, 5–6, 170, 196–201, 271–272
   Governance techniques, 151–153
Governmentality, 154, 190–192, 202–204, 225, 251, 258–259, 264, 323
   Governmentality lectures, 67–68, 175, 190–191, 225
   Governmentality studies, 10–11, 202
Grain, 72–75, 127–128, 319, 322
   Scarcity of grain, 63–64, 68, 72, 127–128
Greco-Roman, 40, 210, 212–213, 221–222, 224–225, 229–236, 252, 254–256, 264, 278
   Greco-Roman culture, 210
Greek antiquity, 125, 195–196, 224–225, 228–232, 237, 245–246
Gros, Frédéric, 253–254

Habermas, Jürgen, 214–215
Hacking, Ian, 187–188, 277–278
Hallward, Peter, 301
Han, Byung-Chul, 208
Harcourt, Bernard, 7, 82, 153, 161–162, 174, 175, 180–181, 269–270, 292–293
Hardt, Michael, 143–144, 264–265
Heidegger, Martin, 15–16, 25–26, 87, 232, 237–238, 268–269, 274
Higher education, 6–7, 87, 173–174
History of ideas, 23–28, 244
Homo criminalis, 3, 155

340 Index

Homo œconomicus, 155, 198–199
Human agency, 212–217
  Human agent, 19, 211, 246–247
Human capital theory, 180, 198–199
Humanism, 3, 22–23, 103, 216, 226, 263–264, 275
  Antihumanism, 22–23, 157–158, 161, 165–166, 200, 228, 237

Ideological state apparatuses, 67–68, 160–165, 167, 174–175, 188–190, 204
Ideology, 5–6, 30–31, 79, 83, 151, 156–157, 160–175, 179–180, 184–185, 196–197, 282–283
  State ideology, 33, 67–68, 179–180, 196
  Ideology critique, 5–6, 83, 267, 282
Impulsive self, 208–209, 265–266
Industry, 12–13, 117, 146, 316–317
  Industrialists, 16–17, 19, 51, 82, 217, 295–296
Instrumental, 95, 121, 274–275
  Instrumentalization, 87–89
Insurance, 66–67, 151–152, 205–207, 317
  Insurance technology, 8–9
Intellectual history, 23–28
Intelligibility, 75, 100, 101–102, 104, 195, 280–281
  Background intelligibility, 114–115, 135, 136–137
  Grid of intelligibility, 124–125, 280–281
Internet, 7, 9, 205–207
Interpellation, 83, 85, 160–162, 167–170, 204, 206–207
  Ideological interpellation, 161–162, 168–169, 200–201
  Freedom in interpellation, 17, 169–170

Jameson, Fredric, 209–210, 215–216
Juridico-disciplinary, 151–156, 174, 175–201
  Juridico-disciplinary techniques, 151–152
Justice, 70–71, 82, 153, 180–181
  Redistributional justice, 19–20, 304, 310

Kant, Immanuel, 25–26, 93
Koopman, Colin, 7–9, 18–19, 33–35, 43, 124, 209–210, 224–225, 247–248, 276–277

Labour, 51–52, 151, 154, 159, 162–163, 175–188, 316–318
  Labour power, 162–163, 175–176, 178, 182–184, 316–317, 319
  Wage-labour, 51–52, 151–152, 175–179, 188–189
Lacan, Jacques, 167–168
Lacoue-Labarthe, Philippe, 245–246
Lambert, Greg, 53–54, 280–281, 298, 300
Latour, Bruno, 20–21, 145, 147, 291
Law, 4–5, 63–76, 116–117, 175–201, 204, 293–294, 314, 320–321
Liberalism, 5–6, 73–74, 155, 200, 203–204
  Liberal governance, 5–6, 170, 196–201
Limit-experience, 257–258
  Desubjectivation, 257–258

Macherey, Pierre, 165–166
Machines, 59–60, 84–86, 88, 126, 131, 177–178, 205, 207
  Machines and organisms, 22, 83–84, 89, 218–219
Madness, 37, 47, 74, 91–92, 269–271
  Mental health, 154, 187
Market, 34–35, 73–74, 153, 184, 189–190, 198–199, 204–207, 271–272, 288, 314–315
  Free market, 30–31, 189–190
  Market as site of veridiction, 73–75, 288
Marx, Karl, 161, 184
Marxism, 17, 52–53, 77, 147, 154, 161–167, 170–202, 214–216
  Marxist theory, 161–165, 171, 173, 177, 179, 282–283
  Freudo-Marxism, 162, 170–171, 179, 180–181
  Nietzscheo-Marxism, 180–181
Materialism, 165–167
  Historical materialism, 78
Metaphysics, 92–93, 100–110, 120, 131–132, 134–138, 142–144, 150, 222–223
  Modern metaphysics, 96, 102–107, 111, 121, 131, 135
  Metaphysicians, 104–109
Method, 18–20, 24, 33–34, 114–115, 202, 267
  Methodology, 285, 287–288, 300–301
  Analytics, 18–20, 33–38, 211, 286
Micro-dispositifs, 54–63
Migration, 313–319
Modern technology, 15, 22–23, 87, 232, 274–275
  The essence of technology, 15–16, 87–88, 95, 99, 110–111, 128, 131–132, 148–149
Modernity, 89–90, 108, 109, 113–114, 131–132, 142–144, 146, 222–223
  The modern age, 89–90, 112–114, 117, 120, 142–143, 148
Montag, Warren, 161–162, 164–167, 171–172, 282–283
Monument(s), 289–291, 309–310
Moralization, 69, 82, 153–154, 174, 177, 179, 180–181, 185–188, 294, 312
  Moral codes, 40–41, 229–230, 234–235, 237, 241, 248, 261, 293

Nature, 75, 87–89, 91–92, 94, 97–102, 147, 150
  Natural resources, 12, 87–88, 103, 106–107, 128
Nealon, Jeffrey T., 50–51, 209–210, 212, 217, 223, 255–256
Negativism, 140, 270, 273–274
Negri, Antonio, 264–265
Neoliberalism, 29–30, 34–35, 155, 159, 191, 198–201, 203, 208, 212, 272
  Neoliberal economics, 198–199
Nietzsche, Friedrich, 15–16, 26–27, 37, 60–61, 68, 91–93, 104–109, 114, 129–130, 138–144, 168–169, 173, 180–181, 186–187, 222–224, 226–229, 236–246, 252–253, 263–266, 268–269, 272–274, 279–280, 283–284, 302

Nihilism, 105, 109, 142–143, 146, 214–215, 226, 241, 243–244, 273–274
  The death of God, 105, 245–246
Nominalism, 27, 270–271, 308
Normalization, 6, 43, 58–59, 63, 64–65, 71–72, 83–84, 115–116, 118–120, 259–263, 280–281, 295–296, 302–303
Nussbaum, Martha, 256–258

Objectification, 87–89, 102–104, 106–107, 112–119, 131, 140, 147–148
Ontology, 15–16, 122–123, 126, 138–139, 141–142, 257–258, 279, 299
  Historical ontology, 122–123, 141–142
  Ontological difference, 100–101, 115, 131–133, 136, 141–142, 150
Optimization, 87–90, 106–107, 131–132, 150, 198–199, 208
  Empty optimization, 87–88
Over-determination, 76–86

Palti, Élias, 93, 139, 299
Panopticon, 54–63
  Panopticism, 54–59, 117, 280–281, 286, 308
  Panoptical surveillance, 54–55, 58–59
Parrhēsia, 251–254
Pastoral power, 69–71, 155–156, 158–160, 164–165, 169, 170, 185, 186–187, 191–196, 219–220, 259
  The pastorate, 191–192, 219–220
  Pastoral-governmental techniques, 153
Penalty, 69, 119
  Penal system, 4–5, 17–18, 58, 68–71, 75–76, 80–82, 129, 153, 175–176, 183–184, 205, 281, 292–294
  Penal reform, 17–18, 69, 82
  Penitentiary, 69–70, 185–186, 292–293
Phenomenology, 92–93, 100–101, 124, 133–150, 222
  Phenomenological notions, 93
Philanthropy, 52, 268, 309–313
  Philanthropists, 309–313
Philosophy of technology, 15–16, 131, 185–186, 232
Physiocrats, 72–73, 291–292
  Physiocratic theories, 72–73
Poetry, 147–149
Politics, 72–75, 144–148, 176–177, 190–191, 194–196, 207, 214–216, 225, 228–229, 249–250, 253–254, 256–257, 271–272
Polyhedron, 287–288, 300–301
  Multiplication of causes, 288
Population, 38–40, 65, 66–67, 76, 89, 112–113, 154–155, 191, 192, 217–218, 306–307, 321–323
  Population statistics, 8, 38–40, 158–159, 190–191, 306, 307
  The living population, 66–67
Poulantzas, Nicos, 204
Prediction, 6–8, 66–67, 88, 152, 205–207, 251–252, 317, 321–322
  Predictive profiling, 6, 205–206

Price, 34–35, 38, 73–74, 212–214, 221–246, 257, 263–264, 273, 275–276
  What does it cost? ('Foucault's economics'), 223–224, 275–276
Prison, 4–5, 17–18, 58, 68–71, 75–76, 80–82, 129, 153, 175–176, 183–184, 205, 281, 292–294
  Correctional prison, 61–62, 69, 70, 81, 185–187
  Cellular punishment, 55–56, 129–130
  Prison-industrial-complex, 80, 82, 153
  Solitary confinement, 43, 185–186, 292–293
Psychiatry, 75–76, 155, 180–181, 186–187, 190–191, 195, 219, 224–225, 259–263, 276
  Psychiatric power, 38, 42, 45–46, 55, 219
  Criminal psychiatry, 50–51, 56, 64–65, 186–187
  Legal psychiatry, 68, 75–76
Psychoanalysis, 167–168, 308–309

Rabinow, Paul, 2, 10, 16–17, 47–48, 136–137, 156–157, 235–236, 244–245, 267–268, 278–280, 297
Raffnsøe, Sverre, 16, 45–46, 54–55, 61–62, 85, 127, 234–235, 272–273, 297–298
Regime of veridiction, 74–75
Relationality, 20–21, 90, 126–128
Relativism, 214–215, 269–270
Repressive state apparatus, 161–163, 174, 179–180, 188–189
Ressentiment, 222, 240, 242–243, 252–253
Risk, 6, 8–9, 29, 65, 251–252, 313–319, 322
  Risk calculation, 5–6, 8–9, 151–153, 204–207
Roman antiquity, 22–23, 212–213, 229–230, 233–234, 250, 264, 299
Rose, Nikolas, 2, 64, 202, 267–268

Security, 5, 14, 16, 65–68, 72–74, 196, 206–207, 313–319, 321–322
  Securitization, 66–67, 314–315, 318–319, 321–322
Self-care, 41, 238–240, 248, 254–255, 259–260, 278
  Care of the self, 221–222, 234–241
Self-conduct, 40–41, 112, 195–196, 207, 220–221, 224–225, 265–266
Self-formation, C 210–213, 221–222, 228–234, 247–248, 250, 256–259, 265
Self-technique(s), 19, 40, 149, 208
  Technology of the flesh, 38–40
Sexuality, 3–5, 19–20, 36–40, 74, 76, 250, 282, 294, 304–309
Skinner, Quentin, 28
Sluga, Hans, 92–94, 106, 142, 144, 148–149
Social constructionism, 277
Social struggle, 16–18, 20–21, 52–53, 80, 83, 137–138, 140, 141, 155, 176, 181, 196, 201, 263–264, 275
  Social conflict, 20–21, 141, 176–177
  Social domination, 204
Social work, 180–181, 185, 193, 303, 304, 309–313
Sociological functionalism, 51, 176–177, 267, 284